New Media Technologies and User Empowerment

Participation in Broadband Society

Edited by Leopoldina Fortunati / Julian Gebhardt / Jane Vincent

Volume 6

Frankfurt am Main · Berlin · Bern · Bruxelles · New York · Oxford · Wien

Jo Pierson / Enid Mante-Meijer / Eugène Loos
(eds.)

New Media Technologies and User Empowerment

PETER LANG
Internationaler Verlag der Wissenschaften

Bibliographic Information published by the Deutsche Nationalbibliothek
The Deutsche Nationalbibliothek lists this publication in the Deutsche Nationalbibliografie; detailed bibliographic data is available in the internet at http://dnb.d-nb.de.

ISSN 1867-044X
ISBN 978-3-631-60031-3
© Peter Lang GmbH
Internationaler Verlag der Wissenschaften
Frankfurt am Main 2011
All rights reserved.

All parts of this publication are protected by copyright. Any utilisation outside the strict limits of the copyright law, without the permission of the publisher, is forbidden and liable to prosecution. This applies in particular to reproductions, translations, microfilming, and storage and processing in electronic retrieval systems.

www.peterlang.de

Acknowledgements

Most of the work in this book originated in the Working Group called 'Users as Innovators' at the COST 298 conference 'The Good, the Bad and the Challenging: The User and the Future of Information and Communication Technologies', 13-15 May 2009, Copenhagen, Denmark. Chapters 1 and 16 are new.

The editors wish to thank the staff at Peter Lang GmbH, Berlin for their support in establishing a new series on new ICT and society called 'Participation in Broadband Society'.

This publication is supported by COST Office, and its staff is gratefully acknowledged, together with COST Action 298 Chair Bartolomeo Sapio and Vice Chair Tomaž Turk, for the assistance provided. Thanks also go to the series editors for their support during the production of this book and to Marinka Verburg for formatting the chapters. Finally we also wish to thank the research centre SMIT (Studies on Media, Information and Telecommunication) at the Vrije Universiteit Brussel, part of the IBBT research department Digital Society, for their support.

COST - the acronym for European Cooperation in Science and Technology - is the oldest and widest European intergovernmental network for cooperation in research. Established by the Ministerial Conference in November 1971, COST is presently used by the scientific communities of 36 European countries to cooperate in common research projects supported by national funds.

The funds provided by COST less than 1% of the total value of the projects support the COST cooperation networks (COST Actions) through which, with EUR 30 million per year, more than 30 000 European scientists are involved in research having a total value which exceeds EUR 2 billion per year. This is the financial worth of the European added value which COST achieves.

A "bottom up approach" (the initiative of launching a COST Action comes from the European scientists themselves), "à la carte participation" (only countries interested in the Action participate), "equality of access" (participation is open also to the scientific communities of countries not belonging to the European Union) and "flexible structure" (easy implementation and light management of the research initiatives) are the main characteristics of COST.

As precursor of advanced multidisciplinary research COST has a very important role for the realisation of the European Research Area (ERA) anticipating and complementing the activities of the Framework Programmes, constituting a "bridge" towards the scientific communities of emerging countries, increasing the mobility of researchers across Europe and fostering the establishment of "Networks of Excellence" in many key scientific domains such as: Biomedicine and Molecular Biosciences; Food and Agriculture; Forests, their Products and Services; Materials, Physical and Nanosciences; Chemistry and Molecular Sciences and Technologies; Earth System Science and Environmental Management; Information and Communication Technologies; Transport and Urban Development; Individuals, Societies, Cultures and Health. It covers basic and more applied research and also addresses issues of pre-normative nature or of societal importance.

Web: http://www.cost.eu

 ESF provides the COST Office through an EC contract

 COST is supported by the EU RTD Framework programme

 COST 298 – Participation in the Broadband Society

Table of Content: New Media Technologies and User Empowerment (Volume VI)

Yves Punie
Introduction: New Media Technologies and User Empowerment.
Is there a Happy Ending? 9

Part 1: Theoretical Perspectives on User Involvement and Empowerment

Enid Mante-Meijer and Eugène Loos
Innovation and the Role of Push and Pull 27

Valerie Frissen and Mijke Slot
The Return of the Bricoleur: Redefining Media Business 45

Serge Proulx and Lorna Heaton
Forms of User Contribution in Online Communities:
Mechanisms of Mutual Recognition between Contributors 67

Part 2: User Approaches in ICT Design and Development

Aphra Kerr, Stefano de Paoli and Christiano Storni
Rethinking the Role of Users in ICT Design:
Reflections for the Internet 85

James Stewart and Laurence Claeys
Problems and Opportunities of Interdisciplinary Work Involving Users
in Speculative Research for Innovation of Novel ICT Applications 101

Marinka Vangengck, Jo Pierson, Wendy Van den Broeck and Bram Lievens
User-Driven Innovation in the Case of
Three-Dimensional Urban Environments 123

Part 3: Differentiation in User Roles and Creativity

Mijke Slot
Web Roles Re-examined:
Exploring User Roles in the Media Environment 143

Philip Ely, David Frohlich and Nicola Green
Uncertainty, Upheavals and Upgrades:
Digital-DIY during Life-change 163

Eva K. Törnquist
In Search of Elks and Birds:
Two Case Studies on the Creative Use of ICT in Sweden 181

Levente Szekely and Agnes Urban
Over the Innovators and Early Adopters:
Incentives and Obstacles of Internet Usage 195

Part 4: Case Studies on User Empowerment

*James Stewart, Richard Coyne, Penny Travlou, Mark Wright
and Henrik Ekeus*
The Memory Space and the Conference:
Exploring Future Uses of Web2.0 and Mobile Internet
through Design Interventions 213

Sanna Martilla, Kati Hyyppä and Kari-Hans Kommonen
Co-Design of a Software Toolkit for Media Practices:
P2P-Fusion Case Study 231

Ike Picone
Mapping Users' Motivations and Thresholds
for Casually "Produsing" News 251

Stijn Bannier
The Musical Network 2.0 & 3.0 271

Enid Mante-Meijer, Jo Pierson and Eugène Loos
Conclusion: Substantiating User Empowerment 285

Editors and contributors 309

Yves Punie

Introduction: New Media Technologies and User Empowerment. Is there a Happy Ending?

Empowerment

Empowerment is a term that is so widely used in science, business, civil society and policy that it risks becoming an oxymoron: everybody talks about it but nobody dares ask what it really means, let alone carry out studies on this in a consistent and empirically reliable way. In general, empowerment refers to the capacity of individuals, communities and/or groups to access and use their personal/collective power, authority and influence, and to employ that strength when engaging with other people, institutions or society. It encourages people to gain the skills and knowledge that will allow them to overcome obstacles in life or work and ultimately, help them develop within themselves or in society (Wikipedia, accessed 14.07.2010). Empowerment is a multi-dimensional social process that helps people gain control over their lives. It is a process that fosters power in people for use in their lives, in their communities and in their society, by acting on issues they define as important (Page & Czuba 1999). The approach to empowerment proposed by Page & Czuba (1999) is based on a literature review, in which three major components to understanding empowerment are highlighted. In the first place, empowerment is multi-dimensional, in that it occurs within sociological, psychological, economic, and other dimensions. Second, empowerment occurs at various levels, such as individual, group, and community. Third, empowerment is by definition a social process, since it occurs in relationship to others.

This book deals with an additional dimension of empowerment whereby users try to gain control over their lives in relation to New Media Technologies and Information and Communication Technology (ICT). It provides a rich and diverse account of both empirical and conceptual/theoretical studies on the use and acceptance of media and ICT – as well as rejection and non-use – by ordinary people in their everyday lives. It builds upon earlier research in this area, a pioneering strand of which was labeled the "domestication approach" (Silverstone & Haddon 1996; Silverstone 2005, 2006). This book looks at these processes from a particular angle: the active role and contribution of users in the innovation process (Von Hippel 2005), the latter being conceived of as the interactive and social process of developing, designing, producing, marketing, adopting and using new media and ICT (Silverstone & Haddon 1996). The book shows that the new roles that are being taken up by users are strongly linked to user empowerment in the sense of users taking control in processes where they traditionally were not expected to play a role. This leads us to raise two key questions: Are users now becoming actors with an influence amongst many other actors involved? Or rather: Are users taking over control from others in certain areas?

The evidence provided in this book helps us to address both questions. In the next two sections, an overview of the contributions to this book is presented according the major questions raised above, thus not in the order as presented in the table of contents. A first series of contributions deals with users as active contributors to the innovation process. They look at understanding everyday users and usages in context and in practice and/or at the role users play in the development, design and adoption of new media and ICT. A second series of contributions deals with the impact of user contributions in the media domain in the wider sense, revealing the changing roles of users and their impact on power relations and control in the media sector. In the next section of this introduction, additional evidence from our own research is presented to document further whether user empowerment is taking place in the domains of work, politics, education and government and if so, how. In the last section, it is argued that while full empowerment has not been reached through ICT, the underlying processes and activities involving millions of people who are now connected online, cannot and should not be ignored either.

Users as active contributors in the innovation process

The chapter by *Mante-Meijer and Loos* (Innovation and the Role of Push and Pull) looks at changing user roles from the angle of how the innovation process is affected. In particular, it looks at the interaction between innovation that is pushed by technologists, economy and politics and the active role of users in the uptake, rejection, use and/or re-invention of the innovation. Using the theoretical frameworks of Weick ("enacted environment") and Giddens ("duality of structure"), they observe a dynamic sense-making process between societal structure and user practice. This is part of a choice making process: people can be forced (pushed) or enticed (pulled) into certain actions. In this process, enablers and constraints are found. Based on an analysis of several cases the chapter concludes that, due to this interaction and choice making process, there is a lag between supply and use of technological innovations. Push can only be successful if the right enablers are brought into play and the innovation fits the capabilities and sense making of potential users.

The chapter by *Kerr, De Paoli and Storni* (Rethinking the Role of Users in ICT Design: Reflections for the Internet) reports on work from an interdisciplinary project which explores the design of future telecommunications services, networks and applications, particularly focusing on the internet. The authors refer to Woolgar and others, who find that every process of innovation, design and development can be characterized as a struggle between competing conceptions of the user and that there is a diversity of users and practices in which users and non-users can be disruptive and dangerous, but also provide value and drive innovation. They also refer to Van Dijck, who argues for a more critical view of Social Media, as many users play relatively inactive roles (lurking, viewing, rating, etc.) and do not create or design themselves. However, there is also the role of the design of ICTs in regulating/controlling user behaviour and user profiles, as the authors show on the basis of two contrasting case studies. The "Multics system" provides an example of a trusted system in which protection and security prevail over user freedom. The open hardware "Arduino case", on the other hand, foresees multiple user roles with little separation between users and designers. The authors conclude that there are no clear–cut, easy answers as to whether we are really moving towards more user freedom ("drift") or rather towards a restriction of this freedom. Further empirical research on the role of users in internet design is needed.

Stewart and Claeys (Problems and Opportunities of Interdisciplinary Work Involving Users in Speculative Research for Innovation of Novel ICT Applications) focus on some of the challenges faced by multidisciplinary teams working on interdisciplinary research into innovation in ICT applications, based on their personal experiences. There are generally four main disciplines brought to bear in research on speculative applications of ICT: engineering, design, social science and business development. Each has its own approach to formulating questions and providing answers, methodologically, culturally and even philosophically. They also have different ways of reflecting on these practices. The key question for this chapter is thus not only what difficulties can arise in interdisciplinary research involving users, but also how the methods and outputs of user research can make interdisciplinary research more successful. The authors provide an overview of the most commonly used research methods and the value generated by the different disciplines. They argue that there is a need to better define and understand these divergences, to identify pitfalls and also to highlight the creative and analytical opportunities arising from the involvement of users in interdisciplinary research.

Vangenck, Pierson, Van den Broeck and Lievens (User-driven Innovation in the Case of Three Dimensional Urban Environments) argue that a thorough understanding of media technology users has become vital in technological design and development, in order to increase the chances of new products and services living up to the expectations, characteristics and practices of future (end) users. Theoretically, the authors envisage linking the perspectives of "User-Centred Design" (UCD) and "User-Driven Innovation" (UDI) with the domestication approach that looks at how media technologies are domesticated in people's everyday lives. The URBAN project, which deals with the effective and efficient handling of 3D data for urban environments, is used as a case study. The authors observe no easy match between current and future user practices (identified by means of the domestication framework) and the objectives and expectations of technological project partners, who are mainly concerned with fine-tuning and experimenting with the basic technology of 3D modelling. However, it is possible to combine both approaches, first by identifying innovation opportunities from the users' point of view and second, by allowing all the stakeholders involved to steer the development process in an iterative way. This could lead to a more thorough understanding of users which would result in finding new opportunities to create value, and a systematic/planned involvement of users throughout the entire innovation process.

Collaborative design involving ordinary users is also discussed by *Marttila, Hyyppä and Kommonen* (Co-Design of a Software Toolkit for Media Practices: P2P-Fusion Case Study). They describe and analyse the development of an open source software toolkit for creating audiovisual Social Media applications which were to be co-designed by communities of everyday people. The authors acknowledge that, in practice, co-design for a large, distributed and multi-disciplinary project is far from simple, requiring, amongst others, a carefully planned strategy for continuous and effective mobilization of the co-design partners. Other challenges relate to a common understanding and timely use of mature enough prototypes. The authors show, however, that despite its challenges, design for openness and for designability is something that designers, technology developers and institutions need to learn, because in the rapidly evolving global and open digital ecosystem, only collaborative and designable systems and components will be able to respond to the increasingly sophisticated demands of the evolution of the practices of people.

The chapter by *Ely, Frohlich and Green* (Uncertainty, Upheavals and Upgrades: Digital-DIY during Life-change) provides an interesting angle on the dynamics of change in dealing with digital technologies when life changes occur. What they refer to as "The Problem of Digital-DIY" can crop up when people experiencing life changes configure and re-configure their domestic entertainment, information and communication technologies. The chapter describes pilot studies and empirical research into people going through a life change, and makes it clear that this not only involves a broad social network, real and virtual, but also that digital-DIY is studded with "problem-solving" opportunities just like those found in traditional DIY activity. The authors conclude that digital-DIY is a very "social" activity that reconnects not only artefacts but also people. Moreover, experts, non-users and non-experts alike give their advice, guidance and support. In most cases, there is a real sense of satisfaction on completing the technical set-up, although tensions also arise when the community activity is undermined by significant infrastructure problems with power, cabling and broadband connectivity. The authors conclude that there is still much to do to support even the most knowledgeable users.

Although the internet is becoming widespread in Hungary, too, *Szekely and Urban* (Over the Innovators and Early Adopters: Incentives and Obstacles of Internet Usage) investigate the incentives and obstacles of internet usage and non-usage, linked to the different user groups identified by Rogers in his work on the diffusion of innovations. Internet usage today is highly influenced by age, education and social status, and as a result, incentives and obstacles can be very varied, depending on these differences. This chapter reports on qualitative research on non-users. Though non-users do not deny the general importance of ICT, they see the more negative characteristics of ICT developments, and in particular those related to physiological effects, mental effects and social effects. Non-users have stereotypes about users: they sit in front of computers all day, and they only have virtual relationships. Interestingly, non-users accept the information and communication functions of the internet, but they consider the entertainment aspects to be harmful, causing serious addiction. Also negative images in the media deter people even more. The authors argue that the reasons for refusing to use ICT are complex, and as result, that strategies to tackle these need to take that complexity into account. They propose an approach to change the attitudes of non-adopters by focussing on the practical aspects of the internet and its strength in information provision.

The chapter by *Törnqvist* (In Search of Elks and Birds: Two Case Studies on the Creative Use of ICT in Sweden) describes and analyses two case studies on how users can function as innovators by using already-established ICTs in creative ways. The two cases are about mobile recreational activities in nature, namely elk hunting and bird watching. The chapter demonstrates that the social context plays a significant role in the introduction and use of ICT and that the development takes place in interaction between individuals. Companies wanting to innovate without a knowledge of the social and cultural structures in which the innovation will take place, face high risks of failure. The difference between the two case studies is that in the case of elk hunting, the hunting association and its web editor are the main actors driving the development of ICT creative uses while in the case of bird watchers, the main actors are both producing users and everyday users (different bird watchers with different technological knowledge and competence) who are active during different development stages. The author argues that, in the process of innovation, both enabling and constraining factors can emerge, depending on which "virtual pocket of local order" the user belongs to. Though everyday users are not innovators in the sense that they (mainly) produce an artefact, they do expand the use of existing equipment and resources which they already are familiar with.

Stewart, Coyne, Travlou, Wright and Ekeus (The Memory Space and the Conference: Exploring Future Uses of Web2.0 and Mobile Internet through Design Interventions) dig into the possibilities of Web2.0 and personal mobile media for collective memory practices. The chapter explores experiments with a "Memory Space", which concentrate on the building and testing of a tool to make the intense and multilayered experience of a conference more productive and reorienting. It particularly taps into the use of place and space as key elements in producing and linking to memories of encounters and ideas. It suggests new ways to record and access informal conversations and encounters using mobile messaging, social networking, text, images, voice and video, and linking these with the formal and informal physical spaces of conferences using the web, GPS, and mobile phone interfaces, thereby creating a much richer record of a conference than formal conference proceedings and private memories. The authors argue that memory practices will probably be radically changed by new media, as we will be able to recall not only "facts" from the Web, or communicate in real-time, but also selectively leave and reuse all sorts of traces of our public and private activities. On the spatial dimension, we have a range of new ways of activating our experience and use of space and place using new ICT that are being widely explored. They suggest that the junction of the two domains of space and place opens up considerable scope for design, technical development and academic enquiry.

Changing roles of users impacting power and control in the media sector

The chapter by *Frissen and Slot* (The Return of the Bricoleur: Redefining Media Business) focuses on the transformation of the traditional media audience since the 1980s and the resulting substantial changes in user/producer relations that have taken place within the media and entertainment domain. To understand this changed role of users, the authors point to a return of the user as "bricoleur" (Lévi Strauss), as opposed to the user as consumer separated from the producer as engineer. Based on evidence from five specific Social Media transitions (P2P file-sharing, podcasting, interactive television, citizen journalism/blogging and internet community games) impacting the media domain (music, radio, broadcasting, the press, gaming) it is concluded that this role of the user as "bricoleur" represents a fundamental shift in user/producer relations.

The chapter by *Proulx and Heaton* (Forms of User Contribution in Online Communities: Mechanisms of Mutual Recognition between Contributors) analyses the types of online user contributions that emerge in five different Social Media applications: i.e. in the collaborative encyclopedia Wikipedia; online citizen journalism; the practices of free software developers; the immersive universe Second Life and audio podcasting. Proulx and Heaton are seeking the unique social form that transcends these new collaborative practices for internet-based content creation and exchange. The author refers to a shift to "participative culture" practices (Jenkins) and to "produsage" (Bruns) to account for these active user roles. A regime of "conflictual cooperation" between mainstream media and new, individualized mass communication media is observed. Which of the two possible scenarios (continuation versus disruption) will prevail remains an open question.

The chapter by *Slot* (Web Roles Re-examined: Exploring User Roles in the Media Environment) examines user roles in online media entertainment. The author refers to both positive views (e.g. Leadbeater, Tapscott & Williams) on active users in the area of web 2.0 as opposed to the passive consumers in the traditional media domain, and to more critical approaches to user empowerment (e.g. Keen, Dreyfus) pointing to problems related to quality, truth, reliability and triviality. The author then draws on her own empirical research (an online user survey) to further deal with the key questions of how important these new user roles are and whether user empowerment is truly a disruptive development. Slot argues that, like no other media before, computers and the internet have lowered the threshold for a very large group of users to take on a variety of roles in the media domain on a large scale. The internet is more integrated into people's lives than ever. Overall, it seems that users are very active online. Consumption and communication roles (more traditional audience roles) are the most popular online. The variety within these roles is large and users engage in these activities very often. Other less traditional roles are carried out by many users, but less often, and a distinction can be made in this case between more active and less active sub-roles. Less active sub roles like customizing, selling, voting and sending content to others via e-mail are more important than activities like writing a weblog or making a website. Slot concludes that the 90-9-1 rule (90% audience or lurkers – 9% contributors – 1% creators) developed by Nielson does not adequately account for the diverse and dynamic picture that emerges when describing user activities in the online media entertainment domain.

The chapter by *Bannier* (The Musical Network 2.0 & 3.0) examines the changes brought to the musical network by current Web 2.0 applications and future Web 3.0 applications, paying particular attention to the role of the user in the processes of creativity, reproduction, distribution and consumption, which together constitute the musical network. Based on a theoretical reflection and a literature review, the author shows that all processes within the musical network are indeed affected by the rise of current and future Social Media. Networks of creativity are changing, now that relations between artists and fans are becoming more direct, leaving the traditional music industry actors to one side. Artists are becoming prosumers as they are able to produce their own albums. This also affects the networks of reproduction as, with digital technologies (e.g. MP3), music is becoming detached from physical support, making room for knowledge-based semantic processes such as filtering, navigating, tagging, etc. The distribution network has also changed now that music can be distributed digitally via internet-based networks, reducing the cost of distribution to almost nothing. Finally, the networks of consumption, covering those places in which musical products are purchased, are becoming connected to all the other networks. Before, record companies and other music industry actors influenced every network, but now they are influenced by the internet user. The same developments can be seen with the advent of Web 3.0. Although Web 3.0 applications may provide users with fewer online content generation possibilities at the expense of the data and metadata they create, their aim is to provide the user with personalised and enriched content.

The chapter by *Picone* (Mapping Users' Motivations and Thresholds for Casually "Produsing" News) presents the results of a diary study and in-depth interviews with 18 respondents on their motivations and thresholds for engaging with the news or becoming "produsers". The author makes a conceptual distinction between consumption (non self-publishing), casual production (occasional self-publishing) and structural production (continuous self-publishing). This chapter focuses on casual engagement with the news, rather than on the more structural activities like blogging about news or citizen journalism. The author argues that production and consumption of news are very distinct activities in the mind of the consumer and that user motivations for engaging with news can be articulated along three dimensions: social (social reflex), personal (self-confidence) and substantive (news content). An additional dimension related to producing news-related user-generated content is the role of the authority of the producer. The author stresses that the consumption/production dimension does not imply linearity. A consumer is not at all bound to become a "produser". The author concludes that a better understanding of the news "produser" role is not only needed academically but that this could also help the news industry to turn the current crisis into an opportunity.

Other high impact areas of Social Media: Work, politics, education and government

During the last few years, researchers – including myself – at the European Commission's Institute for Prospective Technological Studies (IPTS) have undertaken extensive research on the socio-economic impacts of Social Computing, Web 2.0 or Social Media on the European economy and society. Our research has looked into the emergence, breakthrough and use (Ala-Mutka 2008; Cachia 2008; Pascu 2008), and impact – both actual and potential – of Social Media applications in multiple domains and/or sectors: media, entertainment and ICT sector (Punie et al. 2009b); business, work and enterprises (Lindmark 2009); government and administrations as well politics and society (Misuraca 2009; Punie et al. 2009a); education and learning (Ala-Mutka 2010; Redecker et al. 2010), inclusion and integration (Kluzer & Haché 2009); health (Valverde 2009); mobile (Feijóo 2009) and identity (Lusoli & Cachia 2009).

On the basis of this multi-sector evidence (Punie et al. 2009b), we summarized the actual and potential impacts of Social Media according to two trends that are especially relevant for user empowerment. First, new collaboration models, in which users play new roles in content creation (e.g. user-generated content), in providing peer support (e.g. *PatientsLikeMe*) and in service delivery (e.g. *PatientOpinion*) are driving bottom-up social innovation processes. The open, user-centric and participative functions of Social Media applications enable new horizontal collaboration models to emerge which attract users across sectors, institutions and geographical locations, because they are perceived to be empowering by these actors. Second, Social Media-enabled collaboration is giving rise to the creation of collective knowledge as a new peer-created resource (e.g. *Wikipedia, PeerToPatent*) and allows several actors – governments, politicians, civil society, intermediaries and citizens – to use it for new purposes, including the achievement of public goals (e.g. *Theyworkforyou, Wikileaks, Fixmystreet*, etc.). Users join Social Media applications to create, review, refine, enhance and share information around specific topics of interest, e.g. professional, health-related or political. Collective knowledge is thus gathered by employees, citizens and governments, patients and doctors, and teachers and learners, allowing them to use it for new purposes, including the achievement of public goals (Centeno et al. 2009).

As documented in Punie et al. (2009b), both new user roles and collective intelligence gathering have emerged in:

- **Workplaces**, both public and private, where employees play an active role and join interest communities outside the organisational framework in order to have better access to and jointly build new knowledge, improve skills, keep informed about the activities of others, and find out about new jobs or recruit new colleagues. Social Media tools are being increasingly adopted in enterprises to generate and use new knowledge to improve internal work processes, products and services. Concretely, access to user-generated knowledge available on professional social networking sites such as *LinkedIn*, increases the cost efficiency of recruitment processes. Customer-generated knowledge on product performance, usability and design is used by enterprises to improve product characteristics. Employees are increasingly using Social Media peer-produced knowledge to upgrade their skills and knowledge and for networking. Also, the availability of user-generated knowledge on product and service quality (e.g. as on *Tripadvisor)* empowers consumers in their purchasing choices, and increases product competition on quality and price. Overall, these elements could positively contribute to increasing enterprise competitiveness.

- **Politics and society**, where citizens and groups of citizens organise collective action across borders and cultures. Citizens organise themselves to support and complement public organisations. Examples include citizens collaborating in disaster management, or controlling politicians and governments (e.g. *Theyworkforyou*). Social Media collective knowledge can enhance political participation. Social Media empower users and civil organisations to build, manage, access and distribute government and political information, lowering the barriers for the citizen participation and engagement in policy and political decision-making. Social Media also provide tools to gather citizens' opinions on a massive scale. This more comprehensive consultative process allows for better-informed public decision making. Websites like *Peer to Patent, Fixmystreet*, and *MyBikeLane* provide diverse examples of information generated by citizens on the basis of their own local or specialised knowledge, opinions, and needs, which can be effectively used by governments to provide higher quality services that are more citizen-centred and cost-efficient.

- **Education and learning**, where students collaborate among themselves and with teachers, inside and outside formal education boundaries, and also across borders. Social Media support the creation of and access to learning materials such as on-line encyclopaedias, multimedia and immersive environments and podcasts by learners and teachers. These materials can be developed in a collaborative and distributed process, and delivered with flexibility. Examples of applications which support this process include the language learning site *LiveMocha* and the educational material sharing site *Connexions (cnx.org)*. Collaborative learning models open up alternative learning channels by linking learners to experts, researchers and practitioners. Teachers co-develop teaching content and pedagogic methods and provide peer support. Social networks and communities of interest arise around common learning interests and facilitate learning by providing social and cognitive guidance and support. Examples of educational applications include *Cloudworks*, a site for sharing learning and teaching ideas and experiences, *interactivewhiteboardlessons*, a teachers' resource site for interactive teaching, and *RezEd.org*, a resource site on virtual worlds for learning.

- **Government and public administration**, where various stakeholders collaborate on service provision, policy development and enforcement. Examples of such applications include *PeerToPatent*, which harnesses the knowledge of citizen-experts to improve patent quality; *Theyworkforyou*, where citizens track the activities of elected and unelected representatives in government; *Intellipedia*, which links the US intelligence community and provides a peer-to-peer content creation platform. Other applications include *Fixmystreet,* which allows people to report and discuss problems such as speeding cars and broken pavements, and *Mybikelane*, which allows people to report cars which have parked illegally in bike lanes. Social Media user-created knowledge also has a positive impact on multiple facets of public health and healthcare. From the patient perspective, Social Media-enabled user-created knowledge on health facilitates and stimulates self-care and responsibility by empowering both patients and healthy citizens. Social Media communities developed around targeted illnesses, such as in *Patientslikeme*, also provide improved access to medical information, care and social support. From the doctors' perspective, collective knowledge created by doctors can enhance medical knowledge and, as a result, healthcare quality. An example of this application is *Ganfyd*, a user-generated and evolving medical text book. From the health management perspective, the collection of patient experiences through Social Media applications, such as in *PatientOpinion,* provides a tool to improve health service quality management. Knowledge created by wiki tools also helps to organise a coherent, collective and more effective answer to pandemic diseases.

- Social Media provide new tools for **social support and social inclusion**. This is particularly important for groups at risk of exclusion, for instance, in the socio-economic integration and participation of immigrants and ethnic minorities (IEM). In particular, Social Media can support the integration of local and immigrant communities and help them find jobs. Social Media can also provide social networking tools and content that help IEM to maintain and develop connections with friends and relatives in the country of origin. Applications in this area include *CousCous Global,* a website that allows young people all over the world to engage in intercultural dialogue through ICT-mediated debates. However, the need for specific skills to be able to benefit from the advantages of Social Media also brings the risk of a new level of digital divide. Indirectly, Social Media tools also empower Civil Society Organisations (NGOs, voluntary groups, associations, etc.) which play a significant role in fighting social exclusion. Concretely, it enables easier participation, wider knowledge aggregation and broader dissemination, and consequently improves resource collection and utilisation and operational efficiency. Examples of applications in this domain include *Avaaz.org*, a new global web movement to improve the world, and *Mobileactive.org,* a community of people and organisations using mobile phones for social impact.

- **The media sector,** where users collect, report and distribute information about events (Cf. infra). In this way, users produce citizen journalism (e.g. *Twitter*) and become producers of user-generated content (UGC). New user roles are creating novel opportunities for public and private organisations to incorporate user-created *content* and new *actors* into their value chain. Hence, bottom-up user-driven organisational innovation together with dis-intermediation and re-intermediation processes are taking place, transforming the roles of actors and their relationships. For example, learners are taking an active role in their learning as co-creators and evaluators and, as a result, the teacher's role is evolving towards empowering learners to make use of the available resources and tools for their learning. Patients are taking a more active role in managing their health and are becoming much savvier on health and healthcare, which stimulates self-care and responsibility and changes the nature of the patient-doctor relationship. Users are sharing their healthcare experiences, becoming new actors in the quality management value chain of healthcare institutions. Finally, citizens have also become new content providers for the media industry, a trend further reinforced by real-time mobile applications "on-the-go".

This user-driven innovation often challenges the role and functioning of private and public organisations, and thus becomes a potential driver for disruptive change. For instance, changes brought about by Social Media defy traditional actors in the media and publishing industry as discussed above. Changes in learning and teaching are also challenging existing education and training structures and practices. Additionally, Social Media provide opportunities for mass collaboration among citizens, which in turn demands that public organisations and governance processes are more accountable and transparent.

Finally, social innovation is also generated as it is now possible to address effectively sub-critical (long tail) needs which have been until now relatively intractable due to invisible demand or dispersed user communities. Social Media production, sharing and collaboration tools can connect scattered user groups and individuals who share the same interests allowing, for instance, research and advances on rare diseases, the connection of dispersed communities of ethnic minorities or citizen organisations to act as pressure groups around a very specific or minority topic.

The two major trends observed here are based on an analysis of emerging practices and potential uses of Social Media and thus still need to become much more widespread to really have significant and disruptive impacts. Moreover, to realize the full potential of Social Media, a number of challenges need to be addressed: security, safety and privacy risks; the need for institutional innovation and spontaneous and self-governing mechanisms, new skills and digital competences for all actors using these tools. To reap the benefits of Social Media, public sector leaders, decision makers and companies will need to commit to a more open, transparent, dynamic and broader-based dialogue with citizens and consumers. Traditional boundaries will become blurred and new governance models will need to be agreed (Centeno et al. 2009).

Outlook

The practices and examples mentioned above and the many contributions in this book show strong potential for user empowerment and changes in service delivery. There is, however, counter-evidence that existing players and institutions are using Social Media to maintain and/or reinforce their positions or to continue with "business as usual". The debate on empowerment vs. commodification was recently re-activated by Castells and Fuchs: the former argues that a new power struggle is emerging between the global corporate multimedia networks and the creative audience (Castells 2009) and the latter wonders if there is room for real counter-power and autonomy or is it rather about the total commodification of human creativity (Fuchs 2009)?.

This book provides an important contribution to the debate. It delivers evidence for the argument that neither empowerment nor commodification truly reflect the reality, but rather that this is a specific combination and articulation of both, depending on the context, the type of users, their everyday environment, their resources and on the type of technologies, their purpose, their state of development and many other factors and actors. These specific constellations make it very necessary, but also very difficult, to reach a clear conclusion on user empowerment, which also depends on how the latter is defined and made operational. This book, therefore, argues in favour of continued attention for and research on user empowerment and new media technologies. And while no happy ending has (yet) been reached, the activities and contributions of millions of people who are now connected online, enabling them to act together on issues they regard as important, cannot and should not be ignored.

Note: The views expressed in this chapter are those of the writer and do not necessarily represent an official position of the European Commission. Neither the European Commission nor any person acting on behalf of the Commission is responsible for the use which might be made of this publication.

References

Ala-Mutka K. Social Computing: Study on the Use and Impacts of Collaborative Content, EUR 23572 EN, IPTS, European Commission (2008) http://ipts.jrc.ec.europa.eu/publications/pub.cfm?id=1885

Ala-Mutka K. Learning in Informal Online Networks and Communities, EUR 24149 EN, IPTS, European Commission (2010) http://ipts.jrc.ec.europa.eu/publications/pub.cfm?id=3059

Cachia R. Social Computing: Study on the Use and Impact of Online Social Networking, EUR 23565 EN, IPTS, European Commission (2008) http://ipts.jrc.ec.europa.eu/publications/pub.cfm?id=1884

Castells M. Communication Power Oxford University Press (2009)

Centeno C., Lusoli W., Misuraca G., Punie Y., Broster D. 'Key findings, future prospects, and policy challenges' eds. Punie, Y., Lusoli W., Centeno C., Misuraca G., Broster D. The Impact of Social Computing on the EU Information Society and Economy, EUR 26043 EN, IPTS, European Commission (2009) pp. 15-31 http://ipts.jrc.ec.europa.eu/publications/pub.cfm?id=2819

Feijóo C. 'Social Computing and the mobile ecosystem' eds. Punie Y., Lusoli W., Centeno C., Misuraca G., Broster D. The Impact of Social Computing on the EU Information Society and Economy, EUR 26043 EN, IPTS, European Commission (2009) pp. 61-72 http://ipts.jrc.ec.europa.eu/publications/pub.cfm?id=2819

Fuchs C. 'Some reflections on Manual Castells' book "Communicative Power" TripleC' (2009) 7 (1) pp. 94-108

Kluzer S., Haché A. 'Social Computing and social inclusion' eds. Punie Y., Lusoli W., Centeno C., Misuraca G., Broster D. The Impact of Social Computing on the EU Information Society and Economy, EUR 26043 EN, IPTS, European Commission (2009) pp. 97-110 http://ipts.jrc.ec.europa.eu/publications/pub.cfm?id=2819

Lindmark S. 'Web 2.0: Where does Europe stand?' EUR 23969 EN, IPTS, European Commission (2009) http://ipts.jrc.ec.europa.eu/publications/pub.cfm?id=2539

Lusoli W., Cachia R. 'Social Computing and identity' eds. Punie Y., Lusoli W., Centeno C., Misuraca G., Broster D. The Impact of Social Computing on the EU Information Society and Economy, EUR 26043 EN, IPTS, European Commission (2009) pp. 73-85 http://ipts.jrc.ec.europa.eu/publications/pub.cfm?id=2819

Misuraca G. 'Social Computing and governance' eds. Punie Y., Lusoli W., Centeno C., Misuraca G., Broster D. The Impact of Social Computing on the EU Information Society and Economy, EUR 26043 EN, IPTS, European Commission (2009) pp. 121-134 http://ipts.jrc.ec.europa.eu/publications/pub.cfm?id=2819

Page N., Czuba C. 'Empowerment: What is it?' Journal of Extension 37 (5) (October 1999) http://www.joe.org/joe/1999october/comm1.php

Pascu C. An Empirical Analysis of the Creation, Use and Adoption of Social Computing Applications, EUR 23415 EN, IPTS, European Commission (2008) http://ipts.jrc.ec.europa.eu/publications/pub.cfm?id=1684

Punie Y., Misuraca G., Osimo, D. eds. Public Services 2.0: The Impact of Social Computing on Public Services, EUR 24080 EN, IPTS, European Commission (2009a) http://ipts.jrc.ec.europa.eu/publications/pub.cfm?Id=2820

Punie Y., Lusolie W., Centeno C., Misuraca G., Broster D. eds. The Impact of Social Computing on the EU Information Society and Economy, EUR 26043 EN, IPTS, European Commission (2009b) http://ipts.jrc.ec.europa.eu/publications/pub.cfm?id=2819

Redecker K., Ala-Mutka K., Bacigalupo M., Ferrari A., Punie Y. 'Learning 2.0: The Impact of Web 2.0 Innovations on Education and Training in Europe' EUR 24103 EN, IPTS, European Commission (2009) http://ipts.jrc.ec.europa.eu/ publications/pub.cfm?id=2899

Silverstone R. ed. Media, Technology and Everyday Life in Europe: From Information to Communication London: Ashgate (2005)

Silverstone R. 'Domesticating domestication. Reflections on the life of a concept' eds. Berker T., Hartmann, Punie Y., Ward K. Domestication of Media and Technology, Open University Press - McGraw Hill (2006) pp. 229-248

Silverstone R., Haddon L. 'Design and domestication of information and communication technologies: Technical change in everyday life' eds. Silverstone R., Hirsch E. Consuming Technologies: Media and Information in Domestic Spaces. London: Routledge (1996) pp. 44-74

Valverde J.A. 'Social Computing and health' eds. Punie Y., Lusoli W., Centero C., Misuraca G., Broster D. The Impact of Social Computing on the EU Information Society and Economy, EUR 26043 EN, IPTS, European Commission (2009) pp. 111-120 http://ipts.jrc.ec.europa.eu/publications/pub.cfm?id=2819

Von Hippel E. Democratizing Innovation Cambridge, MA: MIT Press (2005)

Part 1 - Theoretical Perspectives on User Involvement and Empowerment

Enid Mante-Meijer and Eugène Loos

Innovation and the Role of Push and Pull

Introduction

In 2000, the European Council and the Commission presented the "Action Plan eEurope – An information society for all", which contained a number of defined actions, clustered around three main objectives. These were (1) a cheaper, faster, secure internet, (2) investing in people and skills and (3) stimulating the use of the internet. The Plan envisioned the evolution of the "Broadband Society": a society in which broadband technology has become the universal medium used by all people in Europe. Widespread broadband deployment would yield benefits for all citizens and would give Europe an innovative competitive edge in today's globalizing society. According to the Action Plan, the eEurope targets and broadband society were to have been realised by the year 2010.

Now, having reached the year 2010, we see that both governments and technologists have developed a plethora of activities in this direction. Nevertheless, eEurope is still a far away goal. A mismatch remains between society and technology, with technology considerably outpacing societal use of its possibilities. What could be the reasons behind the lag between technological possibilities and their actualisation?

To understand the reasons for this gap, it is necessary to look at how technological innovations find their way into the everyday lives of individuals and groups of citizens. Weick (1969, 2001) and Giddens (1984) respectively introduced the concepts of "enacted environment" and "duality of structure". When confronted with demands in their environment, people make sense of structure, "a recursively organised set of rules and resources" (Giddens 1984, 25) by "enacting" their environment. This sense making results in practices, which in turn influence structure ("duality of structure") and is part of a choice-making process: people can be forced (pushed by other instances) or enticed (pulled) into certain practices.

In this process, we find enablers and constraints that facilitate or hinder certain choices. Several theories provide insight into the innovation process and the enablers and constraints that play a role in innovation. In this chapter, sense making in the process of technological innovation is discussed within the perspective of general diffusion theory, domestication theory, capability theory, theories of risk taking and choice making theory. First, we take a close look at how push and pull play a role in the creation of the Broadband Society and the resulting innovational practices by users and we discuss the concept of "innovation" and the role that is played by creativity and time in the innovation process. Then we offer a number of illustrative cases that show the diverse factors playing a role in the innovation process a nd the theories mentioned above are elaborated in order to show how the innovation process is enabled or constrained. Finally, we analyse these cases in the light of the different theoretical perspectives provided by these theories.

Our main questions are:

- What is innovation in the Broadband Society?

- Which aspects of innovation can be distinguished?

- What is the role of push factors and pull factors in this innovation process?

- Which enablers and constraints can be distinguished during this process?

Aspects of innovation

Introduction

Wikipedia gives the following general definition of innovation:

> "The term innovation means a new way of doing something (…) It may refer to incremental and emergent or radical and revolutionary changes in thinking, products, processes, or organizations."

Often defined as "ideas applied successfully", importantly, innovation is always coupled to a practice or behaviour by users (McKeown 2008). Byrd (2003) equates innovation with creativity and risk taking: old ways have to be abandoned; new ways and behaviour have to be adopted.

This process may be completely voluntary, or may be forced by external agents. Innovation may mean completely new, different behaviour; it also may imply small changes in the customary way of doing things by individuals or groups of individuals. Innovation may be imposed under pressure of some external agent or instance, or may be voluntary because the new behaviour is more conducive to reaching a certain goal. Innovation may be the result of push (coerced or enticed) or of pull (engendered by specific needs and wishes of individuals)

In this section, we focus on a special brand of technological innovation: the adoption of broadband technology in order to create a broadband society. In the discussions of Workgroup I of Cost 298 (Users as innovators), four aspects of innovation were distinguished, which span the continuum from completely free and voluntary, user driven pull to externally forced push:

• Creative finding of new uses of existing or new technology by the user. In general, the users themselves customise and adapt technology in order to fulfil a certain desire or need. This is a voluntary pull process (SMS text messaging is a well known example). Users are free to choose whether or not to participate.

• Domestication of adopted new technology into everyday life and work (incremental discovery of possibilities of technology; e.g., use of the pc for increasingly more aspects of everyday life). Choices are influenced by how well users adjust to the new technology and are willing to try out new possibilities.

• Social innovation, another form of incremental innovation: adopting and using new technology under the pressure of significant others (e.g. use of email as a generally accepted communication mode). Choice is restricted or enhanced by the social community of which the user is a member.

• Adopting and adaptation to new devices, prescribed by politics, technology, management, legislation etc., or forced by structural policy (e.g. digital TV, e-government without non-digital alternatives). Such new devices leave no other choice.

Innovation and the role of creativity

From the definitions of innovation, it is clear that innovation is a relative concept. It might mean a completely novel use of something, invented by the user (creative innovation), but it can also mean a new behaviour, in which the person breaks with old habits: e.g. starting to use the internet after years of refusing to because postal services are adequate enough. It can mean the step by step discovery of the wider possibilities offered by a new service or gadget, such in the case of those who at first use the internet only for email and then discover that it is very handy for banking transactions or for booking a trip. Innovation can be individual, or it can be collective for a group of people or for an organisation. Innovative behaviour can be pushed (forced) by external agents like industry, government, organisation or social community, or it can be asked for (pulled) as the result of the actual or perceived needs of individuals or groups.

Innovation and time

Each innovation needs a certain time to reach the users and become an institutionalised way of doing things. Some innovations never enter this stage. A well known example from the eighties is the video telephone, that pundits predicted was to become *the* communication mode of the future. Although the feature was introduced several times, it consistently failed to find a circle of users numerous enough to be economically feasible (Ortt 1998). Only now, as a part of internet telephony, has it finally taken its place among the many modes of modern communication.

At the other end of the spectrum is the phenomenon of SMS text messaging, which emerged as a wholly new and innovative way of using the mobile phone. "Texting" arose spontaneously and succeeded in becoming, within a very short time frame, common technology that is widely used all over the world.

Falling somewhere between these two extremes is the case of pc and internet use, pushed widely by industry and governments. Today's modern society is unthinkable without these technologies. Nevertheless, there is a huge lag between the possibilities that are offered and the actual use that is made of them by individuals and organisations in the different countries of Europe.

What is behind adoption of innovation? What makes people adopt and what makes innovation spread over a wide population of users? What, on the other hand, hampers adoption of (certain types of) innovation in spite of great efforts from industry, governments etc. to make this part of daily life? The next section presents a number of short examples of more or less successful adoption of broadband technology for communication, information and transactions. In some cases, adoption was strongly pushed by external agents, in other cases, pull by users played the most important role.

Some cases

Internet for information and interaction with citizens

One aspect of broadband society is that, within Europe, the internet is assumed to be the main vehicle used by all European citizens to interact with their governmental institutions, whether to obtain information, submit information or to benefit from government e-services and online transactions.

The Netherlands are among the countries in Northern Europe with the highest diffusion of broadband and internet. Particularly, the rollout of broadband occurred at a rapid pace in this country: Between 2001 and the present, a large majority (more than 70%) of all Dutch citizens invested in a broadband connection for their pc, mostly by upgrading their telephone line or using a cable modem . Recent research in the Netherlands, however, shows that despite a constant push and the availability of broadband in the majority of the Dutch households, citizens still do not use the internet as a source of information on relevant issues as a matter of course (Van Deursen et al. 2006).

The most successfully pushed use of on-line interaction between citizens and government is the use of the internet by the Dutch income tax system. The year 1998 saw the introduction of the electronic income tax return. From the very start, citizens were enthusiastically encouraged to file their returns electronically. Since then, a growing group of citizens has made use of this transaction form. In 2006, around 75% of the Dutch citizens who were liable to pay income tax filed their returns electronically. The reasons for choosing the electronic route were mainly the ease of use, speed and the faster result. This does not mean, however, that these returns were all filed by the citizens themselves. Qualitative research by Mante-Meijer & Loos (2007) shows that more than half of the citizens ask for help from others. Around one third relied completely on others, either professionals or trusted third parties.

Another case of push involved a field that was consciously opened up for competition, namely the choice of health insurance company (Loos & Mante-Meijer 2007 and Mante-Meijer & Loos 2008). Up till then, a large part of the population had been covered by a compulsory health insurance system, which assigned people to fixed insurance companies. Under the new system, people were forced to make a choice, evaluating the type of insurance that would best fit their situation. Insurance companies had to compete for clients. Many people were opposed to or very hesitant about this new policy. Not only was there considerable reluctance to change insurance companies, people also failed to make use of all the highly advertised information channels that had been provided so abundantly to make the choice easier. This lack of interest and use could be observed across all age groups and both genders. The main reason for this behaviour was the fact that people had not asked for a change in health insurance system, as they were more than satisfied with the existing system. Furthermore, the analogue media were vastly preferred as information sources. Digital information media were used far less frequently, and mostly in addition to the other media types. The special sites that had been created to enable citizens to compare the various insurance packages available were largely ignored, partly because they provided too much information, and because they were difficult to navigate.

Interactive digital TV

One of the important elements of broadband society is interactivity between users and producers. Digital television is one medium by which this may be realised. Research shows that, although digital will soon be standard for both the TV and the products that may be viewed on TV, the spread of this type of TV is not as rapid or as self-evident as initially expected. Part of this is due to the fact that there are a great many analogue TVs around that still work to the full satisfaction of the user, plus that an extra device (a set top box) is needed to make it possible to receive the digital signal. New TVs have inbuilt digital tuners, but existing TVs do not. As interactive television is still rare, people have demonstrated little interest in purchasing these new TVs or the set top boxes (Pierson et al. 2008; Trkman et al. 2008; see also chapter Vangengck et al. and Tornquist in this volume).

But even when people are offered the opportunity to try out real interactive digital TV for free, they do not necessarily take advantage of the chance to do so (Urban 2008, see also chapter Skezely and Urban in this volume). In Flanders, for example, people were given the opportunity to make use of an interactive digital TV and were observed during a certain period to see how this affected their viewing practices.

Focus group research shows that people say that they like being able to break with the traditional TV system and to fit the incoming flow of content to their own needs. This is also one of the most important triggers for people to switch to digital television. People like being in control, and being able to time shift puts them in control over the existing broadcasting system. However, this does not necessarily mean that people will use the opportunity lavishly. The first test with interactive digital TV in Flanders, e-VRT, showed that people do indeed shift the starting hours of their favourite programmes by means of the PVR and electronic program guide, but in their selection, they often stick to old viewing habits and taste preferences. The time span in which they watched television was also still the typical prime time television hours. This means that the purpose behind this program selection was not to reorganise the viewing time and to adapt the broadcasting schedule to their own needs, but to simply postpone prime time programmes to later on in the evening, when people had the time to watch them (Van den Broeck et al. 2008).

Kitchengate

The Flemish example shows, that it is not so easy to induce people to make use of the opportunities offered by technology. Old habits die slowly. People tend to hold on to practices that have been part of their everyday lives for a long time. They have to discover for themselves how and where to innovate. An example of this was the experiment with Kitchengate Klamer (2005). This was a Danish experiment in 2000 and 2001 in which ICT services were combined within an easily accessible medium that was situated in a central space in the home where the members of the household spent relatively much time (the kitchen): a refrigerator with a computer screen that enabled people to make use of several information and communication, food and family management services:

- Information services: TV, radio, news, traffic information, local information

- Communication services: email, IP telephone, address book, phone book

- Food management such as: recipes, personal cookbook, daily menu, shopping lists

- Family management: calendar, to do lists, yellow notes, voice messages

It turned out that people "discovered" the possibilities, according to their own everyday needs. Dependent on life stage, family composition, age and gender, different types of services were employed. People also started to experiment with new services, such as the internet, of which they had formerly made no use. The field trial was a big success, but was not followed up in the market, because of the costs.

Mobile phone for bird watching

The most well known creative pull innovation instigated by users is the use of SMS as a cheap means of communication to contact others quickly and directly. As the more developed mobile phones offer possibilities to make and send pictures and to access the internet, a new use for the mobile phone was devised by a group of birdwatchers (see chapter Tornquist in this volume). Communities of bird watchers used to pass on information about the numbers and the types of birds that were observed on their bird watching trips on the spot, through notes attached to billboards at certain bird watchers sites. At some point, somebody came up with the idea of developing a special programme on the mobile phone that made real-time communication about the types of bird spotted possible via the internet, combined with photos of the observed birds. The device was easy to operate and soon became very popular within the bird watchers community. The use was a creative innovation on an old theme. People were used to mobile phones and SMS text messaging, but they adapted the extra features to their own specific needs.

Push and pull innovation

Introduction

In the above examples we see technology and policy driven, spontaneous and incremental uses of the technological possibilities provided by broadband. Moreover, they clearly demonstrate that adoption of innovative practices does not occur as a matter of course. Some people are more innovative than others. In general, diffusion is seen to follow the general curve from early adoption to late majority described by Rogers (1962). In the end, even the laggards will start using the technology, although not before the technology has become so embedded in society, that it becomes impossible to neglect. Yet even then, there will be people who consciously refuse to make use of it.

In time, several theories have been developed that explain this phenomenon of diffusion. Each contributes a part of the complete picture. What are the factors that further and hamper the development of e-society? What are the possibilities of push in this respect?

General Diffusion theory

Rogers (1962) developed an economic theory that shows that the adoption of each innovation demonstrates a curve that goes from early adopters or innovators via early majority, late majority to laggards. The idea is that if an innovation is successful, these stages will all be passed through. By the time the late majority has started adopting the innovation, the market will have become saturated and the time will have come to tweak the innovation in order to get the process started again. Innovation adoption is a combination of market push and market pull. Innovation is thought to be mostly driven by economy and technology and the rational choices of people.

This theory does explain in general *how* adoption may develop. It does not explain *why* people want to adopt an innovation in the first place and what happens during the process afterwards.

Domestication theory

The domestication approach (Silverstone & Haddon 1992; Haddon 2004) shows how an innovation slowly becomes embedded in the everyday life of the individual or the household. When people start using it, they gradually develop insights into the diverse ways in which the innovation may be used. Use of the innovation is subsequently integrated into their daily habits. The adoption of the innovation is incremental. Push may start the acquisition, but pull is the determinant factor in the final adoption. This theory does not explain *when* and *why* people decide to start *using* the innovation or decide to forsake it.

Capability theory

Capability theory (Heres et al. 2005) goes more deeply into the circumstances under which adoption may or may not take place. It shows that there needs to be a fit between the person, the person's technological, economical and social situation and the technology offered. If the personal situation or the technical situation does not fit the capabilities and needs of the person, he will not adopt. The whole process is influenced by the structural political, economical, demographical, educational and cultural factors in society. Here, again, push may be used to make people conscious of the innovation, but the fit decides whether people will adopt or not. This theory explains why people *will* or *will not* adopt. It also pays attention to the general societal factors as reasons why societies will differ in their adoption patterns (see Figure 1).

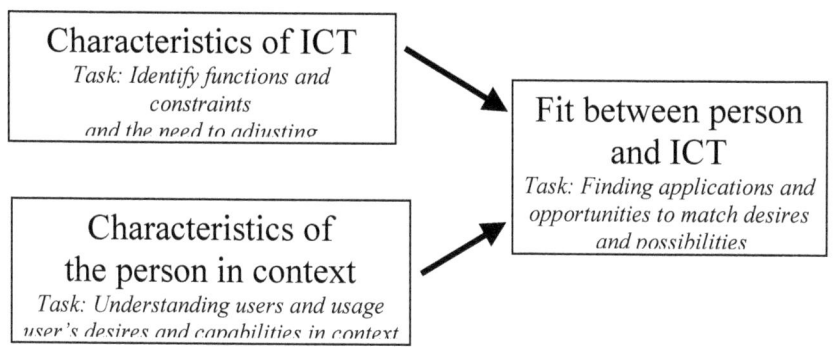

Figure 1: Capability model

Theories of risk taking

Loos & Mante-Meijer (2007) and Mante-Meijer & Loos (2008) explain how theories of risk taking (Schwartz 2004; Simon 1979; Douglas & Wildavski 1982) elucidate the choice-making process itself: perceived risks play an important role in the decision making of people. If the perceived risks are too great, people abstain from making a decision and keep things as they are. However, some people accept higher risks than others. Douglas & Wildavsky (2004) speak of different cultures of risk taking: in individualistic cultures, people look only at personal risk and gain, while in regulated cultures people do not intend to do something that might break the rules. These rules may be the structural rules of society as a whole, or the rules of their own social group.

Analysing the cases

Theoretical framework

Actors make sense of their structural environment and translate this into certain practices by making choices between alternatives. Weick (1969, 27, 64) called this translation process and the resulting practices "enactment":

> "Rather than talking about adapting to an external environment, it may be more correct to argue that organizing consists of adapting to an enacted environment, an environment which is *constituted by* the actions of interdependent human actors. (...) The phrase "enacted environment" preserves the crucial distinction that we wish to make, the most important being that the human *creates* the environment to which the system then adapts. The human actor does not *re*act to an environment, he *en*acts it. It is this enacted environment, and nothing else, that is worked upon by the process of organizing."

The choice-making during this process and the resulting practices can be constrained by sanctions, punitive responses from some other actors or by the given character of structural properties. In the same way, these same properties may enable certain choices and resulting practices. On the one hand, structure influences practices which may push an innovation by enablers and constraints; on the other hand, practices can also influence structure (Giddens' "duality of structure", see figure 2). In both cases it is the sense making of the individual that is decisive for the adoption.

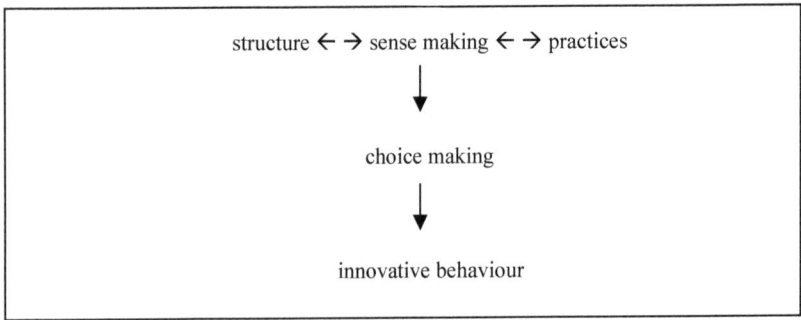

Figure 2: Theoretical frame work

In figure 2, we see the main processes that play a role in innovative behaviour. Both structure and practices guide the ways people perceive and make sense of their situation, i.e., the ways they may translate structural conditions into everyday practices, or standard practices into new structures. Structural conditions may find their sources in the macro structure of the society of which the individual is a part (e.g. economy, cultural, political, educational systems and other institutional factors), but also by the meso and micro structure the organisations of which people are a member, the formal and informal social groups to which they belong and in which they live, work and have leisure activities in their everyday lives. All these structural conditions on different levels act as enablers or constraints of innovation and pose choices that have to be made. But not only structure plays a role, the capabilities of the person himself also influence and drive the choice-making. Intelligence, education, personal economic position, feeling for technology, individualism, adherence to rules, e.g. are filters which are used in the assessment of perceived risks or advantages of innovative behaviour, and the resulting choosing of practices.

Let us now look again at the cases we presented, keeping in mind the different theoretical angles in interpreting the behaviour of the users.

Internet for information and interaction with citizens

First, the case of the government push for innovative ways to communicate with the government: the tax system and the health insurance system. The most interesting difference is that it took a relatively short time and no coercion to seduce the citizen into e-filing his tax return, while the change in the system of health insurance and the use of digital information met with a lot of resistance.

The following differences could be observed:

• Electronic tax filing was strongly pushed by the tax department as it enabled the organization to work more quickly and more efficiently.

• People were obliged to file a tax return anyway, and were used to calculating their taxes themselves and filling in a hard-copy form, a method in which errors easily occurred. The new system simplified the work enormously by doing the calculations automatically. People only had to fill in the given categories, after which the amount to be paid or the refund would automatically be shown. As people were already accustomed to using a pc, it was not a big step away from standing practices. For those reluctant to download the programme from the internet or to submit their return electronically, the system also offers a CD Rom that is sent by ordinary mail. The instructions on how to fill in the form were provided with the program. If desired, more extensive information was also available in hardcopy instruction guides. Using the electronic option posed no risk, and offered ease and security. In this case, the innovation was enabled by the high density of computer use in Dutch households. It made sense to people to make use of the new method, because it saved time. Even if when help was needed from others, using the electronic option simplified the work of the helpers.

In the case of the health insurance system, there was a strong governmental push to choose a new health insurance company, but on what basis and how were not defined. This meant that citizens had to make their own choices, making use of information they had to accumulate themselves. Considerable effort was required to do a thorough job of comparing the possibilities. The authorities assumed that people would go to the websites which had been specifically developed and were being pushed as enablers to help them with their choice. In reality, people turned to analogue information sources and the sites of the insurance companies themselves. This was due to the constraints that these specially developed websites posed:

• Stimulating the use of websites presupposes the ability to make use of these. This proved a far too optimistic assumption: the sites were not easily navigated, information was not always clear. The sites themselves did not fit the specific needs and requirements of the users.

• Another reason for this lack of interest in the use of digital information could be the lack of knowledge and capability to navigate the internet in an efficient way. Indeed, research showed that the websites of municipalities and general governmental institutions were widely unknown and widely unused, despite the enormous efforts to advertise them and make them available to all citizens (Van Deursen et al. 2006). Consequently, intensive research was carried out into the constraints in the use of websites in the public domain. This research showed that, although most people have the technical and operational skills to navigate the internet, they often lack the analytical abilities to select the relevant information (Van Deursen & Van Dijk 2008). There was no fit between the capabilities and the needs of the citizens and the technology provided.

• It was also thought that people would be highly motivated to choose the best package at the lowest price. However, only in a very limited number of cases did economic value prove to be the most important enabler: far more important were values such as loyalty to the current insurance company, the lack of dissatisfaction with the cover provided, a fear that choosing the cheapest package was risky in terms of the quality of service in the future, and a negative attitude towards change as such, which made looking for information a waste of time. In other words: the innovation was interpreted in many cases as being unwanted and risky.

Interactive digital TV

The experience with interactive digital TV revealed other aspects. Although digital TV is being pushed as a standard for Europe, adoption is progressing only slowly. Here are some aspects that potential users were found to take into consideration:

• Conventional analogue TV is still very widespread. Since its adoption in the fifties, people have grown used to it and to the standard broadcast programming. It was adopted as a one way information and entertainment medium, used for the purpose of relaxation after a day of hard work. People are not used to interaction with their TV. Interactive digital TV does not fit into their everyday lives.

• A TV is supposed to be a durable consumption good, to be replaced only if it no longer suffices. Here, budgetary aspects acted as a constraint for buying a new one.

• Due to the rapid pace of technological development, people tend to postpone new acquisitions for some time. Not only do they do so because they are used to the old technology and have no real desire to relearn how to use their appliances, but also because of the fear that newly acquired technology will also become outdated within a short time. The risks are too great. Especially in times of economic insecurity, people put off replacing outdated devices and appliances that still work by newer models.

• Interactive programmes are (still) scarce, limited to voting either by (mobile) telephone or via the internet. Here, the quality of the programmes were a constraint to innovation.

• The set top box is an addition that might or might not fit into the furnishing of the house. More TVs in the house mean more boxes and higher costs.

The case of the video on demand trial in Flanders shows the working of the time frame: People were offered an opportunity to try out a new feature. There was no real obligation to make changes. People were used to certain viewing habits and viewing times. Although they appreciated the idea of being able to watch programmes any time any day, in practice they only made limited use of the possibilities. There were some changes, but they were restricted to certain programmes that were viewed somewhat later on the same evening at a more convenient time. The viewing patterns were not only dictated by the programmes people wanted to see, but also by the time schedules of everyday life. In other words, it took time to domesticate the new features into the viewing habits.

Kitchengate

Kitchengate is an example of an incremental innovation offered by a new gadget. The feature fitted the information and communication needs in the households of the participants in the try out. There was no risk connected to participation. It was adaptable to the different interests of the various household members. Features that fit into daily practices were used, while those that did not were discarded, depending on the person living in the household in question. People did not have to change their habits, but were given means to practise these in a different and more efficient way.

Interesting was the fact that there was also a tendency to try out things that, up till then, had not been used, e.g. the internet function. Here we see that, during the trial, a certain degree of domestication occurred of the new feature in the kitchen. An enabler was the fact that an easily accessible medium was involved that was situated in a central space in the home where the members of the household spent relatively much time, and which provided features that were interpreted as handy and useful. Features such as on-line shopping that were not considered convenient were seldom used.

Mobile phone for bird watching

The mobile phone for bird watching is a typical example of a pull innovation and a grass-roots innovation. A member of the bird watching community discovered a new use for the mobile phone and was able to develop a program that fit mobile telephone use into the hobby of his community. As it simplified communication about the birds observed, it was quickly adopted by the members of this community. It was not freely available on the market. To make use of the program, it was necessary to be a member of the community. Enablers were the availability of a person who could develop and produce the program. It also lent an air of exclusivity to the members of the group and served as a binding factor and an incentive to join the community. Not being part of the community was a constraint to make use of the information the program could provide.

Conclusions

In this chapter we explored the factors that influence the adoption of broadband in European society. We especially paid attention to the following questions:

- What is innovation in the Broadband Society?

- Which aspects of innovation can be distinguished?

- What is the role of push factors and pull factors in this innovation process?

- Which enablers and constraints can be distinguished during this process?

We saw that innovation, in the sense of using new ways for doing something in everyday life, may cover a wide range of practices. Innovation may mean developing completely new practices or building on existing practices. It may be revolutionary, or incremental. It may be due to a creative moment of some individuals or groups in society, it may be part of a hype or a fashion or it may mean slowly getting accustomed to new possibilities. In this sense, even laggards in adopting new technology could be "innovators", as they, too, are won over to doing things in new ways. All these forms of innovation together shape the Broadband Society, a society that will develop into one in which broadband technology will be the universal medium used across Europe. This also means that creating a broadband society cannot be done overnight, but will take time to develop. The question is: What possibilities are there to enhance this development and how to ensure the quality of life of people in this broadband Europe?

Our example cases show that, in modern society, (technological) innovation is greatly pushed by technologists, economy and politics. However, it is clear that push only is not a sufficient means to get people to adopt. The above examples provide some insight into the complicated field of innovation, adoption and use. Starting with Roger's theory on the adoption curve, we examined the factors that play a role in the adoption process and looked at how they can explain why people are prepared to innovate or not. On the one hand, we see the role of domestication, capabilities and fit, and choice making as factors that influence the incremental aspects of the adoption process. On the other hand, the willingness to innovate as such is pushed or hampered by the readiness to take risks. All these theories pertain to the enablers and constraints that play a role in the process mentioned by Giddens, in which innovative behaviour is related to structural environment – sense making – practices. Given the structures people are a part of, and given the perception they have of the usefulness of the innovation in their everyday lives, these enablers and constraints turn people into early adopters/innovators, or make them choose to postpone the adoption or to reject it totally. It is all about the way they "enact" their environment (Weick 1969).

The cases also illustrate that push might come from diverse sources: the macro structure of the social system that forms the general background in which the decision-making process is primed, but also the meso and micro structures in the direct social environment that coerce, invite or constrain the individual to look for innovative practices. Push can be successful, but only if the right enablers are brought into the field and the innovation fits the capabilities and the sense making of the potential users. On the other hand, these same structural factors, sense making and enablers might result in a pull for innovative technology, and spontaneous innovation.

Finally, it is important to keep in mind that, according to Giddens' structuration theory, "structure properties of social systems are both medium and outcome of the practices thy recursively organise" (Giddens 1984, 25). Applied to innovation we could argue that structure is both *a starting point for* as well as *a result of* innovative practices by sense making human beings.

References

Byrd J. The Innovation Equation: Building Creativity & Risk Taking in Your Organization San Francisco, CA: Jossey-Bass/Pfeiffer Aprint (2003)

Deursen A. van, Dijk J. van, Ebbers W. 'Why e-government usage lags behind: Explaining the gap between potential and actual usage of electronic public services in the Netherlands' Lecture Notes in Computer Science 4084 (2006) pp. 269-280

Deursen A., Dijk J. van Digitale Vaardigheden van Nederlandse Burgers, Scientific Report Series Enschede: Universiteit Twente (2008)

Douglas M., Wildavsky A. Risk and Culture. An Essay on the Selection of Technological and Environmental Dangers Berkely, Los Angeles, London: University of California Press (1982)

Giddens A. The Constitution of Society: Outline of the Theory of Structuration Cambridge: Polity Press (1984)

Haddon L. Information and Communication Technologies in Everyday Life: A Concise Introduction and Research Guide Oxford: Berg Publishers (2004)

Heres J., Mante-Meijer E., Turk T., Pierson J. 'Adoption of ICTs: A proposed framework' eds. Mante-Meijer E., Klamer L. ICT Capabilities in Action: What People Do Luxemburg: Office for Official Publications of the European Communities (2005) pp. 19-48

Klamer L. 'Kitchengate: 'The screenfridge innovation: Solutions to fulfill a need?' eds. Mante-Meijer E., Klamer L. ICT Capabilities in Action: What People Do Luxemburg: Office for Official Publications of the European Communities (2005) pp. 49-66

Loos E., Mante-Meijer E. De Kiezende Burger en het Nieuwe Zorgstelsel. De Invloed van Leeftijd, Geslacht en Opleiding op het Gebruik van Oude en Nieuwe Media als Informatiebron Houten: Springer (2007)

Mante-Meijer E., Loos E. Het Gebruik van Oude en Nieuwe media voor Contacten met de Belastingdienst. Multi-channel Onderzoek naar de Invloed van Leeftijd, Geslacht en Opleiding Case Study for the "Alliantie Vitaal Bestuur", Dutch Ministry of the Interior Utrecht: USBO (2007)

Mante-Meijer E., Loos E. 'Risk takers and choice makers: Their (non) use of new media. Age and risk perception during a choice process' eds. Pierson J., Mante-Meijer E., Loos E., Sapio B. Innovation for and by Users Brussels: Opoce (2008) pp. 53-64

McKeown, M. 'About Innovation', Financial Times (2008)

Ortt R.J. Videotelephony in the Consumer Market Leidschendam: KPN Research (1998)

Pierson J., Jacobs A., De Marez L. 'Archetypical users as starting point for exploring wireless city applications: Linking the domestication and diffusion approach.' eds. Pierson J., Mante-Meijer E., Loos, E, Sapio B. Innovation for and by Users. Brussels: Opoce (2008) pp. 107-120

Rogers E.M. Diffusions of Innovations New York: Free Press (1962)

Schwartz B., 2004. The Paradox of Choice. Why More is Less New York: Harper Perennial (2004)

Silverstone R., Haddon L. 'Explaining ICT consumption: The case of the home computer' eds. Silverstone R., Hirsch, E. Consuming Technologies: Media and Information in Domestic Spaces London: Routledge (1992) pp. 82-97

Simon H. 'Rational decision making in business organizations' American Economic Review 69 (4) (1979) pp. 493-513

Trkman P., Blažič B.J., Turk T. 'Broadband development: The importance of enablers and constraints for a consistent strategic policy making' eds. Pierson J., Mante-Meijer E., Loos E., Sapio B. Innovation for and by Users Brussels: Opoce (2008) pp. 181-19

Urban A. 'Mobile television: A hype or a real consumer need?' eds. Pierson J., Mante-Meijer E., Loos E., Sapio B. Innovation for and by Users. Brussels: Opoce (2008) pp. 27-38

Van den Broeck W., Pierson J., Lievens B. 'Confronting video-on-demand with television viewing practices' eds. Pierson J., Mante-Meijer E., Loos E., Sapio B. Innovation for and by Users Brussels: Opoce (2008) pp. 13-26

Van den Broeck W., Pierson J., Pauwels C. 'Does itv imply new uses?' A Flemish case study Paper presented at The EuroITV2004 conference in Brighton (29 March 29 – 1st April 2004)

Weick K.E. The Social Psychology of Organizing Reading Massachusetts: Addison-Wesley (1969)

Weick K.E. Making Sense of the Organization Oxford: Blackwell (2001)

Valerie Frissen and Mijke Slot

The Return of the Bricoleur: Redefining Media Business

Introduction

"The desktop revolution has brought the tools that only professionals have had into the hands of the public. God knows what will happen now." (Minsky 1983, in Friedrichs 1983)

For centuries, the only mass medium available to the public was print – in the form of books, newspapers or pamphlets. Not until the late nineteenth century did new technologies emerge that enabled the rise of other mass media (Croteau & Hoynes 1997; Gorman & McLean 2003). Commercial printing technologies, the development of newer techniques for photography and the phonograph paved the way for, amongst others, illustrated newspapers and magazines, printed sheet music, music records, postcards and children's books (Anderson 2006). In 1895, the Lumière brothers invented the cinematograph, enabling moving pictures.

The array of mass media was extended with the introduction of the radio in 1920, leading to the so-called golden age of radio in the 1930s. In the 1940s, television entered the household. From the 1950s until the 1980s, television dominated the mass media landscape (Castells 2000). Just like radio, television had the ability to reach massive audiences at one point in time with a single broadcast. In the 1970s, game consoles and VCRs were introduced. Game consoles enabled people to play video games at home, such as Pong– one of the first video games (1972). The VCR enabled time shifting: watching broadcasts at a freely chosen moment in time.

As consumers, people used many of these mass media; they read newspapers, magazines and books, watched films and television, listened to the radio and music records and played video games. In the 1980s, the media sector underwent substantial changes. These were, in first place, technological in nature. The personal computer entered the household. Media content was digitized. The scope of publishing expanded to electronic sources. The diffusion of the computer was followed by the roll out of the internet. Computers were linked together in a network, enabling connections between users. The internet was increasingly seen as the most important technological platform for the media and communications sector (Henten & Tadayoni 2008).

More importantly, the internet enabled passive consumers of content to become active users. The internet provides a two-way channel for communication (Shirky 2000; Tapscott & Williams 2006; Leadbeater 2008; Van Dijck 2009). Contrary to mass media, online media enable consumers to talk back and to design and program for themselves. Computers are tools for text processing, photo and video editing, audio recording and playing games. And the internet supplies a massive network for users to communicate with others and to share information. Jenkins (2006) describes this new converged media system as a participatory culture in which both users and producers interact with each other according to a new set of rules.

This chapter focuses on the transformation of the traditional media audience and the resulting substantial changes in user/producer relations that have taken place within the media landscape. These developments are put in a broader perspective and linked to the concept of "bricolage", a concept coined by the French anthropologist and philosopher Claude Lévi-Strauss. Bricolage refers to a way of thinking and making sense of the environment, which is strongly rooted in concrete, everyday experience. The concept has since also been applied in media studies and cultural studies, where it involves a process of resignification of cultural signs or artefacts with established meanings that are reorganised into new codes of meaning in new circumstances (Barker 2004). In this chapter we use the concept to analyse the *changing role of the media-user,* who can be understood as the new bricoleur. The changing role of the user has profound consequences for consumer/producer relations in online media services.

First, the concept of bricolage is explained in more detail. Secondly, the transitions in user roles and user/producer relations are illustrated by two specific developments in the media industry in which users took on other roles then being only consumers: peer-to-peer (P2P) file-sharing in the music industry and citizen journalism and blogging in the press domain. Both developments show how users have used the concrete creative potential of their new media environment and have reworked this into new uses with a disruptive impact on established user/producer relations, which, therefore, can be understood as bricolage.

Our analysis is based on an overview of both quantitative and qualitative secondary literature concerning technological and organisational developments in two media domains, with a focus on changing user roles and subsequently on user/producer relationships. Based on sales figures and industry data, the developments of traditional consumption are highlighted. These data serve to illustrate the changed consumer/producer relations. Furthermore, a number of new developments in the music and press sector are presented, showing how technology enables consumers to become bricoleurs.

Bricolage

The French word "bricolage" (from the verb "bricoler") means "tinkering". In the Merriam Webster dictionary, "bricolage" is described as the "construction (as of a sculpture or a structure of ideas) achieved by using whatever comes to hand" (http://www.merriam-webster.com/dictionary/bricolage). Claude Lévi-Strauss introduced the concept in his book The Savage Mind, to describe the characteristic features of "primitive" mythical thought. The bricoleur, according to Lévi-Strauss, uses all the concrete materials he encounters in everyday life and all the earlier experiences of himself and others around him, to make sense of the world he is living in and to find solutions for the problems he is confronted with in everyday life. He creatively and intuitively combines and recombines the bits and pieces that are available in the "treasury" of his everyday surroundings and experiences. By using what is concretely available, he often – more or less accidentally - creates something new. In this sense the bricoleur can be contrasted with the "ingénieur" (engineer), who deploys a more systematic, structured and rational way of thinking, and is *explicitly* looking for something new. According to Lévi-Strauss, the engineer represents modern, scientific thought, while the bricoleur represents the "savage mind" or a wild kind of thinking.

The concept of bricolage has been used in several disciplines such as the arts, where it refers to the creation of a work of art from a diverse range of materials and things that are already available. In music it has been applied to for instance hip hop and rap music. These styles can be seen as a mix of Afro-American urban culture, elements of traditional oral story telling by "griots" in West Africa, and musical beats and samples taken out of different traditions, all recombined into a new kind of music with the aid of computer technology (Frissen 2008; Von Hippel 2005)

In academic thinking, the notion of bricolage has been used by postmodern philosophers, such as Baudrillard, Derrida, Deleuze and Guattari. In cultural studies, the concept has been applied to understand the cultural practices of subcultures (e.g. Hebdige 2008). In technology studies, Sherry Turkle has used the concept to describe an intuitive and associative style of computer programming that strongly resembles the "wild thinking" as described by Lévi-Strauss. In her book Life on the Screen (1995), Turkle contrasts this style with the conventional, structured and top-down "planner" approach of traditional software developers. The bricoleur-programmer plays with the elements of a program, with the bits of code, applies a process of trial and error, and uses visualization and simulation techniques. He learns about how things work by interacting with them (Turkle 1995, 51-52).

Over the past decade this style has gained prominence in the field of ICT and technology development. In innovation studies, Eric Von Hippel has described many examples of user-generated innovations in his book Democratizing Innovation, while Charles Leadbeater & Miller (2004) have pointed out that professional amateurs ("pro-ams") are more and more important for creative production and are changing the way these production processes are organized. If we take a closer look at the actual practices of this new breed of users, we can see remarkable similarities with Lévi-Strauss' description of bricolage. Pro-ams – or "lead users" as Von Hippel labels them – take their concrete everyday life and user experience as starting point and as toolbox for (accidental) innovation. In a process of trial and error and by smartly and intuitively using the available experience and knowledge of their peers, they improve existing products and processes and develop new ideas.

Many illustrations of this new form of creativity can be found in the media and ICT domain, famous examples being evidently Linux, P2P technology and what is popularly referred to as web 2.0. Influential ICT innovations often are accidental inventions, the result of a process of trial and tinkering, incremental little steps and combinations that are being made in the concrete experience of everyday life and everyday interactions. In this process, users have become more prominent actors in innovation. The current stage of development of ICT and new media offers users many possibilities to start "tinkering". The internet constitutes a rich treasury of building blocks and bits and pieces of software that can be used and recombined to every possible goal and advantage. The current internet has thus strongly enabled the return of "wild thinking" or the return of the bricoleur. And the return of the bricoleur, in turn, has enabled users to take on roles which were traditionally the privilege of business parties. This has transformed the character of the media sector.

Transitions in the media sector

The changed behaviour of internet users and the way this has influenced user/producer relationships are illustrated by the developments in two media entertainment domains; the music industry and the press domain.

Changing consumption patterns and peer-to-peer file-sharing in the music industry

One of the first media sectors that witnessed changing user roles was the music industry. From 1999 on, enabled by file-sharing programmes like Napster, users started up- and downloading music files through peer-to-peer (P2P) file-sharing networks on a large scale. Napster was the first user-friendly program for the audience to transfer and download files (Bender & Wang 2009). At the turn of the century, the usage of P2P file-sharing platforms took off. In 2002, approximately 100 million users had file-sharing software on their computers. They used the technological opportunities that were offered to them to explore music and videos and share it with peers. The decentralized and ubiquitous file-sharing networks proved to be a nightmare for the incumbents in the music industry.

The music industry had faced similar copying threats with the invention of the cassette player and the CD recordable, but these problems were relatively small-scale (Mooney et al. 2010). In those days, the industry did have a problem with professional pirates, but the problem with at home users was to some extent manageable – not in the least because taxes could be put on carriers. Internet proved to be different: users discovered that it offered the possibility to share server space, as millions of computers were linked in a network. As music was available in digital form, the code could be cracked, it could be stored on their computers, and it could be copied and shared in the network. This development made the original physical carrier of content (a CD–disk) more and more obsolete. Millions of users were taking on roles as distributors and started bypassing the traditional players in the music industry; the scope of file-sharing extended. Furthermore, the internet environment encouraged users to take up new roles in the value chain of music production and consumption; by exploring these new possibilities they forced the music industry to revise its business strategy substantially. In the following sections, this development is described in more detail.

Shaking up traditional consumer/producer relations

The reaction of incumbents in the music industry was to a large extent defensive, with the music industry claiming that sales of music CDs were declining at a disastrous rate. In the US in 1997, 753 million CDs were shipped. This number rose steadily to 942.5 million in 2000 (which is actually inconsistent with the popularity of file-sharing in these years) but dwindled after 2000 to 619.7 million in 2006 (RIAA 2007). The recording industry blamed users who were illegally downloading music files. In 2007, the Institute for Policy Innovation (IPI) estimated that the cost of worldwide sound recording piracy to the US was 12.5 billion USD (Siwek 2007). The industry at first started suing the programs behind file-sharing. In 2000, the US court limited the activities of Napster, a file-sharing service with approximately 77 million users. And these activities continued. The International Federation of the Phonographic Industry (IFPI) stated that in 2002, 2003 and 2004 respectively 28,000, 38,000 and 41,000 web and FTP sites were taken down (IFPI 2004, 15).

In addition to suing file-sharing services, the music industry tried several other tactics to ban file-sharing, which included applying strict digital rights management (DRM) to music files, launching awareness campaigns for the public and urging governments to strengthen the copyright protection system (Blomqvist et al. 2005; Bakker 2005; Bender & Wang 2009; Van Eijk et al. 2010). From 2002, lawsuits were brought against individual copyright infringers in several countries. In 2004, the IFPI, for example, reported civil claims against 150 P2P users in Denmark in 2002, 100 criminal complaints filed against 100 P2P users in Korea in 2003 and criminal raids of 75 P2P uploaders and service providers in Italy in 2003 (IFPI 2004).

Changed consumption behaviour

As Van Eijk et al. (2010) point out, although the recording industry was confident that the declining sales were brought about by illegal file-sharing, the measurable effect of file-sharing on music sales is ambiguous (also see Bender & Wang 2009). Over the years, a discussion started about the causality of file-sharing on music sales, with different research outcomes contradicting each other (e.g. Oberholzer & Strumpf 2004; Liebowitz 2004; Bakker 2004; Geist 2005; Michel 2006; Bender & Wang 2009; Liebowitz 2010; Mooney et al. 2010). Some scholars supported the music industry in its claims, while others contested these claims. Oberholzer & Strumpf (2004), for example, used observations of actual file-sharing behaviour. In 2004, they alleged that illegal downloads had a minimal effect on sales, and that the effects were actually statistically indistinguishable from zero. The outcome of their research was contested by others, most importantly Liebowitz (2004; 2010). Most studies show that illegal downloading has a limited effect on music sales. Other factors also contributed to declining CD sales. Authors mention, for example, poor macro economic conditions, a reduction in the number of album releases, growing competition from other forms of entertainment, the sale of vinyl singles, or qualitative factors.

There might be another factor that influences the music industry, and this concerns *changed user behaviour* (apart from sharing music with peers). This can be illustrated by looking at sales data. The United States is taken as an example here. The Recording Industry Association of America (RIAA) provides shipment statistics in the US. These are total statistics of all units sold in one single year (e.g. CD's, cassettes, music videos, digital downloads) For the purpose of this analysis, they are compared from end 1990 to end 2009 (see Figure 1).

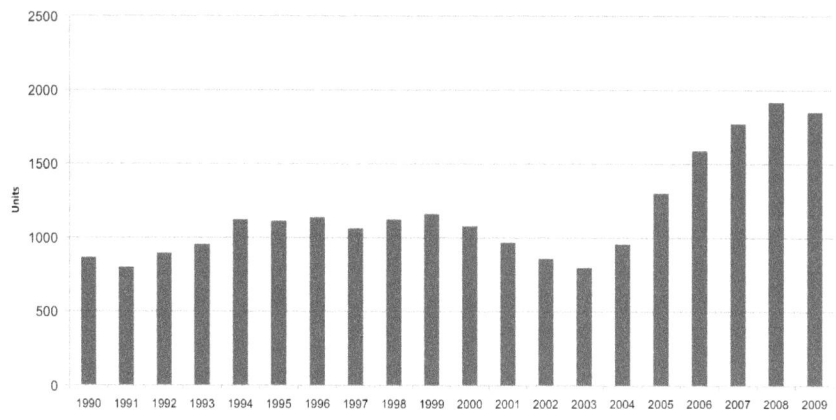

Figure 1: Total shipment music units in the US 1990-2009 (data source: RIAA)

Taking a closer look at these sales data, total shipment in the US showed a slightly upward curve from 1991 to 1994. The years 1994 – 1999 showed relatively stable shipment figures. Sales started declining from 1999 (1,161 million units) to 2003 (798.4 million units) – a decline of approximately 31 percent. This decline coincides with the year that file-sharing gained popularity. But sales took off again in 2004 (in this respect, it needs to be underlined that it was not until 2004 that legal digital downloads were included in the shipment statistics). In 2005 the sales even surpassed the number of 1999 sales (1,302 million units). In 2009, the sales declined slightly.

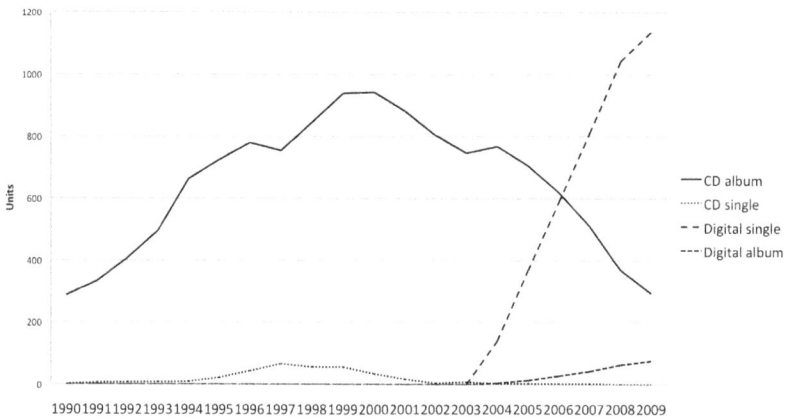

Figure 2: Shipment statistics per carrier 1990-2009 (data source: RIAA)

In figure 2, the shipment statistics of CD's and digital sales of music singles and music albums are compared. The decline in sales of CD albums is clearly visible and starts around 1999. From 2003 on, digital sales take off (and are provided by the RIAA). Between 2006 and 2007, digital single sales surpass the physical CD album sales. It seems that, through the years, digital sale of singles has compensated the decline in CD albums that are sold. The digital music album seems to have taken over the position of the CD single, and is only marginally sold. Looking at these figures, the claim that users have stopped buying music seems untrue. Users even started to buy more music than before. But their consumption behaviour has changed. Rather than buying music albums, online they primarily buy single tracks.

The success of digital sales and other production possibilities

The declining sales in the music industry can thus be put into historical perspective. Researchers showed that *illegal* digital music sharing is only one aspect of the drop in music income from sales. But by analyzing sales data provided by RIAA, it becomes clear that *legal* online music sales *did* affect the music industry to great extent. From 2004 on, the sales of online legal music took off. From that year on, the RIAA started incorporating digital sales into their reports. In 2006, the association of the recording industry worldwide (IFPI) claimed that in two years time, the digital sales of music has gone from nil to six percent of the global worldwide revenues, what accounts for 1.1 billion Dollars (IFPI 2006). In 2007, 15 percent of all music sales is sold online or on mobile and worldwide revenues were estimated 2.9 billion Dollars (IFPI 2008). The number of legal online music services rose from 50 in 2004 to 350 in 2006. In 2007 this number has risen to over 500. And over 6 million tracks were accessible legally for users to download (IFPI 2008). In 2009, more than 25 percent of record companies' revenues could be attributed to digital sales (IFPI 2010). Digital sales had a market value of an estimated 4.2 billion Dollars. Furthermore, IFPI stated that 11 million music tracks were available through 400 legal music websites.

This development is influencing a growing number of companies in the music industry who have adapted to the changed circumstances and started offering online music legally. Apple, for example, introduced the iPod player in 2001 and started selling music online through their iTunes Music Store in 2003, competing with large online record stores like Wal-Mart (in the USA) and Amazon. By 2006, one billion songs had already been downloaded from the iTunes store and in January 2008, Apple surpassed the other online retailers by covering 19 percent of the online market for music downloads (Bangeman 2008). For businesses, legal internet music sales open up a whole range of new business opportunities, including, amongst other things more individualized marketing, an increasingly diverse offering (long tail markets) and other ways to make money, for example, by starting music services based on streaming. Furthermore, internet enables producers to offer their users personalized recommendations like the well-known "people who bought this album have also bought (...)".

Digitization and online distribution of music has had various *other* consequences for user/producer relations. Firstly, it has enabled users to change their consumption patterns. Rather than buying complete digital albums online, users were particularly interested in single music tracks. As the analysis shows, sales of digital singles rose faster than the sales of digital albums. Secondly, users are enabled to take on different roles in music services. Some legal services actively employ their users to distribute the music through P2P file-sharing, leveraging the large costs of servers to store music tracks. Furthermore, services like Weedshare & Altnet reward their users with respectively credits and money when they share their music files with other users. And the internet has significantly lowered the threshold for several new initiatives in the music domain.

Firstly, the internet allows music producers to offer new distribution deals. Online music distribution takes on many shapes. Users are enabled to download music a-la-carte as in iTunes. But increasingly, users have also started subscribing to music services (like MusicStation and Spotify), non-DRM download services, advertising-supported services and brand partnerships (IFPI 2008). Spotify, for example, offers users 15 hours of free streaming music. For a premium subscription, users can stream music without any time limits and commercial breaks. They can even download the music to an offline playlist for portable playback. In 2008, Nokia and SonyEricsson offered mobile phone subscribers unlimited access to music.

Secondly, internet enables established artists to engage in new music deals and become more independent. In 2007, the British band Radiohead released their album *In Rainbows* online for free (Pareles 2007). Users were enabled to download the music and to pay whatever price they wanted for the album. According to ComScore, 62 percent of all users who downloaded the album in October 2007 did not pay anything for it. But still, the average user (payers and non-payers taken together) paid $2.26 per download (ComScore 2007).

Furthermore, the internet lowers the threshold for lesser-known artists to market themselves and sell their music to a large audience. According to a study by Madden (2004), American musicians are using the internet as a tool to create, promote and sell their work. A large majority - some 83 percent - of these American musicians say they provide free samples or previews of their work on the internet. For example, artists have started promoting themselves in social communities like MySpace., Over 1.2 million rock acts and 1.7 million R&B acts are vying for attention on this social network (IFPI 2008). Some of them succeed, like the famous examples of Arctic Monkeys, Lilly Allen and Esmee Denters. Yet next to unknown artists rising to fame themselves, record companies are increasingly starting to interact with these networks. Social networks function as marketing networks for music producers. They sometimes allow users to share music files for promotion. Furthermore, online networks like MySpace function as a breeding ground for new artists. Record companies are paying a lot of attention to these sites, for they might popularize certain acts. They filter the offerings on these sites and try to contract new and popular artists. In this respect, they are once more trying to take on a gate-keeping role.

But (lastly), users are also taking on these gate-keeping roles themselves, engaging in the selection process of bands. In this respect, one interesting new online initiative is Sellaband (www.sellaband.com). This website started in 2006 and allows users to invest in artists who present themselves online. For 10 Dollars, users can buy an interest in a band they like. These users are called believers. Every band that collects 5000 believers, equal to 50,000 Dollars, is allowed to make a CD. The possible profit this CD is going to make is split between the artist, Sellaband and the believers. In August 2008, 8324 artists were registered on Sellaband, of which 25 had reached 5000 believers. At the end of 2009, $3,000,000 was invested by users. In 2010, the service went bankrupt, but was able to find a buyer and re-start (Van Buskirk 2010). Other fan-funded websites for music are Aucadia.com, Pledgemusic.com and Artistshare.net.

The creating user in the press domain: citizen journalism and blogging

The press domain consists of newspapers, books and magazines. In this section, we will focus on newspapers. The first newspapers were published at the beginning of the seventeenth century. Over the years, new and emerging media sectors like television, radio and the internet have become increasingly stronger competitors of the press, which led in fact to a crisis in the newsprint media at the beginning of this century: many newspapers are now desperately trying to survive in this highly competitive market. One of the important drivers behind this crisis is the changing behaviour of the user, who has started to use the possibilities of the internet in many ways.

Newspaper business

Every year, the World Association of Newspapers (WAN) carries out a survey on the newspaper industry. In 2004, they reported that worldwide circulation of newspapers had grown 2.1 percent, taking global sales to a new record of 395 million daily newspapers (WAN 2005). Since 2000, the number of global titles rose 4.6 percent. In 2007, the number of daily newspapers was up to 532 million newspapers and 540 million in 2008. In 2009, the global newspaper industry witnessed a decline of 0.9 percent, due to the economic downturn. In some countries, circulation was already falling, and at an even more rapid pace prior to the economic doldrums such as in the US and in various countries in the European Union like Germany and the Netherlands. From 2003, the European Union witnessed a drop in the circulation for paid-for newspapers by almost six percent (WAN 2007). Traditional subscription newspapers were increasingly competing with free newspapers like Metro and online news sources.

In 1999, 347 million people bought a newspaper every day, while in 2004, this number was up to 395 million (WAN 2005). The daily readership of newspapers was estimated at one billion in 2004 and 1.7 billion in 2007 (WAN 2007). Since the adoption of the internet, however, users are increasingly turning to the internet to read news messages. This is possibly influencing readership of traditional subscription newspapers. In the US, in 1974 around 72 percent of the population could be counted as a regular newspaper reader (Distripress 2005). But in 2000, this figure was down to 57 percent. In the European Union that year, 62.1 percent of the adults read a newspaper every day (WAN 2001).

Digitizing the news

In Digitizing the news (2005), Boczkowski studies how daily newspapers in America have been influenced by technology. He states that the internet had radical consequences for the production and consumption of news. The traditional roles of newspapers as content providers, agenda-setters and watchdogs started changing (Picone 2007). In the 1980s, newspapers started exploring technological possibilities like videotex and teletext. Furthermore, newspapers were increasingly written, edited and printed at a distance (Castells 2000). Reporters were taking advantage of the technological developments and portable computers in their jobs. For example, the TRS-80 portable computer was often used by reporters in the field (University of Minnesota 2007).

Slowly, newspapers started relying on the web as a new publishing environment. In 1980, the New York Times, Wall Street Journal and Dow Jones put their news in an online database. And in 1985, 50 newspapers were offering online access to news texts. In 1992, this number had risen to 150. According to Boczkowski (2005), around 1995, newspapers really started focusing on the web "as their preferred non-print publishing environment". This showed in the numbers of online journals. In 1998, more than 750 American newspapers had internet sites (Boczkowski 2005) and in 2000 this number was up to 1207 (WAN 2001), a growth of 37 percent. After 2000, growth slowed down, but still the number of online websites grew steadily. From 2003 to 2007, the number of online newspaper websites grew by almost 51 percent. From 2006 to 2007, this percentage was almost 14 percent (WAN 2007). According to Boczkowski, newspapers were reprinting original content from the paper to the web, increased their usefulness by adding related content and published new content (for example updates of news stories).

According to Boczkowski, the traditional newspaper business faces several changes due to the dynamic potential of digitization and being online. First, rather than a largely generalized product, news making can now be easily customized for the users. Secondly, newspapers are no longer bound to the spatial limitations of newsprint. They can offer much more (background) information. Thirdly, since distribution costs are lower, newspapers can cater to both the micro-local and the global audience. As a fourth change, Boczkowski states that traditionally, newspapers had a duration of 24 hours. After 24 hours, they were outdated. Now they are permanently available as a digital library for users. Fifth, the organization of the news is much more complex due to the possibility of constant updates. Just like in television, newspapers can cover news stories permanently. Sixth, rather than plain text and still images, newspapers have more multimedia at their disposal. They can incorporate videos and audio into their news report. In that sense, the differences between news organizations have diminished (paper, TV, radio, internet). And lastly, Boczkowski argues that the users are conceived as being increasingly important. Rather than a one-to-many orientation, the relationship between users and newspapers has become much more dynamic.

Consumers of online news

Users, increasingly, are turning to the internet for their news. Research by Horrigan in 2005 has shown that traditional media organizations dominate online news sources. Reading news is the third most popular online activity for Americans on an average day, in addition to checking e-mail and conducting a search (Horrigan 2006). WAN reported that the audience for newspaper websites grew 350 percent from 1999 to 2004 (WAN 2005). Horrigan found that 35 percent of internet users check online news everyday and that almost one-third of all American internet users read traditional newspaper websites. In the Netherlands, researchers found similar figures. In 2007, one out of three Dutch internet users visited a traditional newspaper website at least once a month. In 2008, this percentage was up to 47 percent (Cebuco 2008).

Not only has their consumption pattern shifted to the internet, the roles that users take up in the process of news production and consumption have changed as well. Mainstream media companies are increasingly anticipating on active users by giving them a role on their website. For example, on the BBC website, users can upload their own photos and videos if they have witnessed a news event. Many newspapers enable users to comment on a selection of articles, and some add blogs or user sections to their website.

Changing relationships between users and producers

The changes in the relationship between the newspaper journalists and their audience are further explored by Picone (2007). He links these changes directly to the three traditional roles of newspapers. The first major change can be seen in the role of the newspaper as agenda-setter. Based on research by Althaus and Tewksbury (Althaus & Tewksbury 2000, in: Picone 2007), Picone claims that on the internet, users have much more freedom to compose their own information environment and share it with others. Services like Digg allow users to tag news messages and to rate their popularity. News portals like Google News, citizen journalism and the blogosphere are also demanding attention from users. The internet is a fast, easy and cheap way to gain access to numerous news sources. This enables users to set their own peer-driven news agenda, limiting the power of the newspapers as an agenda-setting force in the process.

A second change is in the traditional role of the newspaper as watchdog or fourth estate. The internet enables users to publish their own versions of the truth or their opinion about news messages online and they indeed use these possibilities. Collective intelligence of the users plays an important part in this respect. The internet audience will most likely have other information about news "facts" and is enabled to contradict traditional news sources online more easily. Websites like *Wikileaks* post secure information online for all users and other journalists to see without editing the information beforehand. Thirdly, the role of the press as news provider changes with the increased competition of other news sources like free newspapers and online news sites and blogs. All news is available for free online. According to Picone, the function of the traditional newspaper is shifting as a result from gathering news to selecting, analysing and commenting news. But Picone claims that newspapers still do not fully embrace the new possibilities presented to them by the internet. They are approaching the new possibilities in "a conservative and rigid way" (Picone 2007, 102).

Obviously, the internet has changed traditional user/producer relations in the newspaper domain. This development is reinforced by the fact that on the internet, traditional news sites are no longer alone in providing the news. Users are also increasingly getting their news online from other sources and starting to create and spread news themselves.

Users as creators of news

In addition to the rise of web portals like Google news that collect news messages from different online news sources, users are increasingly creating their own news. OhMyNews is an online newspaper started in 2000 in South Korea (www.ohmynews.com). Rather than a number of professional journalists, the website generates news written by a small staff and (for the largest part) by its users. In 2000, under the motto "Every citizen is a reporter", 727 reporters started gathering news and posting messages online (Yeon-Ho 2007). In 2007, this number had risen to over 500,000 reporters from 200 countries. Citizen journalists who publish on OhMyNews are paid by the service if they produce a headline story (approximately 50 Euros). They can also receive tips from readers who appreciate their story (Yoo 2007). Citizen journalism services have also started in other countries, for example Purdafash in India (purdafash.com), Vikalpa in Sri Lanka (www.vikalpa.org), iReport, the citizen journalism website of CNN (www.ireport.com) or Newassignment.net, an international "open platform" journalism website, maintained by an investment by Reuters in 2006 (www.newassignment.net).

Weblogs, too, can be seen as a new publishing platform (Pascu et al. 2007). A weblog is a website with regular entries of commentary provided by an author. In 1994, the first weblog was written, but the term was not coined until 1997. On blogs, users provide news or commentary on a large variety of subjects (Pascu et al. 2007). Since 2003, the number of blogs started rising exponentially. At the end of 2003, 2 million weblogs were tracked by Technorati; by 2004, this number was up to around 6 million. In 2005, 20 million blogs were tracked and in 2006, 62 million. By August 2008, Technorati was tracking almost 113 million blogs (www.technorati.com). According to Technorati, each day 175,000 blogs get included in the blogosphere and bloggers post 1.6 million posts a day (18 updates a second). However, it is important to emphasize that not all blogs are active. Blog content can be searched through blog search engines like Technorati, Feedster, Blogsearch (Google) and IceRocket.

Some journalists and publishers reacted to bloggers (just like the music industry in the case of file-sharing) by going on the defensive . They were afraid their traditional journalistic practice would be jeopardized. Bloggers "stole" news messages and published them on their weblogs (Allan 2005). They were also supposed to be unreliable and the quality of most blogs was, according to critics, very bad. But increasingly, traditional newspaper businesses started incorporating blogs on their own websites. The Dutch newspaper de Volkskrant offers visitors of their website a free weblog. And each week, a summary of all blogs of the week is published in the print version of the newspaper. Another example: in Germany, the regional newspaper Opinio is fully composed of weblogs (Tomesen 2006).

By the end of 2004, blogs had become an important aspect of online culture (Rainie 2005). In the US, 8 percent of internet users aged 18 and older reportedly keeps a blog (Lenhart & Fox 2006) – this comes to about 12 million Americans. In 2009, this rose to 11 percent (Lenhart 2010). Most of the bloggers are younger than the average internet population (54 percent is between 18 and 29). In December 2005, 37 percent of American internet users reportedly read blogs (Lenhart & Fox 2006). And nine percent of American internet users read news blogs (Horrigan 2006). According to PEW Internet & American Life

Project, in 2006, 54 percent of US bloggers said they have never published their writings elsewhere (Lenhart & Fox 2006). It should be noted that the survey of Pew in 2006 showed that one-third of all bloggers see blogging as a form of journalism. Most of them see blogging as a hobby. Just how institutionalized blogging in the online domain has become is illustrated by the Bloggies – an award ceremony for weblogs. The prize has been awarded since 2001 and has been emulated by national blog awards like the Dutch bloggies. In 2005, the first conference on blogging was held in Paris (Elburg 2005).

The shifts in the consumption patterns of news show that every role that is enabled in the internet environment and that can be taken by users, is actually taken up. This does not imply that their traditional role as consumer has been completely abolished. More interestingly, what is happening here is that the new environment that the internet offers to users provides them with a concrete toolbox of potential roles, that they can tinker with and improvise. They can pick the role that fits best for that particular moment. In that sense news consumers have become a difficult target and a great challenge for the news industry.

Conclusion

Traditionally, a small concentration of media companies provided cultural products for a mass audience. Great emphasis was placed on hits and blockbusters. The strict hierarchical and one-way organization left no room for a users' role other than that of consumer. Product and process innovation was part of this traditional production and organization model, and in their role of "market", users of the media were not actively involved. Of course, other user roles did exist – users did create, copy, build upon and communicate about cultural products – but on a relatively small scale: none of this really challenged the more or less rigid organization and business models of the media sector. Overall, production and consumption remained two separate domains in the traditional cultural industries.

Since the 1980s, the media landscape has changed significantly. The interaction between users and producers in the online domain is supported and accelerated by technology. The internet makes two-way communication much more direct and faster than other media were able to. It changes, for example, the scope, speed and impact of the interaction within communities, between various user groups and between users and producers. In this chapter, these developments were illustrated in two media domains; the music and press sector.

This transformation of the media audience into active media users may be understood as the return of the bricoleur. This description clearly fits the current trend towards user-generated content, and towards more the participative and active roles that users have taken up in the media value chain. If we look at the developments in the media domain over the last decade - and particularly at the recent user driven development of the internet - there is a striking resemblance between the new media user and the bricoleur as described by Lévi-Strauss.

Creation and production of cultural goods was originally in hands of artists and media companies. But the internet significantly lowered the threshold for users to create, produce and publish their own works. And users do so passionately, deploying everything that is at hand in their everyday life and tinkering with the whole array of creative bits and pieces that was made available to them through the development of the internet. They are creating videos, photos, music, blogs, podcasts and even television programs. They become accidental media stars, give rise to unexpected innovations and have a radical impact on the sector. They publish their own blogs and sometimes commercialize their products and by doing all this, have unintentionally but steadily changed the sight of the media sector. As a result, business parties now increasingly integrate user-created content into their services. Software developers offer their raw material to users to further develop them and adapt them to their everyday circumstances and needs. Users actively use and re-use the vast number of applications and tools that are available through the web and use existing content for mash-ups and modifications. User-created content is stimulated through the wisdom of crowds principle and by collaborative projects. The growing importance of user-created content is illustrated by the fact that this wild thinking is now becoming more and more institutionalized. This can be deduced from the prizes that are awarded to for example blogs and the increased number of authors that seek active contact with their audiences to better their product.

Not only the production, but also the distribution of content has changed significantly. Firstly, users have taken up active roles in distribution processes, as P2P file sharing has shown. Piracy has been a very important issue over the past few years. But looking at sales figures and other research that has been done in this area, the statement that every illegal download is a loss in revenue can be seriously doubted. Increasingly, P2P file-sharing is being adopted to share content legally. For example, in the television domain P2P technology has proven to be a solution for significantly increased server costs. Secondly, artists have more freedom to distribute their own content or engage in innovative distribution deals, thus bypassing the traditional gatekeepers. Users can promote themselves and find an audience. Social networks are a great facilitator for this development. In the traditional media domain, professionals were important gatekeepers to select content. On the internet, these gatekeepers are not as powerful anymore. The amount of content available online has increased exponentially. By rating and tagging content, users are making content more easily findable. By selecting most viewed or high rated content like news, music, videos, books and more, users are increasingly relying on their peers in the selection process. Producers capitalize on this phenomenon to, for example, integrate collaborative filtering into their services.

Just like all the other steps in the value creation process, consumption has changed as well. Consumption through the internet has soared and can be labeled as disruptive. Unlike traditional consumption, online consumption is diversified and fragmented. Users are now much more used to customization and specialization. The music domain has showed that online, users are much more inclined to buy a single track than buying a whole music album. The internet enables users to explore millions of niches with highly specialized content (the long tail). RSS feeds are enabling users to customize new flow of content. And instead of relying on a specialized carrier per media domain, like a CD, a video or a television program on a television screen, users can access all content from the computer screen. This has significantly lowered the threshold for consumption.

Finalizing, we may conclude, that digital media have turned out to be exemplary tools for bricolage, for giving meaning to and structuring everyday life in the information society in new ways and yet in ways that we have seen before. Whereas the ingénieur may have fulfilled a strong role in the first stages of the age of the digital media, by now his role has come to be much more modest. The shape and pace of recent developments in the field are no longer defined by traditional models of engineer-driven innovation, but much more by a mundane, messy, and unpredictable user-driven dynamics. The history of the media has shown that this do-it-yourself spirit is not completely new. Although the radio was invented by a classical engineer (Marconi), amateurs started to tinker with the technology in their concrete everyday context, and to share their experiences with other users. Without the enthusiastic efforts of these radio amateurs, the broadcasting media would probably never have developed into what they are today. Nevertheless, for most media, the agency of users has for a long time been relatively small: users of the media were more or less confined to being passive consumers and to constitute a mass audience. In the twenty-first century, however, the savage mind of the bricoleur has taken over and is shaping the disruptive innovations confronting the media sector today.

References

Allan M. 'Het volk heeft zijn stem hervonden' Vrij Nederland (March 26, 2005) pp. 60-61

Anderson C. The Long Tail. How Endless Choice is Creating Unlimited Demand New York: Hyperion Books (2006)

Bangeman E. 'Apple passes Wal-Mart, now #1 music retailer in US' Ars Technica (2008) http://arstechnica.com/news.ars/post/20080402-apple-passes-wal-mart- now-1-music-retailer-in-us.html (accessed August 2008)

Bakker P. 'File sharing--fight, ignore or compete. Paid download services vs. P2P-networks' Telematics and Informatics 22 (2005) pp. 41-55

Barker C. The Sage Dictionary of Cultural Studies London/Seven Oaks CA: Sage (2004)

Bender M.T., Wang Y. 'The impact of digital piracy on music sales: a cross-country analysis' International Social Science Review 84 (3-4) (2009) pp. 157-170

Boczkowski P.J. Digitizing the News. Innovation in Online Newspapers Cambridge Massachusetts: MIT Press (2005)

Blomqvist, U., Eriksonn, L.E., Findahl, O., Selg, H. and Wallis, 'RReport on technology versus usage and effects' (2005) MusicLessons deliverable 1 http://xml.nada.kth.se/media/Research/MusicLessons/Reports/deliverable_1.pdf (accessed September 2008)

Buskirk E. van Bankrupt, Crowd-Funded SellaBand Acquired by German Investors Wired (February 2010) http://www.wired.com/epicenter/2010/02/bankrupt-crowd-funded-sellaband-acquired-by-german-investors/ (accessed February, 2010)

Castells M. The Rise of the Network Society (second edition) Oxford: Blackwell Publishing (2000)

Cebuco 'Dagbladsites zetten opmars voort' http://www.cebuco.nl/website/actueel.asp?menuid=15&ntype=&nid=816 (accessed September 2008)

ComScore For Radiohead fans 'does 'free' + 'download' = 'freeload'?' http://www.comscore.com/press/release.asp?press=1883 (accessed August 2008) Press release (2007)

Croteau D., Hoynes W. Media/Society. Industries, Images, and Audiences Thousand Oaks, London, New Delhi: Pine Forge Press (1997)

Dijck J. van 'Users like you? Theorizing agency in user-generated content' Media, Culture & Society 31 (1) (2009) pp. 41-58

Distripress Press Business No. 1 http://www.press-business.com/pdf/2005_01_press_business.pdf (accessed September 2008) (accessed September 2005)

Eijk N. van, Poort J., Rutten P. Legal 'Economic and cultural aspects of file-sharing' Communications & Strategies 77 (1) (2010) pp. 35-54

Elburg A. van 'Businessmodellen weblogs niet wezenlijk anders' Emerce *(*April 26, 2005)

Friedrich O. 'Machine of the year: the computer moves in' *Times Magazine* January 3, 1983

Frissen V. 'Digitaal knutselen. De doorbraak van het wilde denken' eds. Frissen V., De Mul, J. De Draagbare Lichtheid van het Bestaan. Het Alledaagse Gezicht van de Informatiesamenleving Kampen: Klement/Pelckmans (2008) pp. 15-27

Geist M. Piercing 'The peer-to-peer myths: an examination of the Canadian experience' First Monday 10 (4) (2005)

Gorman L., McLean D. Media and Society in the Twentieth Century. A Historical Introduction Malden, Oxford, Victoria, Berlin: Blackwell Publishing (2003)

Hebdige D. 'Subculture: The Meaning of Style' ed. Ryan M. ed. Cultural Studies: An Anthology Blackwell Publishing (2008) pp. 587-598

Henten A., Tadayoni R. 'The impact of the internet on media technology, platforms and innovation' eds. Küng L., Picard R.G., Towse R. The Internet and the Mass Media Los Angeles, London, New Delhi, Singapore, Washington DC: Sage (2008) pp. 45-64

Horrigan J.B. 'Online news. For many home broadband users, the internet is a primary news source' Pew Internet & American Life Project http://www.pewinternet.org/pdfs/PIP_News.and.Broadband.pdf (accessed September, 2006)

IFPI IFPI. Online Music Report London: IFPI (2004)

IFPI. Digital Music Report London: IFPI (2006) http://www.ifpi.org/site-content/library/digital-music-report-2006.pdf (accessed Februari 2006)

IFPI. IFPI Digital Music Report 2008. Revolution innovation responsibility London: IFPI (2008) http://www.ifpi.org/content/library/DMR2008.pdf (accessed August 2008)

IFPI. IFPI Digital Music Report 2010 Music how, when, where you want it London: IFPI (2010) http://www.ifpi.org/content/library/DMR2010.pdf (accessed August, 2010)

Jenkins H. Convergence Culture. Where Old and New Media Collide New York, London: New York University Press (2006)

Leadbeater C., Miller P. The Pro-Am Revolution. How Enthusiasts are Changing the Way our Economy and Society Work London: Demos UK (2004)

Leadbeater C. We-think. Mass Innovation, not Mass Production London: Profile Books (2008)

Lenhart A., Fox S. 'Bloggers. A portrait of the internet's new storytellers' PEW Internet & American Life Project (2006) http://www.pewinternet.org/pdfs/PIP%20Bloggers%20Report%20July%2019%202006.pdf (accessed August 2008)

Lenhart A. 'Social media and young adults' PEW Internet & American Life Project (2010) http://www.pewinternet.org/Presentations/2010/Feb/Department-of-Commerce.aspx (accessed August 2010)

Lévi-Strauss C. The Savage Mind Chicago: University of Chicago Press, The Nature of Human Society Series (1966)

Liebowitz S.J. 'File-sharing: creative destruction or just plain destruction?' School of Management University of Texas http://som.utdallas.edu/capri/destruction.pdf (accessed March 2006) (2004)

Liebowitz S.J. 'The key instrument in the Oberholzer-Gee/Strumpf file-sharing paper is defective' School of Management, University of Texas (2010) http://musicbusinessresearch.files.wordpress.com/2010/06/paper-stan-j-liebowitz1.pdf (accessed August 2010)

Madden M. 'Artists, musicians and the internet PEW Internet & American Life Project' http://www.pewinternet.org/pdfs/PIP_Artists.Musicians_Report.pdf (accessed September 2008) (2004)

Michel N. J. 'The impact of digital file-sharing on the music industry: An empirical analysis topics in economic' Analysis & Policy 6 (1) (2006)

Mooney P, Samanta S., Zadeh A.H.M. 'Napster and its effects on the music industry: an empirical analysis' Journal of social sciences 6 (3) (2010) pp. 303-309

Oberholzer F., Strumpf K. 'The effect of file-sharing on record sales. An empirical analysis' (2004) http://www.unc.edu/~cigar/papers/filesharing_march2004.pdf (accessed March 2006)

Pareles J. Pay 'What you want for this article?' New York Times December 9, 2007 http://www.nytimes.com/2007/12/09/arts/music/09pare.html?Pagewanted=1&_r=1 (accessed August 2008)

Pascu C., Osimo D., Ulbrich M., Turlea G., Burgelman J.C. 'The potential disruptive impact of Internet 2 based technologies' First Monday 12 (3) (2007)

Picone I. 'Conceptualising online news use' Observatorio (OBS*) Journal 3 (2007) pp. 93-144

Rainie L. The state of blogging Washington, DC: Pew Internet & American Life Project (2005) http://www.pewinternet.org/Reports/2005/The-State-of-Blogging.aspx (accessed October 2010)

RIAA Year-end Shipment Statistics (2007) www.riaa.com (August 2008)

Shirky C. RIP the Consumer 1900-1999 http://www.shirky.com/ writings/ consumer.html (2000)

Siwek S.E. 'The true cost of sound recording piracy to the U.S. economy' (2007) http://www.ipi.org/ipi%5CIPIPublications.nsf/PublicationLookupFullTextPDF/51CC65A1D4779E408625733E00529174/$File/SoundRecordingPiracy.pdf?OpenElement (accessed August 2008)

Tapscott D., Williams A.D. Wikinomics. How Mass Collaboration is Changing Everything New York, London: Penguin Books (2006)

Tomesen R. 'Webloguitgeverij Michiel Frackers van start' Emerce January 31 (2006)

Turkle S. Life on the Screen. Identity in the Age of Internet New York; Simon & Schuster (1995)

University of Minnesota Media History Project Minnesota: University of Minnesota (2007) http://www.mediahistory.umn.edu/timeline/1980-1989.html (accessed October 2010)

Von Hippel E. Democratizing Innovation Cambridge, MA: MIT Press (2005)

WAN World Press Trends: Newspaper Growth Continues WAN (2001) http://www.wanpress.org/ce/previous/2001/congress.forum/wpt/growth.html (accessed September 2008)

WAN World Press Trends: Newspaper Circulation and Advertising up Worldwide WAN (2005) http://www.wan-press.org/article7321.html (accessed September 2008)

WAN World Press Trends: Newspapers are a Growth Business WAN (2007) http://www.wan-press.org/article17377.html (accessed September 2008)

Yeon-Ho O. '10 Preconditions for the value of user-generated content' Oh My News (2007) http://english.ohmynews.com/articleview/article_view.asp?article_class=8 &no=347268&rel_no=1 (accessed August 2008)

Yoo C. 'Giants of citizen media meet up. Founders of OhMyNews, Wikipedia share visions' (2007) The Tyee http://thetyee.ca/Mediacheck/2007/10/24/WikiVOhMyNews/ (accessed August 2008)

Serge Proulx and Lorna Heaton

Forms of User Contribution in Online Communities: Mechanisms of Mutual Recognition between Contributors

Introduction

In less than a decade, a *social* internet has grown up around us (blogs, wikis, social networking sites). Users of the Web are becoming information producers. Internet users exchange messages, post evaluations, comments and photos, remix music and videos that they can then publish worldwide. Wikis allow the collaborative production of texts that everyone can edit. Social network sites such as *Friendster*, *MySpace* or *Facebook* encourage users to publish their profiles and to comment publicly or semi-publicly on the profiles of others. They invite their users to build a public network of contacts ("friends") and to navigate among a panoply of third party applications. Users thus "collect" contacts and form groups or "communities" of interest around shared passions, hobbies or interests. How do individuals and groups behave in this new digital context? How can we use a sociological vocabulary to describe the new ways that user communities are using social web platforms to collaborate and to produce content in cyberspace?

The notion of community employed here has little in common with the definition the first sociologists used to describe the passage from a social group based on tradition (community) to modern society at the end of the 19th century. Ferdinand Tönnies (1887) defined community (*Gemeinschaft*) as a social form based on emotional and geographical proximity and involving direct, physical, authentic interactions among its members. In the so-called "digital community", however, members typically have no common geographical ties and face-to-face physical interactions are no longer necessary. Today's digital communities also differ considerably from the first internet use communities that Howard Rheingold baptised "virtual communities" (Rheingold 1993). This type of community was much smaller. Strong social ties and sustained commitment to communal goals developed within these online communities, even though users met asynchronously and at a distance.

Since about 2002, the expression "digital communities" has come to refer to large networks of user/contributors who post content on sites such as Wikipedia or Amazon and to social network sites composed of huge quantities of interconnected user profiles. Today's digital communities are often nothing more than aggregations of individual users, ephemeral micro-clubs gathered around shared interests and characterised by partial belonging and similarities in one aspect or another of their lives (consumption, professional, associative life, etc.). The hypermodern identity of the internet user appears to be composed of a constellation of multiple, contradictory sources of identification and subjectivities in action (Rybas & Gajjala 2007). The social ties produced by social Web platforms appear to be sociologically quite different than the ties developed in either traditional communities or early virtual communities (Proulx et al. 2006).

Emergence of *individualized networking media*

In the internet's digital setting, approaches to creating and distributing content have been undergoing significant change for more than a decade, turning cultural industries' traditional models upside down. Four characteristics mark this turn to "participative culture" practices (Jenkins 2006b). First, users are positioned at the centre of the apparatus, encouraged to produce and distribute their own content online: this is generally referred to as *user-generated content* or *user-created content* (OECD 2007). Second, participation appears to be facilitated by the limited level of cognitive and technical competencies required to use the tools of these new platforms – inequalities in access and appropriation notwithstanding – to create a context which favours increased creation and content-sharing among casual internet users (Leadbetter & Miller 2004). Third, these changes are grounded in the development of online collectives and communities, networked and structured in apparently non-hierarchical ways (Surowiecki 2005). Fourth, these transformations spawn new economic models (Gensollen 2006) based on the large-scale aggregation of often minimal individual contributions, and a market rationalisation of the production and distribution of informational goods. Kick-started in 1999 with the propagation of peer-to-peer music file sharing that revolutionized the music recording industry (Moreau 2008), new forms of participation have multiplied, demanding strategic adaptation by a number of sectors of the cultural industries.

New collaborative practices for internet-based content creation and exchange have emerged in a variety of sectors. Consider the following practices, each of which corresponds to a particular kind of online participation:

• Collaborative encyclopaedias: contributors to *Wikipedia* are inventing new ways to dynamically assemble encyclopaedic knowledge (Levrel 2006)

• Citizen journalism: citizen journalism sites are challenging journalism's traditional rules (Gillmor 2004; Bruns 2005)

• Free and open source software: communitarian forms of open source software development increasingly constitute an alternative to proprietary software (Weber 2004)

- Immersive environments: *Second Life* is an original digital environment in which content creation depends intimately on users' ongoing contributions (Boellstorff 2008)

- Podcasting: podcasting practices imply important reconfigurations of the radio broadcasting system (Berry 2006; O'Neill 2006)

Juxtaposed, this diversity of collaborative practices suggests a major evolution in internet use. We suggest that a certain unity underlies this diversity. Like Bruns (2008), who coined the term *produsage* to distinguish these new practices from the traditional process of *production,* we seek to highlight what is particular about these phenomena of *online contribution*. Since users do not receive payment for their online contributions, such uses appear motivated by powerful symbolic rewards instead. This suggests the importance of recognition in internet user practices – that is, peer confirmation of a subject's social value (Honneth 2002).

Recent work in media and cultural studies has described the digital environments that emerge from the convergence between computing, audiovisual media, and telecommunications as privileged sites for widespread cultural creation. After a first movement of technological and economic convergence during the 1980s, we are now witnessing a second movement of convergence between mainstream media and new media (Jenkins 2006a; Bruns 2008). Similarly, recent studies on the uses of technological innovation describe the user as playing an increasingly active role in the innovation process (Oudshoorn & Pinch 2003, 2008). This kind of research initially described the lead users' capacity to identify their "needs"; to devise technical solutions to fill them; and, finally, to build and test prototypes under practical conditions of use (Von Hippel 2005; Cardon 2005). It has since been extended to take into account the larger universe of users who might contribute to a process of *bottom-up innovation*. Rightly or not, Von Hippel thus talks about "democratizing innovation" (Von Hippel 2005).

Analyzing users' contributions

The nature and quality of online communities, and subsequently the legitimacy of online knowledge activity in epistemic communities, has been a subject of debate since the internet has emerged as a major social force. Proulx and Latzko-Toth (2000) review various approaches to the notion of community, relating it to the notions of *public* and *social network*. More recently, there have been several attempts to develop typologies of "commons-based peer production" collectivities (Benkler 2006). Haythornthwaite (2009a) proposes a reconciliation of peer production and virtual community approaches to online collaboration by articulating dimensions of contributory behavior, recognition and reputation mechanisms and affiliation to community along a continuum running from crowdsourcing (Howe 2006; Surowiecki 2005) to community. Vainio et al. (2006) distinguish online epistemic communities according to community size, degree of centralization of decision-making, and how they deal with intellectual property, while West & O'Mahony (2008) identify transparency and accessibility as two key features of openness in online collaboration, and outline dimensions of organization of production, community governance and intellectual property as elements of what they term architectures of participation. Like O'Reilly (2005), they argue that architectures of participation are socio-technical accomplishments in which social considerations such as recognition, reward, motivation and co-orientation are as important as technical features. Even digital communities that appear to be nothing more than aggregations of individuals (crowds) may be able to create content and produce knowledge thanks to their largely invisible social organization.

In some sense, the promise of online knowledge crowds is the promise of participatory democracy, as evidenced in participatory culture and citizen journalism. In this context, the internet provides a platform for citizens to voice their concerns and create an alternate structure for citizen engagement. As Haythornthwaite (2009b) notes, crowdsourcing is the beginning of some larger change or action, with an idea of continued attention and action. While the crowd may not be a community, it is assembled *in the interests of community*. Individuals are independent contributors to a collective enterprise, but not a collaborative one.

We analyze processes of creation and exchange in online environments along four dimensions: (a) the modes of visibility mediated by the system which facilitate social recognition among contributors; (b) the level of expertise displayed by contributing internet users; (c) norms and governance models among collectives of contributors; (d) the insertion of contributory behaviours in the context of an economy of the immaterial based on the exchange of informational goods.

● **Visibility and social recognition in contribution systems**

While remaining attentive to the diversity of uses of any system, we are examining the eventual transformations in visibility that result from relationships between users and systems (Thompson 1995, 2000). The conception and design of second-generation internet tools appears to integrate different visibility models. As users appropriate these platforms and tools, the boundary between what may and may not be seen (Cardon 2008; Boyd 2008) may also shift. Changes in visibility also condition mutual recognition between users, who require visibility as a precondition for mutual recognition (Voirol 2005b). We thus hope to describe the processes and procedures by which users construct the categories of the visible and invisible, on one hand, and to identify the normative assumptions through which what is worth seeing and not worth seeing is determined (Voirol 2005a) on the other. Accordingly, an analysis of reputation management – that is, of symbolic rewards related to recognition – seems relevant.

• **Level of expertise and contribution quality**
New collaborative platforms encourage casual users to participate directly in content creation. However, these informational goods remain generated mainly by "amateurs". This observation leads us to question the status of ordinary/amateur/lay users with respect to that of "professionals" (Leadbeater & Miller 2004) and to examine the processes by which the figure of the expert (re)emerges within user groups, paying close attention to how collaboration and contributions are recognized among users (Dejours 2007). Rather than exploring the distinction between these artificial categories and the asymmetrical relationship it assumes, we seek to assess the nature, quality and degree of effective expertise among ordinary contributors (Collins 2007; Collins & Evans 2007). Expertise, in this setting, refers to mastery of technical devices as well as to the ability to develop specific content or to communicate in digital environments.

• **Norms and models of governance models in contributor groups**
At first glance, contributor groups appear to be non-hierarchical, spontaneous agglomerations. However, participants organize their diverse content in ways that will make it easy for other internet users to find (Auray 2008). Formal and informal rules of governance develop, and communities can be disaggregated into circles of contributors according to various levels of participant engagement (Cardon 2005). Three variables appear to determine the degree of openness of these online group's governance: the permeability of their boundaries to the outside world, the ability to discuss norms for conflict resolution within the community, and the transparency of the criteria linking the merit of users' contributions to their reputations (Auray 2008). This last point is an important one, since "reputation systems" are important elements in groups using second-generation internet tools.

• **Economic models: contribution in the context of the immaterial economy**
From an economic standpoint, media content distributed over collaborative platforms constitute non-rival informational goods: even they have been acquired by third parties, they continue to exist at the point of acquisition (Gensollen 2006). Scarcity thus shifts from the body of information created by users, to the technical procedures and social organisations which facilitate its optimal use. Contributors aggregate information that has already been developed, and whose cost of supply is therefore very low. In order to make efficient use of this patchwork, internet users need tools for research and quality control. We thus move from the attention economy (Goldhaber 1997) of the mass media to an economy of free content in which value is transferred to the equipment and services necessary for its collective use. In this economic

context, there is an eventual risk that the goodwill of contributors may be exploited by the organisers and managers of the masses of information they produce. The owners of collaborative platforms hold information use rights and may employ those rights to increase market efficiency (Dujarier 2008).

The case of citizen cyberjournalism

The use of individualized networking media has brought "citizen cyberjournalism" practices to the fore (Proulx 2009). These include the production, processing, and distribution of journalistic information by individuals who are not professional journalists but who use the tools of the social Web. Everyday users thus participate cooperatively in the online publication and processing of journalistic facts. From the humble status of reader, internet users become *editors* of news, *commentators* of current events, or *recyclers* of information in other formats. However, what does the term "citizen" mean in such a context? Is it simply a way of contrasting ordinary people and professional journalists?

If so, then citizen cyberjournalism appears as a simple complement to traditional media production. Adopting the tactics of crowdsourcing here suggests only the mobilisation of a larger number of persons for processing and publication (Surowiecki 2005), not any particular citizen activism. If, on the other hand, citizenship designates a movement towards speaking out on the part of ordinary people seeking to participate actively in the life of the City, we can then ask ourselves whether participating in cyberjournalistic practices creates a real alternative to conventional mass media in the tradition of engaged citizen media, also referred to as *autonomous media* (Langlois & Dubois 2006; Granjon 2008). This is the position held by Gillmor (2004) and the co-founder of the French citizen cyberjournalism site *AgoraVox* DeRosnay (2006).

In this context, two principal elements are important: the creation of content by Internauts is facilitated by the ease of use of next generation internet tools and platforms, and competition with mass media allows traditional journalistic gate-keeping practices to be short-circuited. Bruns (2005) describes this empowering participation by ordinary citizens as "gatewatching". In this second scenario, the traditionally linear, top-down communicational chain linking the journalist to the public is broken. In its place, we find a circular and continuous chain of communication involving citizens' active participation in online information publishing. News becomes a conversation between professional journalists and community members sharing the online media publishing space, to the benefit of the audience. Active publics such as these could thus potentially echo social movements and activist groups that formulate social, political and cultural demands.

Citizen journalism websites initially appeared in response to what were perceived as significant shortcomings in mainstream news media (Deuze et al.

2007). The common use of "citizen journalism" as a blanket term tends to obscure significant differences in approach between various participatory news sites (see Bruns 2005, for a classification of models for collaborative online news production). In fact, a variety of models employ various degrees of balance between enabling direct participation by citizen journalist contributors in producing the news and some level of editorial oversight by site operators and journalistic staff. In the ten or so years since citizen journalism has come to the fore, citizen-only sites have proved difficult to sustain, and the near term future of citizen journalism appears to lie in collaborations between professional and nonprofessional journalists to produce the news. The following case describes one prominent and successful citizen journalism site. OhmyNews is an example of a site that relies primarily on citizen contributions but which also integrates professional editors and journalists. It is a hybrid between institutional or commercial support and community engagement.

"Every citizen is a reporter"

OhmyNews is an experiment in citizen cyberjournalism that has served as an inspiration to sites of a similar nature around the globe. It was founded in 2000 by Oh Yeon Ho, a veteran investigative journalist, in reaction to South Korea's conservative mainstream press (Kahney 2003). Only a few years later, the big, collaborative online newspaper had become one of the country's most influential media outlets. As a credible institution, its reporters are given access to government ministries and public institutions, putting them on level footing with professional reporters. In 2010, the site attracts an estimated 2 million daily readers. An international English language version of the site was launched in 2004, but it now focuses more on "curating the debate on citizen journalism" than on the news itself.

With "Every citizen is a reporter" as its motto and guiding concept, OhmyNews has changed how news is produced, distributed and consumed. "Journalists aren't some exotic species, they're everyone who has news stories and shares them with others." (Oh 2004) Anyone who registers with the site can contribute and there are no restrictions on membership.

OhmyNews reflects a hybrid model of news production. While the site is based on citizen participation, it is careful to balance participation with professional presentation. The vast majority of the news is written by more than 62,000 registered citizen journalists who contribute about 150 stories a day, over 70 percent of the news content for OhmyNews. A paid staff of about 70 editors and reporters edit articles posted by citizen reporters and write in-depth stories (Ohmynews.com).

The production process resembles that of a traditional newspaper, but is conducted through discussion forums on the site that allow reporters and editors to discuss story ideas with citizen contributors. Citizen reporters decide what ideas they want to follow at their own time and expense. Reporters can post anything on the site, as long as they abide by the site's code of ethics. For example they must agree to stick to the facts and to use their real identities. The site warns contributors that they bear sole responsibility for their posts. Copyright is shared between the site and the reporter, who is free to republish the material elsewhere. Stories are submitted through a Web interface and enter an editing queue before going live. All stories are fact checked and edited by professional editors, but some errors may still make it through. For example, OhmyNews has occasionally had to retract articles, and there have been problems with reporters' undisclosed conflicts of interest (Kahney 2003). Occasional inaccuracies are not necessarily a problem in a peer-production model, however.

> "With OhmyNews, we wanted to say goodbye to 20th-century journalism where people only saw things through the eyes of the mainstream, conservative media. (…) We put everything out there and people judge the truth for themselves." (Oh, cited in Kahney 2003)

The site covers everything a traditional newspaper covers - from sports to international politics, but with a personal and partisan tone. "Stories are often subjective, oozing with emotion and odd personal tidbits. But they also can be passionate, detailed and knowledgeably written." (Kahney 2003) Although citizen reporters may be paid a small fee (from $2 to the equivalent of about $17 if their story becomes Top News), their motivation for contributing is not monetary. "They are writing articles to change the world, not to earn money." (Oh 2004) By making OhmyNews "a public square and a playground for citizen reporters and readers," citizens feel they have a possibility to reflect realities as they see them and to change the world.

OhmyNews' business strategy is one of "selection and concentration" (Oh 2004). The relatively small staff tends to concentrate on particular types of stories that have become the calling card of the site - political and social issues. In discussions, they may decide to focus on a particular issue, in which case all the staff will tackle the same issue that day. What is more, they use the affordances of the internet media to advantage, by reporting speedily and vividly with simultaneous input from readers. For example, in March 2004, two hundred thousand people gathered for a candlelight demonstration in Seoul to protest the impeachment of the South Korean president. Twenty staff reporters and several citizen reporters were there to cover the demonstration with a text-photo-video combination. OhmyNews published a special edition of the weekly paper. They also broadcast the event live on OhmyTV and updated text articles every 30 minutes during the six-hour demonstration. About four hundred thousand readers participated in the demonstration online, and over 85,000 comments on the one issue were recorded on the site (Oh 2004). With coverage of this kind, OhmyNews is challenging and changing the traditional media formula of who is a reporter, what is news or newsworthy, how to write and how to edit news.

OhmyNews follows a for-profit model. It derives two-thirds of its approximately $6.5 million in revenue from advertising and competes with established publications for advertising revenue. After making a profit from 2003 to 2008, it is now struggling financially, but this does not seem to worry them unduly. *"OhmyNews is more concerned with being a social and media movement than a business,"* says Jean K. Min, the site's international communications director. *"Our goal is to empower citizens"* (Min cited in Woyke 2009). The site has been known to turn to its readers for support. That was its strategy in 2008 when readers flocked to OhmyNews for updates on street protests over U.S. imports, driving up its Web server costs. The site posted a plea for donations and covered its costs within a few weeks (Woyke 2009).

When asked why has OhmyNews been successful in Korea, while many similar initiatives have floundered, founder and CEO Oh notes several contributing factors: dissatisfaction with the mainstream conservative media; a sophisticated broadband internet infrastructure and high penetration; the fact that Korea is a small country, in which attention is easily polarized around one or two issues, making OhmyNews' guerrilla strategy (selection and concentration) effective; and most importantly, the desire and willingness of a generation of young Koreans to participate in reforming Korean society (Oh 2004).

Let us revisit OhmyNews in terms of our four analytic dimensions: modes of visibility and social recognition; contribution quality and expertise; norms and governance; and economic model. Citizen contributors sign their stories using their real names, providing them with a certain degree of immediate visibility. Payment for their work is on a sliding scale, according to the popularity of their story. Thus, even if the amount is largely symbolic, a element of supplementary recognition accompanies the payment. In the past couple of years, the site has introduced a system whereby readers can show their appreciation even more directly by "tipping" for stories they particularly appreciate. Frequent contributors to the site will sometimes develop a following.

> "Although there are isolated cases of authors earning thousands of dollars in tips for a story, the tips and payments serve more as encouragement than income. The payment system may send a message to citizen reporters that what they were producing is valuable, but also fits the interactive model of the site." (Joyce 2007, 7-8).

The primary motivation for most OhmyNews citizen journalists remains the opportunity to reflect realities as they see them and to participate in social change.

OhmyNews' model integrates professional and citizen reporters. A staff of professional journalists and editors oversee every story for accuracy and presentation. This maintains standards of quality. The expertise and competency of citizen journalists is recognized, but the role of a core group of professionals in not questioned or contested. The site's code of ethics and the inclusion of citizens in discussions of story ideas likely enhance quality and coherence. They also point to the transparency that governs the site's operations. After ten years of operation, OhmyNews has developed norms and mechanisms for maximizing contributors' contributions. In terms of Auray's (2008) variables for determining openness of governance, membership is open to anyone who wants to contribute, and criteria for attributing merit to contributions are reader-driven and transparent. The site's operating strategy of selection and concentration is well defined. OhmyNews exemplifies an economic model of contribution in the context of the immaterial economy. Information is aggregated and the cost of supply is low. The value-added comes in its presentation and distribution over the collaborative platform. Copyright is shared between the site and the citizen journalist, who can republish his or her article elsewhere, thus limiting the danger of exploitation. As with many citizen journalism sites around the world, the sustainability of OhmyNews' business model has yet to be proven.

Finally, with regards to OhmyNews' mission – empowering citizens – we might ask to what extent a site such as this can effect change? The site is often credited with responsibility for the election of a progressive President in 2002. Closer analysis suggests that, while OhmyNews had an amplifying effect and served as a platform for mobilizing voters during the 2002 Presidential campaign, a number of other factors were also significant in that election. Joyce (2007) argues that the demographic composition of OhmyNews' citizen journalists (a third are students, half are under 30 and half are from the "386 generation" already known for its militancy) challenges the view that citizen journalism will revolutionize the modern democratic process. While it is potentially available to all citizens, only some – primarily those who were already influencing public opinion – take advantage of the forum that OhmyNews offers. We suggest that in her analysis Joyce is forgetting an important part of the journalism equation – the Korean readers, for whom OhmyNews provides an alternative to mainstream media.

Conclusion

Citizen cyberjournalism practices pose social and ethical challenges, as well as questions about the future of journalism. A first challenge concerns the credibility of citizen sources and the quality of the information they gather. Any rigorous practice requires that citizen media establish control and validation mechanisms for information contributed by internet users. The presence of professional journalists on editorial committees appears crucial for ensuring quality control, although some advocates of citizen journalism argue that committees formed solely of citizen spokespersons can do without professional journalists. Whatever the answer, the question remains as to what the ever-increasing presence of non-professionals means for the future of journalism and the news industry. The professional identity of the journalistic profession is being redefined as new dynamics for the production of information develop. The task of informing the public sphere becomes a socially distributed one, beyond the control of professional journalists as increasing numbers of amateurs participate in producing the news.

Another challenge concerns the increasingly diverse associations and collaborative strategies between citizen media, conventional media and major Internet players. Some of the internet's major industry players have demonstrated great interest in integrating citizen-journalism-style practices. New Web 2.0 platforms have given rise to new actors (Wikinews, Yahoo News, MSN, blogs by amateurs, interest groups, political parties and elected officials) as well as new services (for example news aggregators such as Google News). This further threatens the already fragile balance in the media industries (fragility linked notably to the increasing presence of free media). Yet, citizen cyberjournalism remains largely dependent on mainstream news organizations, whose content it debates, critiques and recombines by harnessing large, distributed communities of contributors. The process of increasing hybridization and convergence between bottom-up and top-down models of news production is well underway. It is in this sense that we refer to a regime of "conflictual cooperation" between mainstream media on one side, and new, individualized, networked communication media, on the other.

We can also reframe the emergence of new practices of citizen cyberjournalism in the context of political actors' social visibility. Following Castells, we make two observations to characterize the power of the media in the construction of public space today (Castells 2009). First, the political existence of social actors is subject to their media visibility. Second, until recently the traditional mass media (large television networks and newspaper conglomerates) have tightly controlled the media visibility granted to political actors. Political actors' ability to speak has been heavily constrained by the logic of traditional media which significantly control the topic agenda, the rules of passage, and the amount of time allotted to different political actors use to speak to the public directly. The growth of individualized networked communication media – one of the fundamental characteristics of current changes in the media environment – suggests not only the emergence of plural and heterogeneous public spaces, but also new mechanisms for the public visibility of social actors.

We thus return to one of the central issue of this chapter: can the emergence of these individualized mass communication media echo the principles of participatory democracy? And, if so, how? In analyzing patterns of collaborative contribution in the creation and exchange of media content, our goal is to shed light on the complexity and fluidity of exchanges among amateurs and professionals in various contexts, at the same time building a base of empirical data with which to continue theorizing.

Acknowledgements: This research program is funded by the Social Sciences and Humanities Research Council of Canada (SSHRC) and carried out by the Lab CMO (Communication Médiatisée par Ordinateur) http://cmo.uqam.ca.

References

Auray N. Communautés d'Information et Gouvernance Ouverte: Frontières, Statuts, Conflits Paris: Telecom ParisTech (2008)

Benkler Y. The Wealth of Networks: How Social Production Transforms Markets and Freedom New Haven, CT: Yale University Press (2006)

Berry R. 'Will the iPod kill the radio star? Profiling podcasting as radio' Convergence 12 (2) (2006) pp. 143-162

Boellstorff T. Coming of Age in Second Life. An Anthropologist Explores the Virtually Human Princeton: Princeton University Press (2008)

Boyd D. 'Facebook's privacy trainwreck: Exposure, invasion and social convergence' Convergence 14(1) (2008) pp. 13-20

Bruns A. Gatewatching: Collaborative Online News Production New York: Peter Lang (2005)

Bruns A. Blogs, Wikipedia, Second Life, and Beyond. From Production to Produsage New York: Peter Lang (2008)

Cardon D. 'De l'innovation ascendante' Entrevue réalisée par Hubert Guillaud InternetActu http://www.internetactu.net/?p=5995 (2005)

Cardon D. 'Le design de la visibilité: un essai de typologie du web 2.0' (2008) http://www.internetactu.net/2008/02/01/le-design-de-la-visibilite-un-essai-de-typologie-du-web-20/ (July 23, 2008)

Castells M. Communication Power New York: Oxford University Press (2009)

Collins H. 'A new programme of research?' Studies in History and Philosophy of Science 38 (2007) pp. 615-620

Collins H., Evans R. Rethinking Expertise Chicago: University of Chicago Press (2007)

Dejours C. 'Psychanalyse et psychodynamique du travail: ambiguïtés de la reconnaissance' ed. Caillé A. La Quête de Reconnaissance. Nouveau Phénomène Social Total Paris: La Découverte (2007) pp. 58-88

DeRosnay J. La révolte du pronétariat. Des mass média aux média des masses Paris: Fayard (2006)

Deuze M., Bruns A., Neuberger C. 'Preparing for an age of participatory news' Journalism Practice (1) 3 (2007) pp. 322-338

Dujarier M. Le Travail du Consommateur. De McDo à E-Bay: Comment nous Coproduisons ce que nous Achetons Paris: La Découverte (2008)

Gensollen M. 'La culture entre économie et écologie: l'exemple des communautés en ligne' ed. Greffe X. Création et Diversité au Miroir des Industries Culturelles Paris: La Documentation Française (2006) pp. 285-312

Gillmor D. We the Media. Grassroots Journalism by the People, for the People Sebastopol, CA: O'Reilly Media (2004)

Goldhaber, M.H. 'The Attention Economy and the Net' First Monday 2 (4) (1997) http://www.firstmonday.org/issues/issue2_4/goldhaber/

Granjon F. 'Les nouveaux résistants à l'ère du numérique. Entre utopie sociale et déterminisme technique' eds. Proulx S., Couture S., Rueff J. L'Action Communautaire Québécoise à l'Ère du Numérique Québec: Presses de l'Université du Québec (2008) pp. 59-76

Haythornthwaite C. Crowds and Communities: Lightweight and Heavyweight Models of Peer Production Proceedings of the Hawaii International Conference on System Sciences (2009a) http://www.ideals.uillinois.edu/handle/2142/9457 (February 3, 2010)

Haythornthwaite C. Online Knowledge Crowds and Communities Paper presented at the International Conference on Knowledge Communities, University of Nevada, Reno (2009b) http://www.ideals.uillinois.edu/ handle /14198 (February 3, 2010)

Honneth A. La Lutte pour la Reconnaissance Paris: Éditions du Cerf (2002)

Howe J. The Rise of Crowdsourcing Wired (14.06.2006) http://www.wired.com/wired/archive/14.06/crowds.html (February 3, 2010)

Jenkins H. Convergence Culture. Where Old and New Media Collide New York: NYU Press (2006a)

Jenkins H. Fans. Bloggers and Gamers: Exploring Participatory Culture New York: NYU Press (2006b)

Joyce M. The Citizen Journalism Web site "OhmyNews" and the 2002 South Korean Presidential Election Berkman Center for Internet and Society at Harvard University (2007) cyber.law.harvard.edu/.../Joyce_South_Korea_2007.pdf (October 7, 2010)

Kahney L. 'Citizen Reporters Make the News', Wired News, 17 May (2003) http://www.wired.com/news/culture/0,1284,58856,00.html (October 7, 2010)

Langlois A., Dubois F. eds. Médias autonomes. Nourrir la Résistance et la Dissidence Montréal: Lux (2006)

Leadbeater C., Miller P. 'The pro-am revolution: How enthusiasts are changing our economy and society' Demos (2004) http://www.demos.co.uk/publications/proameconomy/ (August 31, 2008)

Levrel J. 'Wikipedia: Un dispositif médiatique de publics participants' Réseaux 138 (2006) pp. 185-218

Moreau F. 'Numérisation et dématérialisation des échanges internationaux de musique enregistrée' eds. Cohen D., Verdier T. La mondialisation Immatérielle Paris: La Documentation française (2008) pp. 97-115

OECD Committee for Information, Computer and Communications Policy Participative Web: User-Created Content Paris: Organisation for Economic Cooperation and Development (2007)

Oh Y. H. The End of 20th Century Journalism Keynote speech to the 2004 World Association of Newspapers Annual Conference (2004) http://english.ohmynews.com/ArticleView/article_view.asp?no=169396&rel_no=1 (October 8, 2010)

OhmyNews http://international.ohmynews.com/about/ (October 7, 2010)

O'Neill B. 'CBC.ca: Broadcast sovereignty in a digital environment' Convergence 12 (2) 2006 pp. 179-197

O'Reilly T. The Open Source Paradigm Shift eds. Feller J., Fitzgerald B., Hissam S. A., Lakhani K. R. Perspectives on Free and Open Source Software Cambridge, MA: MIT Press (2005) pp. 461–482

Oudshoorn N., Pinch T. eds. How Users Matter. The Co-Construction of Users and Technologies Cambridge, MA: MIT Press (2003)

Oudshoorn N., Pinch T. 'User-Technology Relationships: Some Recent Developments' eds. Hackett J., Amsterdamska O., Lynch M., Wajcman J. The Handbook of Science and Technology Studies 3rd Edition Cambridge, MA: MIT Press (2008) pp. 541-565

Proulx S. 'La confiance: ce qui fait lien au temps de l'incertitude informationnelle' eds. Lobet-Maris C., Lucas R., Six B. Variations sur la Confiance: Concepts et Enjeux au Sein des Théories de la Gouvernance Brussels: Peter Lang (2009) pp. 111-124

Proulx S., Latzko-Toth, G. 'La virtualité comme catégorie pour penser le social: l'usage de la notion de communauté virtuelle' Sociologie et sociétés 32(2) (2000) pp. 99-122

Proulx S., Poissant L., Sénécal M. eds. Communautés Virtuelles. Penser et Agir en Réseau Québec: Presses de l'Université Laval (2006)

Rheingold H. The Virtual Community. Homesteading on the Electronic Frontier Reading, MA: Addison-Wesley (1993)

Rybas N., Gajjala R. 'Developing cyberethnographic rsearch mthods for uderstanding diitally mdiated ientities' Forum: Qualitative Social Research, 8 (3) (2007) article 35 pp. 12

Surowiecki J. The Wisdom of Crowds New York: Anchor Books (2005)

Thompson J.B. The Media and Modernity. A Social Theory of the Media Cambridge: Polity Press (1995)

Thompson J.B. 'Transformation de la visibilité' Réseaux 100 (2000) pp. 187-213

Tönnies F. Community and Society New York: Harper Torchbook (1963 [1887])

Vainio N., Vadén T., Oksanen V., Seppänen M. Elements of Open Source Community Sustainability eds. Helander N., Antikainen M. Essays on OSS Practices and Sustainability Tampere: EBRC Research Reports 36 (2006)

Voirol O. 'Visibilité et invisibilité: une introduction' Réseaux no. 129-130 (2005a) pp. 9-36

Voirol O. 'Les luttes pour la visibilité. Esquisse d'une problématique' Réseaux 129-130 (2005b) pp. 89-121

Von Hippel E. Democratizing Innovation Cambridge: MIT Press (2005)

Weber S. The Success of Open Source Cambridge: Harvard University Press (2004)

West J., O'Mahony S. 'The role of participation architecture in growing sponsored open source communities#Industry and Innovation 15 (2) (2008) pp. 145-168

Woyke E. OhmyNews Chooses Influence Over Income (2009) http://www.forbes.com/2009/04/02/internet-media-video-technology-korea-09-media.html (October 7, 2010)

Part 2 - User Approaches in ICT Design and Development

Aphra Kerr, Stefano de Paoli and Cristiano Storni

Constructing the Role of Users in ICT Design

Introduction

In much literature today, the concept of the "user" has become a point of debate, as, so the argument goes, for any information and communication technology (ICT) service or application there are a diversity of users/actors who exercise their agency in different ways. From digital artisans, to expert users, hackers, players and spectators, users can play a range of roles at different stages of the design/innovation process. Users can be disruptive and dangerous but can also be a source of value and innovation. Non-users and implicated users may also play a role in design, often indirectly (Cowan 1987). Technologies can also play a role and can be considered actors. This discussion takes us beyond simple statements about passive and active users, about diffusion and impacts, and focuses attention on different types of users, differences in power and agency between users and different contexts of use.

According to Woolgar (1994), every process of innovation, design and development can be characterized as a struggle between competing conceptions of the user. Indeed different design approaches offer vastly different roles to users. "Traditional" design methodologies are based on the imagined user, direct and indirect user research and formalized models of user behaviour. Emergent design methodologies try to include users in the design process, e.g. user-centered design, participatory design, and forms of co-design and peer-to-peer production (Storni 2008). Similarly, a range of innovation models exists, from the more traditional linear approach to "open innovation" and "whirlwind innovation" (Callon 2004). The literature in many disciplines now talks about the designer-user relationship in terms of a community or hybrid collective (Callon 2004), a network (Saxenian 1991; Storper 1997), a space of flows (Castells 2000) or an ecosystem. Within this network or community, users may play, or may be invited and allowed to play a range of roles, including that of the designer. Yet despite the prevalence of user empowerment discourses and emergent design methodologies the reality of ICT design, even Web 2.0 internet applications and services, is based on little direct user involvement, little knowledge of contexts of use and focused on user constraint and management rather than empowerment.

The authors of this chapter are working collaboratively on an interdisciplinary project that is attempting to harness emergent design methodologies and social science research in future internet services and applications design. In this chapter we draw upon science and technology studies, innovation studies, interaction design and media studies to problematise the concept of the user and to explore how user roles are constructed in the design of ICT. We do this by critically exploring two contrasting case studies, one historical and one contemporary, where software and hardware respectively constrain and enable user behavior and we conclude with a discussion of the implications of our findings for our understanding of user involvement and empowerment through ICT design.

Co-construction of user roles

Science and Technology Studies (STS) have played an important role in opening up technological design and use to academic scrutiny. STS have questioned received orthodoxies of the neutral engineer or technologist working to develop new products and services, which are later diffused into society as stable products and proceed along a rather standardized s-shaped diffusion curve. STS have challenged technologically determinist accounts of social change and demonstrated that technical design is a thoroughly social process influenced not only by the technologist, or design team, but also by the wider context of design and use.

Early work by Bijker (1995) under the umbrella of the Social Construction of Technology (SCOT) noted that there were a number of relevant social groups involved in the development of a technology, and indeed that they may attach different meanings and play different roles in the development process. It was later argued that technologies and users were co-constructed or formed a socio-technical ensemble. Thus it was not solely a process of users shaping the technology or technology shaping users, but rather an iterative process of co-shaping, an idea clearly influenced by Actor-Network Theory (ANT) (Akrich 1995; Callon 2004), which holds that the need to pay attention to the role of the technology as actor, or "actant", is crucial in any study of users. Also emerging from ANT is the concept of "delegation" or the fact that roles can be delegated to actors or technologies. Both ANT and SCOT researchers have also been interested in how technologies become embedded in society, stabilize and become locked-in.

Studies of designers and technologists at work have highlighted the role that the imagined user plays, as well as the fact that many designers rely on their own knowledge and expertise to design new goods and services, rather than on an understanding of user needs or use contexts. Akrich (1995) calls this the I-methodology. For Akrich, it is clear that designers develop a script that they inscribe into a technology, and this script constrains how that technology may be used and ascribes certain tasks and roles to certain actors. Kerr (2002) found that digital game developers used a similar approach and designed for themselves, i.e. young, white, affluent and technologically literate males. De Paoli et al. (2008) observed that software licenses are themselves scripts that act as boundaries for the inclusion and exclusion of users in Free Software projects. These studies of software design highlight the fact that certain roles can be delegated to a technology and that technologies can exclude as well as include certain uses. Thus technologies are socially shaped, but in turn may also shape their use and users. Users are active and may behave in ways which conflict with the designer's intentions (antiprogram), or act in line with the prescribed behaviour (subscription) or indeed renegotiate it (de-inscription).

Early STS and SCOT studies tended to focus on those highly visible actors who were directly involved in the production/design process. Feminist scholars have, however, contributed to our understanding of the barriers that certain designs can create for certain users, particularly women (Cowan 1987). Pioneering work by Cockburn and Ormrod (1993) followed a technology from production into consumption contexts and started to question the ideologies and boundaries created by technologies. Histories of technologies like the computer and the telephone illustrate how the original designs may have excluded certain user groups but how these technologies were reshaped in various contexts of use. Fleck (1988), in work on complex computer systems in organizations, coined the term "innofusion" to illustrate that users struggle to make technology work and match local needs. Innovation studies more generally have demonstrated that the efficient incorporation of technologies into the workplace is a process of learning by doing through which new practices may emerge (Arrow 1962; Rosenberg 1982; Lundvall & Johnson 1994). In both studies of work and domestic contexts it was noted that if learning is not captured by the producers or designers, such learning may be localized and the technology may fail. The key message of this work for us is that users and use may be prefigured in the technological design process, but that nevertheless technologies may change considerably over time, in many cases due to feedback from users. Indeed innovations may be reinvented or substantially changed through use and negotiation.

Thus using a technology is a much more complex process than merely purchasing the technology and learning how to use it. The learning process has variously been called "appropriation" (Eglash 2004), domestication (Silverstone & Hirsch 1992; Lie & Sorensen 1996) or "social learning" (Williams et al. 2005). The focus in all these approaches is on how technologies are adapted to pre-existing social settings, routines and norms and enter into, shape and are shaped by a range of social factors. Users must symbolically, cognitively and practically grapple with a technology in order for it to be incorporated successfully into their lives. Work by Williams et al. (2005) shows that "intermediaries" play an important role in the process of "social learning" and in translating a technology into everyday life. These intermediaries may be public bodies, private commercial shops, websites or magazines which allow users to experiment and get more information. An important part of the material and symbolic process of appropriation is played by advertising and marketing and these actors may help to imagine new uses and new user groups (Schot & De La Bruheze 2005). Another group, which may play an important role, is that of the non-users. Wyatt (2002) suggests that non-users, whether voluntary or involuntary, may still contribute to the development of a technology.

Early work on the diffusion or impact of technologies in society focused on the user and non-users as a problem. STS has shown us that we need to examine the co-construction of the users and the technology; the ideas, biases and constraints that are designed into a technology and the struggles and processes at work in the use of a technology. Capturing and effectively using feedback from users is now an accepted part of the innovation process and a far from trivial or straightforward process. "Lay knowledge" is at least as important a source of innovation as "expert knowledge". Indeed in certain contexts the user may become a designer, or what Von Hippel (2005) calls a "self-manufacturer" and the designer may also be a user. Instead of focusing on upstream processes, it is important to analyse the network of social actors and intermediaries/mediators involved in producing and consuming a technology over time. This process is what Callon (2004) would call 'translation' or Williams et al. (2005) "social learning". This process changes both the technology and the user/contexts of use.

The key concepts to emerge from this review include: free association and treating human and non-human actors as equally important, co-construction of technologies and users, script and inscription, appropriation and finally, the concept of hybrid communities/networks of innovation. Potential actors to consider include expert, lay, intermediary and non-users, technologies and licenses. Overall, in the study of ICT design, it is important to identify moments of closure and stabilization while also allowing for dynamism. Lievrouw & Livingstone (2002) note that one can "characterize the development and use of new media technologies as a process that involves a constant tension between determination and contingency, that is, between the imposition of order and uncertainty". They argue that at different moments in the development process the prevailing tendency may change from one of determination to one of contingency. In the following section we discuss two case studies that show how the design of a software and a hardware project respectively can offer contrasting levels of contingency and determination of user behaviour.

Case studies

In this section we examine the Multics software system and the Arduino open hardware project. The first case demonstrates the "traditional" approach to ICT design, which is mainstream and widespread, while the second is an emerging approach, which allows new relationships between designer and user to emerge and which appears to empower users in interesting new ways.

In the Multics case, we will see how the behaviour of users was prefigured for "security purposes", a task that was delegated to three simple bits of technology, which in turn effectively created a division of labour between two user groups: normal users and administrators. The case shows that even minimal technological elements (3 simple bits) can, to a great degree, pre-figure the future behaviour and abilities of users. This case was constructed by analysing secondary data, including research reports (Van Vleck 1973), design papers (Saltzer 1974; McCarthy 1992) and manuals related to the Multics and other operating systems (Watson 1970; Silberschatz 2004).

In the Arduino case, we explore an open hardware platform system, which, while placing some "creative commons restrictions" on users, opens up a range of possibilities for user roles and innovation by different user groups. This case study was constructed using analyses of secondary data, including reviews of the Arduino Board in on-line magazines (like Wired, and the official Arduino Web site, www.arduino.cc), in addition to an analysis of some of the on-line discussions about Arduino on technology sites such as Slashdot.com, Make.com and Ponoko.com. This was supplemented with semi-structured in-depth interviews with the original three Arduino developers.

Multics case study

During the 1950s and the 1960s, a mainframe computer consisted of a large machine occupying entire floors of a building, which was mainly used for research purposes by programmers/researchers. With the growth of users in need of computational resources within labs, a data processing method known as Timesharing was introduced. In this case study we provide a simplified account of the Multics protection mechanisms contained in the Timesharing data processing method and how it prefigured user roles and uses.

In a typical Timesharing Operating System (OS) the central processing Unit (CPU) time is equally divided among the users, via a centralized network (figure 1). Using "dumb terminals" users have access to computer resources (memory storage and CPU cycles), hence permitting each user "to behave as though he were in sole control of a computer" (McCarthy 1992), unlike previous data processing methods, where there was a one-to-one relation between a user and the computer. With the growth in the number of users the same computational power was divided/shared among various users (Timesharing).

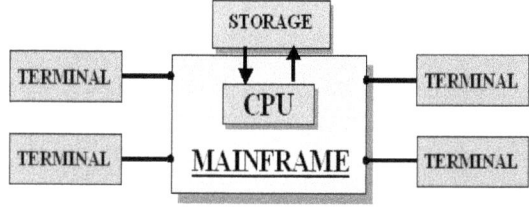

Figure 1: Timesharing system: centralized mainframe used via a series of remote dumb terminals

The creation of the Timesharing technology raised concerns about how best to regulate the increased numbers of users using the Timesharing OS. There was a perceived need for security and protection measures (for example, measures to prevent users from harming the computer system or other users' work), to ensure and support the shared nature of computational resources. The following passages, taken from a book on Timesharing system design (Watson 1970, 111), describes some design principles for creating protection measures in Timesharing computers:

"• Protection of the system from user processes. It is imperative that users not be able to take actions which would stop the system from running or destroy information essential to the system.
• Protection of the users from each other. A user must not be allowed to take an action which would harm the operation of another user's process."

These forms of protection were performed by the Operating System using software solutions. In an operating system, protection refers "to a mechanism of controlling the access of programs, processes or users to the resources defined by the computer system" (Silberschatz et al. 2004, 679). It is this mechanism that is interesting for us because, as we shall see, it embodies a division of labor between users and administrators of computer systems. We can observe this division of labor by briefly describing the protection mechanism of a well-known Timesharing OS: the Multics system.

The Multics system was developed at MIT (from the late 1960s until the late 1980s). For several reasons – including military involvement – protection and security were considered fundamental features of the Multics system. What is important for us is to observe that the memory space (storage in figure 1) of the Multics system was segmented (i.e. divided) into specific parts. Each segment of the memory of Multics is more or less what we today know as a computer file, where the segment can be considered as the "cataloging unit of the storage system, and it is also the unit of separate protection" (Saltzer 1974, 389). Each segment of the system, therefore, was a file with an embodied protection mechanism. Associated with each segment was an Access Control List: a list of users of the system and the permission level they had to access the file/segments.

Once a user accessed the system (via a Username/Password), the user then had access to all the segments belonging to her/him (including segments belonging to the groups of which the user was a member), but not to those belonging to other users. The access control list can be modeled using a matrix (table 1), in which we have the users and the segments. For each file/segment there were different modes of access and in particular: *None* (access denied), *R* (read only), *W* (write only) and *E* (execute). In the example in table 1, *User_1* can only read file 1 & 3, while she is allowed to write over file 2. *User_2* can write on File 1&3, but has no rights at all on file 2. It would appear that *User_2* gave *User_1* the right to read but not to write on files 1 & 3, while *User_1* gave no rights at all to *User_2* for using file 2.

Figure 2 represents a segment of the Multics system. While sections 1, 3 and 4 of the segment represent different parts of the Multics computer file (such as, for example, the specification of the physical address of the file, section 1), it is section 2 which is of particular interest to us. In section 2, are three bits of technology that independently control access to the segment. These three simple bits constitute the core element of the control mechanism of Multics: indeed, it is because of the different settings of these bits that we have an overall division of labor generated by the system.

	File1	File2	File3
User_1	Read	Read & Write	Read
User_2	Read & Write	None	Read & Write

Table 1: Example of Access Control Matrix

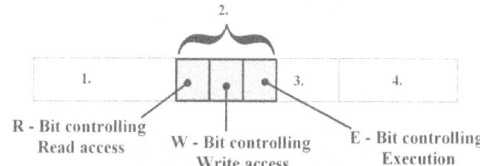

Figure 2: Control bits of the Multics segments, adapted from Saltzer (1974)

In order to understand how these control bits work, let us study the following examples (figure 3). The first example (left side of figure) graphically describes User_2 & File 1 of the access control matrix (read and write access to file 1), while the second example (on the right side) describes User_1 & File 1 (read only access to file 1). These examples illustrate the second protection design principle listed above and how the inner working protection mechanism worked. The file protection bits were able to prevent users from damaging other users' files: User_1 is not allowed to write over file 1. However this form of protection does not characterize the first design principle described by Watson (1970), above.

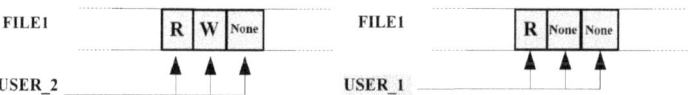

Figure 3: Examples of Multics segment access control and control bits

Within the Multics system, there was a functional division between "normal" users and the "administrator" of the computer system. While both were considered users by the system (i.e. both had their own usernames and passwords), the administrators had particular privileges over the use of the system that the normal user did not have (Van Vleck 1973, 7), such as:

• To certain segments which is not granted to regular users.

• The system will grant them certain requests which it will not grant for normal users.

• Special rights, such as the privilege of being able to patch the system, are available to system administrators.

Some of these administrative privileges, again, were determined by the three control bits. This is apparent from figure 4, where the normal users (in this specific example) do not have the right to write over the OS files or to install a computer application on top of the Operating System. Normal users had rights only to their specific segments and only administrators were allowed to install new programs and to modify and patch the OS segments.

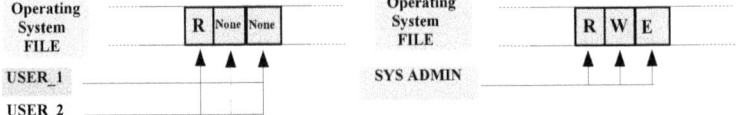

Figure 4: Control bits and division of labor between users and administrators

The control bits clearly act in ways that limit what the users can do with the OS and constitute a concrete implementation of the protection design principle described above. So, while the protection design principles certainly had the acceptable goal of governing the use of computational resources in a network (i.e. to stop the user harming another user's file or the whole system), they also lead to a very specific user role determination.

Arduino case study

The case of Open Hardware (OH) and the recent popularity of some projects in this area represent an interesting illustration of new ways to empower users. Here users are not pre-figured in the design script but become active participants in the design process. Wikipedia defines OH as:

"computer and electronic hardware that is designed in the same fashion as free and open source software (FOSS). Open source hardware is part of the open source culture that takes the open source ideas to fields other than software (...) The term has primarily been used to reflect the free release of information about the hardware design, such as schematics, bill of materials and PCB layout data, often with the use of FOSS to drive the hardware".

OH opens up these design resources to active communities of hobbyists, inviting them to do whatever they want with the original design: build new things on top of it, modify it to adapt to new contexts and exigencies, or radically redesign it.

Certainly, there are differences from FOSS: the replication of software code is definitely less problematic than that of hardware physical components. At the same time, given that electronic components are becoming cheaper and powerful computers are now widely available to run the software to program OH, cost is less and less of a problem. Among the many examples of OH projects, the Arduino board represents a successful instance that merits analysis, as it challenges our traditional understanding of the separation of roles between users and designers. According to the official Arduino community website (www.arduino.cc), the Arduino is:

> "an open-source electronics prototyping platform based on flexible, easy-to-use hardware and software. It's intended for artists, designers, hobbyists, and anyone interested in creating interactive objects or environments. (...) It's an open-source physical computing platform based on a simple microcontroller board, and a development environment for writing software for the board".

Arduino can be used to develop interactive objects, taking inputs from a variety of switches or sensors, and controlling a variety of lights, motors, and other physical outputs – all electronic materials that are widely available, inexpensive and easy to use. Essentially the board is constituted by: a series of ports for inputs that come from whatever sensor is used (motion, light, proximity sensors, etc), a series of output ports connected with whatever actuator is used (motors, lights, computer devices) and a central processor (a micro-controller chip) with a flash memory where written code to process inputs into outputs can be stored. Code is written with a specific FOSS programming language called "Processing" that allows instructions to be written for the processor.

The Arduino board was initially designed for teaching purposes within design education. As one of the main developers of the board recalls:

> "We already work with Processing a lot. At that time Processing was limited to graphical animations. When dealing with tangible and real-time interaction we had to use another language. One day we asked ourselves: why not have Processing to generate programs for our hardware too?"

A specific module for the Processing language was then implemented so that students would not have to learn another language to program hardware in their tangible real-time interaction with design projects. Initially, the programming language was used with Wiring, a more expensive, bigger and less open board than the Arduino. The idea of developing a more agile and open board and an integrated development environment then emerged. In a couple of months, due to a series of collaborations among several volunteers in a design institute in Southern Europe, the first Arduino Board emerged (figure 5). Along with it, a first series of workshops - where the boards were actually given to students and interested teachers – were arranged. Interviewees recall a big design workshop in Madrid in 2005, followed by one in London and in Copenhagen. In a few months, the Arduino board was popular in design institutes all over Europe and - due to word-of-mouth – within many DIY communities.

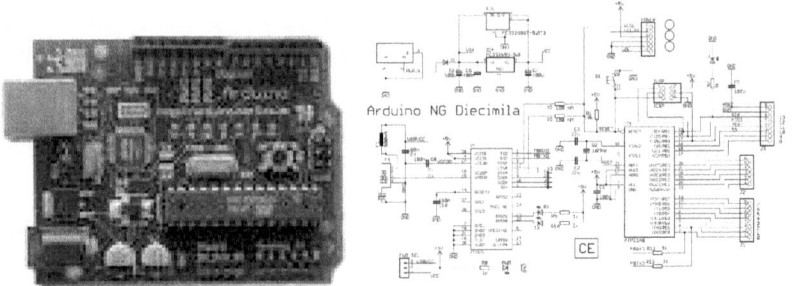

Figure 5: The Arduino Board and one of the schematics used to illustrate its circuit

While in the Multics system roles are prefigured and they and their interdependencies are inscribed in the system, this OH product – and open hardware in general – prefigure roles only partially. The board is intended to be the central core for the implementation and prototyping of interactive products or environments designed by the users themselves. Essentially, the board does things only if it is connected (i.e. soldered) with input sensors, output actuators and programmed. But the design possibilities for users here are endless. Also, Arduino developers have developed very weak forms of control over future uses. The negotiation of the role is not anticipated in the board design but it remains open through a series of strategies that we will now list.

On the Arduino web site, all the schematics, design files and software are posted for anyone to access. Anyone can download them and manufacture their own Arduino. In an extensive article on open hardware boards, Wired wrote about the Arduino:

"You can send the plans off to a Chinese factory, mass-produce the circuit boards, and sell them yourself – pocketing the profit without paying the creator a penny in royalties. Arduino developers won't sue you. Actually, they are sort of hoping you'll do it."

The board schematics and design files are in fact released under the "Attribution share alike 3.0" Creative Commons' license. Under this license, anyone is allowed to produce copies of the board, to redesign it, or even to sell boards that copy the design. You do not need to pay a license fee to the Arduino team or even ask permission. However, if you republish the reference design, you have to credit the original Arduino group (this is the attribution). And if you tweak or change the board, your new design must use the same or a similar Creative Commons license to ensure that new versions of the Arduino board will be equally without fees and open to future modification and redesign.

The language used to program the microcontroller is Processing (Proce55ing.org), an easy FOSS programming language originally intended for graphic design that has been extended - by the Arduino team - to deal with microcontroller physical boards. The Arduino integrated development environment used to write the code and flash it into the board is a piece of software released under the GNU General Public Licence. This license gives the user the power to change and distribute the software source code, provided that new enhancements are released under the same license terms (i.e. the copyleft clause). This breaks down the distinction between users and designers of the software (Callon 2004). The Arduino Web site, where a library of code examples from the user community is growing on a daily basis, is also released under creative commons so that users can freely make use of all the scripts, code and tricks posted there. This will make the appropriation of the Arduino even easier because inexperienced users can take advantage of solutions and tutorials by peers. The only thing that is registered as a trademark is the name Arduino. An interviewee stated:

"The only protection we have in play (is with) regard (to) the name of the board that is trademarked. If you want to make a board and called it Gino, it is ok with me and I do not care. But if you make a board and you called it Arduino you cannot. We want to prevent the diffusion of low quality copies. Arduino for us means that the design respects certain quality (such) as the ease of use, the quality of the components and of their assemblage."

Within months, hobbyists from all around the world suggested changes and improvements to the programming language, to the software and to the physical board. Companies also offered to act as distributors. People used Arduino to build their own robots, amateur Unmanned Aerial Vehicles (UAVs), music electronic gadgets and interactive systems. Expert users published their projects while inexperienced users – even those who knew nothing about electronics – took advantage of the many tutorials available over the internet. For those who were already familiar with the Processing programming language things were even easier. Several unanticipated companies have emerged. A firm called Botanicals developed an Arduino-powered device that monitors houseplants and phones you when they need to be watered: you can buy it online. The web-site Makezine.com inaugurated an Arduino section (an Arduino gift guide) by introducing the board as the best all-around centerpiece to a modern electronics project and listing a huge series of step-by-step tutorials on how to build nifty gadgets with the Arduino. Also Ponoko.com - one of the biggest DIY technology web sites – sells Arduino based products along with a series of add-ons that extend the design possibilities of the board.

However, the Arduino board also divides users. Some, for instance, are not happy with the schematics provided online as making a compatible board is "not easy" (enough) and users must reverse engineer the Arduino. Thus projects like the Freeduino, Saguino and Pinguino have emerged, even if the controversies that generated them are still unsolved in many on-line forums (e.g. http://hardware.slashdot.org/hardware/08/10/24/0343244.shtml).

Implications for ICT design and co-constructing user roles

The Multics case study can be seen as a basic example of what are called "trusted systems" today. Trusted systems are becoming increasingly pervasive, since their role is to create security in computer networks by enforcing security policies. The Multics example, in its simplicity, offers insights into how prefigured and limited the role of users is when interacting with modern banking, government and many commercial sites. It is clear that the role played by (certain) users may be that they are prevented from doing things (such as modifying the operating systems) by the technical infrastructure. It is interesting to observe that in order to limit users' actions, no major technical solutions are required, as three simple bits are enough. These serve to separate the administrators from the normal users. The former have full control over the system and basically can do whatever they want; the latter have prescribed limits. So, we can conclude that while trusted systems have an important goal – that of creating and enabling protection and security over the network (i.e. ensuring privacy or preventing unwanted computer intrusions), sometimes this goal and its implementation has a side effect: that of preventing certain users from doing things. Further, it is worth noting that small parts of system infrastructures can have a great impact on user actions and levels of empowerment.

The Arduino case is an example of a system which allows for multiple user roles. Here, however, the separation between users and designers is far from straightforward. What is interesting here is the way actors and their tools co-evolve within a socio-technical system that have very little pre-inscription of actors' roles. This already teaches us – from a methodological point of view – that the role of the user in ICT can be understood only as a part of a larger socio-technical system that is constituted by human and non-human elements that mutually shape one another. In this second case, licenses and the internet play a key role. Together they afford and invite the formation of creative communities of actors whose role moves from that of designers to that of users. But they are nothing without the actual formation of communities where different people participate, learn from each other, sometimes fight and separate. By developing a series of strategies that regulate a collective creation, we can see how the agency of users of the Arduino are nurtured and invited to appropriate, often in unpredictable ways. The original developers seem to have developed an open-ended design process. There is no side effect for them, as they delegated the creation of Arduino applications and any change to the board's schematics or the programming environment to anyone who is interested. In this case, the strategy repays itself as communities – where use and design mix as well as means and ends – start to contribute and share. Again, learning from our first example, a change in a single element of the whole assemblage and the mechanism can degenerate into something completely different.

The lessons to emerge from our cases would suggest that designers and academics studying ICT design need to be attentive to the interplay between technology, actors and policy documents and pay attention to the fact that even small technical decisions may have considerable implications for users (e.g. create distinctions between users and limit user roles). Furthermore, the role of licenses and policy documents in governing user roles either indirectly through rules or directly through code is also clear from our cases. Thus, while it may not be possible for all ICT systems to be "open" and governed by creative commons licenses it is worth considering the middle ground between a top down approach to design which strictly prefigures user roles and a more open approach to design which invites in users to the design community and empowers them in creative new ways. Our point is not to suggest a best or singular approach to innovation and user empowerment, but to highlight the fact that we need to search for different possibilities, approaches and models if we are to foster user empowerment. This is of paramount importance in the current geo-political climate which is seeing greater and greater levels of computer protection and security delegated to technologies which by definition aim to limit user actions. Further, it is relevant to discussions about the future of the internet and whether and how network neutrality and open standards can be maintained as the numbers of users and uses of the internet grow.

What both these cases serve to do is to relativise contemporary discussions about the user empowerment offered by the internet and, in particular, by Web 2.0 internet services and applications. Such discussions tend to hyperbolize and overstate the creative agency of the user, both in terms of production as well as consumption, and neglect to explore how the wider socio-technical system in terms of the underlying infrastructure, hardware and software may prefigure in quite extensive ways the possibilities for users. The reality in many Web 2.0 applications is that the user has relatively little agency to create new forms of content, let alone reshape the underlying technologies, and that much of the value they create lies in the collective metadata collected behind the scenes. Studies of Web 2.0 users indicate that many users play relatively inactive roles, preferring to lurk, spectate and rate others rather than create or design themselves (Van Dijck 2009). The user, while afforded certain limited productive roles, is nevertheless restricted by the producer/designer/technology of the commercial application and the legal systems and licenses they put in place. At the same time, other cases exist that provide us with examples of new user roles, some of which enable the user to contribute to the design/innovation process in a more equitable way (Storni 2008), for example, crowd sourcing, smart mobs, open source software and hardware developments like Arduino (Auty 2004). The latter, however, are more the exception than the rule.

Conclusion

The two cases proposed in this chapter illustrate two different approaches to ICT design. The case of Multics illustrates the establishment of barriers and control systems that limit users' actions for security reasons. The Arduino case shows the melting of these barriers in the process of defining the user as the lead, or at least a fellow, innovator. The second case opens up channels of communication and feedback between designers and users, the former closes down the channels. The first case clearly defines roles for user groups while the second leaves these roles more open. In both cases technology and license systems work together to prescribe certain user roles and define the degree to which users may become involved in use or design. Both these case might represent ideal – yet opposite - types of users' scripting, with, on one side, a more managerial, top down approach to ICT design, and on the other a decentralized, peer-to-peer approach. The Italian ICT theorist Ciborra (2000) would probably have argued that this is an example of "from Control to Drift".

Conceptualizing the relationships between these two models and exploring other models is one of the challenges for ICT researchers. These relationships cannot be taken for granted, as there is a risk of falling into subtle forms of reductionism, determinism and essentialism. These models are not just out there as matters of fact; their *matters of factuality* are the result of the same socio-technical processes in which even their relationships are implied. Therefore we need to assess whether we are really witnessing the growth of a drift or more open approach to design, or whether there are still forces acting to restrict such approaches. Is this really a change of paradigm? Will this radically change social relations of production? Will this free us from what the German philosopher Martin Heidegger called the enframing of technology (*das Gestell*)? Or will this give rise to certain privileged user groups being empowered, while others are not? What actors, technologies, policies and licensing systems are needed to ensure that users are truly empowered and in meaningful ways? It is clear that it would be easy to assign positive values to just one side hence making any effort to describe power relations or even political struggles between various socio-technical collectives a difficult task. For us and for our agenda, these cases are just a starting point. Further empirical research on the current and potential role of users in the design of internet services and applications in particular domains is ongoing. However, much has already been learnt from these cases.

Acknowledgement: The authors wish to acknowledge funding support from the Irish HEA PRTLI Cycle 4 FutureComm (http://futurecomm.tssg.org) programme.

References

Akrich M. 'User representations: Practices, methods and sociology' Rip A., Misa T., Johan eds. Managing Technology in Society London: Pinter (1995) pp. 167-184

Arrow K. 'The economic implications of learning by doing' Review of Economic Studies,29 (1962) pp. 155-173

Auty C. 'Political Hacktivism: tool of the underdog or scourge of cyberspace?' Aslib Proceedings: New Information Perspectives 56 (4) (2004) pp. 212-221

Bijker W. On Bicycles, Backelites, and Bulbs Cambridge: MIT Press (1995)

Callon M. 'The role of hybrid communities and socio-technical arrangements in the participatory design' Journal of the centre for information studies 5 (3) (2004) pp. 3-10

Castells M. The Rise of the Network Society Oxford: Blackwell (2000)

Ciborra C.U. and Associates. From Control to Drift: The Dynamics of Corporate Information Infrastructures Oxford: Oxford University Press (2000)

Cockburn C., Ormord S. Gender and Technology in the Making London: Sage (1993)

Cowan R. "The consumption junction: A proposal for research strategies in the sociology of technology' eds. Bijker W., Hughes, T., Pinch T. The Social Construction of Technological Systems Cambridge: MIT Press (1987) pp. 261-278

De Paoli S., Teli M., D'Andrea V. 'Free and open source licenses in community life: two empirical cases' FirstMonday 13 (10) (2008) http://firstmonday.org/htbin/cgiwrap/bin/ojs/index.php/fm/article/view/2064/2030

Dijck J. van 'Users like you? Theorizing agency in user-generated content'' Media, Culture and Society 31 (41) (2009) pp. 41-58

Eglash R., Croissant J. L., Di Chiro G., Fouche R. Appropriating Technology Vernacular Science and Social Power Minneapolis: University of Minnesota Press (2004)

Fleck J. Innofusion or Diffusation? The Nature of Technological Development in Robotics Edinburgh: Edinburgh University (1988)

Kerr A. 'Representing users in the design of digital games' ed. Mäyrä' F. Computer Games and Digital Cultures Finland: University of Tampere (2002) pp. 277-295

Lie M., Sorensen K. Making Technology Our Own? Domesticating Technology into Everyday Life Trondheim: Scandinavian University Press North (1996)

Lievrouw L. A., Livingstone S. 'The Social Shaping and Consequences of ICTs' ed. Lievrouw L. Handbook of New Media London: Sage Publications (2002) pp. 1-15

Lundvall B.-Å., Johnson B. 'The Learning Economy' Journal of Industry Studies 1 (2) (1994) pp. 23-42

McCarthy J. 'Reminiscences on the history of time-sharing' Annals of the History of Computing 14(1) (1992) pp. 19-24

Rosenberg N. Inside the Black Box: Technology and Economics Cambridge: Cambridge University Press (1982)

Saltzer J.H. 'Protection and the control of information sharing in multics' Communications of the ACM 17 (7) (1974) pp. 388-402

Saxenian A. 'The origins and dynamics of production networks in Silicon Valley Research Policy 20 (1991) pp. 423-437

Schot J., De La Bruheze A. 'Giving birth to new users: how the mimimoog was sold to rock and roll. How Users Matter' eds. Oudshoorn N., Pinch T. The Co-Construction of Users and Technology Cambridge: MIT Press (2005)

Silberschatz A. Operating Systems Concepts with Java London: Addison-Wesley (2004)

Silverstone R., Hirsch E. eds. Consuming Technologies. Media and information in Domestic Spaces London: Routledge (1992)

Storni C. 'Rethinking the role of designer in future ICT' Proceedings of the Second Irish Human Computer Interaction University College Cork (2008)

Storper M. The Regional World London: The Guilford Press (1997)

Van Vleck T. 'Multics system administrators Manual' (1973) http://www.bitsavers.org/pdf/honeywell/multics/AK50_sysAdmin_feb73.pdf

Von Hippel E. Democratising Innovation Cambridge: MIT Press (2005)

Watson R. Timesharing System Design Concepts New York: McGraw-Hill Company (1970)

Williams R., Stewart J., Slack R. Social Learning in Technological Innovation Experimenting with Information and Communication Technologies Cheltemham: Edward Elgar (2005)

Wyatt S., Thomas G., Terranova T. They Came, they Surfed, they Went Back to the Beach Technology, Cyberpole, Reality Oxford: Oxford University Press (2002) pp. 23-40

Woolgar S. 'Rethinking the dissemination of science and technology' CRICT Discussion Paper No. 44 (May 1994)

James Stewart and Laurence Claeys

Problems and Opportunities of Interdisciplinary Work Involving Users in Speculative Research for Innovation of Novel ICT Applications

Introduction

As professionals, we are increasingly finding that we have to cross traditional disciplinary and institutional boundaries, such as between academia and industry, or between science and design. We are sharing methods and tools between disciplines, but it can be easy to lose sight of the motivations and intellectual foundations of these methods, the tacit knowledge that we bring to their use, and the wide variations in how the results of investigations and interventions are interpreted. We need to understand better these divergences, identifying pitfalls, but also highlighting the creative and analytic opportunities of this approach to working.

This chapter contains many personal experiences from our own everyday work life. For this reason, it is well worth reading our biography that has been included further along in the book. The standpoints adopted in this chapter very much reflect our backgrounds as social scientists.

More and more boundaries are being crossed between institutions and disciplines in the search for innovation in the field of novel ICT applications. Companies like Intel, Nokia, Xerox, Google, Yahoo and Bell Labs have decided to involve professionals other than engineers in their research work. Although some companies have been working with multi- or interdisciplinary approaches for more than ten years, a clear methodological interdisciplinary framework for innovation research within companies has still not been defined. While the added value of bringing together different disciplines is acknowledged, why and how this value is achieved remains unclear. Hence, different companies have developed their own approaches: in one, a separate "human sciences" department has been set up; another has established multidisciplinary and interdisciplinary teams; and there are also engineering companies paying an academic social science research group or a consultant to do certain research.

There is a growing body of literature that focuses on the difficulties of work in multi- and interdisciplinary teams, citing issues of epistemological difference (Penny 2009), conflicts of identity, group membership and cultural capital (Jackson 1996; Nicoll 2000), misaligning of concepts and terminology (Leigh Star 1991), lack of openness to approaches and ideas from other disciplines (Payne 1999), power issues (Suchman 1987), structural biases and failure of management. However, these types of teams are constituted because it is recognised that their varying skills and knowledge are necessary to conduct research for innovation, in the same way as labour and knowledge is divided in most other areas of human endeavour. We, as social scientists, are concerned with interdisciplinary work involving research with "users". Our question is not only what difficulties can arise in interdisciplinary work involving research with "users", but also what ways the methods and outputs of user research can act to make interdisciplinary research successful.

This chapter is presented in three parts. First, we define some common challenges when working in interdisciplinary ways. We summarise the different forms of representations of users that are used in (speculative) innovation research. Second, we describe the challenges of a social scientist entering an engineering team and the way we are seen as a proxy for users. These challenges will be illustrated with personal observations (Laurence) made during her first months work within Bell Labs, and will be situated in a broader discussion. Third, we will attempt to formulate a way that user research can act as tool for making interdisciplinary research a success. Here the personal reflections of James on different projects he worked on are discussed. We end by giving some real-life figures of the utilization of user research methods in the Application Domain groups of Bell Labs and we round up by pointing to some starting points on how user research methods can be handed over in a way that research with users can facilitate interdisciplinary speculative research on novel ICT applications where every member has a different role to play.

Problem definition: Speculative research for innovation

Introduction

Product and service innovation is a long and complicated process – it may start with formal research and development, but equally may emerge from experimentation by users or intermediary organisations in industry networks. It usually takes years of idea generation and experimentation before a supply network and user community with the necessary experience and expertise can be established that will finally implement a successful innovation. In this chapter we are concerned with the early experimental stage and ideas and evidence development in the field of new applications of ICT, rather than in the work of development teams creating products and services according to more immediate business needs. This type of work tends to use requirement-led methods where the environment for use is established, and the problems to be solved are relatively easily identified. The early research is more open-ended, experimental and uncertain. Research is about asking questions, formulating problems based on those questions, the search for ways to answer those questions, analysing results and exploring how those problems might be addressed. It sometimes produces some type of answer: in the form of a prototype technical artefact, a business plan, a report on human activity or a new analytic framework or theory, but its main aim is to explore the uncertainties of the world, and the possibilities of change produced by bringing together people and technology in novel ways.

We term this type of work "speculative research for innovation" – speculative since it is inventive and involves imagining futures different to the present; research, since it involves scientific methods and the exploration of the unknown and the novel; and innovation, since it is directed at informing and stimulating innovation. In this final point it is differentiated from the speculative research of, say, art-science, which has no pretensions of informing innovation.

This final distinction is also crucial in highlighting the institutional context: the speculative research for innovation that we address often occurs in the Research and Innovation (R&I) departments of ICT firms, staffed by engineers and developers trained in technical problem solving, using established software and product development models. Penny (2009) suggests that many people trained in analytic disciplines, such as much of engineering (who are applied scientists) are less equipped to formulate problems, but focus very much on providing solutions and answers (generally in the form of an artefact). It is not surprising, then, that speculative research that attempts to bring together technology and people is difficult to integrate into the still existing dominant waterfall model for innovation within the engineering methodology.

Until recently, the process used to develop an innovative application was considered a linear process involving requirements capture and the definition of the specifications. This was followed by the development of a lab mock-up and finally, the design and implementation of the Graphical User Interface (GUI) and experience design. The designer community has also adopted this software development process; designers integrate design methods and user tests in the different defined development phases of the waterfall model (the so-called UCD Design research cycle). This is probably the core reason for the relative ease with which an engineering team is expanded with designers, although the adoption of "user-centred" design methods, which are by nature oriented to potential customers, has also helped. Designers also use speculative methods when designing novel ICT applications; but they do not engage with the results in an analytical way, only in an inspirational way. Unlike many other areas of technological development, where the design and prototyping can be a long and expensive process, software development is increasingly replacing the traditional 'heavyweight' software development methods (such as the waterfall method) (Beck & Fowler 2001) with agile programming methodology that produces high quality code at a scale appropriate for research. These fast, iterative processes create opportunities for social scientists to be involved in "requirements capture" and to influence the development process during different stages of the programming work, including user testing and trials.

We have observed from our experience that there are generally four main disciplines brought to bear in research on speculative applications of ICT: we can stereotype these as engineers (e.g. software architects, research engineers, software developers), designers (e.g. usability designers, product designers, user-experience designers, graphic designers), social scientists (e.g. anthropologists, sociologists, communication scientists) and business developers (e.g. marketers, business modellers). Each has its own approach to formulating questions and providing answers, methodologically, culturally and even philosophically. They also have different tendencies to reflect on these practices. We start first with some general reflection upon interdisciplinary work and the role of the 'user'.

Production and use of knowledge about "users"

This chapter situates the issues of interdisciplinary work in the context of research into novel applications of new technologies, and in particular around practices that bring potential users and knowledge about users into the development process. Companies acknowledge the benefits of involving users in their research on innovations. By involving users early in the development process they hope to reduce the risks of failure and, more specifically, the development cost of the product. As the insight has grown that innovation is always a socio-technical change in society, early understanding of users or looking for new opportunities via users is becoming more common (e.g. Pals et al. 2008). It is therefore useful to frame "user involvement" within a model of the role of users in design and development. We extended the Social Learning in Innovation approach (Williams et al. 2005) and a concern for the representation of the user (Vedel 1994) in Figure 1.

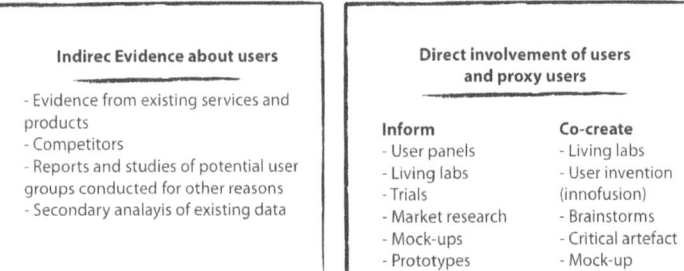

Figure 1: Sources of Representations of Users (based on Williams et al. 2005)

Information about potential users of future products is very important, both practically, and symbolically. Development groups have many sources of user information - some from past experience, some from direct work with potential or proxy users, and others from personal or professional constructions of what users are like and may or may not require. Speculative research on technology applications is rather different from requirements-based research, where suppliers can work with known customers to develop requirements, and work with them to fine tune them. Speculative research departs from visions of technology or the world, and attempts to engage with both in rather experimental processes. The "users" are initially unknown, and potential users hard to identify, and often hard to engage with. It is in this sort of R&I that interdisciplinary teams are important.

While R&D staff can attempt to "go and ask what people want", it is equally likely that technology developers will observe that "people do not know what they want, it is not worth talking to them – just invent something and persuade them to buy it!" This is what Limonard & De Koning (2006) call the dilemma of user involvement: users cannot always articulate their expectations or predict what they expect to do with certain devices or applications they have never seen or thought about before. Of course, most of us do not know what we want in terms of a new technological product or service that makes a significant departure from established provision. However, to suggest that therefore we should not, or need not engage with people who might use our services and products is ridiculous. User-research has values other than prediction: it offers researchers stimulus and opens new avenues of enquiry. However, the methods that can be used - human-centred design techniques, requirements engineering, modelling, and marketing techniques etc - are in many cases the same techniques that designers and engineers and business analysts use in more pragmatic work.

In research we engage with potential users of future technologies, because in the world of uncertainty, and often unsuccessful innovation, knowledge about "users" is seen as very valuable, and has great currency within innovating communities (Nicoll 2000). It is passed around departments and up hierarchies to inform or corroborate decisions, and to illustrate the veracity of business plans and future prospects of technical artefacts. However, as the figure above illustrates, there are many sources of knowledge about "users" (Williams et al. 2005), in the hands of different professionals, derived from a range of sources. As social scientists we hope we have scientific and moderated methods to obtain, assess and use knowledge about the people we study, but it is dangerous to assume that we have a monopoly over this sort of knowledge, or produce the sort of knowledge that is actually useful. Even if we do, there is a clear problem with our ability to communicate this knowledge to those outside our discipline.

Let's go and talk to the user

We have both had the challenge of working in multi-disciplinary teams, doing "interdisciplinary work", charged with providing knowledge about "users", but having to fight for the space to produce it adequately, and to manage its use.

At its simplest, we can involve "users" in the research cycle by saying "Let's all go and talk to users, then we will have a shared understanding of their problems and be able to come up with some solutions". In practice and theory this is highly problematic and raises lots of questions, although it also lets us question our own skills and professionalism. What is the role of social scientists if engineers, designers and business developers can talk to users directly? Have we been educated for four years or more in our discipline, just for something everybody can do? And if not, how can we explain our added value?

The opposite approach is also problematic, as when other members of the research team think that the job of talking to users should be delegated to social scientists who will supply them with material or "requirements" on which to work. Social scientists are generally trained to study people, while those in other disciplines are not (with caveats for market research and human-centred design). But how can we explain that there are a lot of questions without answers, or that answers are much more complex than they would like them to be? When entering Bell Labs as a social scientist I (Laurence) kept a diary to reflect upon my experiences. Now, two years later, I re-read the diary and analysed it to identify the challenges of interdisciplinary work. I will quote from my diary to clarify some of our ideas. I start by admitting that all of the challenges I encountered at the start of my work are still there.

> *"I have a feeling that I didn't even have to defend my research proposal. But I don't trust it. Now they are sending me 1000 more research questions I should answer in my research. How can I make them clear this is impossible?"* (17th October 2006)

When we look more concretely at the practice of research we see that each discipline has different methods of engaging with "users", if they have methods at all. These will often be very different, to do with training, goals, and required outputs (e.g. marketing surveys need numbers to go into business models, design ethnographies need concepts and ideas to stimulate design, engineers need to identify problems to solve and requirements to satisfy). Getting different team members to work together is likely to be tricky. With limited resources, how can we use the same methods in a satisfactory way that works for the different disciplines? The choice of a method is, in our opinion, based on the research questions. But this is not the opinion of the whole team.

> *"I received more comments on the slides that I submitted, which is good. But they are not necessarily from the corner that I expected. Starting from research questions is clearly not the normal course of business here. The non-technical research they did until now, I think, was*

particularly creative, and they also did some usability research. Both are important, but it doesn't stop there of course." (20th October 2006)

Often a method is chosen not because careful assessment has indicated its value for answering a particular research question, but because researchers like it. Although different methods can sometimes be used, there is also the question of *how*. A social scientist entering an interdisciplinary team is often seen as a proxy for the user. Her participation raises expectations, yet misunderstandings about her role abound.

The challenges of interdisciplinary work from a social science perspective

Interdisciplinary teamwork can be hard work. Entering unknown fields and attempting to communicate with disciplinary strangers can be a rather painful affair, as well as stimulating and exciting. Anbar (1973) calls the type of researchers doing this sort of work "bridge scientists". The feeling of being in a minority is normal if the only one with your specialism is you. You may be tolerated, but not accepted by the group. On the other hand, you do not have to compete with the others in their discipline; the sad thing is, however, that you cannot do your job properly if you are not part of the group. The first challenge of interdisciplinary work is becoming part of the group.

When I wrote this for example, I was wondering how I could ever become part of the group, if non-engineers were perceived as follows:

"A remark by J. was very funny, he said 'even people can use it'. And that's what it is. They want it simple and intuitive. But is this what people want? And aren't engineers also people?" (16th October 2006 – my 11th day at Bell-Labs)

In the following pages, different challenges of interdisciplinary work will be described and will be illustrated by my diary quotes.

The feeling of misusing research methods

After many years of academic study and application of carefully developed and argued social research methodologies, it can be hard to enter an industrial research environment where concepts and methods are picked up and tossed around like toys on the beach.

"The day started with a talk with the usability engineer who gave me a pile of information on prior studies that had happened in the team. I think they remain very strong on the high-level interface; a layer on top of the application rather than on the application. But it was very kind of him to share information with me. A real overview of questionnaires used,

methods, research, etc. is not available, and the ones I saw were far from scientifically correct." (10th October 2006)

When working in an interdisciplinary team, we share methods and tools between disciplines. However, it can be easy to lose sight of the motivations and intellectual foundations of these methods. We often have the feeling we are denying our own discipline. This is not evident, but it starts getting really difficult when we feel that a scientist from a different discipline is using "our" methods in another ("wrong") way.

Different feelings about time

As social scientists, we learn to work in research cycles that can take several years. This seems to be in contradiction with the time schedule of creation of novel ICT applications in industrial R&I. Researchers in industrial innovation research can look appalled to hear that you need two years to do your research ... if you dare to tell them at all!

> *"What I hate is that everything must be done so quickly. How do you do user research if you have 14 days to prepare? How can you say something about research when you barely have time to analyze? How can you master the methodology used if you do not have time to read? Or do a proper literature study before you start your research."* (20th November 2006)

Doing interdisciplinary research where we can learn from each other means that a certain alignment in timing of the research happens. Because the core of the research is still to develop new applications, and engineers are most often in the majority, other disciplines are supposed to adjust to their timing. The fact that the development of an ICT application, and in particular the software, has a totally different timeframe than mainstream social sciences research makes the use of certain methods problematic or impossible. However, also it should be noted that the short time scales for particular technical development are rather artificial: there will usually be a great deal of revision later on, and the actual time scales for research are much longer. Social scientists should ensure that they can contribute both to the short and longer-term research and development cycles of those they are working with.

Starting from nothing

As social scientists, we have learned to critically examine and explain every decision we take during our research. We carefully develop questions, and plan research steps in advance on a timetable appropriate to the research method. But when doing speculative research it is difficult to justify what you are doing when you do not really understand it: advance understanding is not always needed, in this kind of research, change comes by doing.

> *"But everything is innovation, even the technology does not yet exist. So combining other existing technologies makes the prototypes, weird, I'm used to examine existing things. I am not visionary, I never was. It points to a form of arrogance, which I dare not. Alla, but we will see."* (9th October 2006)

As social scientists, we are not used to "inventing" new things (even though we invent new concepts). This is far more the case for research engineers: their career choice implies they are interested in creating or inventing new applications. Knowledge about existing technological trends and tools seems important when looking at the future. For social scientists, this is a domain where in which they are strangers.

Another difficulty is the fact that the development of an application is not always an aim in itself. For companies like Intel, Alcatel-Lucent Bell Labs and others applications are often seen as, what Bruno Aïdan calls "instantiations of a technology" (Personal communication, November 30, 2009). The focus on 'user needs' or the development of an application that users would like is then a proxy to create, develop and sell underlying technology. The question then is where to start from during the research process. Should that be from the development of an application, and looking from there at what interesting technologies could lie below? Or perhaps the starting point should be the new technology, searching within these boundaries for possible new applications which and could be interesting for particular users/groups.

Compromising your discipline away

Despite its recent growth in popularity, the academic world is not generally enthusiastic about interdisciplinarity. Social scientists in academia, particularly in sociology and anthropology, have very different goals and values from those in industrial and even policy environments, and they seem to find the use of their research methods for applied sciences rather inferior. An "applied science" version of sociology or communication studies, for example, does not exist, or as Bouwen (2007) put it: "there is a need for communicational engineering". The result is that, once employed in the industrial world, a social scientist rapidly becomes alienated from the academic world, as he or she no longer conforms to the standards of the discipline.

> *"The question is how you can get respect within the academic or scientific world, combining it with speed of research in Alcatel. The only possibility is to formulate the clear boundaries of the research. It will then need some puzzling to get publications or to get something fundamental in way of new research results."* (20th October 2006)

Despite the feeling of misusing research methods, what clearly emerges from these quotes is the importance of maintaining in contact with disciplinary colleagues. Not only do we, as researchers, need their feedback and acceptance of our research, we need to keep abreast of the existing body of literature. We should be professionals who are strongly grounded in a particular discipline, deriving satisfaction in terms of scientific curiosity and recognition by their peers. But we cannot only stay in our discipline; we have to cross borders if we want to work in an interdisciplinary manner.

Modelling and processing the world

The other members of the team have definite ideas about the type of results they wish to obtain from user research. For example, the business developers want figures to write a business case, or stories to sell their concepts. The designers and engineers want models of how people work, and material to write a complete and hermetic scenario to draw up requirements.

"Mental models? What the hell are they talking about? Does there exist a mental model of a man or a group of people? Can everything be put in a model? I can give them 1000 models, but a model is always only one possible representation of a process, structure or mechanism? It never tells the truth, but why is it thought that everything needs to be in a model to capture? And is everybody eagerly waiting for this model to be formulated by me before they go on? Ah, strange birds still here and sometimes very frustrating." (31st October 2006)

It is clear that cognitive models of action are not very appropriate in research for innovation of novel ICT applications. Authors like Suchman (1987) and Leigh Star (1991) were very convincing in their vision on the importance of particular circumstances and situated actions because of the fact that significances of artefacts are related to the circumstances of their creation and their use.

Looking back on these first months

What became clear on observing the new team I had joined was that with a "classical" use of social sciences methods we would never achieve the goal of innovation of novel ICT applications. Nor did the other team members express much interest in reading social science literature, my research reports or theoretical discussion. The encounter point of the different disciplines in their work was mostly found when using creative methods. Creative brainstorming, making-things in group sessions… these were tools that were used without problems, and were perceived as inspiring by all team members. Also when working with users these methods were successful. It is clear that *creativity* is of equal if not more importance than *analysis* when doing speculative research, but it requires another disciplinary language, tools and forms. Unfortunately the goal of this research is not only to find inspiration in interaction with users. Therefore some "proper" scientific methods must be used and end-users must be studied in order to gain more information for the innovation process of a novel application; combining methods and tools to achieve this would be the ultimate goal. So to learn how to do this, I became inspired by the work of James, as described in the next section.

The creative team

My (James') more recent experience, after doing multidisciplinary work with engineers in telecommunications R&D, was to collaborate closely with other researchers more used to working in the disciplines of design and engineering for design. Unfortunately I did not manage to keep a research diary... although latterly we did take to recording video blogs of the outcomes of our meetings. The projects we were working on related to place, and the role of ICTs in shaping our experiences of space, control of place, and the integration of the "virtual" and the "real". The principal issue I found was to move into a speculative design world in a team that was torn between playing with new technologies, developing new applications and exploring social science research themes.

From observation to intervention

A key approach in the academic-design world I (James) found myself was the "intervention". This generally involves creating some sort of out-of-the-ordinary event, such as placing an object in a public place, or bringing people together to experience something unusual. It has elements of performance – the "artist" designs the intervention, but what is sought is the reactions of those who wittingly or unwittingly participate in, and therefore are co-creators of, the intervention. They may be observed, filmed or interviewed, or even asked to make more active contributions. My first experiences were with a group of 30 academics from many disciplines, holding research events in "non-places": a DIY superstore and an airport, where we talked to staff and customers, made presentations, played games and tried to look under the skin of the place. Part of these events involved minor transgressions, which nearly got some arrested, and the production of large numbers of photographs and videos. While I found these events interesting and stimulating, they were certainly not recognisable as a research method despite having elements of participant observation, interview and design. Nonetheless it was clear that for many participants this was a perfectly valid method, and could be the basis of a whole research paper.

This project was considered so successful by funders that a new project was funded, based around the concept of research by design, and "designer workshops". While similar to intensive design "charettes" (Sutton & Kemp 2002) aimed at producing exploitable designs, these could also be considered interventions, as they involved brainstorming, design activities, and live testing by the participants in order to stimulate discussion and reflection on the concepts through inventive practice. However the planning and conduct of interventions was challenging methodologically for me, as someone brought in with expertise in talking to 'users' on their use of technology. I had to do a great deal of work to make the practice fit in with my ideas of how to talk to people with other ideas of the 'active user' and co-creation. There was no space for long user trials, just short (2 hr to 2 weeks) experiments, where the outcomes were not meant to be careful evaluations of the benefits and problems of a particular system, but new ideas and directions for subsequent explorations. We did need some formal 'user research', but I was particularly challenged by the project leader suggesting that "we need some user research – let's get some people into "Second Life" and get them to talk about it for a few hours".

Eventually I managed to situate myself much more in the role of facilitator, and less as an active participant. I found myself asking the other team members to step back from the conversations with the user-designers, as they were always tempted to interrupt and put their own ideas in without listening. There was a constant tension over our role – when should we be observers, and when should be take on a dual role as designers and as observers.

I, and my colleague from social science did mange to do some "conventional" user studies, using interviews, diary studies, and textual analysis of Facebook users to explore the proposition that Facebook, and social-networking sites, have some equivalence to "real" meeting spaces. However the exigencies of the broader research approach made it hard to analyse and incorporate this research into the project while it was running. However, like much research, its value became apparent later, and the interdisciplinary context of research in which it was produced meant that questions were posed and approaches used that are very unlikely to have been developed "independently".

In the final analysis, I am not convinced of the value of much of the collected "user data", but at the same time, am satisfied with changing my skills and using the experience to develop much stronger ideas on the possibilities of involving "users" in speculative research.

User methods in speculative research

Engaging with users is generally seen as important for learning about potential users (to inform development), to test products or services against 'real' users, to allow potential users to influence the innovation more directly (co-create), or to smooth the adoption process. We propose that engaging with users, "making together" or "doing something together for the user", in the process of speculative research can have positive influences on the conduct and outcome of interdisciplinary work: methods to learn and engage with potential users are also methods to bring together an interdisciplinary team. However, what methods should we use, and how can we balance the different expectations and expertise of team members?

When doing interdisciplinary work involving users in speculative research into novel ICT applications we draw on methods mostly used in design, business studies and social science, such as cultural probing, participative observation, conceptual design proposals, intention surveys, creative brainstorms, scenario building with users, long interviews, focus groups, surveys and then use this data to build models, create personas, tell stories, create scenarios, develop theory and extract requirements.

These methods have very different time scales – long-term engagement with a community using multiple methods versus an afternoon in the park with a camera. Most non-social scientists have not had research training or experience to develop good fieldwork techniques and therefore incorporate existing social sciences methods "badly". (Wynne (2009) gives a good example on her blog:

"the way designers discovered ethnography as a "method" without adopting the premise behind ethnography: social context is everything, not just an extra factor that can be bolted on, but ultimately has to be designed out".

This does not necessarily mean they cannot get something out of the experiences, and we cannot learn from them either. On the contrary, social scientists are usually not good at engaging with inventive practices of the respondents and here we can learn a lot from the practices of designers.

We propose a programme of work to better define and understand the divergences, identify pitfalls, and create the possibility to also highlight the creative and analytic opportunities using various methods of user-engagement in speculative research.

The initial version of this chapter involved the compilation of a table of methods, their uses by different disciplines, and their limitations (Appendix 1). This illustrates the ambition of this research topic, and the possibilities of misinterpretation and disciplinary prejudice in classifying user research methods used by others. It is immediately clear that there can be some wild simplification and stereotyping even in drawing up the list.

We are attempting to identify how to align the use of methods with the questions that team members from different discipline would like answered via user research. In practice this may involve the drawing up of a list of questions, both broad and narrow, and the selection of a combination of user methods in order to answer a selected set of questions. Although every discipline has its own frameworks and outputs, the search for collaboration to get there should take a central position. While there will be common team and institutional goals, each team member will be looking for their own outputs from the common set of research (Table 1).

Discipline	Output
Engineering	Prototype or product
Design	Product, interactions, interfaces
Business Development	Insights in business models
Sciences	Empirical results and theory development

Table 1: The desired outputs for each discipline

Research can be conducted in parallel, but will often be developed sequentially, as the team creates new intermediate outputs that lead to new questions and open up the possibility of using new methods (e.g. once a prototype is developed, or a set of interviews makes clearer the needs and wishes of potential users). We can divide every user research plan into three categories: planning (e.g. developing the interview topic list, making the design probe); doing (executing the research with users); and using the results (incorporating the results when creating the wished output). Social scientists can play an important role at all stages, planning, coordinating the "doing together" of the user research and leading the analysis of the results. In order to do this, a social scientist needs to understand the value of the results of different types of research to other team members, not only methods from the social sciences, but those from other disciplines too. Table 2 gives examples of potential uses drawn from our experiences, and observations from the literature and discussions at conferences such as EPIC (anthropologists) and COST 298 (sociologists and economists) .

Method/Tool	Engineering	Design	Business Development	Social Sciences
Cultural probes	Not really interesting or useful. Only as background information	Common design method used for contextual investigation	Nice visual material for presentations	Valuable in combination with method, but mostly generic info.
Long interviews	Over-complex material, without quantitative results	Useful insights, but not creative, visual or tactile	Quotes for use in business pitch, identification of important qualities of potential product or service	Research report exploring meanings and practices through talk
Focus groups	Gets range of views and opinions quickly	Useful insights, but not creative, visual or tactile	Get range of views and opinions quickly	Explore meanings and alternative perspectives
Interventions	A type of prototype testing, but needs some clear method of evaluation	Creation of intervention important design moment. Stimulates the public, and provides tangible inspiration.	Can promote awareness of research in target group, and provide visual and narrative material	Needs to be accompanied by detailed analysis of video, interviews, focus groups etc.

Table 2: The value of different methods and tools for the different disciplines of interdisciplinary teams

What is clear is that no single method is going to provide satisfaction to the team members; even if it can be used to answer particular questions. However, neither is it appropriate that each team member conduct his/her own independent user research. A multi-method approach that provides different types of knowledge, and coordinates the expertise and needs of each members is necessary. For example, focus groups where different team members participate can then be built on by in depth interviews conducted by the social scientists. A simple analysis of the results can then be done by all team members building on common insights from the focus groups, while more in depth analysis of the same material can be done by the business analyst and the social scientist.

Some real-life figures: the Bell Labs applications domain teams

In order to gain an idea of what methods are actually used by researchers in application development, we conducted a survey of members of the Alcatel Applications development group, focusing on the use of five user research methods that are used when doing speculative research for innovation: in-depth interviews, design probes, surveys, focus groups and UML diagrams, and one other method use in development teams: creative brainstorming. The group members work in self-defined fields such as Ambient Media, Emerging Market Applications, Hybrid Communication and HyperMedia.

A short survey was sent to the 112 people working in Alcatel Applications Domain based in several sites in Europe, the United States and India. 27 complete surveys were returned (35 total returns), a response rate of 24%. 18 respondents (66.7%) responded positively to the question "Are you involved in research where the objective is less the production of an operational system, but more the investigation and expression of potential futures" i.e. they are engaged in "Speculative Research". 21 of 25 (84%) said they work in multi-disciplinary teams. When asked to classify themselves, 12 of 27 respondents choose multiple categories, e.g. engineer, researcher, manager and designer, and three more described themselves as just a "researcher". This suggests that many who work in this field consider themselves "interdisciplinary". The largest group of respondents classed themselves as engineers. Only three "social scientists" responded, as was probably to be expected given the relatively recent arrival of social scientists in this type of establishment, of whom two saw themselves "only" as a social scientist (figure 2).

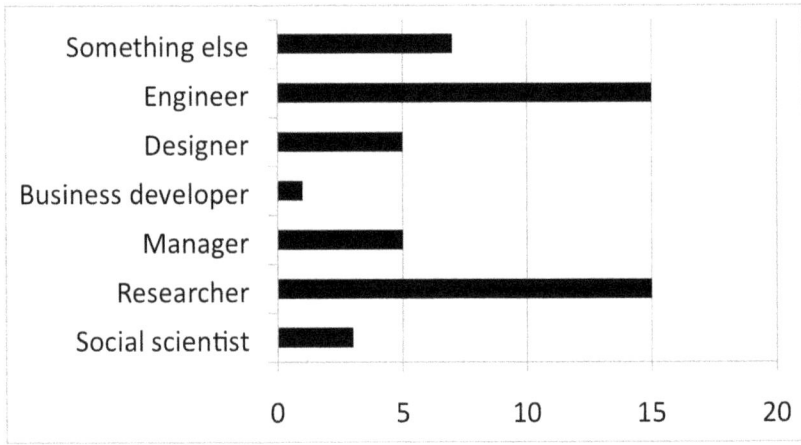

Figure 2: Responses to the question "I am a ... " (different answers were possible)

Despite the low numbers of "social scientists", there was considerable engagement with end-users, using and doing interviewing, focus groups and surveys. 16 of 26 (59.3%) actually worked with end-users themselves. The main methods used were focus groups (18/23, 62.1%), although only four out of 23 respondents actually conducted the focus group and only two out of 23 planned the focus groups (6.9%). 18/25 used interviews, with 8/25 conducting interviews themselves and 6/25 planning the interviews. Design probes were used by 11/24 (39%), surveys by 17/25 (38.6%) and UML by 8/23 (26.7%). A whole range of other methods, such as prototyping and eyetracking were also used. In all cases the results of user-research were used much more broadly than the data collection, suggesting a considerable division of labour. Other results are not presented here, but it is clear that user research is very important, but very much focused on collection by a few, and use by many, and not as a common activity.

Conclusions: User research as a tool for interdisciplinary work

There are a number of ways to make interdisciplinary teams successful. It is important to bridge the gaps in understanding and forming common purpose and identity. To a large degree this depends on the team members: interdisciplinary work needs certain kinds of people, with an open mindset and curiosity. In some ways this is unfortunate, since it means that interdisciplinarity is not structural to innovation processes of organizations or consortia. At a more structural level, a management approach that facilitates this bridging is necessary. The manager must not only be a good interdisciplinarian him/herself, he/she must ensure a culture where there is respect for other viewpoints and a willingness to engage in dialogue, and openness and exchange is encouraged.

We suggest that it is possible to facilitate bridging using research on users. While we, as many others, find interdisciplinary work stimulating, the personal experiences we relate here are often negative in relation to the quality of the work we can conduct as social scientists: we complain of the sidelining of methodology and its replacement with technique. However, we also have very positive experiences of bringing people or 'users' into interdisciplinary research. From this experience we suggest:

• Everyone in a team can engage with users, and we know that each member of the team does so for different reasons and with different expectations and intellectual resources. It is nonetheless a shared process, and unlike internal factors such as vision or goals, user research brings in the voice of people from outside, voices that have considerable value and force.

• Doing research with users opens up the world of people. We are confronted with certain users with whom in everyday life we possibly would never have contact. The fact that we do this with the whole team makes discussions possible that start from the same experience and not only from assessment of technical possibilities or abstract visions.

• We can learn a lot by collective evaluating of research with users. In this way we hear what others found interesting, what it means to them and the work they are doing and the way they interpret certain activities. Thus we can gain more respect for each other's interpretations.

• As social scientists we have to be open to the methods and interpretations of other team members, and help develop programmes of user research that responds to everyone's needs and expertise, in terms of outputs, time scales and effort.

• Speculative research with users makes things happen, away from theoretical constructions. The team should work together to make this happen. The doing together, and the doing-together-for-the-user not only makes the feeling of working together on something strong, but also the feeling that there will be a "real user" somewhere, somehow!

• Finally we can educate each other in methods by doing, and maybe we can generate new methods that are more useful for the different disciplines (see table 3 in appendix).

This book addresses concerns of how users are empowered or disempowered in the development and deployment of ICTs. It is important that the ideas, experiences and creativity of those who may represent future users are incorporated into this speculative research – no only does it make it likely that eventual products and services will be more successful, but the investment decisions and innovation pathways are often based on ideas created by researchers in these laboratories. It is important that these laboratories bring together a diversity of research skills, and listen to, and find inspiration in people as well as technology or business visions. We hope that work on collaboration around user research will not only improve the day to day work experiences of social scientists engaged in technological development work, but also make the eventual products and services available to citizens more inclusive and responsive to their needs.

References

Aïdan, B. Personal communication (Review Meeting Ambient Media Team) (November 30, 2009)

Anbar M. 'The "Bridge Scientist" and his role' Research/Development (July) (1973) pp. 30-34

Beck K., Fowler M. Planning Extreme Programming London: Addison-Wesley Longman (2001)

Bouwen J. Trivial pursuits inputs: Alcatel-Lucent Bell Labs Internal document Antwerp (January, 10 2007)

Jackson, S.E. 'The consequences of diversity in multidisciplinary work teams' ed. West M.A. Handbook of Work Group Psychology John Wiley & Sons Ltd (1996) pp. 53-76

Leigh Star S. 'Power, technology and the phenomenology of conventions: On being allergic to onions' ed. Law J.A Sociology of Monsters: Essays on Power, Technology and Domination London, New York: Routledge (1991) pp. 26-56

Limonard S., Koning N. de 'Dealing with dilemmas in pre-competitive ICT development projects: The construction of 'the social' in designing new technologies' eds. Haddon L., Mante E., Sapio B., Kommonen K.-H., Fortinati L., Kant, A. Everyday Innovators: Researching the Role of Users in Shaping ICT's Dordrecht: Springer.

Nicoll D. W. 'Users as currency: Technology and marketing trials as naturalistic environments' The Information Society 16 (4) (2000) pp. 303-310

Pals, N., Steen M., Langley D., Kort J. 'Three approaches to take the user perspective into account during new product design' International Journal of Innovation Management (ijim) 12 (03) (2008) pp. 275-294

Payne L.S. 'Interdisciplinarity: Potentials and challenges' Systemic Practice and Action Research 12 (2) (1999) pp. 173-182

Penny S. 'Rigorous interdisciplinary pedagogy: Five years of ACE' convergence 15 (2009) pp. 31-54

Suchman L. Plans and Situated Actions: The Problem of Human-machine Communication Cambridge: Cambridge University Press (1987)

Sutton S.E., Kemp S.P. 'Children as partners in the place-making process: Design charrettes as a strategy for developing civic activism' Journal of Environmental Psychology 22 (2002) pp. 171-189

Vedel T. 'Introduction à une socio-politique des usages' ed. Vitalis A. Médias et Nouvelles Technologies: Pour une Socio-politique des Usages Rennes : Editions Apogée (1994) pp. 13-34

Williams R., Slack R., Stewart J. Social Learning in Technological Innovation: Experimenting with Information and Communication Technologies Cheltenham: Edgar Elgar Publishing (2005)

Wynne E. Situated Knowledge and Practical Reasoning as Generalized Usage Models http://blogs.intel.com/it/2007/01/situated_knowledge_and_practic.php, posted on 22 January 2007 (accessed February, 13 2009)

Appendix

Method	Description	Comments	Outputs	Value for disciplines
Cultural probes	Designer technique, creative contextual investigation method.	Do things that SS would take for granted.	Pictures, beautiful probe material, drawings, movies	SS: generic info B: nice visual material for in presentations E: not really interesting nor useful D: love it
Participant observation	Contextual investigation. Observing practices in naturalistic environment. Aiming at giving new viewpoints to the topic.	Not valuable without literature research in advance. Very time consuming and sometime hard to negotiate access, especially when in private or sensitive environments	Pictures, diaries, discussions,	SS: core methods for in depth study and theory development B: not very valuable E: reality check D: background material > designer like it more to work with (individual) people, and if observing, then in lab context.
Participative design / co-design	Taking seriously the input of 'users' – tapping into non-experts' ability to invent and imagine possibilities of technology.	Usually limited to generating ideas by users (e.g. by brainstorming) to use during the use case definition phase or new ideas on design level rather than on application or experience level.	Paper prototypes, pictures, ideas	SS: type of participant observation, but worries about influencing process. B: nice visual material E: new ideas (for features) D: new design ideas
Scenario building with users	Business and engineering tool to define requirements, offer simple range of choices and means to balance risks and potential.	Involves choosing limited number of factors (e.g. 2) and organising ideas and data. If done quickly cannot incorporate carefully researched information	Scenarios	SS: seem simplistic and reductionist; don't know what to do with it B: need it to define business model and choices E: use it for requirement definition D: Imagination tool

Prototype testing	Developers and designers testing their applications with a small group of users, using formal tests (e.g. for usability) or gather feedback.			SS: either formal usability, or rather simplistic feedback gathering B: can be trivial, but can form important part of building business case E: Important gathering of input leading to redesign or confirmation D: Usability testing or confirmation od design
Modelling	Engineering tool, and latterly business and even social science tool. Builds on models of individual behaviour or social system behaviour for prediction	Computational methods can be used to test models using real or test data. Very hard to build the models and choose factors. However can be used to check assumptions, and possibly will become more widespread in future	Models themselves, prediction generated using models	SS: Can seem simplistic and reductionist B: A good model can help decision making and provides quantifiable output. E: reduced social interaction to a model similar to engineering model, but hard to deal with model building D: Not very inspiring, but could be used in design context
Long interviews	Qualitative Social Science method.	Very time-consuming, especially when wanting to analyse it properly	Texts, quotes	SS: research report exploring meanings and practices through talk. B: quotes for use in business pitch E: over complex material D: useful insights, but not creative, visual or tactile
Focus groups	Marketing and now Social Science method to bring a range of 'users' together. Can be a panel of unknowns, or people who know each other well (e.g. family).	Hard to run, and limited in what it can cover, but very illuminating as ideas, practices etc. are challenged in group and not by researcher.	Recordings, videos, texts	SS: explore meanings and alternative perspectives B: get range of views and opinions quickly E: get range of views and opinions quickly, especially on experiences with prototypes D: as above

Interventions	Creating events or objects that would not normally be part of an environment or everyday activities in order to challenge participants stimulate critical thinking and conversations.	A strong design element, very much aimed at stimulating the critical and inventive capabilities of the participants, but unlike cultural probes, often done in dialogue with the creator. Can be lengthy to set up and analyze. Actually similar to user testing, but not focused on validating the object.	Texts, videos, images	SS: Not a usual method, but used in Action Research, or in asking for Interpretations of texts, images. B: very vague, not as concrete as direct feedback on products E: unusual method D: an important human-centred design method, drawn from the arts.
Surveys	Quantitative Social Science method.	Very expensive to do, therefore often done on small scale, with limited value of output	Report, statistics, models	SS: find it interesting when representative part of the population is studied. B: love it, numbers is what they want E: believe it, it's a model D: mostly used for usability research

Table 3: Preliminary sketch of user-research methods and their value to different disciplines

Marinka Vangenck, Jo Pierson, Wendy Van den Broeck and Bram Lievens

User-driven Innovation in the Case of Three-dimensional Urban Environments

Introduction

Innovation has been acknowledged as one of the most important elements in today's economy and business (Edquist 2001; European Commission 2010; European Council & European Commission 2010; Freeman & Soete 1997). We live in a world where change is the only constant and thus innovation is essential for companies of every size in every industry (Chesbrough 2003). Yet, together with the increase in the number of new ICT-products, we also notice an increased number of failed innovations, in the sense that the new products did not meet the expectations of the management (De Marez 2006). As Chesbrough (2003) so forthrightly phrased it: "Most innovations fail. And companies that don't innovate die". According to Von Hippel (2005), only 25% of the innovations are successful. De Marez (2006) identifies the lack of insight into the user and inefficient marketing as the most important causes for innovation failure. Obviously, technological knowledge alone is not sufficient to make an innovation successful, since users often perceive technological innovations in media as too complex or irrelevant. In the end, the user decides if and in what way he appropriates the technology. Some scholars even state that innovation only exists when social practice changes.

> "By defining innovation as something that generates and facilitates change in social practice, we put the user in a central place in the process of innovation. In a very fundamental sense, it is the user who invents the product." (Tuomi 2002, 10)

In this context, the awareness is growing that the involvement of users in the product development process increases the chance that new products and services will actually link in with the expectations, characteristics and practices of future (end) users. This was originally formalized in the field of Human-Computer Interaction in the eighties, with the notion of "User-Centred Design" (UCD) (Holmquist 2004; Veryzer & Borja de Mozota 2005). "User-centred design emphasizes that the purpose of a system is to serve the user, not to use a specific technology, not to be an elegant piece of programming" (Norman 1986).

UCD is frequently defined in different ways. It is a holistic term for development processes and practices within which the user is allocated a central position. Different authors use various terms, such as user-oriented design (Veryzer & Borja de Mozota 2005), human-centred design (ISO 1999), customer-centric design or people-centred design (Wakeford 2004).

Unfortunately, UCD is frequently linked with "usability" and "ease of use" of technologies or applications. Therefore it is regularly limited only to "user testing" and not introduced until the end of the product development cycle. In addition, the user input that is integrated into the design process in UCD is often focused on individual experiences, while the domestication of media technologies occurs within the social context of everyday life. We therefore prefer to refer to "people-centred design", in which the user is not only perceived as an end-user or consumer, but within which the social context and possibly the domestication perspective are included to obtain contextualised user insights (Wakeford 2004). A similar concept is the notion of User-Driven Innovation (UDI), currently readily used in the Nordic innovation policy. UDI can be defined as "the process of tapping users' knowledge in order to develop new products, services and concepts. A user-driven innovation process is based on an understanding of true user needs and a more systematic involvement of users" (Wise & Høgenhaven 2008). Two components are key within UDI: the understanding of users for finding new opportunities to create value on the one hand and a systematic involvement of users as early as possible in and throughout the whole innovation process on the other hand. UDI is therefore defined as the overall interdisciplinary research approach, in which we can apply the participatory design method. However, a few differences should be noted. Whereas in participatory design users are involved as co-designers as early as possible in the design process, in UDI users are involved at the prototype stage of the project. The users involved in UDI are also not viewed as the eventual end-users of the product, but as a source of inspiration, a springboard for further development of interesting ideas. Therefore, people with different requirements are sought for idea generation, as this often opens up different perspectives on the product (Holmquist 2004).

In line with this vision, we can position the domestication framework as a central perspective of looking at the meaning and experiences of media and technology in the everyday life setting of users (Haddon 2007; Silverstone & Haddon 1996). Traditionally, domestication research focuses on the appropriation and use of media technology being introduced in the home. Yet in the context of the wide spread and pervasive domestication of mobile devices, media usage is disconnected from fixed places like the home and is challenging the boundaries of public and private space. So extending the scope of the domestication perspective to outside the home environment, e.g. in the case of mobile urban applications, is inevitable. Hence, we focus on the interrelationship of design and domestication. From this perspective, innovation is much more than solely R&D or product launch. Rather, innovation is perceived as "a process which involves both producers and consumers in a dynamic interweaving of activities which are solely determined neither by the forces of technological change nor by the eccentricities of individual choice" (Silverstone & Haddon 1996). According to Silverstone & Haddon (1996) design and domestication can be seen as the two sides of the innovation coin.

They posit that domestication is anticipated in design, but also that design is completed in domestication. The first part of their proposition (i.e. domestication anticipated in design) refers to how designers and engineers often anticipate on their idea of how a particular technology will or should be used and what place it will be given in the everyday life setting of people. Hence design can be perceived as a kind of pre-domestication. The second part of the proposition (i.e. design completed in domestication) refers to unpredictable ICT user behaviour, as users can adopt ICT in creative and sometimes unanticipated ways that deviate from the initial expectations of the engineers or product developers. Many notorious examples can be found in this regard, like the unanticipated private use of SMS by youngsters (Mallard 2005, 40). In the early stages of new product development (NPD), in which the basic technology is still being fine tuned and a product launch is still far away, it is not possible to investigate the actual domestication or "making the technology one's own" process. It is not possible to investigate how 3D city modelling technology is being incorporated into the existing domestic culture and the routines of everyday life within the scope of the URBAN case study, as the technology has not yet been fully developed or commercialised. Yet involving the domestication approach in user-driven design is still relevant to gaining clear insight into contextualized user behaviour and needs, as well as into the interest for and the meaning attached to the technology that is being developed.

We focus in this chapter on how and to what extent user-driven innovation research conducted from a domestication perspective can be applied in a high-end technological development process. In this context, the URBAN project that deals with 3D city modelling will serve as a case study.

Method

Methodological set-up

The case study in this chapter is based on results of research in the URBAN project. The URBAN project (Uitmeten, Reconstrueren, Bekijken, Animeren en Navigeren van stedelijke omgevingen / Measuring, Reconstructing, Viewing, Animating and Navigating urban environments) was a joint project of the Interdisciplinary Institute for Broadband Technology (IBBT) and several industrial partners in Flanders (Belgium) between 2008 and 2009. This project was first and foremost a technological project that focused on the research and development of computer generated three-dimensional city models. In addition, the project was also directed at exploring potential market opportunities for service innovation in 3D urban environments. This meant that interdisciplinary research was also required on possible usage of future applications. The latter is linked to our specific twofold role in the project: (1) conducting explorative in-depth user research in two iterations to investigate and identify potential service innovation in relation to 3D city models as early as possible in the development trajectory and (2) connecting these findings on current and future user practices of navigation in a 3D environment to the actual technology development process. Only by embedding user input in the design and development process of new products and services will the chance increase that they will actually meet the expectations, characteristics and practices of future (end) users and consumers (figure 1). This fits with the current trend of user-driven innovation (Wise & Høgenhaven 2008). To this end, we opted for an approach consisting of the following four steps: orientation, interaction, exploration and validation.

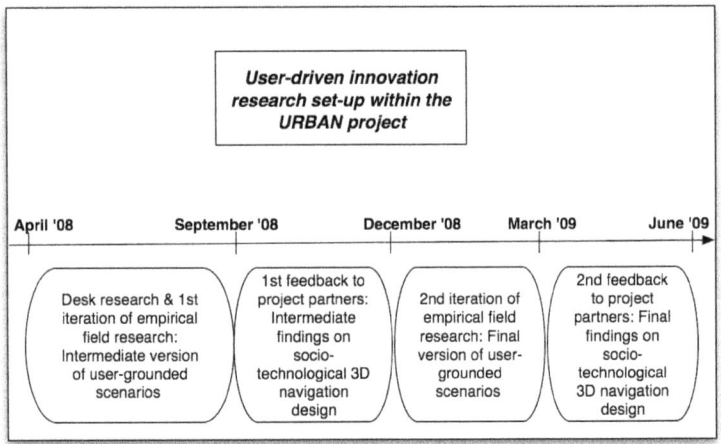

Figure 1: Time line of UDI research set-up within the URBAN project

Step 1: Orientation – First, we conducted a literature study to obtain a horizontal state-of-the-art overview of possible innovative domains regarding the use of 3D city environments. Based on this desk research, we identified several domains in which meaningful user practices occur through interaction with 3D models of real and virtual cities (i.e. fictional cyber-cities that are often used as a gaming environment). These domains are tourism, gaming, navigation and urban planning. Hence, we focused on technological examples of 3D city models in those instances that are used or tested by people in real life. We organised eight expert meetings with different industrial and technological project partners in the first half of 2008. The objective here was to identify services that could create genuine added value for users in a 3D city environment, but that would at the same time be in line with the technological trajectory of the involved project partners. This resulted in the selection of two vertical domains within which a 3D city model and its related services offer innovative opportunities from a user perspective: tourism (in particular city trips) and real estate.

Tourism was selected because the market of (mobile) city applications is gaining momentum in the tourist sector. We therefore sought to analyze the extent to which such existing services can be complemented with 3D city model applications. Real estate was determined by the experts to be a relevant segment, as 3D visualization of cities could offer significant added value for people looking for and assessing a house or apartment. In addition, based on our desk research, this seems to be a domain that has received very little attention in the current literature on service innovation in 3D environments. First, we carried out empirical research in the form of 28 observations in the Brussels tourist office and the Brussels airport, in most cases followed by a semi-structured interview (July 2008). This was followed by expert interviews with two experienced travel agency managers and two realtors. Next, eight archetypal users in both areas (i.e. four respondents who recently went on a city trip and four prospective buyers and renters) were subjected to a first round of in-depth interviews in the period of July-August 2008. The selection was based on purposeful sampling. The goal of this qualitative research part was to assess the opportunities for innovation and to identify sensitizing concepts for user-driven innovation of 3D city services (Pierson et al. 2008).

This research process enabled us to identify and draft two user grounded scenarios: one that deals with tourism and another with real estate. We have chosen to work with user scenarios and not with use cases, since the combination of both technological components and user aspects (especially social and context characteristics) is the perfect mix to enable developers to take the user into account during their everyday research and development activities (Jacobs et al. 2007). As the interaction between user groups and technology developers is not always self-evident, the user scenarios keep everyone focused on the same target and allow an assessment to be made as to whether the technology that is being developed meets the user perspective. The scenarios describe how a particular persona, in our case the city tripper or the person who is looking for a house, enacts a practice or behaves in a given situation and hence brings the user to life. They provide a setting, have actors, objectives or goals, a sequence of events and end with a result. The fictional personas, created to describe the typical city tripper and real estate purchaser, represent a group of end users during design discussions (Courage & Baxter 2005). The two developed scenarios define the possibilities and constraints of a 3D digital city environment and serve as guidelines in the socio-technological development activities within the multidisciplinary URBAN research project. The insights of previous research activities were used to adjust the scenarios. Consequently the scenarios are under constant development - as "living" documents - throughout the whole research and development trajectory and feed back the innovation process (figure 2).

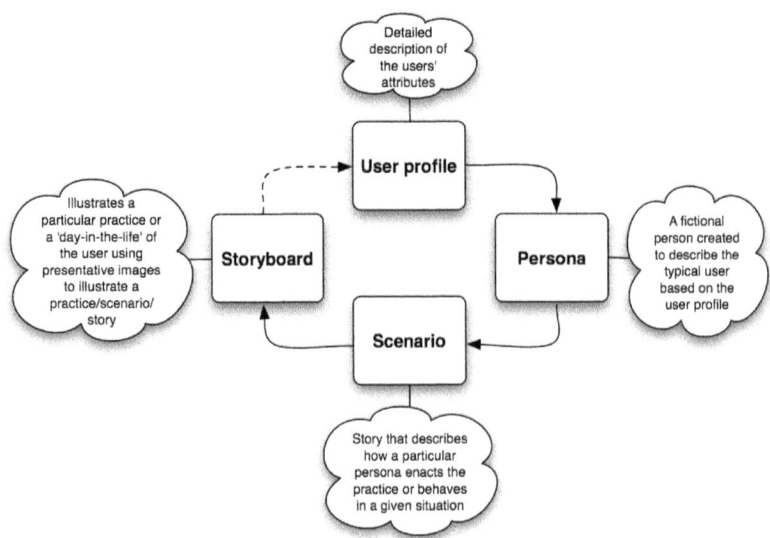

Figure 2: From creating user profiles to personas, scenarios and storyboards

Step 2: Interaction – During the second research phase, we set up a participative design exercise. The integration of user innovation in technology design requires the identification of the technological elements and activities that are susceptible to change. Therefore we first interviewed the involved project partners to trace the "hooks" for user input to guide the development. During these interviews, which took place in the second part of 2008, the partners were also asked to provide input on the technological feasibility of each component of the scenarios from their perspective. Secondly, we involved all the relevant stakeholders in a participative workshop on 15 December 2008. From a mutual shaping perspective, the workshop tried to find a match between users on the one hand and the technological, research and industrial partners on the other hand. During this workshop, we presented user scenarios that were visualised by means of the storyboarding technique. In a setting where the involved parties have a very different background, storyboards offer a common visual language to communicate on design aspects (picture 1). The product design storyboard supports developers in understanding the product-user interaction in context and over time (Van der Lelie 2006). This research process allowed us to fine-tune the user scenarios from a technological and business perspective in order to optimally guide the development process. In addition, a technological assessment of the users needs and requirements indicated to what extent the user scenario input could effectively be incorporated.

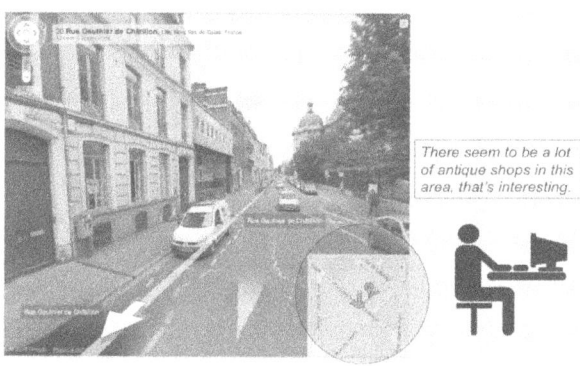

Picture 1: Excerpt from storyboard "Tourism"

Step 3: Exploration – In the third research phase in first half of 2009, we confronted the 12 carefully selected users (based on purposeful sampling) with the first URBAN prototype (picture 2). The latter was the first version of the demonstrator that was developed in line with the user scenarios. This kind of Proxy Technology of the main demonstrator (which was planned to be ready at the end of the project in December 2009) allows users to undergo an (immersive) truthful experience of 3D urban navigation (Torben Nielsen et al. 2008). Moreover, by bringing users in contact with the technology during its development process, the user experiences can (ideally) be integrated as feedback in the following design and development activities. ICT user behaviour is unpredictable, since users can adopt ICT in creative and sometimes unanticipated ways that deviate from the initial expectations of the engineers or product developers. That is why it is vital to investigate users in direct contact with the technological prototype or service that is being developed. However, immature technology that is still linked to fundamental research of engineers and technology developers - which is the case for the URBAN project - is not yet fully "understandable" for future users. Therefore user input will only have a genuine added value in a "semi-mature" technological environment. Semi-mature technologies are adequate to serve as an "objet frontière" (Flichy 1995) and allow all involved stakeholders to discuss the meaning and further development of the artefact (Ballon et al. 2007). Consequently, the first version of the URBAN demonstrator will serve as the "objet frontière" for 3D city modelling technology. This research phase will result in a final version of the user-grounded scenarios based on user goals and practices and will provide an overview of the findings on user navigation in a 3D city environment.

Picture 2: Screenshot URBAN prototype

Step 4: Validation – In the final research phase, we organised a second participative workshop on 16 June 2009 with all the project partners, in order to embed the user research outcome and thus the final user scenarios in the last phase of technology development (picture 3). In this way, the empirical findings from step two could be validated by the different stakeholders in the project, and thus enable the completion of the socio-technological 3D navigation design.

Picture 3: Second participative workshop

Reflections on the UDI project approach: prelude

Within the URBAN case study, we were confronted with three main issues regarding the socio-technological development process: "no single vision on project direction", "no overall cooperation" and "no full embedding of user (research)". All three issues have implications for a UDI research set-up, as they can hinder the integration of user input in the technological R&D process.

- **Project direction**: Within the URBAN project, the project partners have developed mainly a technologically-oriented vision on what should be achieved at the end of the project. As yet, there is no shared vision on the possible future application domains in which the 3D city modelling technology could be embedded.

> "I rather work like I first want to see what I can do technologically and then I will take a look at the user. Of course if you are doing this kind of research you actually do not know what will be the outcome so first I want to see what is possible." (Researcher of a company that is specialised in mobile mapping technology)

The project is considered to be an opportunity to experiment with and fine-tune 3D city technology. However, 3D city service innovation is not (yet) perceived as a priority. Hence the involved partners rank the 3D urban services and functionalities that are integrated in the user-grounded scenarios according to whether these are central or not to their own technological challenges in the project. As a result, mainly user input on visualisation issues, such as the (possible) added value of 3D visualisation over 2D and the required level of realism from a user perspective would match the need of the technological, research and industrial partners.

- **Cooperation**: Cooperation is mainly bilateral, in the first place between partners involved in the same work package(s) (or task) of the project and secondly, between a research group and a data provider. There is less overall cooperation among the project partners. Cooperating with other project partners is perceived as mainly being useful in the case of a win-win situation, i.e., if all partners benefit from working together. In order to optimize cooperation between technological research and user research, the former need to be convinced of the added value of involving the user perspective in their own research trajectory: "What's in it for us?". This could be one means to increase the cooperation within the context of a user-driven innovation development process.

> "I would like the collaboration only if it's suitable for all partners, if it's a win-win collaboration, but it's very difficult since we all have different goals, all different expertises." (Research developer at a high tech research centre)

- **Involving user (research):** User research is generally perceived as an activity typically taking place in the final phase of technology development. The first phase of the project is devoted to the development of the basic 3D city modelling technology. Once this technology is fine-tuned, user input can become relevant to help the technological partners decide on the concrete user-oriented direction of the technology and to guide the development of the demonstrators that will be presented at the end of the project. It is only then that user input can become relevant, which entails that user research only needs to be embedded in the final development phase, i.e., when the technology is becoming "mature".

"I would say the user sometimes is a nice to have more than a must have in this first part of URBAN. But if we want a real demonstrator that is convincing for Immoweb people or others (Immoweb.be is a popular Belgian real estate website), then of course we have to make something that it can be used by people and we cannot guess it completely by ourselves." (Research developer at a high tech research centre)

This substantially limits the leeway for technological changes, often leading to minor adaptations like usability-related interface changes (e.g. enlarging certain buttons, adding FAQ section). Yet the user-driven innovation perspective starts from the idea that successful technological development depends on the involvement of users during the whole product development process, including the early stages. Only then can we increase the chance that new products and services will actually link in with the expectations, characteristics, practices and experiences of future users.

Findings

In this section, we elaborate on the case study URBAN. Finally, we reflect on the methodological lessons we have learned from how we introduced a UDI approach within a basic technology development research project.

Case study: UDI in URBAN

The URBAN project is first and foremost perceived by the different (technological) partners as an opportunity to do basic research on technical issues such as 3D modelling for visualisation, compression, object recognition and omni-directional video. At the end of the project, the high-end research done by each partner was brought together for demonstration (via a demonstrator). The majority of the research partners in the project initially saw little added value in incorporating user research into their (early) R&D activities. The URBAN case illustrates how challenging it can be to fully integrate a UDI approach in a heavily technologically oriented project, with the risk of UDI remaining rhetoric only, without any real impact.

The lack of involvement of the user perspective also became visible through the fact that no prior use case scenarios were defined in the project. These are being developed en route, not so much to steer technological choices but to outline one of the two final demonstrators. In this way, the user scenarios (and the related storyboard) are dependent on the technological choices already made, instead of the other way around. The technological research will determine how the user scenario (and story board) will look, instead of the latter (also) being used to make decisions on technological options. The defensive reflex to add new technological functionalities that originate from the user research is a relevant finding in this regard.

There seems to be a chasm between the functional requirements - which deal with the intended behaviour of a system - as (pre-)defined by the technological partners on the one hand, and the user practices on the other. These practices relate to the use of services and applications that are to be linked with the interaction framework in the 3D city environment. Often, user requirements, a familiar concept in the human-computer interface (HCI) domain for optimizing ICT use (Preece et al. 2002), are used as a first bridge towards these user practices. But in HCI, the concept usually involves the individual level and usability issues. In our approach, we use the concept in a much broader sense, also involving the social dimension and hence the everyday life world of people (Vermeir et al. 2008). Functional requirements concern the operations or actions that have to be performed on the application and are frequently translated into interface controls (Cooper et al. 2007). The following illustrates a number of user requirements - stemming from user practices - that conflicted with the functional requirements identified by the different URBAN partners:

• Location-based, public transport and user-generated content services: We noticed that location-based, public transport and UGC services are considered to be outside the scope of URBAN since these are already part of other, separate research projects. Therefore, only if the services already existed and could easily be integrated into an application, were they to become part of the (URBAN) demonstrator. This indicates that the research setup is sometimes very narrowly defined from a technological perspective, which means that the functional requirements are also very strictly defined and focussed. In these cases, only limited attention is given to possible external factors.

• Up-to-date cultural events and restaurant information: The services that required the involvement of external partners, such as cultural organisations for integrating up-to-date events information or restaurant owners to update their suggestions, were not implemented based on the perception that these were too time-consuming or too complex to integrate.

• User-prefered highlighting of key buildings and locations: We saw that user input concerning the way important buildings or locations should be indicated (e.g. colouring, enlarging, framing, etc.) conflicted with the technological possibilities in the current 3D model. That is why the technological developers had already chosen to have important buildings "glow" in the application (as a functional requirement), which was a more technologically feasible option.

• User-defined search functionalities and object recognition: In addition, we found that the project partners ranked the relevance of the different functionalities (whether or not important for users) according to their own technological challenges in the project. As a result, the "search functionalities" that are very appreciated by tourists, such as the implementation of various kinds of listings (e.g. "Top 10 Belgian restaurants of Brussels", "Top 10 hotels of Brussels", etc.), have little priority within the project. In one scene of the storyboard on city trips, the user entered a particular top sightseeing destination in Brussels - "Marollen" (i.e. the oldest class district of Brussels) - in the 3D city application, but was unable to gain any useful result. From a user perspective, it should be possible to locate the most important sights in a 3D tourist application. However, as only Google Maps had been integrated in the demonstrator, the application could only give the search results that are available through Google (and "Marollen" cannot be found this way). Several research partners declared that finding a solution for such search issues was beyond the scope of the project. Another example regards traffic sign detection and recognition. Although this might be important information for users (e.g. where are traffic lights, where am I allowed to park?), this type of information was not included in the object recognition functionality within the project.

Nevertheless, we also identified areas where the user practices view and the functional requirements view of the technological partners seem to converge. Items where user input could guide the R&D process of the other project partners more directly are the following:

• Apparently, the technological partners particularly struggle with visualisation issues, such as the (possible) added value of 3D visualisation versus 2D images. For example, user research shows that a 2D representation can sometimes provide the user with a better overview of (parts of) a city than a 3D city model. This means that in some instances, 2D images can have an added value in a 3D navigation system.

• Furthermore, the required level of details and thus realism of the 3D model to enable the user to have an immersive experience is another important issue defined by the project partners. The 3D city model that was being developed generates only a general, vectorized 3D representation of urban environments. So while navigating through the 3D city environment, the users will not be able to look at realistic façades of shops, restaurants or other buildings. Observing realistic façades would only be possible by linking omni-directional video (ODV), which is also part of the project, to specific locations. ODV makes it possible to capture 360° panoramic pictures at video speed. Several project partners assume that a detailed front view of buildings is not important for users. However, the user research showed that the outside appearance and façade of a property and its neighbourhood is the first selection criterion when searching for a new home. Tourists too, expected a 3D representation of the most important buildings and attractions. Thus a certain level of detail will be indispensable in the 3D city model, in order to live up to the expectations, needs and practices of house buyers and tourists.

Obviously, user input concerning these visualisation issues would definitely match with the needs of the technological and industrial partners.

Reflections on our involvement in a UDI project

By deploying a UDI approach in a heavily technologically oriented and focused research project, different insights have been gained.

First, in the context of socio-technological research on UDI, it appears to be very useful to make user-related profiles of the actors involved in a project, in particular concerning their relation to possible user research input. Identifying each partner's background, expertise, profile and role within the project is an essential step in the investigation of the UDI process. In this way, it is possible to assess where user input could have a genuine added value in the R&D process. Moreover, it also makes it possible to anticipate on possible reservations of some partners whose daily research and/or development activities are more removed from the user.

Second, the use of text-based scenarios was well received. The suggested domains of tourism and real estate framing these scenarios were perceived as high potential domains. Despite this enthusiasm, we noticed that they were not fully used to focusing on the different research aspects. After analysing the gathered input of all the involved project partners evaluating the different components of the scenarios, it became clear that the input was rather general and that this was no more than a simple evaluation of the potential of the proposed services. Input regarding the technological steps that needed to be undertaken in order to establish the scenarios is largely lacking in these evaluations. Consequently, it is important to guide the input process in order to create a more extended overview of the technological challenges of and possible technological solutions for the different scenario components. Only in this way can it be assessed in detail what will be desirable and feasible to implement in the design process. Although each functional requirement can be coupled with some kind of user input, finding this match is not self-evident. When gathering input from all the involved stakeholders on the user scenarios, the question should be if and how the functional problem created by a particular user requirement could be solved technologically in the current project or possibly in the future. In the context of the URBAN project, this question was investigated further in the final research phase, in which we aimed to embed the final user findings in the socio-technological 3D navigation design. However in a more general sense it is important not to overestimate the breadth of technological feedback, but to only ask the kind of specific feedback in which they are expert.

In addition, sufficient technological points of recognition need to be built in, in order that they know where they can give their input.

Third, the storyboard visualisation of the same scenarios, added with the partners' feedback and discussed in the participative workshop, evoked more (obstinate) responses. Hence storyboarding seems to trigger respondents more than user scenarios, which highlights a crucial added value of this research tool. The resistance seems to be related to the fact that storyboards visualise the consequences of certain decisions and translate abstract ideas in concrete technological choices. In this way the partners were able to assess from their perspective which components of the scenarios would be (un)usable and too time-consuming to implement or too extended.

Finally, on a more practical level, as UDI is not self-evident and sometimes a rather time-consuming and demanding process, it is necessary to adopt a very flexible research attitude and lower the threshold for participating in the user research as much as possible, especially when user research is perceived as less valuable for the overall project goal.

Conclusion

In this chapter we have investigated how and to what extent we can involve the domestication approach in the UDI research, which we have conducted in the context of the URBAN research project. The involvement of the domestication framework enabled us to gain insight into contextualised user behaviour and needs in relation to the everyday life practice of planning a city trip and searching for a home. However, embedding these findings in an early stage of NPD appeared not to be that self-evident.

The case study has enabled us to better understand and assess the kind of obstacles to integrating user research conducted from a domestication perspective, in the technological R&D process. A systematic involvement of all the involved partners aimed at a particular user-driven outcome is an important condition for UDI. Yet there are also partners who hardly come into contact with user issues, especially when conducting more basic research in the early stages of R&D. Clearly there is not always an easy match between current and future user practices identified by means of the domestication framework on the one hand (with regard to the described case-study of URBAN the everyday life practices of planning a city trip and searching for a real estate property) and the objectives and expectations of the technological project partners who are mainly concerned with fine-tuning and experimenting with the basic technology of 3D modelling on the other hand. However, this difficulty in matching should not be generalised for all technologically oriented projects. An increasing number of industrial and technological stakeholders are convinced of the central role of users in technological innovation. In this regard, we observe the rise of test and experimentation platforms like "living labs", which take UDI as their starting point (Ballon et al. 2007). In any case, it is always important that during the development process the door is kept open for the integration of functionalities that in the future can appear to be necessary from a user perspective. In other words, the development process needs to be fed back continuously by user input as every decision that is made during the R&D process can create a lock-in situation in which a certain functionality can no longer be adjusted (e.g. the traffic sign recognition). Consequently design decisions should be driven by user perspective.

The integration of the user perspective especially evoked more resistance in the early phase of development than towards the implementation phase. In the context of URBAN, the user-grounded scenarios have created some awareness among the other (technological) partners about the potential translation of the technological research towards added value for the user. However, the identification of these user aspects has not (yet) led to major technological implementation of other elements than those foreseen from the beginning of the technological research plans. The user input that is taken up is primarily situated on the level of services in the context of the URBAN demonstrator and not on the level of the basic architecture. This coincides with the fact that user input is mainly allocated a place in the final technology development and implementation phase, which leaves little room for strategic user-driven technological adaptations.

Our case study shows how insights into particular user practices can be an important element in technological development processes. We were able to identify a number of subjects where the functional requirements of the technological partners and the user practices do converge and hence where user input could have a genuine added value for the R&D activities. Especially user input concerning visualisation issues, such as the added value of 3D visualisation versus 2D and the required level of details and thus realism, matches with the needs of the technological and industrial partners. Also the involvement of contextual issues, like search issues, is indispensable from a user perspective in order to have clear insight into how users would "domesticate" the 3D city model in the everyday life practice of a city trip or in the search for a house or apartment.

Ideally there should be frequent and intensive interaction between users and engineers throughout the entire R&D process, with openness towards and understanding of each others input. Moreover, the UDI vision that users should be an integral part of the full technological trajectory needs to be shared by all the involved partners, in order to establish a true UDI approach. Although this project showed that it is not easy to integrate UDI in a project with many research partners, each with their own research agenda, we do see it as worthwhile and even necessary step. Optimising the cooperation between the different research partners is therefore a necessity. It is also important to make sure that the technological partners have a clear view on what they can expect of the user research. They often equate user research with usability research, and therefore see it as a nice-to-have instead of a must-have. There should be more awareness about the concrete outcomes of a UDI, as this not only involves small usability improvements, but also necessary affordances and user requirements, thus illustrating its added value.

Based on the above insights, we argue that, in relation to domestication from the concept phase onwards (thus embedding insights on current and future domesticated user practices as early as possible in the R&D process) UDI can definitely play an important role in the development of media technology. First by identifying innovation opportunities, the potential target group and its needs and practices and second by steering the development process in an iterative way, together with all the involved stakeholders. In this way the domestication framework can meet the two key components of UDI.

Acknowledgements: This chapter is the result of research carried out as part of the URBAN project (1 January 2008 until 31 December 2009), funded by the Interdisciplinary Institute for Broadband Technology (IBBT). URBAN is carried out by a consortium of the industrial partners AGIV, Androme, GeoAutomation, SPC, Tele Atlas and Procedural in cooperation with the IBBT research groups EDM, IMEC, VISICS, ICRI and SMIT.

References

Ballon P., Pierson J., Delaere S. 'Fostering innovation in networked communications: test and experimentation platforms for broadband systems' eds. Heilesen S.B., Jensen S.S. Designing for Networked Communications: Strategies and Development London: Idea Group Publishing (2007) pp. 137-166

Chesbrough H.W. Open Innovation: The New Imperative for Creating and Profiting from Technology Boston, Mass.: Harvard Business School; Maidenhead : McGraw-Hill (2003)

Cooper A., Reiman R., Cronin D. About Face 3: The Essentials of Interaction Design Indianapolis: Wiley Publishing (2007)

Courage C., Baxter K. Understanding your Users: A Practical Guide to User Requirements - Methods, Tools, and Techniques San Francisco: Morgan Kaufmann (2005)

De Marez L. Diffusie van ICT-innovaties: Accurater Gebruikersinzicht voor Betere Introductiestrategieën (unpublished Ph.D. thesis) Universiteit Gent, Gent (2006)

Edquist C. 'Innovation Policy - A Systemic Approach' eds. Lundvall B.-Å., Archibugi D. Major Socio-Economic Trends and European Innovation Policy Oxford: Oxford University Press (2001)

European Commission. Europe 2020 - A Strategy for Smart, Sustainable and Inclusive Growth Brussels: Commission of the European Communities (2010)

European Council & European Commission. A Digital Agenda for Europe Brussels: Commission of the European Communities (2010)

Flichy P. L'innovation technique - Récents Développements en Sciences Sociales: Vers une Nouvelle Théorie de l'Innovation Paris: La Découverte (1995)

Freeman C., Soete L. The Economics of Industrial Innovation (3rd ed.) London: Continuum, viii (1997)

Haddon L. 'Roger Silverstone's legacies: domestication' New Media & Society (9), (2007) pp. 25-32

Holmquist L.E. 'User-driven innovation in the future applications lab' Presentation at CHI 2004 Vienna, Austria (April 24-29, 2004)

ISO. Human-centred Design Processes for Interactive Systems (ISO 13407: 1999(E)) Geneva: International organization for standardization (1999)

Jacobs A., Dreessen K., Pierson J. '"Thick" personas: Using ethnographic methods for persona development as a tool for conveying the social science view in technological design' Paper presented at The good, the bad and the unexpected: the user and the future of information and communication technologies - A transdisciplinary conference organised by COST Action 298 (May 23-25, 2007)

Lelie C. van der 'The value of storyboards in the product design process' Personal and Ubiquitous Computing 10 (2-3) (2006) pp.159-162

Mallard A. (2005) 'Following the emergence of unpredictable uses? New stakes and tasks for the social sciences understanding of ICT uses' eds. Haddon L., Mante-Meijer E., Sapio B., Kommonen K.H., Fortunati L., Kant A. Everyday Innovators: Researching the Role of Users in Shaping ICT's (Vol. 32) Dordrecht: Springer (2005) pp. 39-53

Norman D.A. 'Cognitive engineering' eds. Norman D.A., Draper S.W. User Centered System Design: New Perspectives on Human-Computer Interaction Hillsdale: Lawrence Erlbaum Associates (1986) pp. 32-65

Pierson J., Jacobs A., De Marez L., Lievens B 'Archetypical users as starting point for exploring wireless city applications: Linking domestication and diffusion approach' eds. Pierson J., Mante-Meijer E., Loos E., Sapio E.B. Innovating for and by users Brussels: COST 298 – OPOCE (2008) pp.107-120

Preece J., Rogers Y., Sharp H. Interaction Design: Beyond Human-Computer Interaction New York: Wiley (2002)

Silverstone R., Haddon L. 'Design and domestication of information and communication technologies: technical change and everyday life' eds. Mansell R., Silverstone R. eds. Communication by Design: The Politics of Information and Communication Technologies Oxford: Oxford University Press (1996) pp. 44-74

Torben Nielsen K., Jacobs A., Lievens B., Pierson J. (2008) 'Faking the real thing? Proxy technology assessment as a method for participative design.' Paper presented at Participatory Design Conference - Designed for Co-designers' Workshop, Bloomington, USA (October 1-4, 2008)

Tuomi I. Networks of innovation: change and meaning in the age of the Internet Oxford: Oxford University Press (2002)

Vermeir L., Van Lier T., Pierson J., Lievens B. 'Making the online complementary to the offline: social requirements to foster the 'sense of community'' Presentation at Communication Policy and Technology Section for the IAMCR (International Association for Media and Communication Research) congress Media and global divides, organised by Stockholm University & IAMCR Stockholm. Sweden (July 20-25, 2008)

Veryzer R.W., de Mozota B. 'The impact of user-oriented design on new product development - An examination of fundamental relationships' Journal of Product Innovation Management, 22 (2005) pp. 128-143

Von Hippel E. Democratizing innovation Cambridge, Mass.: IT Press (2005)

Wakeford N. (2004) Innovation through People-centred Design: Lessons from the USA Guildford: University of Surrey (2004)

Wise E., Høgenhaven C. User-driven Innovation: Context and Cases in the Nordic Region Oslo: Research Policy Institute - Nordic Innovation Centre (2008)

Part 3 - Differentiation in User Roles and Creativity

Mijke Slot

Web Roles Re-examined: Exploring User Roles in the Media Environment

Introduction: From consumer to user

"In changing the relations between media and individuals, the internet does not herald the rise of a powerful consumer. The internet heralds the disappearance of the consumer altogether." (Shirky 2000)

In the traditional media environment, users have primarily been consumers of content. By choosing, buying, interpreting and discussing media products, they have taken up roles at the end of the value chain. This consumption role has been separated from the creating, producing, gate-keeping and supplying roles of the mass media. In general, media producers do not allow audiences to easily communicate back to the creators or to participate in the value-creation process without invitation. The traditional mass media can therefore best be described by its one-way communication characteristic (Croteau & Hoynes 1997).

In line with the arguments of Mante-Meijer and Loos in this volume, Shirky (2000) states that the internet has enabled users to change this static relationship. Over the past twenty years, new technologies, digitization, convergence and the spread and deployment of computers and the internet have changed the media landscape. With rapid speed, the internet has become an integral part of our daily lives (e.g. Silverstone & Hirsch 1992; Küng et al. 2008). Instead of a one-way channel, the internet provides a two-way channel through which users can "talk back" (Shirky 2000; Tapscott & Williams 2006; Leadbeater 2008; Van Dijck 2009). This lowered the threshold for users to participate. The audience increasingly discovered ways and tools to become digitally active themselves. Computers are tools for text processing, photo and video editing, audio recording and playing games. And the internet supplies a massive network for users to communicate with others and share content and information.

This chapter explores the extent to which users can take on roles in media services online. Based on a user survey, the concept of the active online user will be refined. In the following paragraphs, the methodological aspects of the user survey will be briefly discussed. Secondly, the outcomes of the survey will be presented, highlighting user roles in the online media entertainment domain and comparing the differences between user groups. In the conclusion, the discussion on the activities or in-activities of internet users will be put into perspective. But first, in this introduction the concept of the active user will be further explored.

Participative users

Writers from different backgrounds have coined various concepts for participative users. One example is the concept "prosumer" – a contraction between producer and consumer. Originally this concept was introduced by Toffler (1980), but in the digital era it has also been extensively used to portray producing online users. Another example is the concept of the "pro-am", the professional amateur. Pro-ams are amateurs who pursue amateur activities to professional standards (Leadbeater & Miller 2004). Like prosumer, the pro-am concept is used for for more than just online activities, although the internet does provide a powerful tool for individuals to become a pro-am.

Next to prosumer and pro-am, terms like "user-created" or "user-generated content", "co-creation" and "crowd sourcing"re used in marketing and business to characterize the act of users creating content themselves or participating in design or decision processes. These developments seem to have attracted even more attention since the rise of "web 2.0" (DiNucci 1999; O'Reilly 2005), also called the "participative web" or the "social web" (Frissen et al. 2008). The web 2.0 concept became popular in 2004 and was extensively used to describe a new and potentially disruptive stage in the development of the internet. The term web 2.0 is primarily social in nature. It is used as an umbrella concept to explain the development of new internet applications that exploit connectivity and the collective intelligence of the users (Madden & Fox 2006). These new applications enable users to create, publish and share information on an unprecedented scale (Pascu et al. 2007; Slot & Frissen 2007).

One of the first sectors that witnessed the effect of more user autonomy was the music industry. In 1999, users began taking up distribution roles by up and downloading music files through peer-to-peer (P2P) file sharing networks like Napster and KaZaA. IAlready in 2002, the Pew Internet and American Life Project found that nearly 30 percent of Americans had made use of these file-sharing platforms at least once (Horrigan & Rainie 2002). Record companies and intermediary organizations like the RIAA (Recording Industry Association of America) reacted defensively.

In time, users also became active in other online media sectors. In the press domain, news companies were shook up by online user practices. Instead of relying on journalists as gate-keepers of important news events, users increasingly create their own information environment (Picone 2007). Millions of users publish their own information in the blogosphere – in 2007 blog search engine Technorati was already indexing more than 100 million blogs (www.technorati.com). News portals like Google News (news.google.com) gather news messages from different news sources like newspaper websites and blogs around the world on their websites, free for users to customize. Websites like Wikileaks allow users to publish and access (confidential) information. Applications like Digg (www.digg.com) popularize certain news themes by enabling users to link to and judge news messages - making intermediary parties obsolete in the process. Users take on tasks of traditional journalists in citizen journalist initiatives like OhMyNews (www.ohmynews.com) in South Korea. And via social networks, on which millions of users worldwide have created an account (Boyd & Ellison 2007), content and news events are rapidly shared between users. Surpassing the industries' selection and gate-keeping mechanisms, amateur artists promote themselves through social networking sites, and authors can publish their own books – online or in print. And these are only a few examples of possible user roles online.

Jenkins (2006) describes this new media system as a participatory culture in which both users and producers interact with each other according to a new set of rules. As the quote at the beginning of this chapter shows, Shirky argues even that this change has undermined the traditional role of the mass media, because consumers have changed into "media outlets" themselves. They have started producing their own media content, and therefore the concept of the consumer has become totally obsolete – online, consumers do not exist anymore. But to what extent is this true?

User participation and the devaluation of culture

Although internet positivists like Leadbeater and Jenkins are generally positive about active user roles, applaud online possibilities and see participating users as a solution to many problems, traditional media companies and cultural critics often approach active user roles with caution and scepticism. And from a scholarly perspective, the concept of the "user as an active contributor" is also labelled as ambiguous (Van Dijck 2009).

Existing media companies are not too happy that consumers have found ways to circumvent their services. They take the economic and legal perspective that every illegal download is a violation of copyright law and a reduction of income. Over the years, many industry associations have defended their position and tried to stop users from sharing files through file-sharing services. To take the music industry as an example: in addition to suing platform providers, the music industry applied several other strategies to ban file-sharing, such as applying strict digital rights management (DRM) to music files, launching awareness campaigns for the public and urging governments to strengthen the copyright protection system (Blomqvist et al. 2005; Bakker 2005; Bender & Wang 2009; Van Eijk et al. 2010). From 2002, lawsuits have been brought against individual copyright infringers in several countries. In 2004, the IFPI, for example, reported civil claims against 150 P2P users in Denmark in 2002, 100 criminal complaints filed against 100 P2P users in Korea in 2003 and criminal raids of 75 P2P uploaders and service providers in Italy in 2003 (IFPI 2004).

Online user activity is criticized from a cultural perspective as well. Keen (2007) sounds the alarm about the destructive impact of the digital revolution on culture, economy and values. He argues that self-publishing undermines our sense of what is true and what is false and corrupts our culture. Not only does Keen take the large number of blogs as an example, he also states that services like Wikipedia, Google and YouTube are good examples of users displaying their bad taste, proving the absurdity of content and the devaluation of culture. In taking on producing roles and evading cultural gate-keepers, users might even be undermining "truth". With fewer professional middlemen, truth and trust are compromised online. Plagiarism, intellectual property theft and stifling creativity are all consequences of the devaluation of truth on the internet. Keen argues that we need media professionals to keep our culture at a high standard.

From a more analytical perspective, the extent to which users are truly active and empowered online is questionable. Often, the assumption is made that on the internet all users produce content, but analysis shows that only a small percentage of online users actually create content. Nielsen (2006) argues that in social participatory services, user interaction is actually disappointing; 90 percent of online users don't participate but just "lurk" in the background (Nielsen 2006). They are simply inactive audience members. Nine percent of users are intermittent contributors – they contribute from time to time. These users can be characterized as editors. Only one percent of the users of a particular online community accounts for most activity. They are the creators. According to Nielsen, this inequality of contribution is not only visible in weblogs, but also in Wikipedia and book reviews on Amazon. Although this analysis has not yet been substantiated by large-scale research, more scholars point out that the activity of users should be assessed more carefully (Van Dijck 2009). Furthermore, the power of the producers, both incumbents and newcomers, to influence and steer users should not be underestimated (Jenkins 2006; Van Dijck 2009).

Researching user activity online

Although both positivists and critics agree that the media landscape is changing, they do not agree on the value of or the extent to which users take on roles other than that of consumers. Many uncertainties still exist today about changing user roles and subsequently shifting online user/producer relations. Conversation about online user participation easily degenerates into a discussion about the positive or negative side effects of this development. Although this debate is often very normative in character, the questions raised in these debates are absolutely relevant and should be taken seriously. Siegel underlines that, just like other media, the internet deserves to be challenged by the same fundamental questions (Siegel 2008). And as a starting point - as has been pointed out by Van Dijck (2009) - it is highly relevant to developing a more nuanced model for understanding user roles online. Therefore this chapter will shed light on the developments by studying in practice what roles users are currently enabled to take on.

Concepts

A number of concepts are used throughout this chapter that deserve clarification. In this research, users are defined as individuals using the internet for media purposes in their leisure time. Instead of consumers (using the product or service without adding value) or end-users (a concept that implies that the innovation process is already finished when it reaches them (Bergman & Frissen 1997)), the user concept implies that people who use the internet are active and add something (of value) to the information, product or service that they use. According to Tuomi, the user of a technology is not an individual person, but a member of a community that uses a technology in a certain way (Tuomi 2002); therefore it is better to talk about users in the plural. In this research, the differences between user groups will be taken into account.

The concept of user roles should not be mistaken for user agency or user empowerment. Van Dijck (2009) points out that user agency can be an ambiguous concept. It is often used to point out that users are putting in a "certain amount of creative effort" to create something "outside of professional routines and efforts". User roles are defined more broadly and do not only focus on creating something. In this chapter, user roles are all the different ways users can interact with media and entertainment applications. These roles do not necessarily mean that they have to be active or creative. Consumption, for example, is also a user role.

In this chapter, user roles are divided into six main categories: consuming, creating/customizing, contributing, sharing, facilitating, and communicating. These main categories are divided into numerous sub-categories. Consuming roles are primarily individual roles. Users listen to music, read text, view videos, play games and buy media products online. These roles do not directly add value to the product or service for other users. Creating and customizing is a more active user role. Users make and upload their own content and create value for other users. Customizing also involves creating, but is less creative. Users who customize alter existing products, content or services to fit their own needs. Customization only enables users to choose from pre-defined categories. Contributing is adding context to existing content or services. Users, for example, add information to Wikipedia, vote for the best video on YouTube or object to a reaction that is given in an online newspaper. Sharing is uploading content (music to file-sharing services, for example), or sending content directly to other users. Facilitating can be defined as an activity by which users make it easier for themselves or others to find and use existing content or services. Examples are adding tags, subscribing to an RSS feed or recommending content. Communicating is all the activities that take place between users to exchange information and opinions. Examples are chatting, sending each other messages or discussing on a forum.

As a field of research, this study focuses on the media sector. Media are transmitters of content for (groups of) consumers and they make use of technologies like radio, television, print or internet (Küng et al. 2008). Media companies use these media outlets to transmit packaged content. The sector in which these companies operate is called the media sector. The media sector is partly focused on information and partly on entertainment. In this chapter, user roles are explored in press, music, photo film & video, games & social networks and broadcasting services on the internet.

Users of online media services

Methodology

The user survey was carried out among internet users in 2008. Approximately 600 internet users took part in the survey. Respondents were asked to complete the survey and send the survey to other internet users. An advantage to this approach is that users are probably more willing to complete a (long) questionnaire if they know the person who sent it to them. One important shortcoming of this method is that not all internet users have an equal opportunity to be selected as participants. Therefore, the results cannot be generalized for the entire internet population, but only for a specific user group.

The survey consisted of multiple parts. In addition to general user characteristics, like age and gender, users were asked about their media use in their spare time. Furthermore, the respondents were asked how many minutes a day they spend on the internet in their spare time. In the second part of the survey, respondents were asked to indicate their offline and online media activities, ranging from consumption activities to creating content to facilitating roles, like recommending or tagging content, to communicating.

In this study, internet users are not viewed as a homogeneous group of people. Differences in age and gender might influence the use of online media entertainment services. Therefore, in addition to an analysis of frequency and average use, the group of respondents is divided into different categories and compared. In this chapter, the respondents are compared on age and gender.

User characteristics and media use

Of the respondents, 43 percent were male and 57 percent female., with an average age of 32 years old. The 25-44 age group was the largest group of users (53 percent), followed by the 13-24 age group (29 percent). Although the survey was posted online in Dutch and English, most respondents were Dutch (92 percent).

The respondents reported spending on average approximately 1.5 hours per day on the internet in their spare time. Younger users spend significantly more time online than older users.

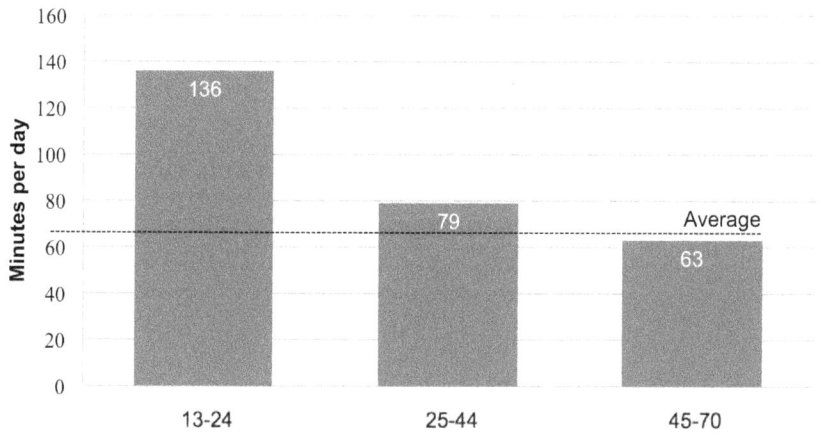

Figure 1: Time spent online per age group

The youngest group of respondents (13-24 years old) are online for an average of 136 minutes a day, well above average. They spend more time online than the 25-44 age group (79 minutes) and more than double the time respondents between 45 and 70 years old spend online in their spare time (63 minutes) (see Figure 1).

Participating users

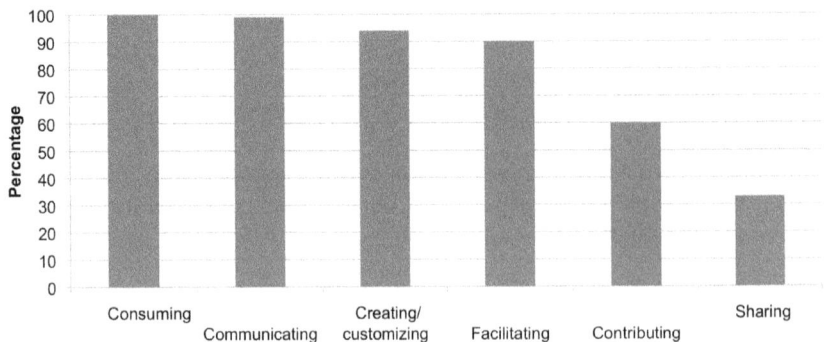

Figure 2: Online user activities

Figure 2 presents the activities of the respondents in the main user role categories. The most popular online activities involve consumption; a full 100 percent of the users who completed the survey were consumers of online media content. In addition to consuming online content, practically 100 percent of the respondents use the internet to communicate with others. A large percentage of users (approximately 94 percent) creates or customizes content. Facilitating activities, sending content to other users via e-mail or rating content and products, for example, is carried out at least once a year by almost 90 percent of the respondents. More than 60 percent of all respondents say they engage in contributing activities. Sharing content by uploading films and music is less popular among the respondents; one third takes on these roles at least once a year.

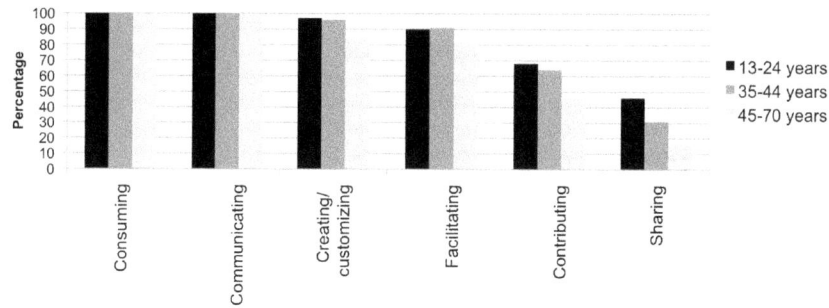

Figure 3: User roles for different age groups

Figure 3 shows the varieties between age groups. In all three groups, 100 percent of the users engage in consumption and communication activities. The percentage of users that creates is high in all groups, but highest in the youngest age group. Almost 97 percent of all users aged 13-24 engage in one or more creating activities, compared to 84 percent of oldest users. And while 68 percent of the users between 13 and 24 and 64 percent of the users between 25 and 44 contribute to online media services, less than half of all respondents in the oldest group contribute. The percentage of users that shares content is even lower; 17 percent of the oldest user group shares content, compared to 31 percent of the users between 25 and 44 and almost half of the youngest user group.

But in spite of these differences, and at first sight, users seem to participate very actively online. Let's take a more detailed look at user activities.

All users are consumers

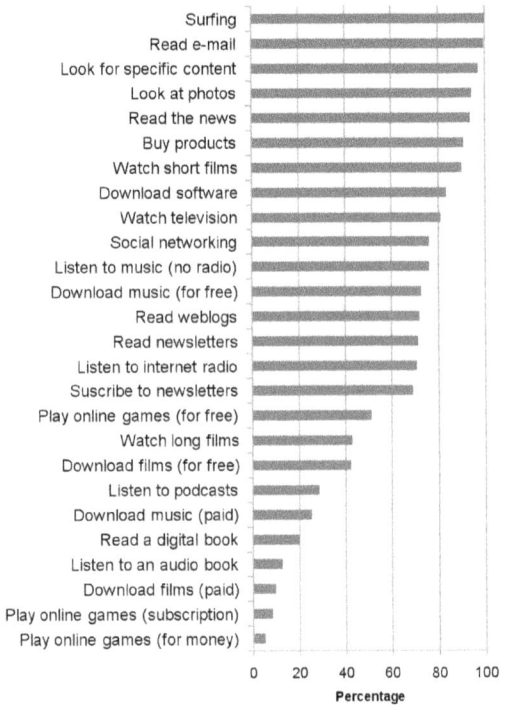

Figure 4: Online consumption practices

All users who completed the survey are consumers of media content online (see Figure 4). They surf the internet, read e-mails and spend time looking for specific content. Many users view photos online and read the news. Approximately 72 percent of the respondents download music for free at least once a year. And more than one-quarter of the respondents indicate they pay for downloaded music at least once a year. More than 90 percent of all respondents watch short films online, on YouTube, for example. More than half of all respondents play online games. Slightly more than 80 percent watches television on their computers. More than three-quarters of all respondents are active on a social networking site and lastly, almost 91 percent buys products online, books and DVDs, for example. Respondents even engage in lesser-known activities like reading digital books (almost 20 percent) or listening to podcasts (almost 29 percent) at least once a year.

Looking at differences between user groups, younger users are more active in consumption activities in general. They are, furthermore, more likely to look at photos, watch videos and television, listen to music (not internet radio), download music and play online games. Younger users particularly spend more time on social networking services; 43 percent of the 13-24 age group respondents claimed to be active on a social network multiple times a day, against 9 percent of the 25-44 age group and 0 percent of the 45-70 age group. Looking at gender differences, men tend to read online news on a more regular basis, download more films and software and play online games for money more than women.

It can be concluded that all users online are consumers engaging in a wide variety of consumption roles covering all media sectors. Consuming media content is a rather traditional activity that does not differ very much from offline media use.

Communication is key

The internet facilitates communication on an unprecedented scale (see Figure 5). In the survey, ten online communicating roles were presented, of which respondents on average chose 5. Sending messages, public or private, via e-mail or through a specific service is very popular. Almost 99 percent of all respondents send someone an e-mail at least once a year (approximately 80 percent sends e-mails at least once a day).

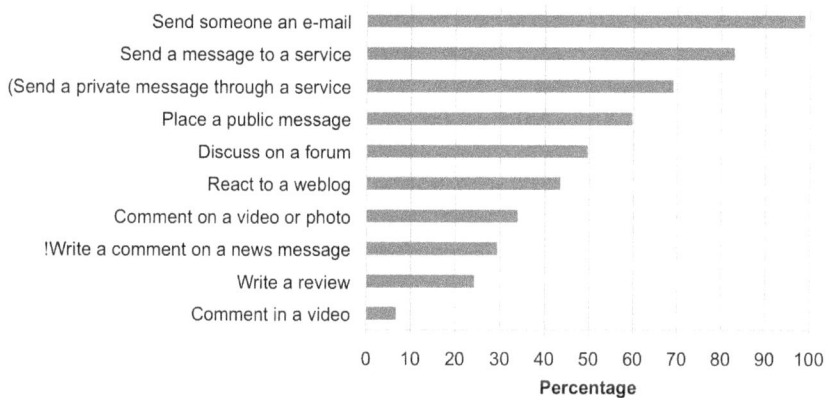

Figure 5: Online communication practices

How interactive is online communicating? Respondents communicate most often directly and one-on-one (for example through e-mail or by sending a message directly to the producer of a service). More interactive ways of communicating, like discussing on a forum, reacting to a weblog or writing a review, are done less often. But still the percentage of users that actively engages in discussion online is high. Almost half of all respondents take part in a discussion on a forum at least once a year. Almost 44 percent of all users who completed the survey react at least once a year to a weblog post. Almost 30 percent of all users write a comment on a news message at least once a year. Writing a review is less popular – almost one-quarter of the users engage in this activity.

Younger respondents are far more active in communicating online than older respondents. Users between 13 and 24 are more likely to comment on videos or photos than the user group aged between 45 and 70 (53 to 14 percent), send each other private messages through social networks, for example, (84 percent versus 33 percent), place public messages (81 versus 27 percent), react to weblogs (63 to 25 percent) and discuss on a forum (64 percent versus 28 percent).

As the results above show, the respondents frequently engage in consuming as well as communicating activities. But these roles are still rather traditional. As was pointed out in the introduction to this chapter, the internet enables users to become much more active. And the results of the online survey indicate that internet users engage in a large variety of other activities as well. Only two percent of all respondents do not engage in any activities other than consuming and communicating.

Making the internet easier

Facilitating activities, sending content to other users via e-mail and other services or rating content and products, for example, is carried out at least once a year by almost 90 percent of the respondents. The respondents engage on average in 4 facilitating activities.

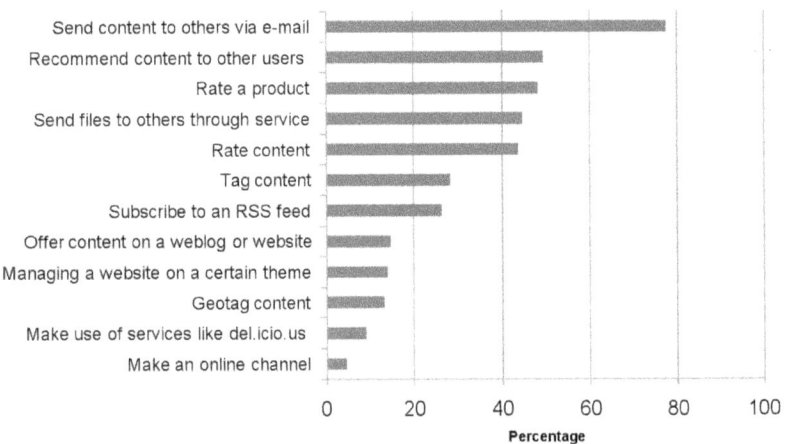

Figure 6: Online facilitating practices

More than three-quarters of all respondents send content to others via email (see Figure 6). Recommending and rating content is done by approximately half of all respondents. Geotagging content (adding geographical data to content) is not a frequent activity, but more than 13 percent of all respondents still do this at least once a year. Tagging content is more popular; more than 28 percent does this at least once a year. Analysis of the data shows that users often combine these activities; almost 90 percent of the users who use geotags, also tag content.

Choosing customization over creation?

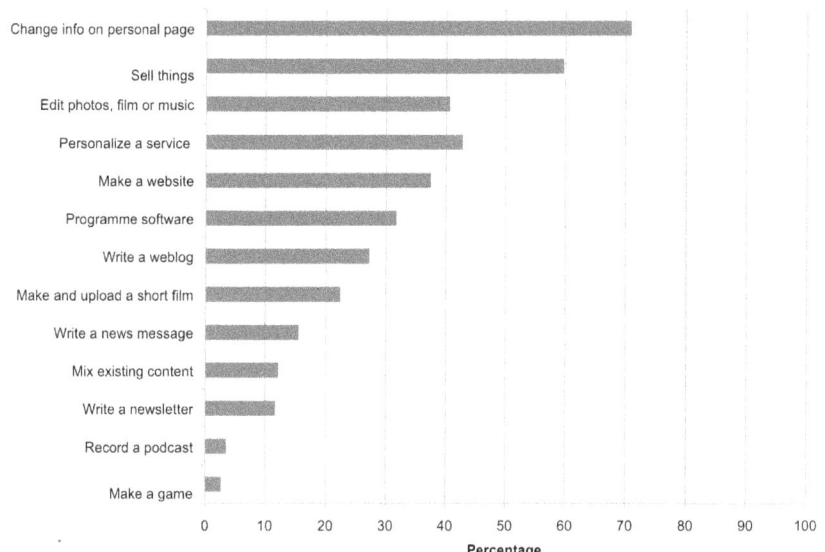

Figure 7: Online creation/customization practices

A large percentage of users (approximately 94 percent) creates or customizes content on the internet. The respondents were offered 13 different online creation roles. On average, they chose 4 categories. Most popular activities are: changing information on personal pages (for example on a social network), personalizing, editing and selling (see Figure 7). In these cases, users have a limited number of options to be truly creative. More creative activities, like writing a weblog, making a website or a short film, are carried out less often by the respondents. Nevertheless, the number of creative users is still significant.

Almost 71 percent of all respondents change their profile or personal information on a website at least once a year. This is consistent with the percentage of users who are active on a social networking site (76 percent). Approximately 41 percent of the users edit photo, film or music files. More than

37 percent of all respondents have their own website and 27 percent write a weblog at least once a year. Recording a podcast (4 percent) and making a game (3 percent) are the least popular activities among users.

Differences between user groups are primarily visible in age categories. The youngest age group (13-24 years old) is more likely to engage in editing photos (56 versus 37 versus 25 percent) and more often changes information on a personal page. Almost 85 percent of the respondents between 13 and 24 years old change the information on a personal page at least once a year. Approximately 14 percent does this at least once a day.

Contributing and sharing

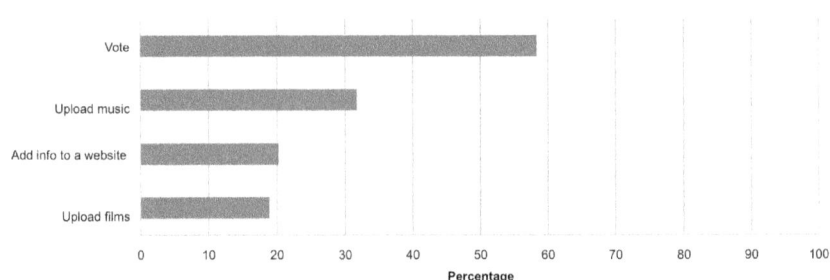

Figure 8: Online contributing and sharing practices

More than 60 percent of all respondents say they engage in contributing activities (see Figure 8). Approximately 60 percent of all users contribute to online services by voting for specific content. Only 20 percent of the respondents actively add information to websites, Wikipedia, for example.
Compared to the previous user roles, sharing content by uploading films and music is less popular among internet users; approximately 32 percent uploads music at least once a year. Compared to the percentage of users who download music for free, this indicates that uploading and downloading are not always combined. Users probably download content without also using P2P networks, for example through Usenet groups.

Level of activity: Low, medium and high-level participation

The research outcomes above show that users are enabled to take on a large number of roles in online media services. But not all roles are equally active. Consumption, for example, is primarily a low level activity, while creating content is acquires a higher level of user involvement. In other words: users have to put in more effort to make a video and post it online than to update a profile on a social networking site.

To gain a better understanding of the level of user participation, all sub-roles that users can take on are classified into low-level, medium-level and high-level participation. Writing a weblog, making and uploading a video and making a website are classified as high-level user activities. Writing comments on news messages, discussing on a forum, sending e-mails and uploading music are classified as medium-level user activities. Low-level user activities are consumption activities like reading, watching, buying and downloading. Voting, tagging and rating are also included in this category. The average percentage of users that take on activities is calculated for each category.

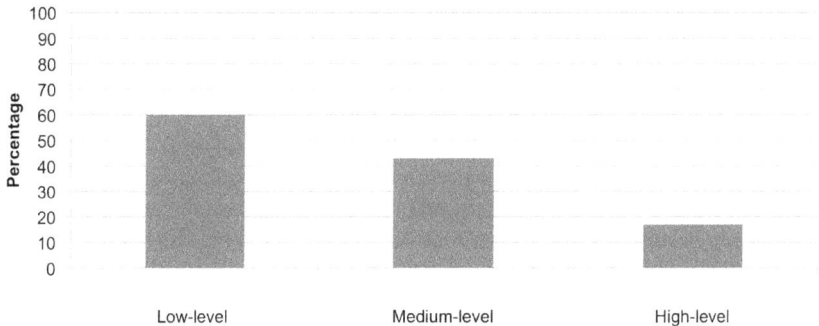

Figure 9: Average level of user participation

Figure 9 shows the average user participation for low, medium and high-level user activities. More users take on low-level activities then high-level activities. On average 60 percent of the users of online media services engage in low-level activities, 43 percent in medium-level activities and 17 percent in high-level activities.

Conclusion: Extended consumers

Let's go back to the quote at the beginning of this chapter. Shirky claims that online, each user has developed into a media outlet and this has brought about the disappearance of the consumer altogether. Although the use of active user concepts and the research results presented above substantiate part of his statement, Shirky's claim about the death of the consumer on the internet can be nuanced. Even online, users can still be classified as consumers of content. They read newspaper articles on websites, watch television shows on their computer screens, listen to music and play online games – on the internet, every user is also a consumer. The fact that consumers are enabled to take on other roles online can be seen as a complementary development rather than a complete turnaround. Therefore, it can be argued that because of the internet and networked media, users are enabled to take on other roles *besides* being consumers. Perhaps they can be best labelled *extended consumers*. Instead of only focussing on the user as a producer (prosumer), or creator of content, the active-user concept can be broadened to include all kinds of roles.

Computers and the internet have indeed lowered the threshold for a very large group of users to take on a variety of roles in the media domain on a large scale. The internet is more integrated into people's lives than ever. Overall, it seems that users are very active online and take on a variety of user roles. Contrary to primarily acting as consumers, users create, facilitate, share and communicate.

Age differences

Except for a small number of activities (like engaging in social communities or more technical activities like programming and downloading software), gender is not an important variable in explaining the differences in internet use. The differences between the age groups are particularly striking. Internet use seems to be much more dependent on generational than on gender differences. Of the user groups, 6 percent of the oldest users do not engage in any activities besides consuming and communicating. This is a significantly higher percentage than the user group between 25 and 44 (1 percent) and the youngest group between 13 and 24 (2 percent).

Younger users tend to be online longer each day and engage in more activities than older users. The younger age groups, for example, are over-represented in communicating – they communicate on more levels than older users, who primarily send e-mails. They are, furthermore, significantly more active on social networking sites. But this chapter has also shown that older age groups are also taking on many active online roles. It can be concluded that they might be online less often and engage less frequently in activities, but they still engage in a large variety of user roles.

Active user roles in perspective

If we were to adopt a very literal definition of Nielsen's 90-9-1 rule, the research outcomes would cast doubt on this theory. A far larger percentage of users create content online than only one percent. Almost 38 percent of all users have built and maintain a website, more than 27 percent of the respondents write weblogs, over 15 percent engage in writing news messages and four percent record a podcast at least once a year. And most users are audience, community and active participant at the same time. Taking these outcomes into account, the

90-9-1 rule seems irrelevant for describing user activities in the online media entertainment domain.

Looking more closely, the findings suggest that the level of user participation can be nuanced. Low-level and more traditional participatory activities, such as consuming content, communicating and customizing, are among the most popular user roles. The variety within these roles is large and users often engage in these activities. On average, far fewer users engage in truly creative and high-level user participation, like building websites and uploading self-made videos, than users who engage in easy and low-level activities. Nevertheless, online, the traditional consumer role has extended significantly into multiple user roles, and this has challenged existing user/producer relations.

The outcomes of this user survey can be taken as a starting point for further research on the impact of online user behaviour on user/producer relations. As Jenkins and Van Dijck have underlined, producers are also influencing user behaviour. Who stands to benefit most from user activity? Is it the user or is most user activity simply a marketing ploy from commercial players to obtain personal data? Are users able to influence the way these parties behave? Internet users are increasingly aware that their personal data is being stored and used to gain a profit. In 2010, Facebook users started a Facebook Users' Union. They demand that Facebook gives its users a say in how the money earned from user data is spent (Kiss 2010). Up until August 2010, this Facebook group had gathered approximately 1,100 users. It will be interesting to see if this group grows and if these users can make a difference. The coming years will show to what extent users are truly empowered online.

References

Bakker P. 'File sharing--fight, ignore or compete. Paid download services vs. P2P-networks' Telematics and Informatics 22 (2005) pp. 41-55

Bender M.T., Wang Y. 'The impact of digital piracy on music sales: a cross-country analysis' International Social Science Review 84 (3-4) (2009) pp. 157-170

Bergman S., Frissen V. 'De eindgebruiker bestaat niet. De dynamiek van het gebruik van ICT in het leven van alledag' Informatie- en Informatiebeleid 15 (2) (1997) pp. 68-74

Blomqvist U., Eriksonn L.E., Findahl O., Selg H., Wallis R. 'Report on technology versus usage and effects' MusicLessons deliverable 1 (2005) http://xml.nada.kth.se/media/Research/MusicLessons/Reports/deliverable_1.pdf (assessed September, 2008)

Boyd D. M., Ellison N. B. 'Social network sites: Definition, history, and scholarship' Journal of Computer-Mediated Communication 13(1) (2007)

Croteau D., Hoynes W. Media/Society. Industries, Images, and Audiences Thousand Oaks, London, New Delhi: Pine Forge Press (1997)

Dijck J. van 'Users like you? Theorizing agency in user-generated content' Media, Culture & Society 31 (1) (2009) pp. 41-58

DiNucci D. 'Fragmented Future' Print 53 (4) (1999) pp. 32-33

Eijk N. van, Poort J. and Rutten P. 'Legal, economic and cultural aspects of file-sharing' Communications & Strategies 77 (1), pp. 35-54 (2010)

Frissen V., Staden M. van, Huijboom N., Kotterink B., Huveneers S., Kuipers M., Bodea G. Naar een 'User Generated State'? De Impact van Nieuwe Media voor Overheid en Openbaar Bestuur Delft: TNO (2008)

Horrigan J.B., Rainie L. 'The broadband difference. How online Americans' behavior changes with high-speed Internet connections at home' Pew Internet & American LifeProject (2002) http://www.pewinternet.org/pdfs/PIP_Broadband_Report.pdf

IFPI IFPI Online Music Report' London: IFPI (2004)

Jenkins H. Convergence Culture. Where Old and New Media Collide New York and London: New York University Press (2006)

Keen A. The Cult of the Amateur. How Today's Internet is Killing our Culture New York: Doubleday/ Currency (2007)

Kiss J. 'Facebook should be paying us' The Guardian Monday 9 August (2010)

Küng L., Picard R., Towse R. eds. The Internet and the Mass Media London, Thousand Oaks, New Delhi, Singapore: Sage Publications (2008)

Leadbeater C., Miller P. The Pro-Am Revolution. How Enthusiasts are Changing the Way our Economy and Society Work London: Demos UK (2004)

Leadbeater C. We-think. Mass innovation, not Mass Production London: Profile Books (2008)

Madden M., Fox S. 'Riding the waves of Web 2.0. More than a buzzword, but still not easily defined' Pew Internet and American Life Project (2006) http://www.pewinternet.org/pdfs/PIP_Web_2.0.pdf

Nielsen J. Participation Inequality: Encouraging More Users to Contribute (2006) http://www.useit.com/alertbox/participation_inequality.html(assessed September 2008)

O'Reilly T. 'What Is Web 2.0. Design Patterns and Business Models for the Next Generation of Software' O'Reilly.com (2005) http://oreilly.com/web2/archive/what-is-web-20.html (assessed August 2010)

Pascu C., Osimo D., Ulbrich M., Turlea G., Burgelman J.C. 'The potential disruptive impact of Internet 2 based technologies' First Monday 12 (3) (2007)

Picone I. 'Conceptualising online news use' Observatorio (OBS*) Journal 3 (2007) pp. 93-144

Shirky C. RIP the Consumer, 1900-1999 http://www.shirky.com/writings/consumer.html (2000)

Siegel L. Against the Machine. Being Human in the age of the Electronic Mob New York: Spiegel & Grau (2008)

Silverstone R., Hirsch E. Consuming Technologies. Media and Information in Domestic Spaces London and New York: Routledge (1992)

Slot M., Frissen V.A.J. 'Users in the 'golden' age of the information society' Observatorio (OBS*) Journal 3 (2007) pp. 201-224

Tapscott D., Williams A.D. Wikinomics. How Mass Collaboration is Changing Everything New York, London: Penguin Books (2006)

Toffler A. The Third Wave. The Classic Study of Tomorrow New York: Bantam Books (1980)

Tuomi I. Networks of Innovation. Change and Meaning in the Age of the Internet Oxford: Oxford University Press (2002)

Philip Ely, David Frohlich and Nicola Green

Uncertainty, Upheavals and Upgrades: Digital-DIY During Life-Change

Introduction

"Domestic life stands at the intersection of various currents of social change. (…). In circumstances of (…) [dull] labour (…) [with it's] empty routines in everyday life, personal relations in the domestic sphere may indeed appear as a refuge from a 'heartless world'" (Giddens 1986)

Domestic life may not be the refuge that Giddens describes above any more. Contemporary domestic settings are the place of homeworking, domestic labour, home improvement and home entertainment. The intersection of domestic life and the currents of social change have moved indoors, evident in the regular changes to our everyday lives (moving home, getting married, giving birth, getting divorced) and evident on the screens of our home entertainment and information & communication technologies as we bring our work home, keep up-to-date with current news events, and entertain ourselves.

Particularly when moving, improving or adapting our homes, many of us engage in "do-it-yourself" (DIY) activity. With varying degrees of expertise (and success) we construct, glue, paint, install, knock-down and build-up our homes until, perhaps, we feel comfortable to live wherein we dwell. Our competencies in DIY activity vary, and the way we DIY varies too. We enrol partners, friends, family, builder's merchants, shop owners and work colleagues to help us re-build our homes in the way that we want them. The phrase "do-it-yourself" emerged as early as 1912 in America (Gelber 1997) when homeowners were encouraged to do their own interior painting rather than hire skilled professionals, but it is in the post-war economic boom of the 1950s (during the time of an unprecedented increase in home building and home ownership) that "do-it-yourself" came into its own as a practice (Goldstein 1998). The emergence of the acronym "DIY" instead of "do-it-yourself" appears to be very specific to the UK, and it has proven problematic to date the origin of the shortening to "DIY" (Shove et al. 2007). In both the UK and the USA, "do-it-yourself" activity is seen as self-initiated home improvement activity. In France the equivalent of DIY may be "bricolage" or "making do" (Dant 1999, 69-73).

One form of DIY, however, is less evident and goes largely unreported – that of "digital-DIY". We use the term digital-DIY here to mean the configuring and reconfiguring of domestic entertainment, information and communication technologies; a digital equivalent of "bricolage" or "making do". The term is to be seen as one that Blumer (1969) might call a "conceptual device" or "analytical tool", and describes the repairing, replacing, installing, moving, wiring, updating and inter-connecting of the plethora of domestic entertainment, information and communication technologies (EICTs) during the life of a home and its inhabitants. Such technologies, for example, include televisions, DVD-recorders, laptops, game consoles, portable music players, radios, digital telephones and wireless hubs. We conceptualize DIY here in a democratic sense – as a "democratizing agency" allowing home inhabitants to "create more personal meaning" in their homes (Atkinson 2006).

Whilst a great deal of non-digital DIY activity occurs amongst young homeowners and those who have recently moved (Bogdon 1996; Baker & Kaul 2002), predicted and unpredicted life changes (for example through birth, marriage, death or divorce), still often bring about significant technological changes in the home. Individuals affected by changes in income, status and health are often forced to re-evaluate their domestic environment and the material objects therein and, as we will discuss, it is EICTs that come at the forefront of homeowners' considerations in their everyday life. Indeed, recent Mintel reports (2004-2009) suggest that engagement in home improvement DIY has lessened in favour of less active leisure pursuits like television viewing or internet accessing. However, in the latter part of 2009 and early 2010 there has been a "levelling" of the downward trend in traditional DIY and a turn toward money-saving on the part of homeowners as fiscal pressure continues to impact household spending in the UK (Mintel 2010).

Changes in the number of home inhabitants or the location of the home are more likely, then, to precipitate DIY activity (Baker & Kaul 2002), but what of the digital domain? Shklovski & Mainwaring (2005, 621-622) see the "disruptions" of residential moves as being a period of unsettlement, a time in which there is a "pull of the things left behind and the demands of the new and the unknown". For Shklovski & Mainwaring, this gives us "opportunities for new technologies to provide valuable, foreground support" to families, and they suggest ways in which online services can maintain social contacts, can manage the acquisition or disposal of digital technologies, and how new services might mediate new relationships.

Our interest in this chapter, however, lies less in the way that new innovations in the home can support life- changing moments, but more in the way that inhabitants both (re)configure pre-owned (and perhaps previously defunct) technologies *and* how they introduce new digital entertainment and information and communication technologies (EICTs) into this digital ecology. How are the "old" and the "new" integrated? How do people "handle" EICTs during life-change? What technologies do they select, buy and use? Which ones do they reject? How do people "make do"? How do they digital-DIY?

The home and technology

In attempting a user study of digital-DIY activity, it is important to acknowledge key contributions from a number of disciplinary perspectives so that we might understand better just what happens when (and if) people digital-DIY. If a digital-DIY ecology may be seen as not only about *things* but also about *people* and the *knowledge, actions, behaviours and values* that they hold – the social setting, the technical infrastructures, the individual artefacts and individual (and collective) capabilities – then we should likewise draw from the intellectual traditions of a number of contingent disciplines that reflect these areas of enquiry. There are concepts emergent from such disciplines as human-computer interaction (HCI), science and technology studies (STS), and material culture studies and design studies, each of which may aid our understanding of digital-DIY.

Human-computer interaction (HCI) studies, for example, provide us with both empirical and methodological resources in trying to understand digital-DIY in the domestic domain. HCI studies are orientated towards the design of new ICT products and services (and in particular on the "user experience") in the home, and there is a comprehensive literature in this area giving both empirical insights and guidance on method (see "Case studies" for our interpretation of one such method). For instance, Taylor & Swan (2005) introduce the idea of organizing systems, the material evidence around the home of "informational artefacts" (calendars, to-do-lists, notes), and prompt us to consider the domestic reconfiguration of organizing systems during life change with respect to digital-DIY in our fieldwork. Furthermore, Kirk et al. (2007, 68-69) discuss their ethnographic study of home moviemakers which reveals a videowork lifecycle, indicating the importance of personal labour ("lightweight" and "heavyweight") in both the use of digital technologies and the creation of digital content in domestic settings.

The tendency in HCI, however, is to focus on individual technologies, often driven by corporate research demands (Murphy et al. 2005; Bell et al. 2005; Kirk et al. 2007) or on questions of technical infrastructure (Dourish & Bell 2005; Aipperspach et al. 2008). HCI remains, we suggest, focussed on the innovation afforded by and for technological artefacts, and tends to prioritise the object at the expense of an understanding of people, their mundane innovations and the messy challenges of everyday life.

If HCI studies have privileged the *technical* over the *social*, feminist scholars in the social sciences have at least turned our attention to the people who use the technologies: their *users*. Oudshoorn & Pinch (2003) believe that we are in debt to feminist scholars (Cockburn 1983, 1985; Schwartz Cowan 1987; Cockburn & Ormrod 1993) for bringing attention to users (primarily women) and their use of (mostly) male-designed technologies in the domestic space. For Cockburn, recognising the gendered character of technology allows us to address the ways in which technologies are embedded in (particularly gendered) power relations, as they are played out in the domestic sphere – what Cockburn refers to as "power-play" (Cockburn 1985). How these relations of power are configured in domestic settings with respect to d-DIY is a significant question in our analysis.

If users are gendered, they are equally located as consumers. Schwartz Cowan's work (1987), putting the focus on the consumer in her study of the evolution of home heating and cooking systems in the United States, became the trigger for further exploration of how users interact with technological change (Woolgar 1991; Akrich 1992; Kline & Pinch 1999; Kline 2000). Schwartz Cowan recognised the place of actual or potential customers of technological artefacts at the centre of a network of social relations – the so-called "consumption junction" – which Schwartz Cowan argues is the place at which not only technological diffusion occurs, but also "where technologies begin to reorganize social structures" (1987, 292-293). Our fieldwork interests are therefore informed by the ways that digital-DIY activities within the home are organised as a juncture of consumption between the user within the domestic sphere, and the wider social relations of consumption that configure both technologies and the people that use them.

We are equally interested, however, in going beyond the point of consumption by also exploring the ongoing use/non-use of ICTs, and the domestic production of ICTs, in a digital-DIY ecology. Accordingly, we also draw on a large body of theoretical and empirical work located in science and technology studies. STS gives us a fertile ground from which we may gather insights or concepts that can help us understand domestic digital-DIY, and there are three particularly relevant approaches that we draw on: domestication, social construction, and actor-network theory.

One potential way to understand the mediating technologies seen in a digital-DIY ecology comes from Silverstone & Hirsch (1992) and Silverstone & Haddon (1996), whose ideas towards the "domestication" of ICTs in the home setting have spawned an expansive literature (Haddon 2004, 2006; Berker et al. 2006). This taming of media technologies is explained by distinct phases in what Silverstone & Hirsch describe as a household's "moral economy" (1992, 20). These phases include the *appropriation* of the technology into the home (the act of buying or acquiring), the *objectification* of the technology in the home (where it is located into the wider aesthetic of the home), the *incorporation* of the technology into home use (into the routines of daily life) and the *conversion* of a technology whereby the technology becomes so embedded in domestic and wider social life that it begins to define the relationship between the home and the outside world (for example in the way that television becomes the vehicle for discussion both in and out of the home). According to Mante-Meijer and Loos (this volume) however, one limitation of the domestication approach is that it does not explore *when* and *why* people use and consume (or conversely, continue to use or decide not to use) certain technologies. Accordingly, our approach broadly addresses the processes outlined in domestication, while also exploring the ways in which domestication processes are recursive – that is, domestication is multiple and ongoing when the everyday domestic practices of digital-DIY produce a bricolage of EICTs.

This attention to the "how" of the everyday appropriation and configuration of EICTs is drawn from approaches in the social construction of technology (SCOT). SCOT approaches broadly argue that "social groups" play a key role in the definition of, and solutions to, technological problems. These "social groups" adopted what Bijker and Pinch call "interpretative flexibility" - each social group has its own understanding of a particular technology, and that interpretation of the technology shapes it's development. In one case study - the development of the "safety" bicycle - Bijker et al explain how "relevant social groups" (in this instance both users and non-users of the "Ordinary" or "Penny-farthing" bicycle) shaped the development of the bicycle as we know it today through their concerns with safety, speed and ease-of-use (see Bijker et al. 1987, 17-50). Accordingly, in practices of digital-DIY, we are concerned to trace users' interpretations of their EICTs, and how these inform the configuration of technologies within the home.

Elements of these approaches come together in actor-network theory, developed by Michel Callon (Callon 1987; Callon 1998) John Law (Law 1987; Law 1992) and Bruno Latour (Latour 1987; Latour 1991; Latour 1996; Latour 2007). Early actor-network studies considered the part that non-human artefacts play in social relations. Particularly important here were Latour's now classic text (1992), in which he describes the delegation of agency from human to non-human in the form of the automatic door-closer (or groom), and the work of Akrich (1992) in which she proposed the notion of technological artefacts becoming "inscribed" with the vision of innovators (and the consequential analysis of the actual use and users described as the "de-inscription of technological objects"). While actor-network theory has been criticized for placing too much emphasis on objects and their designers at the expense of an analysis of their users and their activities (Oudshoorn & Pinch 2003), MacKenzie & Wajcman (1999) point out that actor-network theory's most significant contribution is to re-examine the social: it encourages us to look beyond purely the social and the technological, and consider the heterogeneous aspects of social life – artefacts, systems, social networks, users, policies, economics. For us, actor-network theory is not a theory at all, but a way at looking at the world, that we attempt to engage throughout our approach to digital-DIY.

While STS has largely directed its focus at the broad relationship between "technology" and "the social", material cultural studies take as their starting point the specifics of material objects, and the cultures embedded within and through them. The sociology of material culture has taken its lead from anthropology (Clarke 2001; Miller 2001; Miller 2008; Miller 2009) and considered that material objects, like the social structures and cultures in which they are embedded, are equally worthy of sociological investigation (Dant 1999). As Dant summarizes, material objects ("things", artefacts) are: signs of status and identity; vehicles that carry meaning within and between cultures; bearers of aesthetic value; components of ritual; indicators of lifestyle and identity; [centres] of knowledge and ideas; potentially inalienable; and the focus of discourse about their value (Dant 1999, 38). As Molotch (2005) explains, products, objects, artefacts, "stuff" are enrolled in everyday life in the same way as individuals and organizations are: "Objects (...) sustain social practices just as those practices sustain them." (Molotch 2005, 2) Molotch (2005, 3) also helpfully recognises that change is normal and inevitable, believing that "[t]racing the connections in products can show how the social and the material combine to make, depending on circumstance, both change and stability happen in the world."

Empirical work in material culture studies usefully highlights the place of digital technologies in the home and the inter-connectedness of users and their technologies. Lehtonen's (2003) study of 14 people in Finland, for example, tracked the stages of the "domestication" of home technologies (televisions and mobile phones in particular) and proposed the concept of "trials" – stages of engagement between people, their technologies and their practices, stages during which users are able to determine just how well equipped they are to acquire, install and use and "domesticate" technologies into their everyday life. More recently, Shove et al.'s (2007) study of traditional DIY and digital photography, alongside an analysis of kitchen "renewal", the product design profession and on the social science of plastic (Shove et al. 2007) mirrors the contemporary shift in material culture and our own multi-disciplinary perspective in this chapter, acknowledging the contribution of actor-network theory, domestication theory, and design and human-computer interaction studies. Shove et al. (2007, 10-11). set out to fill what they see as "gaps and cracks that lie between the disciplinary development in sociology, science and technology studies, design research and studies of material culture" through a theoretical and empirical assessment of how "things are appropriated and used and how (...) they make particular social and practical arrangements possible", by studying not just one single artefact but the "stuff of everyday life", by "analyzing and understanding the ongoing dynamics of everyday life" and finally "investigat[ing] the different ways of understanding value, need and utility(...) in daily life." We adopt a similarly broad framework here through which to explore the notional concept of digital-DIY. How are people innovative in digital-DIY practice? What encourages or prevents digital-DIY creativity?

Case studies

The theoretical concerns and the methodological approach for our empirical work have emerged from two pilot studies which are described in this section. The pilot studies are significant and relevant because of their role in revealing the sensitizing concept of digital-DIY. The ethnographies described below form part of what Marcus (1995) might call a "multi-sited ethnography". This form of ethnography acknowledges the role that a number of sites of enquiry have in creating "juxtapositions" allowing for a comparative account of cultures (in our case digital-DIY) to be composed where theoretical or descriptive models do not yet exist. We prefer to consider them as complementary ethnographic methods. Table 1 below describes the basic properties of our study sample:

	Participant, Gender, Age	Occupation & Status	No. of 1-to-1 Recorded Interviews	Technology Tour	Photos	User Mapping
A	Nigel, M, Age 53	Air Traffic Control Engineer. Single. Job location changing in next year	1	1	✔	
B	Martin, M, Age 62	Retired Electronic Engineer. Married. Two children M&F (Aged 40). Retired aged 55	1	1	✔	
C	Morgan, M, Age 68	Retired Bank Manager Married. Two grown-up children and 6 grandchildren. Retired 14 years ago.	1	1	✔	
D	Tim, M, Aged 66	Retired Civil Servant Married. With one stepdaughter and 1 granddaughter. Retired aged 55.	1	1	✔	
E	William, M, Aged 64	Retired Civil Servant Divorced. Living with Partner. Has two children (grown-up) and two stepchildren. Retired Aged 50.	1	1	✔	
F	Philip, M, Aged 40	Lecturer/Researcher (March 2007-May 2007) Separated then Divorced. One child. Downsizing.	0	1	✔	

	Participant, Gender, Age	Occupation & Status	No. of 1-to-1 Recorded Interviews	Technology Tour	Photos	User Mapping
F	Emma, F, Aged 29	Public Service Administrator. (December 2009/May 2010) Single, recently divorced (1 year). New job. No children. Moved home twice in last year. Downsizing. Less household income.	2	1	✔	x

G	Vicky, F, Aged 32	Designer/Lecturer. (Sept 2009/March 2010) Single. Recently separated from partner, in new job and moved home. Upsizing.	2	1	✔	x
H	Jenny, F, Aged 41	Carer/Part-Time Health Worker. (November 2009/July 2010) Divorced. Recently moved home. Job-hunting. 2 children (F aged 8, Male aged 9). Downsizing	2	1	✔	x
I	Ross, M, Aged 36	Sales Director. (March 2009/Sept 2009) Married (to Annabel). Recently moved home to "upsize". Three children (M, aged 3, F aged 5, F aged 7)	2	1	✔	x
J	Annabel, F, Aged 36	Housewife. Married to Ross (above)	2	1	✔	x
K	Alison, F, Aged 34	Part-Time Public Service Administrator. (November 2009/June 2010) Partnership (with Herbie below). Newly-born son, Aged 9 months. Not moving home	2	1	✔	x
L	Herbie, M, Aged 42	Tree-Surgeon. Partnership with Alison (above).	2	1	✔	x
Total Participants: 13						

Table 1: Properties of case studies

In all cases, a qualitative, ethnographic approach was employed in gathering and analyzing data, giving first-hand experience of people's interactions with their home technologies. Our emphasis was on exploring the digital domain in the home and, in particular, how people engaged in digital-DIY activity – and just how "innovative" they were.

Pilot studies

Our research project began as an exploration of how users innovate with the plethora of home EICTs, rather than a specific focus on one technology (Who would have begun an investigation of home EICTs with the intention of finding the "digital projector" at the heart of the home? See Picture 2, below). We began by revisiting Silverstone & Haddon's (1996) domestication theory on user innovation, by taking a closer look at a group of expert computer users. This is a hobbyist group that Haddon (2006) might expect to be those likely to be designing or redesigning ICTs or developing new applications. Indeed, in the past, the group been approached by manufacturers such as Sony and Microsoft as expert users likely to inform product development.

This first study employed the "technology biography" method for gathering data for the reading of everyday objects and situations previously used by Blythe et al. (2002). The technology biography allows the researcher to question participants on their previous history of engagement with home technologies, their current, everyday practice and their aspirations or needs for the future. Such a method is likely to reveal "rich and interesting data" (Blythe et al. 2002, 658). An element of the technology biography was the conduct of a "technology tour", mapping EICTs in the home and talking through their deployment and construction.

Participants in this study were all professional white males, either retired or in full-time employment. They included a working air-traffic control engineer and a retired civil servant, retired electronic engineer, retired bank manager, and a retired senior tax executive respectively. Though each participant had "stabilized" their living conditions, had settled into retirement or in professional employment and were well-established in terms of setting up and configuring their domestic EICTs, the research uncovered a diverse and innovative approach to creative digital-DIY practice. In some cases, this was manifest in a relatively mundane adaption of a coat-hanger, timer-switch and FM radio to create an alarm-clock radio that hung on a chair (see Picture 1). Through the simple reconfiguration of the coat-hanger into an attachment for the radio and the inter-connected use of the electric timer-switch, this user was able to redefine the use of a radio by using it to automatically wake him up in the morning.

Picture 1: "Alarm-clock radio"
Photographs ©Philip Ely

By contrast, a more elaborate example of digital-DIY is in evidence (see Picture 2) where traditional DIY skills were employed to augment digital technology.

Picture 2: Self-made data projector-holder-cum-coffee-table
Photographs ©Philip Ely

In this example, the user had designed, prototyped (left) and constructed (right) a discreet holder for his data projector that could also be used as a coffee table either during (or after) home computer "slide shows". Using his woodturning, marquetry and electronic engineering skills, William was able to integrate the manufactured prosumer (professional/consumer) product into a piece of lounge furniture (Ritzer & Jurgenson 2010)

As an expert group, these users were both sceptical about new (pushed) product innovations, enjoyed developing their own (pulled) innovations and were eager to maintain a level of stability in the digital ecology, but this raised further questions for us. What happens when less "expert" users are faced with uncertainty and change? How important and how difficult is it to work with digital technologies when faced with personal upheaval? What happens to "things" when we move home? As researchers, changes in our own lives give us the opportunity to experience at first-hand what our research informants experience. Ely was himself about to experience moving home and living alone due to marriage break-up. Now, we wondered, what happens when people are *forced* to reconfigure their EICTs through changes in their personal circumstances? When technological artefacts and the home itself become destabilized, how do people digital-DIY? Here was an opportunity to experience digital-DIY from a "native's" perspective (Geertz 2000).

One method for understanding the participant's perspective in sociological research is that of autoethnography. Autoethnography allows the researcher to become, for a short time at least, the centre of research enquiry through reflecting and writing on their personal experiences within a given social situation. One might argue that the act of embedding oneself in the field is part of being an ethnographer (Fielding 1981). However, we distinguish autoethnography here from ethnography by its emphasis on data analysis and interpretation of the *researcher's data as research participant data* collected in the field – including photographs and field notes, continuing with and expanding on the use of the "technology biography". We use and refer to a form of autoethnography that recognises the role of the individual narrative combined with cultural analysis and interpretation (Chang 2008, 46) or an "analytic autoethnography" suggested by Anderson in which one uses "empirical data to gain insight into some broader set of social phenomena than those provided by the data themselves" (2006, 378)

What emerged from the auto ethnography during analysis (Ely & Shed 2007) is that significant life-change (and "moving home" in particular) is full of problems. It is compounded not only by the emotional upheaval involved but also by the ongoing challenges presented by the "siting" of EICT artefacts (alongside those artefacts of a less technologically complex nature), the evaluation and re-evaluation of their use/usefulness, and the material challenges presented by connecting or rewiring. And it isn't just artefacts themselves enrolled in the digital-DIY activity. "Non-users" like neighbours may have a role to play in the use and position of them too, and friends and family may also be enrolled – initially as "non-users" but eventually as users too – giving both helpful and (on occasion) unhelpful advice. The pilot studies therefore identified the most significant activities, networks and relationships involved in the reconfiguration of EICTs, particularly during life-change, and informed the direction and scope of the main user study.

Main study

The main empirical study focuses our attention on digital-DIY during life-change, looking at how the consumption, production and use of digital EICTs are intertwined with the changing lives of householders. We define life-change as the change in circumstances at home brought about by residential move, a new job, the birth of a new baby, the end of a marriage or partnership and/or a combination of these.

Our empirical examination of digital-DIY adopted the same ethnographic and interpretive approach as the pilot studies, with a slight variation in method. The empirical data collection aimed to "co-construct" the user world and their digital-DIY ecologies with the introduction of a "mapping method" drawn from contextual design (Beyer & Holtzblatt 1998) alongside the technology tour and interviews. This method, used in human-computer interaction studies, is used as a way of helping to define so-called "customer-centred systems", and invites participants to draw visual maps of where their digital artefacts are located, how these artefacts are inter-connected, and who the "influencers" (or helpers) in choosing and installing digital technologies are in a social network map drawn by each participant.

While our results are still emerging and are currently in their formative stages, some intriguing themes are beginning to emerge from the data, suggesting a complex and nuanced creativity on the part of the participants involved in digital-DIY.

Inside the home

Our empirical research around the concept of digital-DIY reveals a fluid world of old and new technological artefacts, personal values, individual skills and knowledge, financial resources, social networks, structural societal values and corporate entities, set against a temporal backdrop of the movement of material (non-digital) belongings and life circumstances. It is, as Latour (2005) might say, an *assemblage* of artefacts, manuals, help files, websites and humans, a *collective* of people and their practices, values, tastes and knowledge. Despite this messy world of mundane, everyday innovations there are, nevertheless, clear paths to new ideas and concepts that challenge an otherwise stable theoretical idea of technological development. We outline some of these below.

Capital resources

The financial resources of our participants play an obvious role in affecting the appropriation, objectification, incorporation and conversion of digital technologies in the home. This is evidenced by Emma (F,29), who acknowledges that without money decisions on whether certain home EICTs should be bought are postponed until she can afford to buy them or, in Jenny's (F,41) case that, with the future in mind, bought artefacts have to be seen to be reliable (quality, trustworthy brand names) so that money is well allocated.

When economic capital wealth is limited, users become equally innovative in appropriation. Take, for example, Herbie (M, 42) and Alison (F, 34). Herbie works as a tree surgeon and spends a lot of time on client sites both outdoors and indoors. It is during this time that he is able to spot abandoned technologies (in this case, a PC in a skip) and, with the help of Alison once it is at home, is able to install software (with existing licenses) so that they can use it "for free".

However, economic capital is not the only resource that life-changers need – social capital is important too, and there are two types of social capital that our participants draw upon in a digital home. The first is the kind that is manifest through the exchange of material goods, through "gifting". By the time of our second visit, Herbie has been given an unused Apple Mac by one of his clients, already wealthy enough to virtually give it away. Likewise, Vicky (F, 32), is given an old Bang & Olufsen amplifier that she has inherited from her father. The amplifier is a signifier of her childhood past and though she doesn't use the amplifier (it lies unplugged when we arrive) she is reluctant to give it away. The amplifier has become "inalienable" in the same way that precious gifts in Maori communities are never thrown away (Miller 2009, 67).

Vicky didn't just inherit artefacts – she inherited infrastructures too when she bought her new home, infrastructures that she is less happy with. She inherited electrical and aerial wiring to receive television broadcasts, but was frustrated that these were in the wrong place to suit her needs. She also inherited a number of wires and speakers for a home audio network from her partner in her old home and is reluctant to "rip up" the floorboards to install them in her new home.

The second type of social capital is that of social networks and the knowledge embedded within them. Both immediate familial connections and wider friendship networks support our participants in selecting, installing, repairing and reconfiguring home technologies. Despite holding a great deal of personal knowledge and expertise in electronic consumer goods, sales director Ross (M, 36) nevertheless draws upon his personal and professional networks to help him make decisions about the right laptop or desktop computer to buy. Emma not only calls upon the benefits of an online local recycling network to acquire a second-hand PC, but enrols her brother-in-law ("a bit of a geek") in adding hardware components and installing the software she needs. When things break, or she sees error messages on her screen, he is happily on-call to give over-the-phone advice.

Gender still matters

In all of our cases, differences between the male and female genders are still evident. Men are given the hardware building tasks (Ross, Herbie, Emma's brother-in-law, Vicky's brother-in-law, Jenny's brother) whilst the women concentrate on software (Emma and Alison). Though Vicky likes to attempt to understand the more material, physical acts of repairing and installing that home EICTs require, she has always let the men in her life (ex-partner, brother-in-law, father) take the lead in showing her how to do it first. Annabel sees almost all hardware and software tasks as being Ross's domain, preferring to focus on the children as *"when they break (...) well, boy, you have trouble"* (Annabel). Our sample may be small, but the wider family engagement with digital-DIY reveals gender divisions between fathers and mothers, sisters and brothers.

Digital exclusion

Herbie suffers from electromagnetic hypersensitivity (EHS), symptomized by headaches, irritable behaviour and loss of concentration. As a result, Herbie and Alison's home is wireless free – there are no 3G or wireless-enabled devices allowed in the home. Fortunately, their current neighbour is in his eighties and does not have a broadband wireless connection, otherwise they would have to move home to another remote countryside location. Herbie cannot sit or walk in public spaces (supermarkets, bars, cafes, railway stations) for longer than twenty minutes. Herbie and Alison's lives are dictated by the technical infrastructure around them and they have adapted by using wired internet technologies, computers and musical recording and instruments at home. Herbie confesses that he is dominated by this condition and it has a significant influence on their digital-DIY activities and the technologies they use.

By contrast both Emma and Jenny have chosen, at various moments during the year we have spent in contact with them, to temporarily withdraw themselves from certain internet services (e.g. Facebook), television viewing, or digital music archiving for questions ranging from privacy, to limited time available, to personal prioritisation. Haddon (2004) and Wyatt (2003) have already brought our attention to the discourse around non-users of ICTs and our own study contributes to this debate through examples of digital non-use. Our cases show that some users choose to become *former users*, whilst others have no choice at all.

Discussion

Picture 3: Where the television goes
Photographs ©Philip Ely

The cases across our three studies revealed all different types of user innovation – ways of doing digital-DIY or new material configurations in the home. We mean user innovations here in a broad, "soft" sense (Rogers 1962 [2003], 13) – innovative practice, innovative assemblage or innovative design. We privilege some of these not because of their paradigm-shifting contribution to new product development, but as an example of the everyday mundane ways of *doing* and ways of *building* that is congruent with the world of traditional DIY. Examples include:

• Vicky's use of an old newspaper stuck to the wall of her lounge (Picture 3) indicating the planned position of a new flatscreen television and the use of a radio bought from a DIY retailer as a radio to use during decorating because it was cheap and therefore disposable and less problematic if paint dripped on it.

- Herbie's regular plundering of skips for computer and music recording components and recycling of old computer components in reaction to meeting their needs whilst having limited resources.
- Jenny's (and her two children's) regular use of their digital music players to help themselves go to sleep. Or, the use of games consoles to help "level" and calm her son who suffers from attention-deficit-hyperactivity-disorder (ADHD), contrary to what Jenny believes is a misconception that computer games increase hyperactivity rather than reduce it.

These are not ground-breaking innovations likely to stimulate marketing departments, but softer innovations of the everyday that reveal a digital-DIY world of rich user creativity.

Conclusions

Changes in life circumstances bring about material changes in the home, and we have seen that this is a period during which the movement of people and their belongings is brought to the foreground and is helpfully open to ethnographic enquiry. Our analysis suggests that digital-DIY shares many of the attributes of its traditional (and widely recognised) home improvement equivalent. "Old" and "new" technologies and practices are undeniably linked to changes in social, cultural and economic capital, to user's abilities and knowledge in connecting and reconnecting, and to people's shifting values and priorities. At a time of uncertainty for some and excitement for others, people (users) are both empowered and disempowered by their ability or inability to enrol friends, family, neighbours, helpdesks, manuals, websites, bank accounts, and the technologies themselves, in setting out to meet their needs and desires. Despite the promise of technological progress, the design of products and services (and in particular the interfaces to them), the material "soup" of artefacts, the assumptions of gender and the limits of users' own creativity suggest that being empowered to "do-it-yourself" might not be as easy at it looks.

References

Aipperspach R., Hooker B., Woodruff A. 'The heterogeneous home' Proceedings of UbiComp (2008) pp. 222-231

Akrich, M. 'The de-scription of technical objects' eds. Bijker W. and Law J. Shaping Technology/Building Society, Cambridge, Mass. USA: MIT Press (1992) pp. 205-224

Anderson L. 'Analytic autoethnography' Journal of Contemporary Ethnography 35 (2006) pp. 373-395

Atkinson, P. 'Do it yourself: Democracy and design' Journal of Design History 19 (1) (2006) pp. 1-10

Baker K., Kaul B. 'Using multi-period variables in the analysis of home improvement decisions by home owners' Real Estate Economics 30 (4) (2002) pp. 551-556

Bell G., Blythe M., Sengers P. 'Making by making strange: Defamiliarization and the design of domestic technologies' ACM Transactions on Computer-Human Interaction 12 (2) (2005) pp. 149-173

Berker T., Hartmann M, Punie Y., Ward K. Domestication of Media and Technology Maidenhead: Open University Press (2006)

Beyer, H., Holtzblatt, K. Contextual Design: Defining Customer-centered Systems. San Francisco, Calif.: Morgan Kaufmann (1998)

Bogdon, A.S. 'Homeowner renovation and repair: The decision to hire someone else to do the project' Journal of Housing Economics 5 (1996) pp. 323-350.

Bijker W. Of Bicycles, Bakelites, and Bulbs: Toward a Theory of Sociotechnical Change Cambridge, MA: The MIT Press (1995)

Bijker W., Hughes T.P., Pinch T. The Social Construction of Technological Systems: New Directions in the Sociology and History of Technology Cambridge, MA: The MIT Press (1987)

Blumer H. Symbolic Interactionism: Perspective and Method Englewood Cliffs, N.J.: Prentice-Hall (1969)

Blythe M., Monk A., Park J. 'Technology biographies: Field study techniques for home use product development' SIGCHI Conference on human factors in computing systems: Changing our world, changing ourselves Minneapolis (2002)

Callon M. 'Society in the making: The study of technology as a tool for sociological analysis' eds. Bijker W., Hughes T.P., Pinch T. The Social Construction of Technological Systems: New Directions in the Sociology and History of Technology Cambridge, MA: The MIT Press (1987) pp. 83-103

Callon M. ed. The Laws of the Markets Oxford: Blackwell Publishers / Sociological Review (1998)

Chang H. Autoethnography as Method Walnut Creek Calif.: Left Coast; Oxford: Berg (2008)

Clarke A.J. 'The aesthetics of social aspiration in home possessions: material culture behind closed doors' ed. Miller D. Home Possessions: Material Culture Behind Closed Doors Oxford: Berg (2001) pp. 23-45

Cockburn C. 'The material of male power' Mackenzie D., Wajcman J. eds. The Social Shaping of Technology: How the refrigerator got its hum Milton Keynes: Open University Press (1985) pp. 123-146

Cockburn C. 'Caught in the wheels' Marxism Today (1983) pp. 16-20

Cockburn C., Ormrod S. Gender and Technology in the Making London: Sage (1993)

Dant T. Material culture in the social world: values, activities, lifestyles. Buckingham: Open University Press (1999)

Dourish P., Bell G. 'The Infrastructure of experience and the experience of infrastructure: Meaning and structure in everyday encounters with space' Environmental Planning 34 (3) (2007) pp. 414-430

Ely P., Shed R. eds. 'Single lives, personal spaces: Autoethnography and design for solo living' Not in the Manual: User Interventions in and around the Home Farnham: University College for the Creative Arts (2007)

Fielding N. The National Front London: Routledge and Kegan Paul (1981)

Geertz C. Local Knowledge: Further Essays in Interpretive Anthropology New York: Basic Books (2000)

Gelber, S.M. 'Do-It-Yourself: Constructing, Repairing and Maintaining Domestic Masculinity' American Quarterly 49 (1997) pp. 66-112.

Giddens A. Sociology: A brief but Critical Introduction London: Macmillan Press Ltd. (1986)

Goldstein C. (1998) Do It Yourself: Home improvement in 20th-Century America New York: Princeton Architectural Press (1998)

Haddon L. 'The Innovatory Use of ICTs' Haddon L., Mante E., Sapio B., Kommonen K.H., Fortunati L., Kant A. eds. Everyday Innovators: Researching the Role of Users in Shaping ICTs Netherlands: Springer (2006)

Haddon, L. Information and Communication Technologies in Everyday Life. Oxford: Berg (2004)

Kirk D., Sellen A., Harper R., Wood K. 'Understanding videowork' CHI 2007, San Jose, CA (2007)

Kline, R., Pinch T. 'The social construction of technology' eds. Mackenzie D., Wajcman J. The Social Shaping of Technology: How the Refrigerator Got its Hum Milton Keynes: Open University Press (1999) pp. 113-115

Latour B. Reassembling the Social: An Introduction to Actor-network-theory New York: Oxford University Press (2005)

Law, J. 'Technology and heterogeneous engineering: The case of Portuguese expansion' eds. Bijker, W., Hughes, T.P., Pinch, T. Social Construction of Technological Systems Cambridge, Mass.: MIT Press (1987) pp. 111-134.

Law, J., Callon, M. 'The life and death of an aircraft: A network analysis of technical change' Shaping Technology/Building Society: Studies in Sociotechnical Change, Bijker, W., Law, J., Cambridge, Mass, USA: MIT Press, (1992) pp. 21-52

Lehtonen T. K. 'The domestication of new technologies as a set of trials' Journal of Consumer Culture 3 (3) pp. 363-385

MacKenzie, D, Wajcman, J, eds. The Social Shaping of Technology: How the Refrigerator Got its Hum Milton Keynes: Open University Press (1999)

Marcus G. 'Ethnography in/of the world system: The emergence of multi-sited ethnography' Annual Review of Anthropology 24 (1995) pp. 95-117

Miller D. ed. Home Possessions: Material Culture behind Closed Doors Oxford: Berg (2001)

Miller D. The Comfort of Things Cambridge: Polity (2008)
Miller D. Stuff Cambridge: Polity Press (2009)
Mintel. DIY Review UK: June 2010 (2010)
Molotch, H. L. Where Stuff Comes from: How Toasters, Toilets, Cars, Computers and Many Other Things Come to be as They are. New York ; London: Routledge, (2003)
Murphy J., Kjeldskov J., Howard S., Shanks G., Hartnell-Young E. 'The Converged Appliance: "I love it ... but I hate it"' OZCHI 2005 Canberra (2005)
Oudshoorn N., Pinch T. 'How users and non-users matter' How Users Matter: The Co-construction of Users and Technology Cambridge, MA: MIT Press (2003) pp. 1-25
Ritzer G., Jurgenson N. 'Production, consumption, prosumption: The Nature of capitalism in the age of the digital "prosumer"' Journal of Consumer Culture 10 (2) (2010) pp. 13-36
Rogers E.M. Diffusions of Innovations (5th edition) New York: Free Press [1962] (2003)
Shklovski I., Mainwaring S. 'Exploring technology adoption and use through the lens of residential mobility' Proceedings of CHI 2005 Portland, Oregon: ACM (2005)
Shove E., Hand M., Ingram J., Watson M. The Design of Everyday Life Oxford: Berg (2007)
Silverstone R., Haddon L. 'Design and the domestication of information and communication technologies: Technical Change and Everyday Life' eds. Mansell R., Silverstone R. Communication by Design: The Politics of Information and Communication Technologies Oxford: Oxford University Press (1996)
Silverstone, R., Hirsch, E., Consuming Technologies: Media and Information in Domestic Spaces London, New York, NY: Routledge (1992)
Schwartz Cowan R. 'The industrial revolution in the home' eds. MacKenzie D., Wajcman J. The Social Shaping of Technology: How the Refrigerator Got its Hum Milton Keynes: Open University Press (1985)
Taylor A.S., Swan L. 'Artful systems in the home' CHI 2005 Portland, Oregon: ACM Press (2005)
Woolgar, S., 'Configuring the user: the cause of usability trials' ed. Law, J. A Sociology of Monsters Sociological Review Monograph 38 London: Routledge, (1991)
Wyatt S. 'Non-users also matter: The construction of users and non-users of the internet' eds. Oudhoorn N., Pinch T.J. How Users Matter: The Co-construction of Users and Technologies Cambridge, Mass.: The MIT Press (2003) pp. 67-79

Eva K. Törnqvist

In Search of Elks and Birds: Two Case Studies on the Creative Use of ICT in Sweden

Introduction

The aim of this chapter is to understand how users collectively function as innovators when they use already established information and communication technology (ICT) in creative ways. This will be done by trying to answer following questions:

- How do the community members experience the use of ICT?

- How is ICT used and developed by the community members to provide and share information?

- How can ICT be a resource and/or a restriction?

The chapter will describe two case studies that are both about mobile recreational activities that take place in nature-namely elk hunting and bird watching. In the first case, Svenska Jägareförbundet (the Swedish Hunting Association) has introduced a new way of using cellular phones during elk hunts. The second case, which will be presented in greater detail, describes how bird watchers have found new ways of sharing information among themselves regarding where to spot rare birds.

Theoretical framework and methods

This study is based on three main concepts: structural theory, communities of practice, and pockets of local order. All three concepts share the fact that they state that structures and actors can never be seen as two separate entities. Structures, communities and pockets of local orders are created, maintained and transformed by the individuals' actions.

The model showing the connection between social structure, sense-making and practices used in this study is based on Giddens' structural theory (see Chapter 1 for a detailed presentation of the model). Giddens points out that even though people are not completely free to choose their actions and that their knowledge and competencies are in some way limited, it is they who ultimately create the structures of society and are responsible for developing them. In other words, we choose what to do but within given limits and in relation to certain specific conditions.

An organisation (such as the Swedish Hunting Association or the bird watchers) is a social construction that consists of different constellations of practices (Wenger 1998). The people engaged in the practice negotiate their own activities, even if these activities are sometimes responses to regulations. The communities of practices are created, developed and dissolved through learning. Practices also create boundaries, which may be the same as in an institution, but not necessarily so. The boundaries are especially interesting because they are resources for learning—they give rise to scope for new interplay between experience and competence. The process of being engaged in a practice involves the entire human experience, including language, tools, documents, symbols, roles, regulation, and so on. While all of these can be visible, just as important are unspoken norms, embedded understandings, tacit agreements and the like. Wenger points out that a practice involves acting and knowing, manual and mental, concrete and abstract.

A pocket of local order, or PoLO, is a concept used in time geography and resembles communities of practice, although the focus lies on time space. Time and space always come together in order to simultaneously keep track of both spatial and temporal dimensions of material geographical events. In order to understand a process, it is important not to take it out of its context. It has a certain duration in time and it takes place in a physical location in time space. In this time space, goal-oriented enterprises consisting of different projects take place in a certain order. PoLOs are organised to facilitate the performance of the projects, which are not only connected to individuals but also to groups, organisations and companies. The individuals taking part in the project activities have different roles and different authorities. Resources (enablers) and restrictions (constraints) are also important components in the PoLO, yet precisely what a resource or restriction, respectively, constitutes in accomplishing an activity or project is not given, as this can differ between different people taking part in the project, but also over time. Different personnel skills and competencies can give rise to different perceptions of what represents a resource or restriction, respectively. In the same way, technological changes may alter the conditions (Hägerstrand 1985; Ellegård et al. 1997; Lenntorp 1998).

The methods used to collect the empirical data were participatory observation, interviews with members of the two communities, and text studies. The studied texts include web pages and manuals.

The creative user

Both of these cases show that the social context plays a significant role in the introduction and use of ICT and that the development of the technology, its use, and new ways of using it takes place in the context of the interaction between individuals. In the first case examined, a producing user (the hunting association and its web editor) starts and in some way monitors the development of the technology. In the second case, both producing users and everyday users (different bird watchers with different levels of technological knowledge and competencies) are active in the adaptation and development of the technology during different stages of the process. Both cases show that it is a process of innovation, which could be enabling or constraining at the same time, depending on which virtual pocket of local order (Törnqvist 2004) the user belongs to.

Close encounter with a bull elk

The annual elk hunt during the autumn is a significant event that engages a huge number of people (non hunters included). Hunters can share their hunting experiences through the homepage of the Swedish Hunting Association (which has approximately 180,000 members).

Since autumn 2007, it has been possible to upload movie clips to the association's reviewed and monitored web page. Sometimes clips are removed for ethical reasons or because the content is not deemed to be interesting to the public (e.g., "No one is interested in looking at the top of a spruce fir for five minutes") (Lewander 2008). The service has proved popular; since it launched, the web page has had roughly 530,000 visits. At most, the web page has about 5,000 visits per month (for instance, during the elk hunt), although the average is 2,000. Altogether, total viewing time is about 11,500 hours. In 2008, 61 movie clips were uploaded to the homepage, with a length of anywhere between a few seconds to almost five minutes (although the recommendation is that the clip not be longer than two minutes) (Svenska Jägareförbundet 2008) (figure 1).

Top 10 Movies
1. Crow hunt in Ingarp
2. Rulle confronts a badger
3. Close encounter with a bull elk
4. Nappe confronts a cow (elk) with a calf (elk)
5. Calf elk
6. Weasel
7. Small shot towards roe deer
8. Allured male goat
9. Fox drive in Gotland
10. Confronted wild boars

Figure 1: The most popular movie clips (Svenska Jägareförbunder 2008)

The service has become so popular that the Swedish Hunting Association launched a new project during the elk hunt of 2008. The project meant that hunters could share their hunting experiences directly from the forest, using cellular phones and the internet. This new service was a joint initiative of the company that had developed the technology that makes it possible to upload movie clips from almost any cellular phone model, together with the web editor at the Swedish Hunting Association who was responsible for the campaign. The editor said that *"(...) it feels right to be able to offer (...) a technology that makes it possible to upload the files directly from the forest, as well as to see what other hunters have succeeded in catching, in pictures, directly on the cellular phone."* However, she also said that the campaign was launched *"(...) mostly for fun"*. (Lewander 2008). The hunters could also check hunting, sunrise and sunset times via their cellular phone. A follow-up survey (not yet published) was conducted after the 2008 elk hunt in order to, among other things, find out what needs the hunters have for future development.

According to the web editor, some early findings of the survey are that hunters do not seem to be interested in using this new opportunity, and that a total of only 10-15 movie clips were shared. One reason may be cost. Many do not know the price of the service, and are afraid that it would be too costly to use. Another potential cause may be the main reason they are in the forest in the first place - to concentrate on the hunt. In other words, they are focused on prioritising their own activities and not the real-time experiences of others.

I have seen a (rare) bird!

Yet another mobile outdoor activity is bird watching. This case shows how people that are interested in bird watching have changed the way they share information when a certain interesting species of bird has been spotted.

Bird watching is like hunting - a social activity that consists of several more or less different components. One of these components is the wish to share information that makes it possible for other bird watchers to observe exceptional species. Another component, involving a more exclusive group, has taken the form of the Club300 (C3) organization, which from the start has consisted of people who have independently identified 300 different species of birds within Sweden. The organisation was created in 1984 and was formed as an exclusive club for "species hunters".

During the birds' spring and autumn migrations many bird watchers, both those with a more general interest and the species-chasing Club300 members, gather on the island of Öland in the south of Sweden. Due to the large number of people involved, many bird observations occur and there is a mutual need both to share information about the birds spotted and to take part in other peoples' experiences. Indeed, having made the trip to experience the migration, no one would want to fail to observe an exceptional bird, for example, sitting just 500 metres away.

Disseminating information on the observation of a rare species used to take a relatively long time, since this usually happened through personal contacts or with the aid of a news item in the radio or newspapers. Understandably, time was an issue and the process was more about informing the general public that certain species had been seen and less about sharing information that was vital to others so they could take advantage of the opportunity and actually see the bird themselves.

Some twenty years ago, those wanting to share or take part in this kind of information had to be physically present at the specific geographic location at Öland, where *a piece of paper* was posted on a sign with notes on the observation. Apart from the species that had been seen, the notes could also include dates, times and whether the observed bird moved and, if so, in which direction. Sometimes there also was a comment about the gender and age of the observed bird. There were no requirements for how the comments should be formulated as this notice board had been created spontaneously and was managed informally. In order to obtain this information, the only requirement was that a person had to be interested in and know about the paper's existence and where to find it.

In 1985, Club300 established *an answering machine* service that disseminated the same information as the paper, which was managed by a Club300 volunteer living in Öland. This development meant that the requirement to be physically present to obtain information about observations had been eliminated. Those who knew about the service could now sit at home and obtain information from across the entire country, and not just a limited geographical area. The information became more updated over time and also more detailed, although the reporting was limited to rare species sightings. This form of information dissemination became so popular that a number of problems arose. The tapes in the answering machine often broke down due to frequent use, and even the telephone traffic in and out of the small village where the answering machine was located was blocked when a special, exceptional bird had been observed. This problem was dealt with gradually, by creating a wireless connection to a central hub in a bigger town and by using several answering machines for separate geographical areas (Samuelsson 2006).

About ten years later, new technology came into use; not only could the bird's song be heard, a "beep" from the pockets of bird watchers was also audible. This beep made the bird watchers more or less simultaneously grab for their *pagers,* which displayed a group of numbers. They then opened a small booklet, which they used to translate the numbers into a specific bird, place and time.

What had happened was that, during the autumn of 1996, the original paper note and the answering machine was now being complemented by pagers. On the pagers' displays, a combination of numbers replaced the typed and spoken word. RiXlarm, as the new service was called, was a system in which a code composed of numbers was sent to a pre-programmed pager. Unlike the answering machine service, which was available to all bird watchers, RiXlarm was a service exclusive to Club300 members, who could buy these special pre-programmed pagers and thereafter subscribe to reports from the geographical areas of their choice (Club300a 2008).

When a special bird had been observed, the observer sent out the information to every pager through a tone-dialing telephone. Originally, the code that was sent out (which was called an "alarm"), only consisted of 5 digits symbolising which species had been observed and in which geographical area. This later became a 20-digit code when the demand for detailed information increased.

A code on a pager's display could thus look like the following (figure 2):

| 32710124199006519999 |

Figure 2: Code on a pager's display

In plain language, this means that it is an exceptional (3) bird, a Terek Sandpiper (271) observed in Skåne (01) and, more precisely, at the location Sandön (241). The bird is stationary (0) and the observer is certain (0) and that the bird is adult (6) and is <500 meters South (51) of Sandön. Charlie X (9999) spotted and reported the bird.

The pager system was in use until 2005-2006. Half a year earlier, however, a new cellular phone-based system - the Club300 Bird Message Service, or C3 BMS - had been introduced. Today, the cellular phone is replacing both the paper on the road sign and the pagers, and the amount of information at hand has increased even further. In order to access the information, one must be a Club300 member (the requirement of having identified 300 species no longer exists, only a membership fee is required), subscribe to the service, and have a cellular phone that meets certain technical requirements. Below are figures of the way a bird alarm can look on the cellular phone's display. Figure 3 shows a display organised according to geographical area and then the species, and Figure 4 shows a display organised by species and then the geographical area. In both cases, it is possible to choose between the observations of the day, the previous day and earlier observations. Figure 5 shows the additional information available under the second observation shown in Figure 4 (Club300b 2008).

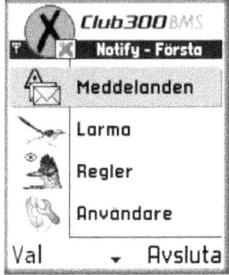

Figure 3: Message display (Club300a)

Figure 4: Todays obervations by geografical area. (Club300a)

Figure 5: Detailed information concerning one of the observations. (Club300a)

Connecting to the internet via a cellular phone means that it is also possible to combine different applications and internet sites to obtain GPS coordinates, maps, driving directions, pictures, sound clips and more information about the species. Many internet sites are created and maintained by individual bird watchers.

Trends in media development

How, then, would future developments look? The company Kairos Future has been commissioned by Radio-och TV-verket (the Swedish Radio and Television Authority) to analyse current media trends and their impact on tomorrow's media (Radio- och TV-verket 2007).

With the breakthrough of the internet, media range has reached enormous levels; among other things, this means that it has become difficult to navigate the large amount of information available to users. The ability to see and, more importantly, to understand the big picture is no longer an option. This means that users face new challenges, but also new possibilities for using Gidden's terminology of constraints and enabler (Giddens 1984).

Our increased ability to download and time shift information also creates greater possibilities for a more personally-organised media consumption. In everyday life, a significant part of the population commutes daily between home and the workplace, and travelling for leisure has also increased. Different forms of mobile media that we can take with us when we move around are expected to have a stronger impact on when and how we use media. Examples include portable media libraries and on-demand television and broadcasts to cellular phones. Kairos analysts also believe that almost all media will be available everywhere and on all platforms. Different platforms have different weaknesses and strengths and therefore innovative ideas will be needed on how they can best be used.

Indeed, the analysts believe that the power of the media will be displaced from the producer towards the "end" user, while intermediaries such as television channels and record companies decrease in importance. This is due to the fact that the content manufacturers can now reach the end users directly. In addition, users can reach each other directly and act both as transmitters and receivers of information. (Il)legal file sharing is an example of the latter. Kairos Future believes that it is more than plausible that consumers will increasingly monitor, combine and transform their media. This will lead to micro-media (i.e., media that can be adapted to and for individual users). The development of media does not mean that mass media will disappear, but the analysts believe that the users/consumers will alternate between a sequential mass media flow and a self-elected micro-media selection that is personal and arbitrary. Sometimes, one will want to choose and sometimes one will want help choosing; this relationship creates requirements for technology and infrastructure that must support both the active and the passive, either as an "all-in-one" solution or as infrastructure that functions in a parallel way.

The findings from the two case studies support the future observations presented by the Kairos media analysts with regard to, among other things, mobile solutions. Both of the presented cases demonstrate that heavy demands are made on the infrastructure, not only in cities but also in sparsely populated areas—since hunting and bird watching mostly take place outside population centres where one could expect to see developed infrastructure. That the chance to be a content producer for the everyday user and the opportunities to combine and adopt different media according to one's own choosing appeals to users is also supported by the empirical material from the cases.

Lessons learned

What, then, is the users' role in relation to innovation? It is important to study the role of the user now that new trends and developments in today's information society influence and are influenced to a greater extent by users, such as through different convergences and Web 2.0 technologies. Previous research on micro-level (i.e., everyday user) practices has shown that the users are creative in terms of fitting ICT into their activities or using them to find solutions to the everyday problems that they already encounter (Toumi 2005; Dourish 2006). Everyday users constitute approximately 90% of micro-level use. Other levels (using producers and producing users) (Hinchcliffe 2007) are different "manufacturers" and can be compared with Rogers' concept (Rogers 1983) of innovators and early adopters. This does not mean that members of this group (the everyday user) are passive users of pre-defined technologies; on the contrary, they collectively create the context and the consequences of and for these uses (Toumi 2005). Therefore, according to Haddon there is no "end user" per se, since there is a permanent, ongoing process of deconstruction and reconstruction (Haddon 2003).

As the title of this chapter states, it is not a product that constitutes innovation in the two described cases but rather the use of already existing devices that are innovative. It is in the process of sharing and not just disseminating information and, in a way, keeping contact with friends and like-minded people that innovation occurs. ICT is a tool for supporting the two communities.

Pocket of local order (Hägerstrand 1985) is a concept used in time geography; although it resembles communities of practice (Wenger 1998) the focus lies on time space. A process has a certain duration in time and takes place in a physical location—a specific location in time space. In this time space, goal-oriented enterprises consisting of different projects take place in a certain order. These projects are not only connected to individuals but also to groups, organisations and companies. PoLOs are located in time space and are organised to facilitate the performance of the projects, such as bird watching and elk hunting. The individuals taking part in the projects by performing activities have different roles with different authorities.

Resources and restrictions are also important components in the pocket of local order, but what constitutes a resource or respectively, a restriction is not a foregone conclusion. It can differ between different people taking part in a pocket of local order but also over time. Both psychological and physical tools are seen as structuring resources and are used to interpret and arrange components in new situations. Naturally, skill and competencies as well as technological changes can alter these conditions.

Communication is central in communities of practices and pockets of order. When members of an organisation talk to each other and with people outside the organisation, they are not only communicating, but also constructing the organisation (or the network) through the process and substance of the communication. It can be said that a network is created, maintained and activated through communication. As different technologies are developed, information flow increases and makes it possible to reach more people over greater distances. This, in turn, results in a larger number of people reacting to, for example, a bird alarm. Through this technological change the PoLO develops into a virtual pocket of local order (Törnqvist 2004).

The narrative of the hunt

The reasons for users' ambivalence towards implementing this special technology (downloading, uploading and taking part in others' movie clips directly in the forest during the hunt) depend on several different factors. One of the contributory factors is that we as individuals, or as members of a community, experience reality differently and therefore act differently when we act to create it. The original initiative for the experiment did not come from hunters or their association. Rather, it came from a company that was external to the community of practice and which had little or no experience with the structures that create the hunter community.

Narratives create and maintain these structures and have a crucial function when it comes to how we understand and handle our lives (in this case the activity of hunting). A conversation researcher has described this in the following way:

"When the elk hunt begins the eternal narrative about it comes to new life. It is developed around bonfires and in the car's heat during journeys or at the dinner table's togetherness. In the hunter's voices the common storytelling echoes of the ancient statement that has been given birth around the very the first bonfires and during all times is also nourished by the group's listening. The statement of the hunt is ancient and collective and at the same time it is private and always renewed." (Adelsvärd 1996)

The light from the cellular phone's display cannot replace the light generated by the bonfire, since it is not during the hunt itself that the hunters share their thoughts, feelings and experiences. It is later, when they do not need to focus on the pursuit that the storytelling and sharing becomes an important function. Within this context/structure, the technology does not create an arena for social and cultural production, which is a criterion for innovative use (Toumi 2005).

To not only film an event but also to connect oneself to the internet and upload the movie requires both concentration and time. This means that the hunter has to make a choice-either to hunt for animals or to take movies to share with others. The size of the cellular phone's screen can also be of importance; since it is small, it can be difficult to see pictures in certain light, which contributes to its limitations in mediating the hunters' nature experiences.

Thus, the possibility of uploading movies did not become an enabling function but rather a constraint, since it did not answer the needs of the hunters during the hunt. In their opinion, it had no useful function and therefore only a few used the technology. On the other hand, functions that would better support the practice of hunting, such as the abovementioned posting of hunting, sunrise and sunset times, would work as enablers.

From paper to cellular phone

When it comes to the innovation of the information process among bird watchers, other conditions helped it succeed. Most notably, it was initiated and developed by the members themselves and according to their needs. Moreover, the use of ICT took place in harmony with existing structures.

The pocket of local order allowed "new" technologies to be introduced - in this case, the pager and later the cellular phone—removing the need for physical vicinity, or being "at the right place at the right time". The time room expands and the pocket of local order becomes virtual. The technology became a resource that was enabling, but only for those who met the requirement of membership of Club300. Those who did not meet the requirement or did not want to become a member had limited or no access to information that was previously free of charge. For these individuals, the technology became a restriction or a constraint in their attempts to access the information.

The use of the pager, however, showed that there were a large number of people who were willing to pay for the information. Since there was a commercial opportunity to charge for the information, the requirement of having identified 300 species in order to become a Club300 member was dropped, and the entry criteria for the community of practice were changed. Today, it is not unusual for someone to become a Club300 member just to access the information. The information is once again accessible to those who have the ability to buy a specific model of cellular phone.

Summary

To use Hinchcliffe's terminology (Hinchcliffe 2007), in the first case the producing users, the Swedish Hunting Association, started and in certain ways monitored the development, implementation and use of ICT. In the bird watcher case, both producing users (the bird watchers with knowledge of the different technologies' possibilities) and everyday users (the "common" bird watcher) were active at different stages of the process of developing how the bird watcher community uses ICT as a tool.

Micro-level users (the everyday users) are not innovators in the sense that they (mainly) produce an artifact, but they expand the use of existing equipment and resources with which they are already familiar. The innovations come to life in the users' practices, since the tools are not only innovative but also used differently in new or specific contexts.

Last but not least, both cases illustrate that creative use takes place within larger systems and institutions. The social context plays a significant role in the introduction, development and use of ICT, and partly dictates whether it is going to be successful or not. The cases also show that the implementation and use of ICT takes place in the interaction between individuals in social communities of practice. A company that is external to the community cannot successfully start an innovative process without knowledge of the social and cultural structures in which the innovation will be used.

References

Interview

Lewander Interview in 2008 with Madeleine Lewander, web editor at Svenska Jägareförbundet.

Publications

Adelsvärd V. 'Att förstå en berättelse – eller historien om älgen' (To understand a narrative – or the story about the elk) Stockholm: Brombergs Förlag (1996)
CLUB300a: 'BMS manual v. 1.4x' http://www.club300.se/files/docArchive/C3BMS-S60-UIQ-Manual.pdf
CLUB300b: 'C3 BMS Larmsystemet för fåglar' (C3 BMS The alert System for Birds) http://www.club300.se/C3BMS/Default.aspx 2008-11-29
Dourish P. Implications for Design Montreal: CHI 2006 Proceedings

Ellegård K., Nordell K. Att byta vanmakt mot egenmakt. Självreflektion och förändringsarbete i rehabiliteringsprocesser.(To change powerlessness against own power. Self reflexion and change in rehabilitation processes Stockholm: Johansson och Skyttemo förlag (1997)

Giddens A. The Constitution of Society: Outline of the Theory of Structuration Cambridge: Polity Press (1984)

Haddon L. 'What is innovatory use? A thinkpiece' eds. Haddon L., Mante-Meijer E., Sapio B., Kommenon K-H., Fortunati L., Kant A. The Good, the Bad and the Irrelevant: The User and the Future of Information and Communication Technologies Conference Proceedings Helsinki (1-3, September 2003)

Hägerstrand T. Time-Geography: Focus on the corporeality of Man, Society, and Environment (Reprinted from The Science and Praxis of Complexity, New York: The United Nations University) (1985)

Hinchcliffe D. Building Web 2.0: AjaxSoa and the Web as a Computing Platform London: Addison-Wesley (2007)

Lenntorp B. 'Orienteringsanvisning i ett forskningslandskap' (Orientation directions in a research landscape) eds. Gren M., Hallin P.O. Svensk kulturgeografi. En exkursion inför 2000-talet. Lund, Studentlitteratur (1998)

Radio- och tv-verket: 'Medieutveckling 2007' (Media Developments 2007) http://www.rtvv.se/_upload/infomatrial/25-1303672584874491230625.pdf

Rogers E.M. Diffusion of innovations New York: Free Press (1983)

Samuelsson P. Ser du tärnan i det blå? En studie av föreställningar om galenskap inom Club300 (Do you see tern in the blue? A study of attitudes about folly within Club300) Avdelningen för Socialantropologi Sociologiska institutionen vid Lunds universitet (2006)

Svenska jägarförbundet Välkommen till Jägareförbundets mobila portal http://www.jagareforbundet.se/mobil/ 2008-12-11

Törnqvist E.K. 'Bland grynnor och blindskär. Kommunikation, lärande och teknik i samarbetsprojektet Sjöräddning' (In shallow waters and among submerged rocks: Communication, learning and technology in the cooperation project Swedish Maritime Search and Rescue) Linköping Studies in Art and Science, no 297 (2004)

Toumi I. 'Beyond user-centric models of product creation' eds. Haddon L., Mante E., Sapio B., Kommenon K-H., Fortunati L., Kant A. Everyday Innovators: Reaching the Role of Users in Shaping ICT's. Springer (2005)

Wenger E. Communities of Practice: Learning, Meaning, and Identity Cambridge (1998)

Levente Szekely and Agnes Urban

On Innovators and Early Adopters: Incentives for and Obstacles to Internet Use

Introduction

The communication and media landscape of the world's developed countries have changed a great deal in recent years. Technological deployment has resulted in the introduction of new gadgets and services, and changed consumption patterns. Research into these changes in the communication and media sectors has typically focused on the behaviour of innovators and early adopters. These segments are well covered by the diffusion of broadband services: in Hungary almost half of the population uses the internet. According to Roger's terminology, it borders on the early majority and late majority groups. Less research has been carried out into these segments, although the differences between the pioneers and the majority are clear.

In the case of innovators and early adopters, technology orientation itself can explain the intensive use of the internet and other communication tools. Finding the usage motivation in the case of the majority is more challenging: attractive services or availability of certain information can be more important than attitude.

The aim of our research is to find the incentives for and obstacles to internet use. We do not focus purely on the innovators as defined by Rogers, but instead use this term in a broader sense. Internet use today is highly influenced by age, education and social status. Older or less educated people use the internet less, so people in these segments who become users can be considered innovators in a certain sense, even if they are linked to the majority groups described in Rogers' theory. The main aim of the research is to identify what motivates people to use the internet and why various groups are resistant to such use. The incentives and obstacles can vary a great deal, depending on age or social status. The research was carried out using qualitative and quantitative methods.

Theoretical background

The trend in the diffusion of new products and services can be explained by Rogers's well-known S-curve. According to this theory, which was developed in the sixties and since then has been validated at various points in time, the formation of a consumer group that uses a new service tends to be slow for most innovations. As the group reaches the critical mass (mathematically: the point of inflexion of the diffusion curve), market expansion accelerates, and more and more people join the group of consumers.

Looking at the acceptance of new products and services, five more or less well-differentiable groups of consumers can be distinguished: innovators, early adopters, early majority, late majority and laggards. The categories are characterized by different socio-economical status, different personalities and different communication behaviour.

Yet the success of innovations and the rate of diffusion not only depend on consumer attitude but also on the characteristics of the product or service in question. Rogers identified five factors that have a central role in the diffusion of innovations: relative advantage, compatibility, complexity, trialability, and observability (Rogers 2003).

Considering the characteristics of broadband services, their relative advantage, i.e. the wide range of interactive services they offer, is evident. Compatibility and complexity are a different matter, as one of the factors hindering development may very well be the fact that many consumers find using it much too complicated. Also, the nature of the experience differs from that provided by traditional media and communication modes. User-friendliness and simplicity are therefore considered fundamental requirements in the interactive services market. Theoretically, there are no worries about trialability, since consumers can gradually familiarise themselves with the new services without any significant negative consequences. Above a certain level of market penetration, observability may not be a problem either.

According to Rogers (1986), three characteristics should be considered when dealing with new communication technologies. One is the critical mass, as the value of any communication service is actually created by the fact that others use it as well. A frequently quoted example is the phone: the practicality of this device was virtually zero for the first owners up until the time they could reach others on the phone. Behind this approach is the network effect, known from microeconomics, which states that the utility of any product or service increases exponentially in proportion to the number of its users. This is only partially true for interactive media services, as the number of users does not directly influence the utility perceived by others. What we have here is a kind of indirect effect: with the number of users growing, more and more actors invest in content and infrastructure development, and thus more and more services become available. Due to Web 2.0 and P2P (peer-to-peer), the services network effect has appeared in content services, too: more and more people use these applications, and the quantity of content is growing.

Second, it should be emphasised that the industry in question is characterized by tool technologies. The techniques can be applied in a variety of ways to diverse situations. The popular applications are shaped by consumer habits and by re-discovering the devices themselves. In regard to the internet, researchers mainly focused on the substitutability of television and newspapers in the beginning, the popularity of chat and forums, while social networking only became apparent somewhat later. The popularity of SMS in mobile telephony was a surprise, as well. Accordingly, even though the development of info-communication technologies is the result of well-planned business and engineering activities, the decision as to whether a specific service becomes popular or not rests with the people. In any case, the resistance to certain devices (e.g. the computer) directly influences the use of info-communication services.

The third factor to be considered is that in the case of info-communication technologies, the acceptance of innovations and the mere fact that they are consumed is less significant than the intensity of use. According to Rogers, the dependent variable of related studies should not reflect the decision about whether to use a product or not but rather the extent of its use. Livingstone (2002) follows the same approach when stating that policy programmes should not primarily focus on providing access to these services but rather on motivating people to use them – which is significantly more problematic. Galacz & Sagvari (2008) found that quantitative indicators of the digital divide should be replaced by qualitative measures. Access in itself does not say a lot; dimensions of use are more interesting: why and how someone uses the internet. At the theoretical point of 100 percent diffusion rate the digital divide can still remain, since there are differences in usage.

Comprehensive research on the adoption of interactive services based on the diffusion model by Rogers has not yet been completed, yet some technologies have already been researched. Research in recent years has concentrated more on the factors determining adoption or non-adoption.

Lin (1998) studied the diffusion of home personal computers. His results showed that adopters, likely adopters and non-adopters constitute well-distinguishable groups according to demographic structure, media consumption characteristics and the ownership of communication technologies. In line with other research, it was concluded that while there is a relationship between television viewing and home PC use, there is no significant relationship in regard to other media (newspaper, radio).

A study on the spreading of fax and audio-information services confirmed the importance of variables related to personal communication. Life quality explained acceptance to a moderate degree, but variables related to media usage did not yield a significant result. Social indicators could only be used to predict acceptance in the case of the fax and not for audio information services (Neuendorf et al. 1998).

Research carried out by Atkin et al. (1998) on the diffusion of the internet confirmed the existence of demographic differences between adopters and non-adopters. Results proved that technological orientation plays a decisive role in acceptance.

Goldfarb & Prince (2008) found that internet access and usage depend on income and education. Interestingly, while income and education positively correlate with adoption, they negatively correlate with time spent online. A likely explanation is that low-income individuals spend more time online because of fewer opportunities to enjoy other leisure activities due to prohibitive costs.

Broos & Roe (2006) analyzed the internet use habits of Flemish adolescents. They proved that, in addition to socio-demographic factors, psychological concepts also contribute to explaining differential levels of computer and internet use. Although the digital divide is often seen as a generational phenomenon, it seems to be more complex. Moreover, significant differences were found on the basis of gender, as even this factor was previously considered significant in older age groups.

Research on so-called computer anxiety can also explain the non-adoption or the cautious use of new technology. It can be defined as a fear felt by individuals when using computers or even considering the use of a computer. Computer anxiety is correlated with age and educational level, but it can be also measured among young and highly qualified users (Beckers et al. 2008). Beckers & Schmidt (2003) emphasized the role of first computer experience(s) in the development of computer anxiety. The initial feeling has a long lasting effect on the attitude to computers and providing friendly, relaxed and professional support to first-time users contributes to a positively rated first experience.

The technology acceptance model (TAM) is a widely used theoretical framework for studying the adoption of a new technology. The internal variables in the TAM are: perceived ease of use (PEU), perceived usefulness (PU), attitude toward use (A) and behavioural intention to use (BI). (Davis 1989). Further empirical research validated the model, and some revisions also occurred in the literature, but the core ideology of the model remained unchanged. Turner et al. (2010) indicated that it is important to measure actual use objectively, as there is a difference in the relationship between the TAM variables and subjective and objective measures of actual technology use. They found that relatively few papers considered objective measures of actual use and when they did, sample sizes were too small. Their paper proved that PU, and particularly PEU, are not as good at predicting actual technology use as BI and associations were lower for objectively measured technology use than for subjectively measured use. In the case of the model, they point out that perceived use and actual use are not the same. Purkayastha (2009) found that Perceived Ease of Accessibility (PEA) also determined the adoption of a product or service.

Internet and computer usage in Hungary

We analyzed the digital divide in Hungary based on the data of World Internet Project (2001-2007). The World Internet Project (WIP) was initiated in 1999, by UCLA and the NTU School of Communications Studies in Singapore. WIP focuses on the social effects of the internet among internet users and non-users. Sample sizes were sufficiently large (about 5,000 respondents) as to enable the in-depth analysis of internet users. For the first three years (2001-2003), it was a panel sample (i.e. our interviewers tried to ask the same respondents every year). However, sample additions were also made in order to overcome the "panel aging" effect. Cross-sectional surveys have been conducted since 2004. The sample was prepared by a multiple-stage, proportionally layered probabilistic sampling method. Data collection was conducted according to address listing, with a decreasing sample method. Field work, i.e. questionnaire interviewing was done in every mentioned year. In 2007, interviewers visited 6,462 addresses and 3,059 persons were successfully interviewed; the percentage of respondents was 47.3%.

Results of the World Internet Project in 2007 proved that the digital divide is an existing phenomenon in Hungary (Galacz 2007). The data proved that 41% of the population were internet users, while 7% can be called computer users: they use only computers, but do not use the internet. More than half of the whole population (52%) is completely excluded from the information society; they do not use computers (or the internet) at all (laggards).

If we look at the socio-demographic characteristics of the three groups, the inequalities become obvious (table 1). In certain groups, the usage parameters are very low, and it is an important policy goal to increase adoption in the most critical segments.

Socio-demographic characteristics	*Internet users*	*Computer users*	*Laggards*
Gender			
Male	48%	7%	45%
Female	42%	7%	51%
Education			
Elementary	31%	5%	64%
Technical school	27%	8%	66%
Secondary school	62%	9%	29%
University	81%	5%	14%
Type of settlement			
Village	34%	8%	58%
Town	47%	6%	47%
Budapest (capital)	59%	6%	35%
Subjective financial situation			
Living without problems	81%	3%	16%
Fairly good situation	56%	7%	37%
Monthly income just cover the costs	34%	8%	59%
Living on the breadline	25%	6%	69%

Age			
14-17	94%	5%	2%
18-29	76%	7%	17%
30-39	63%	12%	26%
40-49	45%	9%	46%
50-59	29%	8%	63%
60+	7%	2%	91%
Activity			
Student	95%	3%	2%
Entrepreneur	69%	7%	24%
Employee	56%	10%	34%
Inactive	39%	9%	51%
Retired	8%	3%	90%
Ethnicity			
Roma	21%	10%	69%
Non-Roma	46%	7%	47%

Table 1: Socio-demographic characteristics of certain user groups

The results confirm the usual gaps among certain socio-demographic groups. According to Rogers' categorization, internet penetration is almost full in certain segments (e.g. students, 14-17 years old). The diffusion rate occurs in (early or late) majority in several groups, but in some other segments the curve is in the early adopter stage (retired, 60+ years old).

Changes in access and use: Digital divide index

According to the recent findings of the World Internet Project, computer and internet access at home have produced significant growth in Hungary in the last five years. About half of households have a computer, and slightly more than one third of households also have internet access. This means that nowadays in Hungary, over one million households have a computer and nearly 1.5 million have an internet subscription.

In the following, we examine how the digital divide has been changed in regard to access and use. We summarise the digital divide according to settlement type, age, gender, school qualifications, financial status, and social background in an aggregated index, which is an aggregated index number similar to the Digital Divide Index (DIDIX). The value of the index shows the proportion of access to and use of ICT tools in a given disadvantaged group (e.g. women, the elderly etc.) and the entire population (e.g. home internet use in the 50+ age group as a proportion of the main average). The value of the index is set between 0 and 100. The lower the index value, the more a disadvantaged group lags behind compared to the average. The index value can be computed for individual disadvantaged groups. DIDIX is obtained by the weighted aggregation of the indices. Weighting means that the access and use indexes have a different weight in the summative DIDEX value (For a detailed description of DIDIX see SIBIS New eEurope Indicator Handbook 2003; Hüsing-Selhofer 2002).

Based on the DIDIX methodology, we examined computer and internet access in the home and also computer and internet use (anywhere).

- We adjusted the proportion of access and use of the group that was disadvantaged in regard to access and use ($\frac{x_L}{x_T}$).

- Next, we weighted the proportions obtained, ascribing 0.3 to use and 0.2 to access and summarised them in each index ($Dj = \sum_{i=1}^{n} w_i \frac{x_L}{x_T}$).

- We computed the annual aggregated index using the arithmetical average of the partial indices ($INDEX = \sum_{j=1}^{n} \frac{Dj}{N}$).

The partial indices that we created and the aggregated INDEX contain the same indicators relating to access and use of computers and the internet. During the time interval studied, the value of the aggregated INDEX rose from 53 points to 65, which can be regarded as a significant result. On the one hand, we found that internet access and use principally depend on age, social background and income. On the other hand, the conclusion that can be drawn from the graph below is that small settlements have been more successful in whittling down their disadvantage than others and that financial differences have also decreased relatively quickly (figure 1). All of this means that in Hungary, age and differences in social background are more significant factors, that are slow to change.

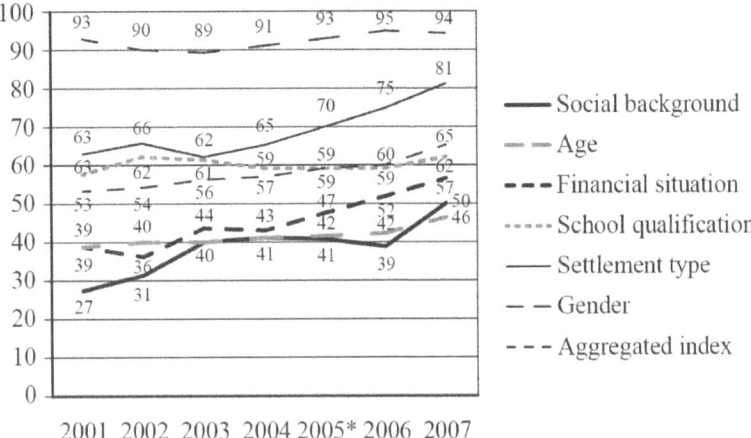

* Estimated data because of methodological shortcomings
Figure 1: Changes in the digital divide (WIP 2001-2007)

After a study of the use and proliferation of ICTs, it is also worth looking into why certain people refrain from using them (figure 2). Based on the opinions of those who do not use the internet, two large groups can be distinguished: those who have financial considerations, i.e. they cannot afford to use the internet, because of the high costs of doing so. The other group is composed of those who refrain from using the internet for cognitive reasons, i.e. they do not need it, they are not interested in it, they cannot use it, etc.

According to those who reported that they do not use the internet for cognitive reasons, they did so because they have no need of the internet, are not interested, do not know how to use it, are afraid of technology, consider it unsuitable for children, see it as a source of pornography, seek to protect their personal data, are afraid of viruses, think it has is too much advertising, or simply lack the time for it. The financial reasons given included: the computer was not good enough, they did not have a computer, technology was too expensive, access was too slow, or difficulties in establishing a connection.

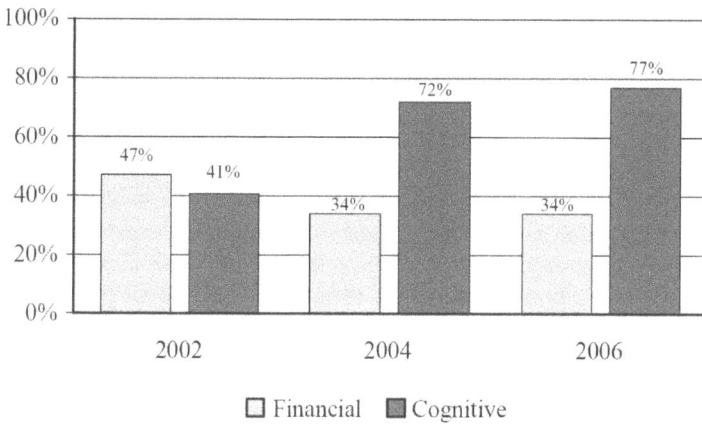

Figure 2: Reasons for refraining from internet use (WIP 2002-2006)

Among those who do not use the internet, the proportion of those who refrain for financial reasons has steadily been decreasing since the first WIP measurement, i.e. since 2001, while the proportion that refrains because of a lack of interest has been steadily rising. This gives rise to the question as to whether the limit of the increase in use has been reached, since further price decreases most probably cannot influence cognitive inhibition, thus allowing for a possible increase in the gap between users and non-users. (Csoto-Szekely 2007)

Empirical research

The aim of our research was to find the incentives for and obstacles to internet use. We tried to identify motivation for internet use and resistance in various groups, since the incentives and obstacles can vary widely, based on socio-demographic characteristics and attitude.

The empirical research set out to gain a deeper understanding of non-users with qualitative methods. Six focus groups and 8 sociological interviews were conducted in Hungary (Budapest and rural areas), in October and November of 2008.

The locations of the focus groups were Budapest (capital; 1.7 million inhabitants), Miskolc (170,000 inhabitants), Szekszard (34,000 inhabitants), Pecsvarad (4,000 inhabitants). Participants were selected by trained instructors. The selection methods were random calling and random walking. The selection criteria we used were: does not use computer and the internet and does not have internet access at home. Every focus group had 7-8 participants. The focus groups were based on three categories (2-2 groups in each of them):

- non-users with a positive attitude to ICT

- non-users with a negative attitude to ICT

- light users who used a computer and the internet, but did not have access at home.

The interviews had a broader scope; we identified some special groups that can be relevant from the point of view of incentives and obstacles:

- heavy users

- light users, who used the internet only for communication purposes\

- beginner users.

The interviewed subjects were recruited from a wide circle of acquaintances. We did not use a random selection method. The goal was not to have a representative sample; we wanted to gain a thorough knowledge of the different types of users. We asked those who claimed to be heavy users; light users, who used the Internet only for communication purposes; and beginner users.

Altogether we were able to form a picture about the main types of fears and stereotypes concerning ICT. It was extremely interesting to become familiar with the opinions of non-users about users and vice versa.

Results

Attitude to ICT

The importance of ICT is accepted even among non-users, and this forms one of the main results of the research. Use of ICT is considered a kind of "must"; and recognized as necessary to preserve individual competitiveness. Besides this general acceptance, several negative characteristics of ICT development were mentioned:

- physiological effects (eye problems or backbone problems because of less sport)

- mental effects ("addiction similar to drugs or alcohol")

- negative impact on personal relationships.

Non-users had no lack of stereotype ideas about users: *"they just sit in front of the computer and they have only virtual relationships"*; *"they only use the internet and do not care about anything else"*. Interestingly, non-users accept the information and communication functions of the internet, but the entertainment aspects are considered harmful, even causing serious addiction (table 2). In brief, only a limited use of the internet is morally acceptable for non-users.

Role of the internet in various activities	*Light user (without access at home)*	*Non-users*
Information seeking	The internet has a primary role	Traditional media and personal contacts
Contacts – communication	The internet has a certain role, but it is not exceptional	Telephone and personal contacts are important (the internet leads to isolation)
Work – study	The internet has an exceptional role	It is the only field in which the internet can be important
Entertainment	The internet has a role in entertainment, but it is limited (otherwise it causes addiction)	Entertainment functions of the internet cause addiction

Table 2: Evaluation of the internet by light users and non-users

There are some controversial aspects pertaining to these pronounced stereotypes. Sitting in front of the television can cause similar kinds of addiction, and it can also push personal relationships into the background. It can be also assumed that non-users are unaware of the communication functions of the internet: VoIP software like Skype can substitute the telephone perfectly, and other communication forms (e-mail, chat) can fully supplement personal meetings.

Reasons for non-use

We found that life stage primarily determines the question of use or non-use. There are many old people among non-users, but the issue is more complex than a simple socio-demographic factor. The real question is whether a person had prior experience with the internet (e.g. at work before retirement, or via a young user in the family) or not. Without any experience and personal support, beginner users have a lot of difficulties to deal with. Computer fear is critical in many cases: old people, without previous experience with computers, believe that it is very difficult to learn how to use them.

It was also found that families with small children often reject the internet and computers. There are major concerns about children using it too much, generating continuous conflicts and pushing other activities (studying, book reading, sport) into the background. Parents know that, above a certain age computer use and internet access is a necessity, because of school homework. In the case of smaller children, however, the cons of internet use can outweigh the pros, so there is a kind of rationality behind these decisions.

The high costs were also often-mentioned factors to explain non-use. It was found that the one-time cost of a computer was extremely high for non-users, but that the monthly subscription fee for internet access was a less frequently mentioned reason for non-adoption. It was also mentioned that there was no point in buying second-hand computers, since they are completely out of date, but that new computers were too expensive: "There is no point in buying a new notebook (which costs 1,000 Euros) just to write a few messages and to look at a few pages (…) there are already cheaper notebooks (which cost 250 Euros) but they are not so good." (Note, however, that in reality, second-hand computers can typically fulfil the needs of beginner users.)

Surprisingly, lack of time was often mentioned as a reason for non-use. Those, who reject the internet, spend their free time on other activities (deeper relationships with family members and friends, reading, gardening, etc.) and the internet would decrease the amount of time devoted to these activities. However, here again, the stereotypes mentioned above came into play: non-users believe that users spend too much on the internet and thus have no time for other activities. The non-users want to avoid this situation and the potential conflicts caused by the re-allocation of free time.

In some cases, the fear of dependency was also mentioned. This is somewhat controversial and shows that non-users respect the power of the internet, and do not trust their ability to control their own use. The stereotypes about users (e.g. they are addicted to the internet, they have poor personal contacts, etc.) are reflected in these fears.

In summary, the financial aspect is only one reason for non-adoption. The decision making process is more complex and there are many aspects to be taken into consideration concerning the decision to adopt or not to adopt the internet. One of the main results of the research was that the often-cited reason for non-adoption ("lack of interest") did not play a role in this case. Presumably because of the relatively high use of the internet in Hungary (it has already reached the level of critical mass), it is somehow embarrassing for someone to say they are not interested. Maybe it is a kind of self-justification to find a more or less rational argument for non-adoption.

Conclusion and implications

We found that the reasons for rejecting usage are complex, so there are several ways to change the attitude of non-adopters. They have a highly practical approach; use of the internet is morally acceptable for them if it serves work or study. Thus it is important to underline the practical aspects of the internet and its strength in providing information. Because of strong stereotyping of impersonal features, it is important to outline the internet's capability to substitute more traditional communication channels (postal mail vs. email, telephone vs. Skype).

It makes the gaining of user practices more difficult. Users typically become familiar with new technology through games: the games and entertainment content are appropriate tools to improve user practices and to enhance the self-confidence of beginner users.

The new content must also be attractive for older generations, whether as information or entertainment. The demand from older people for old concert videos as a kind of youth nostalgia was mentioned several times by the research participants. There is also a clear need for more content in health care and medical treatments, a topic that proved very interesting and important for older people.

It is also crucial to defeat the fears and technophobia of non-users. Because of the lack of confidence, support is required in the first period of usage. The role of younger family members (or other people in the personal network who use the computer) is crucial and this seems to be of more practical help than courses for bigger groups.

Family members and friends have another role in motivating older people to use computer. Physical distance and the relatively high costs of phone calls can provide an incentive to start using the internet. Various research participants mentioned that the internet could be a useful tool for communication with family members living abroad or in other towns.

In any case, it is important to clear up the non-users' stereotypes about using the internet and users. The numerous media reports about extreme situations related to internet (computer addiction, isolated young people, suicide announced in chat, lots of pornographic content, practical information about bomb making, etc) can lead non-users to believe that the internet is mainly used by addicts and criminals, and as a whole to view this as harmful and dangerous. Non-users are also extremely wary of viruses and "virus attacks". Thus greater emphasis on the practical advantages of the internet is required. Obviously, however, this has little to no news value in the media.

Policy makers and market players must make further efforts to attract non-users to ICT in general, and especially to internet use. The traditional incentives (financial support, courses) have to be supplemented by more positive communication about the advantages of the internet. It is important to dispel the stereotypes about the dangers of the internet and develop more content that makes using it more attractive to non-users.

References

Atkin D.J., Jeffres L.W., Neuendorf K. A. 'Understanding internet adoption as a telecommunications behaviour' Journal of Broadcasting & Electronic Media 42 (4) (1998) pp. 475-490

Beckers J., Schmidt H. 'Computer experience and computer anxiety' Computers in Human Behavior 19 (2003) pp. 785-797

Beckers J., Schmidt H., Wechters J. 'Computer anxiety in daily life: Old History?' eds. Loos E., Mante-Meijer E., Haddon L. The Social Dynamics of Information and Communication Technology Aldershot: Ashgate (2008)

Broos A., Roe K. 'The digital divide in the playstation generation: Self-efficacy, locus of control and ICT adoption among adolescents' Poetics 34 (2006) pp. 306–317

Csoto M., Szekely L. 'The indicators of internet usage: Does the net conceal or reduce inequalities according to regions and settlement size in Hungary?' ed. NETCOM - Geographical Journal on ICTs, Networks and Information Society (2007) http://www.ittk.hu/netis/doc/textbook/Csoto_Szekely_The%20indicators%20of%20internet%20usage.pdf

Davis F. 'Perceived usefulness, perceived ease of use, and user acceptance of information technology' MIS Quarterly 13 (3) (1989) pp. 319-340

Galacz A. ed. A digitális jövő térképe – Gyorsjelentés a World Internet Project évi magyarországi kutatásának eredményeiről. ITHAKA, Budapest (2007)

Galacz A., Sagvari B. Digitális döntések és másodlagos egyenlőtlenségek: a digitális megosztottság új koncepciói szerinti vizsgálat Magyarországon. Manuscript (2008)

Goldfarb A., Prince J. 'Internet adoption and usage patterns are different: Implications for the digital divide' Information Economics and Policy 20 (2008) pp. 2-15

Hüsing T., Selhofer H. 'The Digital Divide Index 1997-2002. Draft Measurement approach and results' Empirica: Internal Working Paper (2002) http://is2.lse.ac.uk/asp/aspecis/20020042.pdf

Lin C.A. 'Exploring personal computer adoption dynamics' Journal of Broadcasting & Electronic Media 42 (1998) pp. 95-112

Livingstone S. Young People and New Media. Childhood and the Changing Media Environment London: Sage (2002)

Neuendorf K.A., Atkin D., Jeffres L.W. 'Understanding adopters of audio information innovators' Journal of Broadcasting & Electronic Media 42 (1998) pp. 80-93

Purkayastha S. 'Predicting behavioral intentions of consumers: A framework' IUP Journal of Management Research 8 (12) (2009) pp. 31-43

Rogers E.M. Communication Technology: The New Media in Society New York: The Free Press (1986)

Rogers E.M. Diffusion of innovations (fifth edition) New York: Free Press (2003)

SIBIS New eEurope Indicator Handbook (2003)

Turner M., Kitchenham B., Brereton P., Charters S., Budgen D. 'Does the technology acceptance model predict actual use? A systematic literature review' Information and Software Technology 52 (2010) pp. 463–479

Part 4 - Case Studies on User Empowerment

James Stewart, Mark Wright, Penny Travlou, Henrik Ekeus and Richard Coyne

The "Memory Space" and "The Conference": Exploring Future Uses of Web2.0 and Mobile Internet through Design Interventions

Introduction

New digital media offers many opportunities to record, organise and review our activities, communications and thoughts. Much of this activity is conceived of in terms of "real-time" communication, or abstract, disembodied information access. It is becoming clear, however, that Web2.0 and personal mobile media also have important implications for collective memory practices. We need to understand how this is happening, and how new facilities and practices associated with Information and Communications technologies (ICTs) are support changes in memory practices within the context of particular practices, communities and localities.

This chapter describes some of the work of a project, "Branded Meeting Places: Ubiquitous technology for meaningful social encounter in urban spaces", that explored the changing use of space and place for formal and informal meetings and social encounters, using ideas from practice and theory of branding. The project deployed a "research by design" methodology, and used exploratory studies, and speculative design, and workshops with "user-designers" to create prototype digital games in urban spaces, extensions of social networking systems, and virtual environments using new technologies of space and place.

Through a series of "research by design" experiments, it became clear that as well as facilitating real-time information and communication, these technologies and practices incorporated important memory practices, as physical and digital spaces merge to create a new form of "memory space". In order to explore the "memory space" through design, a collective intervention and experiment was conducted in the theme of the future of "The Conference". A "memory engine" was built to explore how the intense, and multilayered experience of conferences could be made more productive and reorienting. This taps in to the use of place and space as key elements in producing and linking to memories of encounters and ideas The "memory engine" facilitates new ways to record and access informal conversations and encounters using mobile messaging, social networking, text, images, voice and video, and linking these with the formal and informal physical spaces of conferences using the web, GPS, and mobile phone interfaces, creating a much richer record of a conference than formal Proceedings and private memories.

A speculative journey: An exploration of locative and digital media for social encounters in branded places

We have arrived at the current research focus through a development path of several years in terms of technological configurations and theoretical perspectives. The initial work was a series of workshop interventions on the concept of "non-place" (Augé 1992), exploring the past and future of public spaces such as airports and shopping centres. Communication and media technologies were identified as being very important drivers for change of the design and our experience of these places, and indeed a wide range of researchers have been exploring these issues (e.g. Meyrowitz 1985; Laurier 2001; Brown et al. 2005)). Funding was obtained from the AHRC-EPSRC Design for the 21st Century Programme in the UK for a project entitled "Branded Meeting Places: Ubiquitous technology for meaningful social encounter in urban spaces" (ACE 2008). This was to explore the way we use contemporary public places using a "research by design" approach and a tool developed by one of the team members, "Spellbinder", which uses image recognition of photos sent in by MMS (multimedia message from a mobile phone) to trigger a range of responses from a server, such as "unlocking" invisible images "embedded" in the environment. It conceptualised places and objects as the site of digital content and as physical instantiations of hyperlinks. This tool was used as the initial basis of the research method. The goal was to use a series of experiments to extend our conceptual view and open up new directions for research based on work with people, technology and theory.

Rather than taking an atheoretical or ad-hoc approach to place-based content, the research was informed by practice and theory of branding, and the changing use of space and place for formal and informal meetings and social encounters. Brands and branding plays an important role in how we define ourselves individually and collectively, and in how we are addressed by a organisation, both commercial and non-commercial (Holt 2002; Klein 2005). Branding defines much of the textual and graphical content that pervades contemporary public space (Chmielewska 2005), and is one of the axes of contested meaning and control of place, where commercial goals and municipal image-building, and often conflict with the practices and meanings of citizens making use of public space (Klein 2005). However, branding is not a stable set of practices: in the same way as technologies are socially shaped, the production and use of brands and branding is in constant flux, and in the 21st Century, deeply integrated with ICTs (Lury 2004)

The "memory space" concept was first developed in 2008 in a 2 day workshop setting with 25 academic participants from across disciplines who developed an analysis of conference attending, and set a brief for the development of a tool for an "intervention". This brief was to develop a tool to provide a means of recording and accessing the informal conversations, notes and social encounters that occur in the formal and interstitial spaces of conferences. This tool was used as part of the following day's workshop, populating a database of geo-tagged notes, observations and conversations by participants that could be accessed via a map, time-based web and GPS-triggered mobile interface. The intervention was not intended to produce a fully working prototype, but to pose new questions and open new research avenues, stimulating investigation on emerging memory practices in a world where we can record so many of or activities, but need tools and new social practices to make sense and use of these vast databases.

Following a brief discussion of collective memory practices from the literature, this chapter elaborates on the idea of memory practices and "memory spaces". This is followed by a short discussion of the research methodology (Stewart et al. 2007). The main part of the chapter describes the series of experiments leading up to and during the final "research-by-design" event. This includes a discussion of "The Conference" based on the ideas of "branded meeting place", and the inputs by the "designer-users" who participated in the research by design workshop. The chapter concludes with some thoughts on the future of memory practices in the world of social networking, mobile internet and user-created multimedia databases.

Social memory practices and the "memory space"

While our practical implementation of a "memory space" emerged from interdisciplinary conversations and our experiments, we can also explore the idea through a rich literature on memory, archives, space, and social practice. Our concept of memory is not primarily a cognitive one, but a social one, following Halbwachs (1992). Memory is not about "things remembered, or forgotten" but collective, social, or cultural practices that not only involve people, but objects, texts and places (Crang & Travlou, 2001) - mnemonics that exteriorize cognitive memory, and are incorporated into future spatial and social practices. (Olick et al. 1998)

We have long associated places and objects with relationships and events, and we all create artefacts such as photo albums, home videos, and hold commemorative events, such as anniversaries and reunions to relive and celebrate particular events in the past. These objects and events keep alive past episodes that help define present individual and collective identity. This is well documented in the political sphere (Olick et al. 1998), and is not less the case in the everyday and domestic world. We are all familiar with a range of conventional domestic memory supports, such as pin boards, fridge doors, or notebooks. With today's technology we have ever more ways to record events as they happen, store them, share and recreate them, from chat logs to blogs, to Facebook and online photo albums (Coyne & Triggs 2007). These practices have recently been explored by authors such as Van Dijk (2007). New possible artefacts and systems are continually being suggested – including 3D virtual places, dynamic online maps, and tagging objects with stories (Leder et al. 2010). These artefacts not only provide opportunity for reminiscence, but also act tools for the performance of future activities and relationships

The same practices occur in the world of work. We minute meetings, build databases of events such as sales, decisions, hold workshops and conferences to share experiences and build common pasts and visions of the future. There are a variety of tools available to help organise and make meaningful this information, and use it to help create our identity in work relations. Slowly we are starting to see the use of new web and mobile tools that go beyond these conventional CSCW or knowledge management systems to enable ricer memory practices that leverage the tacit and informal knowledge and relationships so essential in team work.

Our concept was first developed upon reflecting on memory practices associated with specific events - weddings, births, holidays etc; events that we take special care to document in photographs, diaries, videos, address books etc that can that we then reuse at later times. This reuse can have many aspects - nostalgia, sharing collective memories to reinforce collective identity, and to initiate new community members into collective identity. As well as descriptive records, we also associate events with places, objects, music etc , either specially chosen, or that just happen to intervene. Our initial design concept was to create a "Second Life" space to celebrate a wedding, or as a recreation of a holiday resort that people could visit to remind themselves of the visit, but also to "meet" others who were there with them, or liked the same place. A virtual space would be created in which to enact common memory practices. Later work on tagging physical spaces, reflecting on the appropriation of space to produce places with personal and collective meaning lead us to introduce the possibility of linking online information systems and the physical space. As we moved into examining online, user-tagged maps the idea of the "memory space" re-emerged. We now had a technical concept of memory space as an electronic repository of media objects that could be populated and referenced with a visual, spatial model - a map - but also in the "real" space. However, a generic tool to "capture" and "revisit" media objects is only part of the process of design - the next stage is to re-embed it with the type of situations for which we already have strongly developed memory practices. The following sections describe the emerge of memory space concept, and the intervention done to situate it within the concept of "The Conference".

Research by design

ICTs are continually offering new possibilities for innovation and use. Social researchers who observe current trends may often get led into studying a particular technology – we have seen the rise of "mobile phone" studies, and "internet studies", examining the use of current technologies. We are used to trying to drawing conclusions about the future, using theoretical concepts and empirical evidence of the past and present. Is this sufficient, when we know practices and technologies will change? One way to extend methods based in the present is to conduct speculative future-oriented research by doing experiments and engaging in design activities that that are informed by our knowledge as social scientists, while also using the practices of designers and engineers to explore emerging socio-technical configurations, and indeed influence them.

This work used an exploratory method which we have called "Research by design". This research method combines the power of theoretical perspectives with tangible "human-centered" design activities, "designer-user" approaches and exploration of the affordances of emerging technologies. In the field of design and study of technology-based practices these design-based methods that create "prototypes" or "probes" have been explored in a variety of forms over recent years (Suchman et al. 2002; Gaver et al. 2004; Coyne & Triggs 2007) although often over protracted periods of time. We used shorter, more iterative interventions (e.g. Crabtree 2004), combining social science and design methods in the style of design charrettes (Sutton & Kemp 2006). Although certainly inspired by insights into user inputs to innovation (Williams et al. 2002), and participatory design discourses (Argyris & Schön 1989; Buur & Matthews 2008), the experiments were not intended to engage with "real" users developing "real" products and services, but as a way to leverage the practices of design, and the exigencies of use within "semi-real" situations of a few days to a few weeks.

Our core research group was multi-disciplinary, from informatics, digital media, architecture and social sciences). This already required the development of methods that would facilitate productive interdisciplinary research: it was hoped that a focus on design, and on working with "user-designers" would help focus the research team (see chapter Stewart & Claeys in this volume). A series of events involving "user-designers" was created, carefully set up by preparing a toolkit of technologies and concepts from which to assemble a technical system that could be used to explore the research questions and issues identified by the participants. The technical development was pursued using lightweight mobile applications, tying together of existing web and mobile services and content, with the help of professional developers and designers. Unlike design methods that use limited mockups and older technologies of physical objects, we worked with IT products, which can be developed in a very short time, especially assembled from a toolkit of custom components, generic online services, and open source frameworks and tools. We still are at a stage where need professionals to help with this assembly, and a long term project is needed to build the toolkit and become familiar with interfaces, limitations and affordances of the material.

The design processes occurred with theoretical' priming', introducing the designer-users to the basic concepts we were interested in exploring, the provision of the toolkits based on previous iterations of design. Through group discussion on the theoretical themes, very open design briefs were set for the design work. Prototyping and "street trialling" and reinvention based on these experience were encouraged through out the process. The design, prototyping and trial uses were documented with observations and individual and group interviews, to provide evidence for later reflection on the struggles and creative moments of design and use.

Early experiments

The early experiments were place we started to develop the practical implementation of the "research by design" method. They were conducted with groups of postgraduate digital media students acting as the designer-users. The designer-users were briefed around the theoretical ideas we were exploring - "the use of ubiquitous technology for meaningful social encounter in urban spaces". Memory was not explicitly a topic on the research agenda, but the project was informed by ideas of place as having cultural "depth" in time, and our use and interpretation of spaces being closely linked to memory practices (Coyne, Wright, Stewart, Ekeus & Travlou (2008); De Certeau 1984). Theoretical priming was followed by technological familiarisation, where the designers and researchers both explored the practical aspects of using the Spellbinder system, which, in common with many bleeding edge technologies, proved less that stable and predictable. In hindsight the need to work around the limitations of the technology was a source of considerable invention and brings us back to the limits of "real life". The designer-users then developed ideas in small groups of 3-4 that we discussed individually and in the whole group. These were then developed technically to create mockups and working demos. The user-designers then had to use their creations, along with their colleagues and friends. The whole design and experimentation process was documents, designers and were interviewed. This matieral was all assembled by the research team to inform the next iteration of research by design.

Successful early interventions included experiments named *Invisible Art* and *Comera* and *PhoneTag*:

- *Invisible Art* enabled artists to embed "invisible" art works in the facades of public buildings. On an application level this was envisioned as a public art or a civic heritage tool. However we then began to conceive of user-generated art and a simple interface for the public to upload images to the same facades. This was the beginning of the notion of a shared social practice of embedding and retrieving geo-referenced digital media, to enable anyone to add signs or tags to the urban landscape, a practice usually limited to government and commercial organisations. Geo-referencing can use any technical system to pinpoint location, not necessarily numerical coordinates. We recognise places by sound, smell, vision, branding, and the people who occupy a place. One challenge is to create technical systems that support the way that human beings recognise place, not just machines.

- *Comera* was a social network application which allowed people to "log in" to buildings and inform friends where they were. People logged in by taking a picture and sending it to a server. Those using the system were updated by SMS text and on Facebook as to the whereabouts of their "friends". The system left a short-term working memory of people's location as well as a long term record of their paths. After the initial group of design-users had left, this idea was developed over a series of interventions with students using and abusing the system. As well as supporting useful learning around the value and limitations of "realtime" knowledge of where friends were, the logs of images turned out to have their own fascination, as we could explore through often obscure images where we and our friends had been, reconstructing paths and routines. It also gave us a way to see what images users chose to portray the places they used, and therefore have meaning for them. This type of system has been developed commercially in many forms since this experiment, with the most successful in 2010 being the US start-up Foursquare, and the Places feature on Facebook.

- *Secret Postcards* was a simple application similar to Invisible Art but the released content was a personal text message. It enabled one to send a picture of a place or object to ones friends who would then have to find and visit the same place to photograph the same object/place to unlock a secret message: for example, telling the receiver that the sender had arranged to pay for the drink in the café if they showed the message to the staff. This took the emphasis beyond the visual and also democratized the embedding and releasing of "content to all".

Memory, meta-verse and universe

At this stage a new technical tool was introduced that appeared to offer new opportunities to explore place, space, branding, design and social encounter: Second Life. This concept of "memory space" was evoked by the possibility of of a meta-verse or 3D social world such as Second Life being used as a catalyst for memory sharing. One envisioned application was as a "reunion" perhaps of students or holiday makers. The "memory space" would be a semi-literal imagining of a real place such as a city or institution evoking the landscapes in the work of Salvador Dali such as his painting "The persistence of memory". Memory objects could be placed in the space and social encounters created using avatars in the space. Iterative design interventions looked at sharing these spaces more literally by walking into a mixed reality room. A concept of "augmented duality" was finally considered as not a single space but an extended social metaverse parallel to the real world and with portals between them (Wright et al. 2008). In terms of cultural memory we theorised the use of such a social duality to encounter cultural memory in the context of museum encounters with heritage.

The Tag

We also introduced a new research theme to carry the research forward: the "branded document". On reflection, and through experiments with "leaving" digital traces using *Invisible Art* and *Secret postcards* the design team converged on the notion of "the tag" as a core concept. "The tag" was explored extensively in a research-by-design workshop in 2008, exploring the many different types of physical and online tagging, how they work semantically, socially, politically, visually and electronically. They involve practices such as labelling, marking ownership, classification, signalling that one has seen or noted an object or text, or passed through a place, or more generally they act as a means to symbolically and electronically link two concepts, objects or people together. In the field of mass tagging practices, the concepts such as folksonomy have been developed to try and understand "bottom-up" tag practices with emergent classifications. We propose that tagging is an appropriation process, a means making sense of the world and establishing an individual order on experiences, that eventually leads to emergent collective meaning making and social order or conflict.

Mass tagging is already a practical fact, rather than a theoretical concept. For example, one of the main services that we have tapped into is the Flickr geo-tagged image database, where users simultaneous tag their images with geographic coordinates, and tag a map with their images. A research-by-design workshop that involved 2 days of design and reflection workshops with 30 practionners and academics was run in May 2008 to explore how we might take the rich use of tagging that now occurs in online environments – especially in Web2.0 services, and link that more closely to tagging of physical space. The application that came out of the "tagging" workshop was named *Visual thumbs* and extended the media content to spoken words. To overcome the problem of lack of "call to action" that using virtual tags has, paper tags were left in the street to indicate that someone had left a voice message that could be unlocked by sending a message to a special phone number. Text messages could also be embedded and shared through Facebook. The emphasis was not just on a preoccupation with geo-spatial referencing but on the sharing of social discourses on topics with a geographic dimension such as the impact of urban development. This was to a certain degree inspired by the Yellow Arrow project (http://yellowarrow.net/), and various systems for citizens to complain about their urban environment that are now being implemented in mobile and online forms around the world. Readers maybe familiar with the more recent AudioBoo application based on the same principle.

Placemaking by placemarking

The final workshop of the Branded Spaces project was planned to be on the topic of "brandscapes", but we reframed this in the light of our experimental journal as "tagscapes". Not only are our urban and private spaces shaped and labelled with the logic of commercial and corporate branding (Coyne, Wright, Stewart & Ekeus (2008) and with the "tags" of spray-paint wielding youths, but are likely to become the site of mass, individual tagging practices overflowing from digital spaces to real spaces. The workshop of some 20 participants was convened to explore the possibilities of completely open electronic tagging systems as forms of appropriation of space: what we termed "placemaking by placemarking" The common use of user-tagging on online mapping systems, and the availability of these on internet-enabled mobile devices also meant we could explore this new platform as a way of visualising where tags and messages were both from a desktop computer, but now out and about on the street.

By this time we had assembled a rich network of technologies, applications case studies and theoretical perspectives. "Memory space" was now more than a literal virtual space but had social and experiential dimensions, both virtual and real, spatial and symbolic, across many forms of media and application. Tags in any form – text, images, voice, video could be left and shared online or in virtual or real urban environments. Technologies now included various place recognition technologies such as image matching, GPS or street indexes, comprehensive content and location services with open APIs such as Flickr and Google Maps, and established social network systems including Facebook and Twitter to be used in mashups. We had all of these accessible through mobile devices via voice, SMS, WAP, and HTML. In the following section we describe the context within which we asked our user-designers to explore tags, and the re-emergence of the "memory space" concept.

Recent directions: Google street level and flickr geo-referencing

Before moving on to the exploration of "The Conference", it is worth mentioning other work that continued these experiments sequentially. This focused on the use of images from public internet applications such as Google Street Level and Flickr. We have developed methodologies to harvest these applications spatially and temporally to access narratives and perspectives which capture the general and the ephemeral and personal. Examples include photographic trails through the Obama inauguration, or glimpses behind the windows to private events in the buildings along urban walks. A particular influence here is Michel de Certeau and in particular "walking the city" (De Certeau, 1985). De Certeau theorises the inhabitants of the city as invisible authors unaware of the "text" their activity "writes" on the fabric of the city.

Bringing these ideas into the 21st century, Coyne (2010) explored the insights from these tagging experiments, among others as a set of practices we now have to *tuning* space. Perhaps the cultural significance of developments in social and locative media, of which our work is a part, is to provide new tools and media to make visible these narratives, and do this "tuning" work.

"The Conference" and the "memory engine"

In order to run a final research-by design workshop we wanted to choose as the topic the types of events that involve intense communication, engagement with other people, creation and annotation of new knowledge, and with strong symbolic and emotional factors. Given the participants were of academics drawn in the majority from creative arts and design and overall brief of the project to study work-oriented meetings, we chose "The Conference" as the topic. This choice had the advantage in that any technical system developed could actually be used as an intervention in an actual conference setting. The workshop consisted of about 25 participants chosen to be a balance of age and gender, and with a broad mix of interests in the field of design, space, ICTs and human-computer interaction. The workshop consisted of one day of brainstorming sessions, practical explorations of the use of the tools developed over the project rand work in 3 groups to propose a design brief. All the workshop participants then voted on which brief should be implemented overnight. A group of 4 designers (including one of the authors) spend the entire night until 11 am creating and building a tool inspired by the brief. The following day the tool was demonstrated, and used by workshop participants in the streets and rooms around the workshop venue. This was followed by a further period of reflection on the idea of "The Conference", and the possibilities for developing new social media practices and tools.

The concept of "The Conference" as formulated by our workshop participants

The following discussion of conferences was largely draw from the discussions of the workshop participants and the work of the investigators in earlier meetings (which are available as podcasts).
   Conferences are a particular form of meeting that is intense and demanding on physical, interpersonal and intellectual levels. From being the preserve of politicians and academics, they are becoming a normal part of many people's working activities, thus deserve more critical analysis and practical innovation.
Conferences have a whole range of formal and informal aims and uses: explicitly, they bring people together to share ideas and experience they have developed elsewhere, and often to develop common understandings and to negotiate future activities. They are highly social, enabling us to meet new

people, re-establish old relationships, share ideas, and develop new ideas, and plan future cooperation. Conferences are seldom one-off – like other meetings, they are part of a series (Coyne, Wright, Stewart, Ekeus & Travlou (2008), with an established structure, a cohort of regular attendees drawn from a larger community. Conferences are often central to a larger occupational community, or community of interest or practice, and used to help create a common identity, involving rituals such as election of officials, giving prizes, celebrating current leaders, and deceased members. These are important practices of memory and identity.

There are many different sorts of conferences. Smaller workshops and conferences are easy to develop and attend - the groups are small enough for everyone to interact and share common experiences. Our concern is for the super-conference, with hundreds or thousands of participants, often taking place in a vast conference centre in a strange city. These types of conferences can be disorientating in many ways, with high risk of getting lost, physically, socially and emotionally. They are not clearly focused in one location and with a clear social group, but occur in a network of formal and informal venues, attendees forming a network rather than a precise community. The workshop participants explored a variety of issues related to this type of event, and were keen to imagine how they could be improved.

As well as existing as a series, conferences are not just the few days of the event itself. The workshop participants focused on three stages of a conference: before, during and after.

- **Before:** as we submit our abstracts, find co-authors, struggle to meet the deadline, book flights, and hotels, receive and study the programme, try to find out who else is going etc. When we are travelling to "The Conference" we finish our presentation, study the programme and try to decide what sessions to go to, look up details of the presenters, so that by the time we arrive "The Conference" has already been underway for a long time. It would be very useful to know who was attending a conference in advance, and use this to help plan how to attend it.

- **During:** There are a large number of way finding activities: find the hotel, finding the venue from the hotel, finding old friends and colleagues, deciding on and finding the right sessions, finding the social events and getting home again. Workshop participants highlighted a number of important problems with conference, for example: the parallel session problem, and how to decide which to attend, and on what criteria; the getting lost for dinner problem; nerves pre-presentation; avoiding people one does not want to meet; the problems of social hierarchy – how to integrate new attendees, and create the balance for old hands between meeting old acquaintances and playing the role of building the community. It was felt that there was lots of basic information that is not available that would be very useful to know, such as who else is in the session, the names of those are those asking the questions etc.

- **After:** After "The Conference" there is the problem of making sense of all the new ideas, and following up new contacts or promises to share work and collaborate. We may have to make a formal report to our colleagues, send off some papers, but frequently a conference is forgotten all too quickly.

Conference organisers implement a range of formal devices to help each stage of a conference, as do regular conference goers. Here we see an interesting relationship between the design of a conference, and the activities of the attendees who perform "The Conference". Social events help to introduce attendees to each others, lists of other attendees, artists in residence, even musicians (e.g. Pegasus Communications conferences). These are intended to help people get the most out of the event.

In recent years we have seen the emergence of new ICT tools to facilitate conference attendance. Some of these are provided by conference organisers, some are deployed by attendees. The PICNIC series of conferences has experimented with a whole range of ICT-based interaction tools for conference attendees. Example of the former include setting up social networking sites for participants, or creating groups on systems used by many of the attendees (e.g. the "Linkedin" Mobile City conference http://www.themobilecity.nl/) These are sophisticated version of the participant list, enabling people to see who will go, look up people afterwards, and sometimes, start and continue discussions, as well as share pictures, documents etc - these are "memory spaces" that link the three stages of "The Conference".

With the arrival of mobile phones and Wifi, we now see the actual conference emerging as a moment of high ICT use. Mobile phones have made attendee's lives much easier of course, but there are other innovations. For example, live online discussion boards projected in conference halls which allow whose not in the room to comment, to create dialogues between audience and speakers and at the end of the talk to have more than the individual notes available. These could also be wikis and blogs open to conference attendees to create dialogues, which become a repository of information, links and views that exists after the event. Other experiments include RFID badges to find people with common on interests or to register meetings on a social network service, for example, the RFID system developed by the Dutch firm Mediamatic for the PICNIC conference).With mobile social media now in common usage, group messaging, and systems such as Twitter in widespread usage (O'Hear 2007; Reinhardt 2009) the discussions in and out of formal sessions are can be shared in real time, but also recorded providing a textual and visual record of events. These real-time communications make it easier to identify the underlying concerns that are being expressed by participants or in other words "catching the vibe".

After conferences it is becoming more common to post images of the event on Web2.0 sites such as Facebook and Flickr. These images are sometimes formally posed, but often images of the many informal activities conferences. These new uses of ICTs start to provide records of many of the informal interactions not usually captured by the formal preparation and reporting processes.

In short, "The Conference" is a complex and rather taken-for-granted activity, an activity that may seem simple, but is actually multilayered and exists in many and fragmented place and times. As conferences become every more common, there is considerable scope for rethinking how they work and can be experienced in light of new technologies and technology mediated practices.

The design intervention

The workshop participants then reflected on what aspects of "The Conference" raised in their discussions they would like to focus on as a design intervention. Ideas include better preplanning and coordination tools, and ways to deal with uncertainties and social problems. However a key interest was to explore the informal aspects, especially those conversations and moments of idea creation that occur in interstitial moments: to capture something of the many informal exchanges and meetings that occur that are not recorded centrally, but exist in the memories of participants, and the rows of empty coffee cups and beer glasses. To this end, the designers proposed the development of a shared "memory space": a system which would catalyse and record informal social interaction off the main conference stage. The key technical outcome proposed was the creation of a general platform for media embedding, retrieval and memory making completing what we call the "memory space engine". Images, text, video can all be embedded and shared and accessed. Geo-referencing can be by image matching, GPS or Google place search on street and city names.

The technical developers spent the night developing and extending the "Memory space engine", choosing to base its operation on GPS devices linked to mobile phones, and a website with a map interface. The next morning the workshop participants were briefed as to the progress and shown how to access and use the "memory space engine" online and with their mobiles.

Workshop participants could send text messages from wherever they were, including the street name in order to place it on a map automatically; record and send audio and video blogs of conversations with GPS coordinates and submit their notes from discussions or personal thoughts. These could then be visualised on a map of "The Conference" area, that showed where these media objects had been created, and by whom. These could be tagged with any extra information. An added feature was to be able to find these on a mobile device – receiving a text message triggered by GPS, to see notes or hear recordings that other participants had had in the same place at another time. Workshop participants were then asked to use the system online and in the city. By the end of half a day of activity the map was being populated and paths and ideas could be explored.

As can be seen from Figure 1, the map view of the "memory spaces" gives a spatial visualisation of "The Conference" posts, most clustered around the main conference venue, but other located in bars, restaurants and in the street.

Figure 1: A screen shot from the map-view of "The Conference" "memory space"

Of course the implementation allows much scope for improvement. We propose integrating it with social network tools, with visualisation of data based on time and social network as well as space, and automatic linking of different sorts of texts. The receiving of location-based "pushed" text messages was interesting experience, but a far from ideal interface for deposited media. For the purposes of the intervention it was the part of the system that created the most interest, probably since it is the most novel: most participants had not experienced location-based media on their own phone before.

Reflections on the method

This intense workshop method showed some benefits and some limitations. There were few immediate conclusions in the workshop: the workshop format is very tiring to all concerned. The insights come later, with the project researchers going through the results and documentation, looking for new ideas, bottlenecks, inspirations, reflecting on the discussion both before and after the design intervention. A two day workshop format does not give much time to develop ideas, unlike the longer 10 week interventions. In many ways, the research team had to give too much guidance to the workshop participants, rather than let them develop ideas at their own pace. It was hard to explain the toolkits and for the participants to fully understand the possibilities of the tools: the organisers must be careful to allow participants to be the creators and performers and not just the audience. Those who had attended a number of the workshops were much better equipped to contribute than those attending for the first time. However the short time period also imposes its own discipline, the equivalent of hard editing of a text: the limited time to produce a brief, to design a tool and to test it provides focus that unfettered speculation can lack, and prevents the unhindered adding of functionality and options that software-based design inevitably leads to. It could well be worth exploring methods and ideas from Rapid Prototyping and Extreme programming, particularly in the design of the "street" tests.

Final Remarks

We have attempted to describe a research journey, taken with a multidisciplinary approach that engaged with practices of design and intervention to explore and enrich conceptual ideas. We proposed an intervention that explored an increasingly common form of professional meeting – "The Conference", but one that could clearly be improved a great deal with a set of tools to capture and integrate a wide range of interactions and information. However, while this is technically possible, the technologies are also limited, and would require considerably more work to explore how new practices might emerge.

During the period between conducting the research and publishing this chapter, the world has moved on. Many of the ideas we explored have been developed elsewhere, and practices such as "logging-in" to places taken up by millions of people. This reveals the strength of the method – finding a way to open a research path that reaches a short distance into the future in terms of design of technology, and also opens up new directions in social and technical research that might not be evident by only looking at existing technological practices.

Unlike more pragmatic, goal oriented work, we were not trying to invent products or services to solve social problems or to get rich, but to explore and extend theoretical and conceptual agendas, The process of abstraction and generalisation is hard, some such highly contingent and localised experiences. But this is the normal problem in social research – and the process of documentation and reflection allows the formulation of new research questions and make unexpected connections of ideas. Using these methods we moved conceptually from ideas of brand, place and business meetings, to ideas of tagging and memory practices. Many insights were drawn for successful and unsuccessful research and writing projects (e.g. Coyne 2010). We would like to continue the work to explore different types of intense, place-based mass events: festivals, political demonstrations etc, activities of significant symbolic value that mark both individual lives, and broader political and cultural life of a community.

We are keen to develop the "memory space" concept along the axes of both memory and space. Memory practices are likely to be radically changed with new media as we are able to recall not only "facts" from the Web, or communicate in real-time, but selectively leave and reuse all sorts of traces of our public and private activities. On the spatial dimension, we have a range of new ways of activating our experience and use of space and place using new ICTS that are being widely explored. We suggest that the junction of these two domains opens up considerable scope for design, technical development and academic enquiry.

References

ACE 'Branded Meeting Places' http://ace.caad.ed.ac.uk/branded/ (2008)
Argyris C., Schön D. 'Participatory action research and action science compared: a commentary' American Behavioural Scientist 32 (5) (1989) pp. 612-623
Augé M. Non-Lieux: Introduction à une Anthropologie de la Surmodernité Paris: Éditions du Seuil (1992)
Brown B., Chalmers M., Bell M., MacColl I., Hall M., MacColl I., Rudman P. 'Sharing the square: collaborative leisure in the city streets' Proceedings of ECSCW 2005 Paris: Springer (2005) pp. 427-429
Buur J., Matthews B. 'Participatory innovation' International Journal of Innovation Management 12 (3) (September 2008) pp. 255–273
Chmielewska E., 'Logos or the resonance of branding: A close reading of the iconosphere of Warsaw' Space and Culture 8 (4) (2005) pp. 349-380
Coyne R., Triggs J. 'Training for practice-based research: adaptation, integration and diversity' ed. Bianchi T. Creativity or Conformity: Building Cultures of Creativity in Higher Education Cardiff: Metropolitan University (January 8-10, 2007)
Coyne R., Wright, Stewart J., Ekeus H. 'Virtual flagships and sociable media' ed. Kent Flagships: Concepts and Places London: Routledge (2008)
Coyne R., Wright M., Stewart J., Ekeus H., Travlou P. 'Meetings on the move' Mobility, the City and STS workshop Technical University Denmark Copenhagen (November 20-22, 2008)
Coyne R. The Tuning of Place. Sociable Spaces and Pervasive Digital Media Cambridge: MIT Press (2010)

Crabtree A. 'Design in the absence of practice: Breaching experiments' Proceedings of the 5th Conference on Designing Interactive Systems: Processes, Practices, Methods, and Techniques, Cambridge: ACM Press (2004) pp. 59-68

Crang M., Travlou P. 'The city and topologies of memory, environment and planning' Society and Space 2001 19 (2001) pp. 161 -177

De Certeau M., The Practice of Everyday Life Berkeley, CA: University of California Press (1984)

De Certeau M., 'Practices of space' ed. Blonsky M. On Signs Blackwell: Oxford (1985)

Dijk J. van Mediated Memories in the Digital Age Cambridge: MIT (2007)

Gaver, W. Walker, B., Pennington, S., Boucher A. 'Cultural probes and the value of uncertainty' Interactions XI.5 - September / October, 2004

Halbwachs M. On Collective Memory Chicago, IL: University of Chicago Press (1992)

Holt D.B. 'Why do brands cause trouble? A dialectical theory of consumer culture and branding' Journal of Consumer Research 29 (2002) pp. 70-90

Klein N. No Logo London: Harper Perennial (2005)

Laurier, E. The Region as Socio-technical Accomplishment of Mobile Workers. eds. B. Brown, N. Green and R. Harper Wireless World London: Springer (2001)

Leder K., Karpovich A., Burke M., Speed C., Hudson-Smith A., O'Callaghan S., Simpson M., Barthel R., Blundell B., De Jode M., Lee C., Manohar A., Shingleton D., Macdonald J. '"Cohesion" tagging is connecting: Shared object memories as channels for sociocultural cohesion' M/C Journal 13 (1) March 2010

Lury, C Brands: The logos of the Global Economy Routledge: London (2004)

Meyrowitz, J. (2005) Rise of Glocality: New senses of place and modernity in the global village ed. Nyíri K. A Sense of Place: The Global and the Local in Mobile Communication Vienna, Passagen Verlag. (1985)

O'Hear S. 'Twitter, the ultimate conference "backchannel"' ZD Net (March 12, 2007)

Olick J.K., Robbins J. 'Social memory studies: From "collective memory" to the historical sociology of mnemonic practices' Annual Review of Sociology 24 (1998) pp.105-140

Reinhardt W., Ebner M., Beham G., Costa C. 'How people are using twitter during conferences' eds. Hornung-Prähauser V., Luckmann M. Creativity and Innovation Competencies on the Web Proceeding of 5. EduMedia conference Salzburg (2009) pp. 145-156

Stewart J., Wright M., Coyne R. 'Research by design: A probe to explore social encounters, urban space and mobile ICT' Paper to COST 298 Conference The Good, the Bad and the Unexpected Moscow (May 2007)

Suchman, L. 'Practice-based design of information systems: Notes from the hyperdeveloped world' Information Society 18 (2) (2002) pp. 139-144

Sutton S., Kemp S. 'Integrating social science and design inquiry through interdisciplinary design charrettes: An approach to participatory community problem solving' Am J Community Psychol 38 (2006) pp. 125–139

Wright M., Coyne R., Stewart J., Travlou P., Williams, R. 'Augmented duality: overlapping a metaverse with the real world' Proceedings of the 2008 International Conference in Advances on Computer Entertainment Technology' Yokohama, Japan (2008) pp. 263-266

Williams R., Slack R., Stewart J. Social Learning in Technological Innovation: Experimenting with Information and Communication Technologies Cheltenham: Edgar Elgar Publishing (2005)

The video blogs of the preparation for and events of the workshop are available here: https://ace-podcast.ace.ed.ac.uk/groups/branded/blog/

Sanna Marttila, Kati Hyyppä and Kari-Hans Kommonen

Co-Design of a Software Toolkit for Media Practices: P2P-Fusion Case Study

Introduction

In this chapter, we will explore several aspects of user empowerment through a case from a project called P2P-Fusion, in which an open source software toolkit and media applications were collaboratively designed together with communities of everyday people. By analyzing the lessons learned from this case, we aim to shed light on the following issues: What benefits and challenges are there in empowering and engaging everyday people in the co-design of a software toolkit? What kinds of strategies, methods and work practices are needed to facilitate this kind of co-design process?

The case presents several aspects that are relevant when discussing the empowerment of people: first, the intentions and motivations behind the project; second, the process and activities within it; third, the constraints of the project's context as a EU co-funded R&D project, and the obstacles encountered with the available technology; and finally, fourth, the results and outcomes of the project. We will touch upon these aspects throughout the chapter.

Open source projects have a long history in engaging a distributed community of software developers and end-users into a collaborative design and development process with a number of established tools, methods and work practices (Raymond 1999; Von Hippel 2001; Tuomi 2002). However, end-users without technological expertise or knowledge of specific coding languages or programming skills have had rather limited opportunities to take part in these projects. In recent years, emerging social media platforms, applications and a large number of Web 2.0 tools on the internet have made it possible for everyday people to participate in cumulative peer-production of knowledge (e.g., Wikipedia), creation of content (e.g., YouTube), enrichment of meaning and even the construction of custom, individualized applications (e.g., Facebook). While this development has created a tremendous opportunity for anyone with internet access to take part in creative content production with global distribution, it offers users rather limited possibilities for innovation in designing the actual social media systems on which this revolution is based.

One way to facilitate participation of everyday people in the creation of future technologies is to use design methods that include peoples' point of view in the design. User-centred design methods have become common in the development of interactive technology systems, devices and services in the field of information and communication technologies (ICTs) (ISO/IEC 13407 1999). Moreover, getting everyday people involved in design processes has become a recommended strategy in digital design (Sanders & Stappers 2008). Approaches such as participatory design (PD) and co-design provide means to engage people in collaborative design of technologies and systems they use (Schuler & Namioka 1993; Muller 2002). The level of engagement in such approaches has varied from users informing and inspiring design to user-driven innovation (Haddon et al. 2005).

Our work builds upon the tradition of participatory design that recognizes potential future "users" that are not trained in design as active co-creators and partners for the duration of a design process (Sanders 2002; Sanders and Stappers 2008). Furthermore, co-design, which we consider both as an approach and set of principles as well as activities carried out in a design process (Botero & Kommonen 2009), forms the theoretical as well as practical core in the software design case presented in this chapter. Appropriating Sander's vocabulary from her mapping of design practice and design research, the project's design process was "design-led" with "participatory mindset" applying "thinking tools" for understanding people's wishes, needs and current media practices (Sanders 2008).

Engagement of people in the design of the technologies that they use can be also facilitated by providing flexible systems and services, such as customizable applications and software toolkits, which can be tailored and developed further by their users. Fischer describes this *Meta-Design* (Fischer & Scharff 2000; Fischer 2003) as a type of design that "characterizes objectives, techniques, and processes for creating new media and environments that allow "owners of problems" (or end-users) to act as designers" (Fischer 2003). Fischer focuses mainly on end-user developers (EUDs) whose "activities range from customization to component configuration and programming" (Fischer 2003). As the Fusion software system was developed with several types of users in mind and with different levels of expertise, we use the term "end-users" to refer to people who are potential or future users of the system or its parts developed in the project. Our concept of end-users includes not only developers, but also people who may not have any programming expertise.

The concept of Meta-Design is important for the creation of environments that empower users. From a designer's point of view, the challenge of Meta-Design is to design for designability: how to design something that is not only a final product to be "used", but also becomes a resource that is available and presents a potential for designing. While Fischer talks about people as "owners of problems", we extend his approach in the case presented in this chapter, and focus on everyday people as designers by being "owners of their practices". The notion of practice is incorporated into our design philosophy; we aim to understand people's practices and translate them into software toolkit design.

The chapter is organized as follows: Section 2 introduces the project and describes the chosen design philosophy and approach. Section 3 reports the case study and demonstrates the practical work carried out. Sections 4 and 5 discuss the findings and lessons learned, evaluating the outcomes of the case and identifying strategies of empowerment, while Section 6 summarizes the conclusions.

Introduction the case: P2P-Fusion

The work described in this chapter was conducted in the context of P2P-Fusion, which was a three-year research and development project (2006-2009). The project's aim was to create a novel peer-to-peer platform called *Fusion* for creating audiovisual social media applications (Figure 1, left). The Fusion system binds together a peer-to-peer network, a distributed metadata layer, social processing and enrichment features, support for embedded licenses, and a component-based toolkit called *Social Media Application ToolKit (SMAK)*. Specific, practical goals for the system were to support social activities that include the creative use and reuse of audiovisual content, and to provide a software toolkit with re-usable components. The aim was that people could use the media applications implemented with the SMAK to share, edit and enrich videos collaboratively (Figure 1, right). With the toolkit capabilities, the applications could also be tailored, and new applications be built to support particular media practices.

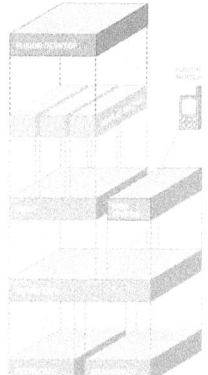 

Figure 1: An illustration of the Fusion software architecture (left) and a screen shot of one media application prototype built with SMAK components (right).

The P2P-Fusion project included a variety of large-scale research and development activities with several stakeholders (e.g., research institutions and audiovisual archives). In this chapter, we discuss the research and co-design activities in the early phases of the SMAK toolkit design carried out by University of Art and Design Helsinki (TAIK) in Finland during the first two years of the project. A core aim of the SMAK software design was to develop tools for constructing desktop social media applications that can be tailored for specific media practices of different user communities. It should be noted, however, that other software design and development activities took place in parallel to the activities described in this chapter (e.g., mobile client development; see Visanen & Rista 2009). The lower layers in the software architecture (e.g., *Mediaspace* and *Peerscape*) were designed at the same time, but this was accomplished through a more traditional software design process by computer scientists, with end-user application development and easy system management in mind.

From understanding practices to toolkit design

The study of people's practices has been of a longstanding interest in various fields of research (e.g., social science, cultural studies, philosophy), and has also been adopted in the field of design and design research (see, e.g., Botero et al. 2002). A practice is commonly seen as patterns of behaviour that include several units of activities which are interconnected to each other. Social practices are embodied and materially mediated arrangements of human activities that describe a particular way of going about an activity with its associated resources (Reckwitz 2002). Traditional software development and human–computer interaction (HCI) analysis usually focus on users' functions and execution of individual tasks. However, when the focus of attention is on the everyday practices of people, "practices" are taken as units of analysis instead of "problems" or "user needs". When translating practices into design language (e.g., description or illustration), a practice is manifested in a certain pattern or workflow that involves certain actors, employs a set of tools and relies on certain resources. Our particular aim, in the context of a toolkit design, is to identify the patterns and elements of the practices, and map them into the larger ecosystem of digital tools, systems and services (see, e.g., Botero et al. 2008).

In the project, this practice-oriented approach was essential, as it was envisioned that the Fusion platform would continue its evolution after the project's duration in the practices and development efforts of its user community, and could be connected with other software modules, libraries and APIs. Compared with many other R&D projects that aim to create technology or products for business, this project was designed from the beginning with the intention that it should lead to end-user empowerment in various ways, such as giving access to resources (i.e., Fusion software) from code level to ready-made applications; connecting communities with joint interests in international co-design workshops; and, through making the communities' practices visible through design tasks, enabling communities to identify and recognize their skills, strengths and potentials better.

The project's outcomes were to be licensed as open source software, so that anyone could have access to the code in all levels of the software architecture. However, as the modification of open source software requires software design and programming expertise, competences that are not easily available to most people, we felt that Fusion should go further than that and aim to be adaptable, extensible and designable by the end-users. To this end, the Fusion platform design included the Social Media Application ToolKit (SMAK) that was designated as the topmost layer of Fusion, and would contain a set of components for constructing applications. The aim was to design the software components in such a way that they would make sense to people from the point of view of their practices, and to make it in this way possible for them to enter the design environment and act as "everyday designers" (Wakkary & Maestri 2008). Thus, they could bring the inherent knowledge of their practices into the co-design process.

Co-design approach in P2P-Fusion

Designers of technology systems and tools are not generally able to alone foresee the great variety of interests and potential practices and understand the motivations of people. Furthermore, even when people act as designers in their everyday life, end-users themselves cannot easily foresee all the possibilities of how the tools can be applied or how some modifications in the software tools can open up possibilities for completely new practices. By bringing the designers of software tools and the "owners of practices" together, helping them to see one another as designers with different sets of skills and interests but with a potential mutual benefit ahead, they may be able to enter a more fruitful design dialogue, that may, as a result, create better tools and interesting new practices. This strategy created the foundation for the co-design activities in P2P-Fusion. The aim was to actively engage people as experts and owners of their practices in the design process. Therefore, our collaborative design activities took mainly the form of workshops, in which interaction designers and software developers collaborated with communities that have practices in using and sharing audiovisual media (rather than using, e.g., applied ethnographic methods).

The name *Content Community* was used in the project for the communities that participated as co-design partners in the project, bringing their practices to inform the design. The Content Communities can be characterized as communities of people that share activities together in a common environment or space, and have social and mediated interactions in multiple ways. We adapt and adjust Lave and Wenger's concept of "Communities of Practice" and deploy it as an approach in relation to communities' activities (Lave & Wenger 1991; Wenger 1998). In the context of P2P-Fusion, audiovisual content or content creation was the common denominator for the communities (hence Content Communities). We collaborated with different types of communities, as we hoped to obtain a broader view of media practices this way. We considered this essential, as the project was developing a toolkit that could be applied for a variety of activities.

The following goals of the software strategy set the objectives for the co-design process: 1) to explore Content Communities' needs, social practices and media use, and to re-use and translate these findings into design language (i.e., specifications, descriptions and technology solutions); 2) to support easy development of customizable applications with a component-based platform; and 3) to test the feasibility of the applications with representatives of the Content Communities. The ultimate design objective of the co-design process was to produce design descriptions for toolkit components that would form feasible Fusion designs based on the identified community's media practices. In addition, the Fusion design process was planned so that the software design and co-design efforts were feeding each other in dialogical process; the software development team obtained input from Content Communities for producing early prototypes of media applications which were built with a reusable software toolkit or building blocks (that were called SMAK software components), and Content Communities received the prototypes for use in evaluating designs and developing their own future applications.

The co-design process had three main phases: 1) initiating the co-design process, 2) co-designing activities and 3) exploring and testing the Fusion software. The co-design activities were continuous, programmed interactions (e.g., interviews, design tasks, workshops) that aimed to integrate the communities into the design process and enable forming of a design partnership between different parties in the project. In the following section, we will present and describe the first two phases in detail.

Co-designing the Fusion system and the reusable software toolkit components (SMAK)

Foundations for the co-design work were established in the first phase of the P2P-Fusion project. This included creating a shared co-design framework as well as finding new co-design partners, the Content Communities, that would participate in the design of the Fusion system based on their media practices, and possibly use and develop the software later. The partners in the project consortium came from multiple organizations and disciplines (e.g., software development, interaction design, archival institutions, legal and social sciences), and not all were familiar with co-design or similar approaches. Collaborative effort was therefore made to involve all the project partners in the co-design work. Ideas and expectations concerning the project, the Fusion system and its applications were collected in workshops. This facilitated creating a co-design plan and a development roadmap for Fusion, as well as recruiting Content Communities.

Recruitment of the Content Communities for the co-design activities started by mapping altogether 33 communities in Finland, Hungary and the Netherlands, some based on the project team's personal contacts. The communities ranged from amateur filmmakers and media educators to groups centred on skateboarding, music and family activities. Based on the mapping and pre-set criteria, a few communities per country were selected and invited to meetings in which the project was introduced and the community members were interviewed about their media use and interests regarding the project. In the following, we briefly introduce the Content Communities with which we mainly collaborated in Finland.

- **A music makers' community**

The community is an online music community, which supports music and band-driven activities, focusing on developing the real-world activities (concerts, promotion). They have a web portal that provides a common space to communicate and promote the activities of the bands, which are members of the community. The community supports open licensing (e.g., Creative Commons) and promotes remix-culture.

- **Extended family**

The extended family consists of geographically separated members and small groups who share their life events with each other using technologies such as blogs and photo sharing services to keep the family connected. The community was particularly interested in sharing and creative reuse of video, as they did not have a practical way to do this. Video clips shot with a digital camera of family members and events were usually stored on a CD and shared face-to-face.

- **Community organizing activities for children and youth**

The volunteer-based community consists of local groups in different parts of Finland, which organize activities for children and youth including singing, drama, play and performances. The community has various types of media content ranging from the instructors' learning materials to documentary photos and videos captured by the children's parents. Finding new tools for archiving and sharing media files within the community was relevant for the community.

- **Two sports enthusiast groups**

Common activities of the groups, comprised of acrobatics and parkour enthusiasts, include training and organizing events together. Learning moves and tricks are at the core of both communities' interests, which includes sharing of one's skills and obtaining feedback from others - videos can also be used for these. Although these communities were already using servers and available online video sharing services for sharing audiovisual content, they were interested in having a tool that would enable private sharing of photos and videos, including collaborative enrichment of their metadata. Some members were also interested in editing and remixing videos.

Co-design with the content communities

In the second phase of the project, close collaboration with the Finnish project team and the Content Communities took place. Co-design activities were organized that aimed at: 1) creating a shared understanding and design language among the co-design partners, and 2) mapping of the Content Communities' media practices, needs and ideas in ways that could inform the development of the Fusion software, and SMAK in particular. At this point, the software development team needed input for producing early prototypes of media applications built with initial SMAK components (i.e., reusable software building blocks).

The collaboration with the communities took place mainly face-to-face and via emails, proceeding gradually towards a more in-depth understanding of the communities' current and potential media practices (table 1). Semi-structured interviews were conducted first, in order to understand the social structure and current media sharing practices of the communities (themes included, for example, what kind of activities the community has and how media is shared currently). After this, two co-design workshops were organized, which engaged the project team (researchers, interaction designers and software developers) and the community members in collaborative design activities, producing further insight to the communities' media practices and needs, as well as design ideas and artefacts. The interviews and workshops were organized individually with each community so that a couple of members per community participated in the activities (usually the same members, men and women, aged around 30 years) with two to four people from the project team. These approximately two-hour meetings were documented on video in addition to notes and photos. Ultimately, the findings of the co-design activities were summarized and communicated in the form of Community Application Concepts for each community to inform the development of SMAK. The methods used in the co-design workshops are described in the next sections.

Activities with the Content Communities	Outcomes	Design document
I. Interviews	Initial understanding of the communities' structure and current media sharing practices	Community Application Concepts
II. SMAK Toys workshops	Mappings of interesting and useful media usage and sharing considering community practices	
III. Scenario and paper prototyping workshops	Further info on the communities' media practices and concrete design ideas regarding media applications	

Table 1: Activities and their outcomes in the second co-design phase.

Designing the SMAK Toys co-design tool

The project team at TAIK designed a collaborative design tool called the SMAK Toys for the co-design workshops with the communities. This was done in small, iterative workshops among project researchers, interaction designers and software developers. SMAK Toys is a set of about 30 magnetic cards that represent different types of media content, as well as ways to use and share the content (Figure 2, left). The individual cards are "building blocks" intended to facilitate creation of a shared design language, a common understanding about practices and a strategy for how they could be translated into the design of a component-based software toolkit (SMAK). The tool is inspired by methods that utilize low-tech elements to engage users in the design process such as PICTIVE (Muller 1991), and similar tools that have been used to help in making the features and functions of intangible digital systems more concrete and easier to connect to everyday life practices in the design and ideation activities (see, e.g., Botero et al. 2002). This toy-like design tool was motivated by the complexity of the software being designed (toolkit) plus the fact that most of the community members had not participated before in software development, and some had only limited experience of new digital technologies and social media.

Mapping with SMAK Toys

The first workshops with the Content Communities focused on finding out what kind of media usage and sharing would be useful and interesting for the communities, considering their practices. With this collaborative design exercise, we attempted to find initial answers to the following questions to provide input to the software development: 1) What types of media content did the communities want to use and share? 2) How would the communities like to use and collaboratively enrich the media content? 3) What kind of privacy and access management issues are relevant for the communities in media sharing?

The workshops began with an introduction, which included elaboration of the SMAK toolkit-in particular, how the aim was to develop not a fixed application, but a toolkit for building media sharing applications. The ideas of components and of applications built using such "building blocks" were illustrated with simple example pictures. After this, relevant SMAK Toys cards were selected and grouped collaboratively. The set of SMAK Toys cards used consisted of six subsets of pre-defined, colour-coded cards grouped by their functions (e.g., media content types, tools for adding metadata such as tags, user roles with different access rights), as well as empty cards on which new ideas could be written. The community members chose cards that they found relevant for their community practices, and also created new ones using the empty cards. The sessions usually started by picking out the media content types (e.g., video), and then selecting and prioritizing how the community members would like to use or manipulate the content (e.g., by commenting or annotating). The cards were attached onto a whiteboard, which enabled dynamic grouping and rearrangement of the cards as well as adding of complementary drawings and text next to the cards. The outcome of each workshop was a "map" that illustrated the community's media practice (Figure 2, middle).

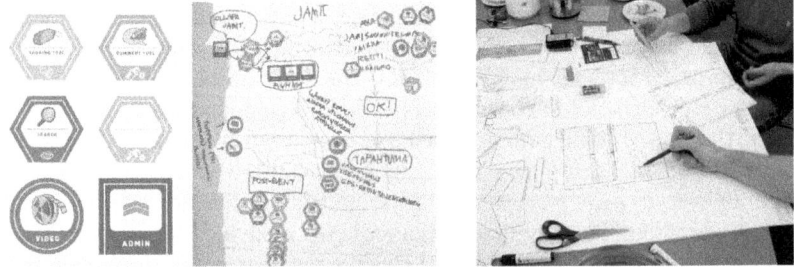

Figure 2: SMAK Toys cards (left) and mapping (middle), and paper prototyping (right)

Creating scenarios and paper prototypes

These workshops aimed to provide further information on the communities' media practices as well as concrete design ideas regarding media applications. We discussed first briefly the mappings created earlier with the SMAK Toys and any thoughts or ideas that the community members had since the last workshop. After this, the community members created and wrote down with the help of the project team one or two scenarios which described potential media-sharing situations for the community (e.g., sharing of photos and videos of a community event). The scenarios were based partially on the discussions in the last workshop and outlined how the community members would like to use and share audiovisual content, ignoring their current restrictions. Next, the community members were asked to create a paper prototype of a media application on a large paper sheet using paper elements, colourful stickers, pens, scissors, sticky notes and glue as materials (Figure 2, right). The aim was to summarize and concretize the design ideas developed during the previous activities. No particular instructions were given regarding the prototypes except that we asked the community members to make a sketch of a media application that would show functionalities they find important to have readily available (a kind of application "main page").

Results of the co-design process

The main outcomes of the first co-design phase were a mapping of different types of potential Content Communities, co-design partnerships with the Content Communities, and establishment of an initial roadmap and co-design framework with the co-design partners. The co-design activities with the Content Communities in the second phase provided multifaceted insight to the communities' media practices, as well as insight into the feasibility of the potential software toolkit structure.

Although there was some overlap between the communities' needs, each of the Finnish Content Communities had unique media practices, which could be potentially facilitated with new tools that enable sharing and collaborative enrichment of audiovisual content. For example, locative information, such as GPS coordinates and routes, were found to be important for one of the parkour enthusiasts' training and video practices. A mobile interface for sharing audiovisual content was also essential for this community, as their activities usually take place on the move. The extended family, for one, was interested in sharing videos and video compilations via "channels" among the family members, and also exporting some of the content to their existing blogs. On the other hand, being able to collaboratively comment and tag media files was relevant for the practices of all the communities.

The findings of the interviews and workshops organized with the communities were summarized in rich Community Application Concepts for each community. The purpose of the concepts was to provide concrete ideas for implementing gradually initial SMAK component and media application prototypes. The concepts were communicated among the project partners using a common template including text and pictures in order to facilitate identification of overlap between the different concepts and issues that needed more input. They also served as a basis for functional specifications for the

SMAK software components. The concepts provided the following types of information for the software development team: 1) types of media content that the communities want to use and share (e.g., video, photos); 2) descriptions of the communities' media practices; 3) list of basic functions needed for accessing the content (e.g. video player); 4) list of more complicated and social functions (e.g., tagging, commenting and annotating of content, video editing, additional interfaces such as APIs); and 5) list of functions needed for access management (e.g., "administrator" user role).

The co-design process also provided valuable input for the whole Fusion platform design. As the Content Communities had an existing social network and identity online, it was essential for them to be able to integrate new software into their existing digital ecosystem of tools and services. This led to the development of the Web Bridge application that serves as a bridge between the P2P network and the World Wide Web.

After evaluating the Community Application Concepts of the Finnish, Hungarian and Dutch Content Communities with the project partners, three demo applications were developed. These did not match any individual concept, but aimed to capture components and functions that could support most of the common, and some of the more specific, media practices identified in the co-design. For example, one of the applications provided ways to integrate locative information with media, as this type of practice was identified in some of the Finnish and Hungarian communities. The prototype applications were then explored and evaluated in the 3rd co-design phase with the Content Communities and some new people that had not participated yet in the co-design.

Discussion and lessons learned

In this section we will discuss the experiences and main lessons learned from the case study described in this chapter. We will address, for example, the challenges of developing a co-design framework and approach in a multidisciplinary environment and design partnership. We will also evaluate the success of the co-design methods and tools used during the process. Based on our experiences, we will propose strategies and means to support and facilitate people's activities, and how to empower them to act as "everyday designers".

Co-design framework in multidisciplinary environment

The P2P-Fusion project's context set some fairly strict constraints: the consortium, budgets, project activities and deliverables had to be fixed before the project started, and had to follow the original proposal quite faithfully. However, the commitment to the co-design approach from the beginning of the project made it possible to have the resources to devote to the work, in terms of personnel, work hours, and workshops. Effort was invested in facilitating formation of a shared co-design framework among the project partners. Although this was, in retrospect, a positive experience, initiating and maintaining the co-design approach turned out to be more challenging than anticipated. The co-design approach is still relatively uncommon in software design, although the ideas underlying participative design approaches are not new (Sanders & Stappers 2008). It therefore seems that for the co-design approach to be applied in such a large, distributed and multi-disciplinary project as ours, it requires a very carefully planned strategy for effective mobilization of the co-design partners.

In addition, it is essential to include early as well as periodical activities dedicated to developing a shared co-design framework and language. Nurturing the co-design approach and concretizing the value of each of the co-design partners' efforts to the design process is important, as the lack of common design philosophy may blur the design goals and decrease the partners' motivation.

Design partnerships: collaborating with the Content Communities

It seemed relatively easy for the Content Communities to grasp their role as co-designers in the project and the idea that their input would form the basis for developing the Fusion system and SMAK. This was a positive finding, as the P2P-Fusion project was the first software design experience for most of the community members. The challenges in the collaboration with the communities were related mostly to communicating the idea of a software toolkit as well as the underlying P2P technology, with its potential and limitations. Another important factor that affected the sustaining of the co-design relationship with the communities was that the project team had difficulties in providing mature enough software for the communities to explore. Developing high-fidelity prototypes fast is particularly challenging in large and distributed projects dealing with issues of overall system/service architecture and integration (Kurvinen et al. 2006). Not being to able to provide concrete examples of the system being designed, or providing prototypes that do not match expectations, had a negative effect on the enthusiasm of the communities. Timing of user involvement is crucial in the software development process, and in retrospect, it might have been better to collaborate in the beginning mainly with some lead users or developers instead of several communities, and later on, when the technological foundation had been solidified, involve a larger number of people in the process.

Another observation from the co-design partnerships with the communities is that it is important to choose motivated co-design partners and create an open atmosphere from the start. It is essential that the people who participate in the collaborative design process have real life needs and/or practices that can provide input to the design process. This does not mean that the participants need to be technology experts or familiar with software in general. Also, their practices do not have to be directly related to the domain of design-sometimes practices that are in some way marginal may provide innovative insight for design (see, e.g., Ljungblad & Holmquist 2007; Naukkarinen et al. 2009). For example, in the P2P-Fusion project, the parkour enthusiasts gave a lot of useful information for the designers, helping them to envision how locative information could integrate with audiovisual media sharing. Collaboration with different kinds of communities was suited well for the software toolkit design in the project, but naturally the selection of design partners depends on the type of software being designed, as well as on its maturity.

Some more practical observations were also made during the project regarding the co-design partnership with the Content Communities. When co-designing with people who are not paid professionals working for the project, it is advisable to discuss the level and nature of engagement among the collaborators periodically during the design process. As these people participate often in projects on a volunteer basis, there should be common understanding of how much time and effort the participants are willing to invest in the project. In addition, an emphasis should be on planning and articulating what are the concrete and intangible benefits for communities to participate in the co-design process; in other words, what do co-design partners obtain in return for investing their time, skills and expertise in their practices? Although the communities were given access, for example, to the open source Fusion software and practical knowledge produced in the project, other compensation mechanisms might also have been implemented. It should also be recognized that people have various skills and expertises, and different motivations to take part in a co-design process; therefore, the process should be open-ended to support flexible agency without predefined roles.

However, it should also be noted that choosing motivated co-design partners in the beginning of a project does not lead automatically to a sustained and successful design partnership. Good communication and openness are essential in interaction among design partners; it is important to keep everyone periodically updated about the status of the project and the use of different parties' design input in the process. It should also be kept in mind that collaboration with design partners might be interrupted or finished for reasons such as changes in participant's needs, interests, available time and resources. Longer projects in particular should thus be flexible with respect to these factors. The inclusion of many communities in the design process facilitated coping with these issues in the P2P-Fusion project, as it enabled adjusting the level of engagement of different communities according to their interests.

Co-design methods, tools and work practices

Several methods and tools were used during the co-design process to engage people in collaborative design. The use of low-fidelity design tools such as the SMAK Toys and paper prototypes in the ideation and feature-harvesting phase seemed to work well in creating a common language among the design partners, as they enabled the communities to express their practices, needs and interests without needing to know technological details. The use of hands-on exercises also concretized the design ideas. However, the ideas that came up in the collaborative design sessions were not always in line with the project objectives that were defined before the process by the project plan and thus our contract with EU. Also, many more ideas were produced than what was possible to implement in the software prototypes. These imbalances challenged the ideals of the co-design approach, and in retrospect, should have been better anticipated. For example, a process could have been designed regarding how to share the so-called supplementary ideas developed with communities so that the future developers of the Fusion system and SMAK toolkit, or other similar systems, could utilize them easily (i.e., sharing ideas and scenarios with external developers and other OS projects in online cooperative platforms).

One of the key insights of the co-design process was that the professional designers should provide access to resources and tools to encourage communities to share their experiences, knowledge or designs with their peers. The interactions between the project team and the communities were based largely on face-to-face meetings and e-mail. Although some wiki-based tools for online collaboration were made available (e.g., learn.p2p-fusion.org), they were used mostly for publishing instructions and tips related to the Fusion software prototypes. Looking back, professional designers should have provided access to the project's resources with contextualization of data and guidance for multiple levels of appropriation of the software (e.g., customization, configuration, coding modules) that would enhance different agencies. As well, more interactive and sophisticated online tools could have been used to promote discussion among the co-design partners. This could have facilitated exchange of experiences, ideas and knowledge between, for example, Content Communities in different countries who had similar interests, and make the design process more transparent across groups and organization boundaries. However, using online tools for fostering discussion among software developers and user representatives to inform design is challenging even when a dedicated online community of product enthusiasts already exists (Hess et al. 2008). Existing tools such as wikis and discussion forums do not necessarily work immediately without customizing and require active updating and moderation in order to be satisfactory.

End-user empowerment: challenges of developing a toolkit

The P2P-Fusion project's fundamental hypothesis was that social video creation and sharing within communities of interest would greatly benefit from certain kinds of new tools. The Fusion system was also designed with various empowering intentions, such as freedom from centralized servers and commercial services and the inclusion of a software toolkit for designing custom applications. The process was designed to be inclusive and collaborative, with an emphasis on the discovery and collaborative evolution of the Content Communities' audiovisual practices, and on the potential creative interactions between the various user communities involved in the project. The chosen strategy also acknowledged people as potential designers of the Fusion software system, and provided an open access to different levels of software from source code to APIs and CSS.

At the core of the project's end-user empowerment is the produced SMAK ToolKit, which contains reusable software components that interested parties can use and develop further in various purposes. Toolkit development is much more difficult from a software design point of view than developing fixed applications (see, e.g., Suzi et al. 2009). A designable toolkit introduces an additional layer of abstraction into the design process, which makes it cognitively more challenging for all participants to envision the target of the design. A great challenge in developing SMAK was determining how the features of the not-yet-existing software toolkit could be discussed in a way that was not too technical, abstract and confusing. How could the available functionality be presented concretely enough to make sense, but without too much rigidity, to make its potential for new designs evident? We attempted to tackle these issues, for example, by designing and using the SMAK Toys in the beginning of the co-design process. The SMAK Toys proved to be an effective way to concretize the complexity of toolkit components, help in creating a shared design language, and facilitate connecting the communities' practices to the toolkit functions. Similar low-fidelity co-design tools could be developed in the future to support early phases of software toolkit design. However, in the later phases of the development, hands-on experimentation with functional prototypes is recommended in order to obtain more realistic input regarding the adaptability of toolkits into people' practices.

In P2P-Fusion, the development of the toolkit to a level that could be easily demonstrated took longer than expected. In terms of results, the final system did not fully meet the goals we had set for ourselves, due to severe limitations we encountered in key technologies, and hence did not fully realize the empowering impact that we had hoped for. Had we known in the early phases of the project what we know now, the overall co-design process would have been easier to plan, starting from the technological roadmap to the co-design input. Despite the difficulties and challenges, we generally believe that there is now more than ever a need for this type of approach to design due to the opportunities created by, for example, Web 2.0 resources and techniques (e.g., mash ups, widgets, APIs and even simple skinning through CSS). We anticipate that it will be hard to develop integrated toolkits that could satisfy the massive diversity in end-user practices, and instead it will be increasingly common that popular software systems will be constructed by connecting diverse designable and adaptable components together, and that these components and their capabilities will increasingly become familiar to end-users through everyday practice. It will thus be a worthwhile effort to design these kinds of tools with ecosystemic compatibility and end-user designability in mind.

Conclusions

We have presented a case in which a software toolkit was co-designed together by communities of everyday people whose media practices formed the starting point and the core of the design and development process. The chosen community practice-driven design approach, together with appropriate co-design tools, proved to be a suitable method for a software toolkit design. Our case also indicates that "everyday designers" without programming skills or knowledge of complex technology solutions (e.g., P2P technology) can be engaged in the design process if their participation is facilitated and supported via multiple means of interactions.

The co-design with Content Communities provided an abundance of material that provided insight to the current and emerging media practices of different types of communities. Using practices as a unit of analysis in the software design process helped in contextualizing the communities' media use in larger ecosystems of people, tools and resources. The Community Application Concepts also proved to be useful in transferring the co-design findings as shared design documents to efficiently guide and structure the software design and development process. The most challenging aspect in the co-design was to establish a shared understanding of the software toolkit, as the concept of toolkit is rather abstract, and people are not familiar with toolkits. However, our experiences in using the SMAK Toys for connecting the real-world community practices with the toolkit component design were positive, and encourage development of further low-fidelity co-design tools to support early phases of software toolkit design.

We conclude that, in the long run, an open-ended system with development options may be a more sustainable investment than a specific application, allowing for more independence for end-users as well as flexibility in systems. In spite of its challenges, design for openness and for designability is something that designers, technology developers and institutions need to learn, because in the rapidly evolving global and open digital ecosystem, only collaborative and designable systems and components will be able to respond to the increasingly sophisticated demands of the evolution of the practices of people.

Acknowledgements: This chapter is a result of research carried out as part of the P2P-Fusion project, co-funded by the European Union through the IST programme under FP6. We wish to thank the members of the Finnish Content Communities and our colleagues at the Arki research group at TAIK who participated in the P2P-Fusion project. We also thank the project consortium, which included, in addition to the University of Art and Design Helsinki (coordinator), the Helsinki Institute for Information Technology from Finland; Delft University of Technology, Sound and Vision and KnowledgeLand from the Netherlands; and the Budapest University of Technology and Economics and the National Audiovisual Archive from Hungary.

References

Botero A., Oilinki I., Kommonen K.-H., Salgado M. 'Digital tools for community building: Towards community-driven design' Paper presented at the Participatory Design Conference, Malmö, Sweden (June 23-25, 2002)

Botero A., Naukkarinen A., Saad-Sulonen J. 'Mapping social practices through collaborative exercises and visualizations' Proceedings of NordiCHI 2008 Using Bridges Lund, Sweden ACM (18-22 October , 2008)

Botero A., Kommonen K.-H. Coordinating everyday life: The design of practices and tools in the "Life Project" of a group of active seniors. Proceedings of the COST 298 Conference: The Good, the Bad and the Challenging.   Slovenia: ABS-Center (2009) pp. 736-745

Fischer G., 'Meta-design: Beyond user-centered and participatory design' ed. Stephanidis J.J.A.C. Proceedings of HCI International 2003 Lawrence Erlbaum Associates, Mahwah, NJ: Crete, Greece (June, 2003) pp. 88-92

Fischer G., Scharff E. 'Meta-design: Design for designers' eds. Boyarski D, Kellogg W. A. Proceedings of the Third International Conference on Designing Interactive Systems ACM New York (2000) pp. 396-405.

Haddon L., Mante E., Sapio B., Kommonen K.-H., Fortunati L., Kant A., eds. Everyday Innovators: Researching the Role of Users in Shaping ICTs Dordrecht: Springer (2005)

Hess J., Offenberg S., Pipek V. 'Community-driven development as participation? - Involving user communities in a software design process' Participatory Design Conference – PDC'08 Bloomington, IN, USA (2008)

ISO/IEC.13407 Human-Centred Design Processes for Interactive Systems ISO/IEC 13407 (1999)

Kurvinen E., Aftelak A., Häyrynen A. 'User-centered design in the context of large and distributed projects' CHI '06 Extended Abstracts on Human Factors in Computing Systems Montréal, Québec, Canada, (April 22-27, 2006) CHI '06 ACM New York, NY, 995-1000. DOI=http://doi.acm.org/10.1145/1125451.1125642

Lave J., Wenger, E. Situated Learning: Legitimate Peripheral Participation Cambridge University Press (1991)

Ljungblad S., Holmquist L. E. 'Transfer scenarios: grounding innovation with marginal practices' Proceedings of the SIGCHI Conference on Human Factors in Computing Systems San Jose, California, USA (April 28-May 03, 2007) CHI '07 ACM New York, NY, pp. 737-746

Muller M. J. 'Pictive - an exploration in participatory design' Proceedings of the SIGCHI Conference on Human Factors in Computing Systems: Reaching Through Technology eds. Robertson S.P, Olson M., Olson J.S., New Orleans, Louisiana, United States (April 27-May 02, 1991) CHI '91 ACM New York, NY, 225-231. DOI= http://doi.acm.org/10.1145/108844.108896

Muller M. J. 'Participatory design: The third space in HCI' eds. Jacko J., Sears A. The Human-computer Interaction Handbook: Fundamentals, Evolving Technologies and Emerging Applications Mahwah, New Jersey: Lawrence Erlbaum Associates (2002) pp. 1051-1068

Naukkarinen A., Sutela J., Botero A., Kommonen K.-H. 'Designing locative media for creative misuse: learning from urban intervention' Proceedings of the 13th international Mindtrek Conference: Everyday Life in the Ubiquitous Era Tampere, Finland (September 30-October 02, 2009) MindTrek '09 ACM New York, NY, pp. 124-127. DOI=http://doi.acm.org/10.1145/ 1621841.1621865

Raymond E. The Cathedral and the Bazaar: Musings on Linux and Open Source by an Accidental Revolutionary Cambridge, MA: O'Reilly (1999)

Reckwitz A. 'Toward a theory of social practices' European Journal of Social Theory 5 (2) (2002) pp. 243-263

Sanders E.B.-N. 'From user-centred to participatory design approaches' Frascara J. (ed.) Design and the Social Sciences Taylor & Francis Books Limited (2002)

Sanders E. B.-N., Stappers P. 'Co-creation and the new landscapes of design' CoDesign: International Journal of CoCreation in Design and the Arts 4 (1) (2008) pp. 5-18

Schuler D., Namioka A. eds. Participatory Design: Principles and Practices Hillsdale, NJ: Lawrence Erlbaum Associates (1993)

Suzi R., Saad-Sulonen J., Botero A. 'Co-designing with web.py: Urban Mediator' Python Magazine 3 (2) (2009) pp. 27-34

Tuomi I. Networks of Innovation: Change and Meaning in the Age of the Internet New York: Oxford University Press (2002)

Visanen K., Rista A. 'Fusion mobile: Challenges of designing a P2P social networking application' Mindtrek (September 30 - October 2, 2009) Tampere, Finland

Von Hippel E. 'Innovation by User Communities: Learning from Open-Source Software' MIT Sloan Management Review 42 (4) (2001)

Wakkary R., Maestri L., 'Aspects of everyday design: Resourcefulness, adaptation, and emergence' International Journal of Human-Computer Interaction 24 (5) (2008) pp. 478-491

Wenger E. Communities of Practice: Learning, Meaning, and Identity New York: Cambridge University Press (1998)

Ike Picone

Mapping Users' Motivations and Thresholds for Casually "Produsing" News

Crisis in the printed news sector: An opportunity for user empowerment?

Since the emergence of audiovisual media, defeatists among both industry and academia have been announcing the death of the newspaper. Admittedly, the Western newspaper business has been in a downturn for several years now, losing almost half of its readership in the last 15 years (The PEW Internet Research Centre 2008). Up until now, the presses have not stopped printing newspapers, though. Radio bulletins made newspaper extras less urgent, for example, while the nightly news hastened the death of the evening paper. Still, newspapers survived. However, adapting to the most disruptive technology of them all, the internet, is something newspaper companies are still dealing with (Knowledge@Wharton 2009). Furthermore, the recent economic crisis is likely to strike hard in this two-sided market. First, paid subscriptions and readership continue to decline. The strategic choice of many news publishers to offer online news for free has been fruitful in terms of increased readership (World Association of Newspapers 2008), but so far this has not been monetized. The revenues of online advertisements do not live up to the expectations and are not likely to do so in the near future (Krol 2009).

The impact of this evolution is making itself felt, as newspapers in general have failed to obtain new revenue streams out of the so-called Web 2.0. The newspaper industry had already been struggling to mount an appropriate response to the coming of age of the Web and the increased cross-mediality it engenders in the news business – and beyond –, and the current crisis is not making this any easier. Unless, that is, I see the current developments as an opportunity for innovation. Dutch journalist, talk show host and internet specialist Francisco van Jole (2009) argues that this crisis is forcing newspapers to examine why other players are becoming the most important news sources online, referring to the newspapers inability to adapt their product to the public's changing way of life. I agree with Van Jole that it is important to take into account the user and the role news plays in his or her daily life when searching for innovative answers to the malaise. But I could go one step further in this more user-oriented approach to the matter, not only seeing it as an opportunity to create new revenue streams, but also as a way of empowering news users.

In today's discourse on new media Web 2.0, applications are in general considered empowering technologies, giving users the ability not only to use information offered by the media, but also to actively contribute to it. This certainly applies to the news industry. The possibilities the user has to participate or contribute to the news by personalising it, sharing it, blogging it, capturing it, etc. are endless. Through these activities of *produsage*, a syncopation of production and usage coined by Bruns (2007), they challenge the traditional news(paper) business in many ways from the strategic to the editorial level (Geens et al. 2007; Picone 2008). Through Web 2.0 technology, the articulate consumers of news get the chance to voice their opinions.

However, experts on new media tend to paint users in their own image: tech-savvy, always on, news junkies. Through our research on this topic, I have had the opportunity to attend several presentations where internet or Web 2.0 specialists preached the end of the traditional news offerings. But thinking that people will use these participative possibilities just because they can is a rather technologically deterministic point of view. Trebor Scholtz warns against the false newness that is aimed at luring investors into new media ventures, which reminds him of the techno–economic utopianism of the 1990s (Scholz 2008). In an online – positive – critique on Web 2.0 Coleman (2008) puts it as follows:

> "The discourse around Web 2.0, in referring to the well-known suite of social media technologies, including blogs, wikis, and social networking sites, is often accompanied by a misguided mixture of hope and pronouncements rooted in a soft form of technological determinism that asserts that using these technologies can bring into being a cluster of democratic forces and impulses – collaboration, transparency, participatory democracy, and decentralization."

Now that the Web 2.0 hype is slowly subsiding, it is important to establish the degree to which the reality meets the expectations created by the hype. In other words, it is important to get to know the user. How are people (not) using these possibilities, why and to which ends? This chapter aims to contribute to the knowledge I have of the user and his/her attitude towards the technological possibilities to engage with the news. I therefore want to look at the motivations and thresholds which dictate whether regular, non-lead-users participate, or not, in the news. I am aware of the fact that user orientation creates inertia for change and that listening only to traditional, "non-participative" news users is likely to stress the benefits of the status quo (Ihlström et al. 2006). Nevertheless, technological evolution is not necessarily linear and non lead-users – or the early and late majority in Rogers' diffusion theory (Rogers 2003) – can give us clues to the thresholds or opportunities confronting users in the process of adopting or domesticating these new ways of using news.

The possibilities of participating in the news online are both technological and social in nature (Ihlström et al. 2006), and it is the later I will focus upon. I believe that users have the power to shape technology in the various ways they use it to their own ends, and hence, that they can be a driver for their own empowerment. In order to understand the impact of this self-empowerment, I cannot solely look at high profile users, but must also take into account the overall majority of today's news users.

The online news produser: Lost in the hype?

Before I look at the conceptual framework needed, let us turn to the literature to illustrate the necessity of a more user centred approach to the topic. I would like to make two points. First, news produsage has been abundantly researched over the last few years, but no single answer has yet been formulated to the question of whether this is reality or mere hype. On the one hand, this phenomenon is depicted as a fundamental one. Örnebring (2007, 2) states:

> "The blurring of the distinction between producers and consumers is not just hype but empirical reality. The blurring of the role and profession of the journalist (cf. the discussions of whether bloggers are journalists, for example) can thus be viewed as a "special case" within the general blurring of boundaries between media producers and media consumers."

Cardoso (2007), on the other hand, finds little evidence of disappearing boundaries between producers and users and between professional journalism and non-professional activities.

Second, this research tradition focuses mainly on news produsage from the point of view of practitioners and media organisations, at the cost of news users. Plenty of studies have been undertaken on the larger subject of user influence and interactivity in online newspapers (Örnebring 2007). The impact of the increased interactivity of the public on the news production process and the role of the traditional journalist is often central to those studies (Paulussen et al. 2007). Referring to the first point of hype versus reality, these studies seem to put forward a rather critical approach to the matter. Ugille et al. (2008) point out the – in our opinion very important – discrepancy between the optimistic views held by the believers of citizen journalism like Dan Gillmor (2004) and Axel Bruns (2007) and the reluctance of traditional mainstream media newsrooms to deal with user-generated content (UGC) for fear of loosing their top-down gatekeeper role. David Domingo (2008) emphasizes this gap between the participatory potential of the web and the actual use of interactive features and speaks of the myth of interactivity. He points to the professional culture of traditional journalists and their rigid news production routines as an important factor for this gap.

However, users as well do not seem to massively embrace the possibilities offered by the web to engage with the news. A study showed that 58 percent of the Dutch citizens never even read the news posted by "regular" people, and only 6 percent casually put news online (Vermaas et al. 2008). Quandt (2007, 19) argues that users and journalists both rather stick to the "good old journalism", following the traditional news values, which reflect the relevance for the user. This seems to correspond to the idea that the social structure of (online) publishing is not changing as fast as the constantly improving technological capacities of the online medium (Kling & Callahan 2003).

But there is little research investigating to what extent users are actually interested in interacting and participating on news sites (Bergström 2007). As Boczkowski (2002) notes, there is a lack of research on the actual ways of consuming news through online newspapers, on the habits of online news consumers and the import of online newspapers to them. How does the user see these evolutions? What are important incentives for him/her to engage? But also, what are thresholds, motivations not to do so? I believe that looking at produsage from a user point of view will not only contribute to the understanding of news produsage as a social practice, but also as a political and economic process in society. Therefore, gaining insight into the attitude, the motivations and the thresholds for users to produse news is important. This can help us understand the phenomenon significantly and especially make us see more clearly into this blurring divide. This leads us to our first research question:

Q1: What are important factors determining whether a user will engage or not with a certain news item? In answering this question, I will try to find motivations underlying different kinds of news produsage, such as commenting, blogging, sharing, etc. independently from the medium or channel. I will first consult the existing literature on the general motivations to produse, which will mostly involve lead-users, focussing on news-related produsage. This will be expanded with the results of our own qualitative research amongst 18 non-lead-users of news, as explained below. In order to research this blurring divide, I must come to a workable conceptual framework that allows us to look at the right factors from a user perspective. In accordance with the point made before about the lack of a user perspective in existing research on user-generated news content, I will start from the framework presented by Örnebring (2007), and adjust it to the needs of a user-oriented approach to user-generated news.

Towards a conceptual framework

I believe that the interactivity between users and producers, while still a vague domain, should certainly be taken into account when looking at online (news) use. It can after all challenge the traditional roles of the news media like gate keeping and agenda setting. Indeed, people are blogging, sharing, tagging, etc., in other words, engaging with content and producers online. When I conceptualise the user, I must therefore operate a framework that encompasses these actions (Picone 2008). As Van Dijck (2009) argues, both conceptually and methodologically, media scholars will need to devise new ways to assess user trends across these new platforms.

I propose a more constructivist approach based on Giddens' structuration theory as outlined by Mante-Meijer & Loos (see their chapter in this volume). Structure, or in this case technology, both shapes and is shaped by the way it is used. The focus lies on the enablers and the constraints of people's (innovative) use of new technologies or services. The user is central in our research, both in our methodology and conceptually. As an analytical framework, I will build on our framework proposed earlier (Picone 2008) to classify activities of produsage from a user's point of view, rather than from an organisational, economical or professional one.

When looking at UGC, I must know what I am looking for. Örnebring (2007) points out the vagueness of UGC as a catch-all term, recalling Alvin Toffler's idea of the prosumer and how it can refer to almost any user activity. He suggests a conceptualisation of the role of UGC in online newspapers along three dimensions based on the ideas of Alvin Toffler (the prosumer), Henry Jenkins (convergence culture), and Yochai Benchler (the wealth of networks): customization versus production, popular culture-orientation versus news-information orientation and centralised versus distributed production. However, not all of these three dimensions are equally important from a user perspective. Especially the latter, as Örnebring himself is first to admit, is difficult to apply directly to online newspapers. Still, I build on the first two to come to a conceptualisation of news-related UGC practices from a user perspective. Via our qualitative research I try to empirically ground the comments and additions I propose to Örnebring's work.

Consumption versus production

Örnebring makes the distinction between acts of customization and acts of production. The former applies when the user does not generate actual content, but rather comments on existing content or generates relatively small amounts of it. The latter applies when content is actually being produced for other users to consume, e.g. through blogs, podcasts, etc. The question is whether this distinction prevails in the eye of the user. Indeed, I could raise some questions as to why Örnebring would classify certain forms of content creation, even if small, as customization. From a professional point of view, this seems acceptable, as comments might not be directly competing with the provision of news articles by journalist.

For a user, however, the fact that he is adding his idea or his vision to the news might very well be an act he would consider as producing, even if this only involves the rating of an article. The fact that Örnebring classifies commenting as both customization (on articles) and production (on forums) might also point to some confusion on his side Customization appears to be an act of produsage that specifically relates to the consumption of news. Therefore I propose a distinction between news produsage actions where the users produce content in any form whatsoever, and those where the user customizes news for his consumption, without producing any form of content. I translated this into the following research question:

Q2: Are actions whereby the user produces content distinctively different than actions where information is merely processed? In order to answer this question, I will turn to the users motivations to examine possible important differences in the motivations to engage with news and the motivations to consume news-related UGC.

Strictly news content versus news-related content

From Galtung & Ruge's (1965) famous list of news factors on (for an overview of the research see Harcup & O'Neil (2001)), the newsworthiness of facts and stories has been studied extensively – albeit mostly from a journalistic, gate-keeping point of view. What makes news worth engaging with, however, is less clear. Örnebring acknowledges the role of the type of content. Again, he looks at it from a production perspective when he ask the question what type of content users are invited to generate and what parts of the online newspaper they are allowed to manipulate. He links this question to the idea of empowerment and from this perspective it is certainly important to look at whether the user is given the opportunity to also engage in "hard news" or primarily in other types of content.

Again, from the perspective of a user, content will be important too, but the hard news - soft news difference, may be of less relevance. For a football fan, the act of participating by commenting on a bad review of his team might seem as relevant as doing the same on some political issue. In order to understand the importance of content for the produsage of news, other criteria appear more relevant. When researching the list of most emailed articles of the New York Times, Thorson (2008) found that articles offering advice about life issues tended to stay on the list for a disproportionate length of time, suggesting that users are proactively sending these articles to their social networks. Here, the type of content becomes important in the light of the social network of the user. Whether news is hard or soft seems less relevant than whether it is worth sharing or not. This results in our third research question:

Q3: Does news content play a role in users' willingness to engage with the news and if so, to what aspects of the content does it relate. The underlying hypothesis is that, in the mind of the user, production and consumption are clearly distinct activities, but move on a continuum from merely usage to production.

Motivations to participate online

As a starting point, I would like to look at users' motivations to generate online news information in various ways. I expect the literature to provide us more insights on lead users, whereas our own research explicitly focuses on less tech-savvy, casually participating users who are more likely to address thresholds. I therefore make the distinction between people who contribute on a more casual level and so-called citizen journalists, which often work together with the media in a more formal way.

If I follow the typology of blogs made by Herring et al. (2004) some kind of blogs are more interesting than others in the light of news produsage. Filter blogs, where users skim the net for information and comment on those topics they think are relevant, are more interesting than online diaries with daily personal stories. So are knowledge blogs (K-log), where users gather information on a specific knowledge domain as opposed to travel blogs, photo blogs, memory blogs or conversation blogs. Filters and K-logs compete more directly with news media's role as gatekeeper, agenda-setter or news producer (Picone 2008).

From a user perspective, however, the motivations to participate in news or merely to tell a story on a blog are not necessarily that distinct. Nardi et al. (2004) distinguish five, not-mutually exclusive motivations for blogging: documenting one's life, providing commentary and opinions, expressing deeply felt emotions (blogs as catharsis), articulating ideas through writing, and forming and maintaining community forums. When I put this next to the typology of blogs offered by Herring et al., documenting one's live is likely to be linked to the journal, travel or photo blogs. Forming community forums rather relates to blogs as a way of conversation, as a communication tool or an alternative communication channel (Stefanone & Jang 2007).

The blog tracking site Technorati (2008a) puts some figures to these facts as 79 percent of American bloggers write to speak their mind on areas of interest and 73 percent do it to share expertise and experiences with others. Only 32 percent use it to keep families and friends updated on their life. Another interesting fact is the measure of success of someone's blog, where personal satisfaction is mentioned by 75 percent of the American bloggers, whereas only 58 percent and 53 percent mention the number of posts and unique visitors respectively (Technorati 2008b). All these figures seem to reflect the very personal nature of the motivations to blog. This corresponds to the image Papacharissi (2004) presents of the blogger as being chiefly motivated by the self-fulfilment of personal expression. But why would certain people put a lot of effort in their writings, almost treating the topics they write about with a journalistic rigueur?

Part of the answer might come from the professional amateur or Pro-Am (Bruns 2007). Leadbeater & Miller (2004, 20) have a very interesting view of the Pro-Am:

> "A Pro-Am pursues an activity as an amateur, mainly for the love of it, but sets a professional standard... they pursue it with the dedication and commitment associated with a professional. For Pro-Ams, leisure is not passive consumerism but active and participatory; it involves the deployment of publicly accredited knowledge and skills, often built up over a long career, which has involved sacrifices and frustrations."

Here, two aspects can be linked to news produsage. First, I can see a link with the concept of the enjoyer. Irene Costera-Meyer (2005) coined this term in her research on television audiences. She states enjoying is not necessarily equal to relaxation or entertainment. For someone who is interested in politics it could be watching a political debate. Likewise, for a thorough laptop user with good writing skills, commenting on a news article can be less lean-forward than having to click a link is for a television fan with no interest in contributing whatsoever. Pro-Ams enjoy actively contributing and do it passionately. A Pro-Am citizen journalist will then cover topics with the professional rigueur of a journalist, maybe even to become one. According to Technorati (2008b) 1/4th of American bloggers write to get published or featured in traditional media. Second is the link with the content, as a Pro-Am could also be e.g. a passionate follower of 17th century Japanese calligraphy, mastering the art. If he decides to blog about it, he will be driven by his passion for the art, not necessarily by the love of the journalistic game.

The most engaged users in terms of time and effort they put in the interaction with journalists are probably the citizen journalists. The central motivation for citizen journalists to participate in collaborative news projects stems from a feeling of impending loss of values. They swing into action because professional journalism is not fulfilling its role (Paulussen et al. 2007). This role now also includes responding to users' input. Schultz (2000) believes that more readers might be attracted to contribute and be motivated to get rid of their passivity if the feedback given by the mass media would be less strategic and more communicative.

The importance of feedback when producing UGC also becomes clear in the role of online communities in the participation in online news, whether they correspond to the offline social network of the consumer or merely exist online. Beyl & Van Passel (2008) identify more general motivations for the participation in online communities, like the national culture, the personal preferences of the user and the relation to other community participants. Interesting here is the importance of self-confidence and the way in which consumers show themselves to the others in the community, linked to a form of timidity (Ryfe & Mensing 2007). The importance of the social network is also acknowledged by Ames & Namaan (2007). According to their study on the motivations to tag pictures on photo sharing sites, users tag to make content searchable and retrievable, as a way of both managing a personal collection and sharing it with others. They also use it to ad context to content, as a way of both personal recollection and communicating the context of the content to others. They notice a predominance of social motivations for tagging and come to the conclusion that the social dimension greatly increases the likelihood that users will tag their photos.

Looking at these different studies, I can already identify motivations to produse that will also serve as a guiding principle for the analysis of our qualitative data. First, bloggers are generally driven by an overall private, sometimes even narcissistic motivation (Papacharissi 2004). For Pro-Ams this goes even further, as they are driven by a passion for their subject of interest. On the other hand, personal timidity, linked to self-confidence can also form a barrier for online engagement. Second, as I saw especially with citizen journalists, is the impending loss of values, driving them to contribute to the news. Here, the interaction with journalists will be decisive, too. Third is the significance of the social network, as it stresses the importance of having an audience when engaging with news.

Methodology

The data gathering took place within the framework of the FLEET project (Flemish E-publishing Trends), in which in total 38 respondents participated: 18 for a short period, 20 others for several months. For this chapter, I analysed the data from the first 18 respondents. A qualitative multi-methodological research design was set up. This design grew organically through an iterative process where new theoretical and empirical insights were constantly incorporated into the design.

During a first phase, an online survey was set up, which was completed by 658 persons. From this data sample, the actual respondents were selected via maximum variation analysis (Polkinghorne 2005). The aim of such a selection is to incorporate an as wide as possible array of different visions and opinions on a topic, by selecting people who strongly correspond on one variable, but differ strongly on others. Hence, all respondents were matched regarding their internet use: all used it daily and were familiar with online news. They differed on three aspects.

First, the degree of general news consumption differed, in order not only to have so-called news junkies amongst the respondents. Second was the difference in degree of new-media mindedness, allowing people with and without affinity for social media to be incorporated. Third regarded their degree of participation in public life, to ensure that people with a vibrant community life and others less active were amongst the respondents. I should note that this method of selection does not focus on demographic factors. However, I made sure that gender, age and means were proportionally even among the respondents, with the exception of youngsters. As digital natives, they form a very atypical group when it comes to online media use. For this reason, all respondents were between 20 and 72 years old.

In a second phase, one-week diaries and in depth interviews were held with 20 respondents. The diaries were used as a reflexive tool for the respondents and as an eliciting tool for the researcher during the interview (Carter & Mankoff 2005). These interviews used the laddering method (Grunert & Grunert 1995; Reynolds & Gutman 1988) to collect and analyse the data, allowing different actions of a respondent to be linked to his/her underlying motivations. The existing motivational concepts, as mentioned in the previous section, were checked through these interviews.

Analysis

Before looking at the respondents' motivations, I would like to highlight a few points. First, a lack of computer literacy, possibly resulting in a reduced usability of such services, can be an obstruction to get the right or relevant information from a respondent (Lievens et al. 2006). By selecting respondents who go online daily, I could generally avoid this problem. Reading on screen is the only threshold related to usability that turned up frequently in the interviews. Second, I found one factor generally undermining produsage: time. Although this is certainly not the most important factor, it emerged from our research as being an important element shaping respondents' engagement in produsage, both in the consumption and in the production of UGC. This is hardly surprising, as studies show that lack of time is the main reason for people not to use the internet more than they already do (Federale Overheidsdienst Economie 2007). Third, I will focus on casual news produsage, which I understand as reactions of common people to the news, mostly in the form of comments (on a blog or news site) or the sharing of this news. As I did not include citizen journalists or bloggers in our sample, the actual production of news was rare. Non-news-related motivations for produsage will only be taken into consideration when they say something about the respondent's use of or attitude towards news produsage.

Thresholds and motivations for consulting news-related UGC

Central to the thresholds or motivations for the respondents to consult news-related UGC is the interest in the opinions of other people. These opinions are valued in the light of the respondent's own interests and the producer's – the author of the comment or the blog post – relation to the topic. The former refers to the respondents' willingness to learn or to simply enjoy, the latter to the producer's authority on the matter. Here I find two clusters of factors. On the one hand, respondents are interested in other opinions on certain news facts, as this enables them to set their own opinions against those of others. By expressing their opinions and comparing these to those of other people, they engage in a self-reflexive activity. This seems related to what Nardi identifies as articulating ideas by writing, but without actually contributing. On the other hand, they see it as fun, meaningless entertainment.

A second cluster is the producer's authority. When looking for other opinions, the authority of the poster becomes important. This authority is granted in different ways: he or she is a first-hand witness, emotionally involved or even a "hands-on" expert. At that point, the often vulgar or irrelevant contributions from other posters are an important threshold. Nevertheless, when looking for entertainment, the relation to the producer becomes irrelevant, as people are looking for funny (or stupid or ridiculous) opinions. Figure 1 shows these relations in a schematic way.

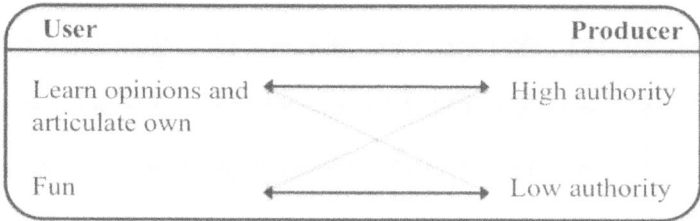

Figure 1: motivational dimensions for the use of user-generated news

Finally, regarding customization, the most common way to personalise news amongst the respondents is the e-mailed newsletter. The reason mentioned most is that they happened to casually subscribe to one e.g. in order to participate in an online contest. Newsletter use does not seem very conscious. The thresholds against customization in any form can be clustered as a preference for general news and people's need to know what is seen as important by society. Customization isolates people from the mainstream news. The data do not allow us to devote more attention to it, but I will definitely go deeper into it in our further research.

Thresholds and motivations for producing news-related UGC

When looking at the respondents' motivations and thresholds to take action and share, post or react to news, I am able to identify three interrelated clusters of motivations that work as conditions for engaging in news participation: social reflex, self-confidence and involvement. I will go deeper into each of these clusters, but already point out that the greater number of these conditions are met, the more likely the respondents are to engage.

Social reflex

A first cluster of motivations can be grouped under the term "social reflex". These are linked to Thorson's conclusion that people share online news with their social network. The respondents all seem to take the potential receivers of their contribution into consideration. Their contribution should help people, interest them or at least contribute to the discussion e.g. by pointing out possible mistakes or raising awareness for the topic. This has both a private and a public dimension. "Private" refers to people they know personally and whom they would address as such, "public" to the potential, unknown audience out there. They ask themselves questions like: will they read it? Will they think it's funny? Will it be useful information to them? Will I bother them? Their potential public not using their contribution is enough reason not to engage with the news. This also seems to be the underlying reason why sharing news via mail is less of a bother than commenting on an online news site: the more you know your public, the more you can foresee its reaction, the likelier you are to contribute.

That bloggers are driven by motivations linked to personal gratification or self-fulfilment does not emerge from the interviews. Conversely, I find important thresholds for participating in online news that illustrate a kind of reluctance on a personal level: the fact that someone else has already stated one's opinion or the prospect of a contribution getting lost in the myriad of other contributions. Hence, I believe that contributing to the news is possibly much less motivated by self-fulfilment, and much more oriented towards a more altruistic engagement with a personal or public audience.

Self-confidence

A second cluster of motivations is related to the respondents' self-confidence. This implies aspects of authority like knowing one's facts and being certain about one's statements, but also aspects of skills like writing skills or the ability to tell clear and coherent stories or the wits to fascinate or entertain people. Participating seems to give different respondents a kind of vulnerability. They have to be certain of their ground to overcome this. This is illustrated by some recurrent participation thresholds: being afraid of getting hooked on (i.e., spending too much time trying to deliver something good), preferring to engage in real-life discussion, not having to write or respecting the opinions of others too much to engage. What is surprising is the fact that even when reacting in a funnier, trivial way, aspects related to skills surface. This is already an indication of the line that needs to be crossed in someone's mind before contributing to the news. Actually contributing to the news, especially in a more public way, seems to be a distinctively other activity than consulting other peoples' contributions.

Involvement

I termed the last cluster involvement. It concerns the respondents' relation to the content of the news. For all respondents, the kind of news to a large extent defines their willingness to contribute to it. This relation is characterised by the respondent's involvement to the news item his fields of interest or the degree to which he is touched or shocked by the news fact. This is certainly linked to the self-confidence mentioned earlier as someone is likely to feel more at ease when reacting to topics in his or her fields of interest. The involvement can also be linked to the nature of the news, such as when something dreadful happens in one's hometown or people he/she knows are affected. These rather emotional reactions seem to be strong triggers to participate. The nature of the news item is also related to the dimension of social reflex, as the respondents are likely to link the story, or their eventual reaction to it, to their potential public.

A good illustration of this, and at the same time of how all three dimensions are intertwined, is one respondent's contribution to an online news story reporting the commotion about parking spots reserved for the disabled. This person admits she is not a good writer and feels reluctant to contribute online (self-confidence). However, the fact that a relative of hers is disabled and that she experiences daily how useful those parking spots are (content), prompts her to post a reaction. If only she can convince 20 people of the necessity of those spots, she would be satisfied (social reflex).

The overall majority of the respondents' motivations to participate can be articulated around these three clusters. The likeliness to participate can be understood in the light of these three pillars and will increase as more conditions are met. Nevertheless, failure to meet one condition can also definitely stop the willingness to participate. The three dimensions allow us to answer the third research question positively. The content indeed seems to play a role in the willingness to participate to news and this in different ways. First, having the social reflex, the content defines whether one's contribution can be of any interest to anyone else. Second, the content determines the degree of involvement a user shows towards the news and hence triggers the eventual engagement. Third, the aspect of self-confidence is linked to the nature of the news and users' knowledge or authority on the subject.

The consumption – production dimension

In order to see if the consumption and production of UGC are indeed distinct activities in the mind of the user, I clustered all motivations and thresholds involving the consultation of UGC and compared these to those relating to the production of UCG. As I saw earlier, more conditions have to be met before engaging in production than before consulting UGC. The latter occurs rather casually when looking for online news. Another indication for this distinction is the occurrence of similar motivations to consume and produce news: to learn from or inform others, and the relation to the news story. Still, even though this would appear sufficient to consume UGC, it is not enough for people to actually produce it, as a lack of self-confidence can easily be enough for users not to contribute. This is a strong potential threshold that needs to be overcome before engaging in the production of news-related UGC.

A second aspect in this regard is the social reflex and the importance of the potential public when engaging in news. When contributing to the news the respondents seem to take up the role of publisher and bear in mind their target audience. Interesting is the fact that this social reflex also occurs when sharing existing content with others. Even if this would not account as production from a professional point of view, from a user perspective the same rules apply. This leads us to the conclusion that indeed, from a user's point of view, consumption and production are distinct activities, and should be understood as respectively non self-publishing in contrast to self-publishing.

Finally, I noticed all respondents have a rather cool relationship with news-related UGC, as if it were something you would only do in certain circumstances. This attitude could be described as being generally positive about the possibilities to participate, while being rather indisposed to do so. I did not gather enough data on the respondents' attitude to make strong conclusions. Some respondents, however, held interesting views that I would like to investigate in our further research. For some respondents, e.g. contributing seems to be something that is not their role, as they have never been asked to do it before, and do not see why they should do it now. Interesting is also that not only some of the older respondents make an allusion to this, but also the younger. This standpoint therefore is not merely generational, as one could expect, and deservers further investigation.

Conclusion

In this chapter, I hope to have provided evidence that production and consumption of news are very distinct activities in the mind of the consumer (Q2) and that the nature of the news fact (content) plays an important role in the willingness to participate (Q3), along with a social reflex and self-confidence (Q1). I hereby accentuate the fact that these findings are specific for news produsage, although certain aspects can be related to produsage in general. By identifying the distinct personal dimension needed for the respondents to produce news-related UGC (Q1), I show that more conditions need to be met before contributing to the news. Therefore, I propose a model for looking at news produsage from a user perspective that makes a clear distinction between the sphere of production and consumption by speaking of self-publishing and non self-publishing.

The motivations to consult news-related UGC are articulated around a social and a substantive dimension. An extra personal dimension comes into play when producing news-related UGC. The role of the authority of the producer for consuming news-related UGC could be considered a personal dimension either, but not on the same level, as it concerns the other as producer in contrast to the self as producer. Referring to the literature on more structural produsers like bloggers and citizen journalists, I can cluster the identified motivations and thresholds to engage with UGC around the same dimensions. This conceptual model is illustrated in figure 2. The black arrow refers to the interplay between the different motivational dimensions. These could also be seen as the social requirements needed for a user to engage in the news. Amongst our respondents I noticed that the more of these requirements were met, the more likely they were to take action. Structural factors like writing skills and self-confidence show that self-empowerment through online news participation is not self-evident. The social reflex and the potential public should be acknowledged as elements news makers can capitalize on if they want to convince people to engage with the news. This however should be submitted to further research. Finally, I want to stress that the consumption - production dimension does not imply linearity. A consumer is not at all bound to become a produser.

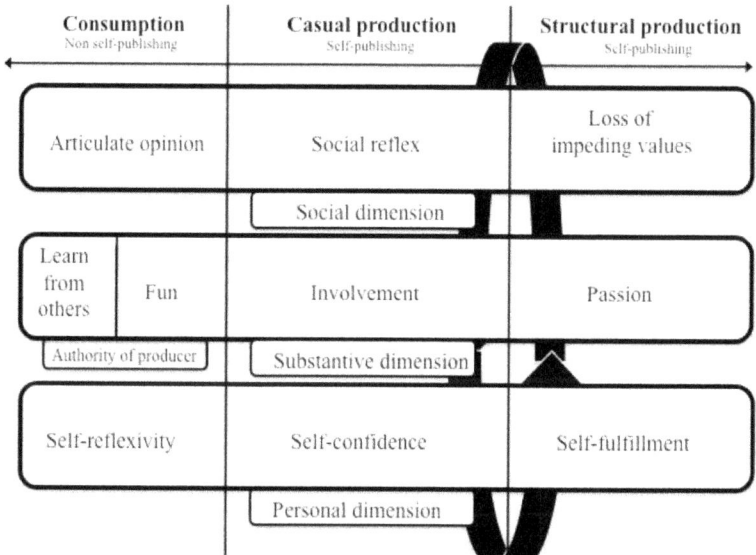

Figure 2: motivational dimensions for news-related produsage

I acknowledge the need for further research to get more insight in users' motivations and attitudes towards news produsage. In this chapter, I focussed on casual news produsage, and more specifically on the consumption and production of news-related UGC in contrast to other aspects of news produsage, like customization and personalisation. Even though I believe our findings relate to more general motivations underlying news produsage, these other aspects merit investigation for their specific purpose. There are a number of leads in that respect that I would like to follow up in our further research.

The most important concerns the effort it demands to participate to the news. Thinking of something to write, how to write it, how to make it interesting to others, etc. all seem related to a certain effort that needs to be made. Time also plays a role here, as the more effort produsing demands, the more time it takes. Depending on the three conditions I described, the respondents consider whether or not to invest time and effort in contributions. The non-self-publication – self-publication dimension appears to be so strong that simply reducing the effort is not enough reason to participate. Effort must be overcome, but is not the actual motivation or threshold to participate. Therefore I would like to scrutinize more in detail different forms of more and less time- and effort-consuming engagement in news and the relation to people's likeliness to participate.

I hope that this and further research can contribute to a better understanding of the produser and how people engage – or do not – with the news through new media. This is important from an academic point of view. I need to understand this socio-technical evolution and the role of the user in the shaping of new ways of using news. However, also from a business perspective I believe that insights about the user are necessary for executives, editors, journalist and entrepreneurs to be able to address their audience in an appropriate way. By looking at users as self-empowered innovators, the news industry might be able to turn the current crisis into a welcome opportunity.

References

Ames M., Naaman M. 'Why we tag: Motivations for annotation in mobile and online media' Paper presented at the SIGCHI conference on human factors in computing systems, San Jose, California (2007)

Bergström A. 'Audience participation in publishing' Paper presented at the Future of Newspapers Conference Cardif (September 12-13, 2007)

Beyl J., Passel E. van 'Analyse praktijken van 'producing users' van community media' CoCoMedia Project Deliverable Brussels: IBBT-SMIT-VUB (2008)

Boczkowski P.J. 'The development and use of online newspapers: What research tells us and what we might want to know' eds. Lievrouw L.A., Livingstone S. Handbook of New Media: Social Shaping and Consequences of ICTs London: Sage (2002) pp. 270-286

Bruns A. 'Produsage: 'Towards a broader framework for user-led content creation' Conference proceedings, Conference on Creativity and Cognition, New York (2007) pp. 99-106 http://eprints.qut.edu.au/ archive/ 00006623/ 01/ 6623.pdf

Cardoso G. The Media in the Network Society. Browsing, News, Filters and Citizenship Lisbon: CIES – Centre for Research and Studies in Sociology (2007)

Carter S., Mankoff J. 'When participants do the capturing: the role of media in diary studies' Conference proceedings, the SIGCHI Conference on Human Factors in Computing Systems, Portland, Oregon (April 02.03.2005)

Coleman G. 'Toward a positive critique of the social web' Re-public http://www.re-public.gr/en/?p=288 (2008) (accessed 19 January 2009)

Costera-Meijer I. 'Impact or content. Rating vs. quality in public broadcasting' Journal of European Communication 20 (1) (2005) pp. 27-53

Dijck J. van 'Users like you? Theorizing agency in user-generated content' Media, Culture & Society 31 (1) (2009) pp. 41-58

Domingo D. 'Interactivity in the daily routines of online newsrooms: dealing with an uncomfortable myth' Journal of Computer-Mediated Communication 13 (2008) pp. 680-704

Federale Overheidsdienst Economie. ICT-indicatoren bij Individuen - Bezit en Gebruik van Computer, Internet, e-Commerce, e-Government, soort verbinding Brussels: Federale Overheidsdienst Economie (2007)

Galtung J., Ruge M. H. 'The structure of foreign news.' Journal of Peace Research 2 (1) (1965) pp. 64-90

Geens D., Picone I., Vandenbrande K. 'Another breach in the wall: organisational dynamics of today's news ecology' Conference proceedings, the Future of Newspapers Conference Cardif (September 12-13, 2007)

Gillmor D. We the Media. Grassroots Journalism by the People, for the People Cambridge: O'Reilly (2004)

Grunert K.G., Grunert S.C. 'Measuring subjective meaning structures by the laddering method: Theoretical considerations and methodological problems' International Journal of Research in Marketing 12 (1995) pp. 209-225

Harcup T., O'Neil D. 'What is news? Galtung and Ruge revisited' Journalism Studies 2 (2) (2001) pp. 261-280

Herring S.C., Scheidt L.A., Bonus S., Wright E. 'Bridging the gap: A genre analysis of weblogs' Conference proceedings, the 37th Annual Hawaii International Conference on System Sciences, Hawaii (2004)

Ihlström C., Akesson M., Svensson J., Fredberg T. 'Audience view on new technology for media consumption' Conference proceedings The JIBS workshop on Consuming Audiences Copenhagen (2006)

Jole F. van 'Nieuws in tijden van crisis' De Nieuwe Reporter (2009) http://www.denieuwereporter.nl/?author=149 (accessed Februari 19, 2010)

Kling R., Callahan E. 'Electronic journals, the internet and scholarly communication' Annual Review of Information, Science and Technology 37 (2003) pp. 127-177

Knowledge@Wharton. 'Urgent deadline for newspapers: Find a new business plan before you vanish' (2009) http://knowledge.wharton.upenn.edu/article.cfm?articleid=2130 (January 7, 2009)

Krol C. Newspapers in Crisis: Migrating Online (Analyst Report Summary) New York: eMarketer (2009)

Leadbeater C., Miller P. The Pro-Am Revolution: How Enthusiasts are Changing our Economy and Society London: Demos (2004)

Lievens B., Van den Broeck W., Pierson J. 'The mobile digital newspaper: embedding the news consumer in technology development by means of living lab research' Conference proceedings The IAMCR 2006 Conference in Cairo (23-28 July, 2006)

Nardi B., Schiano D., Gumbrecht M., Swartz L. '"I'm Blogging This": A Closer Look at Why People Blog' Unpublished paper submitted to Communications of the ACM (2004)

Örnebring H. 'The consumer as producer - Of what? User-generated tabloid content in The Sun (UK) and Aftonbladet (Sweden)' Conference proceedings The Future of Newspapers Conference Cardif (September 12-13, 2007)

Papacharissi Z. 'The blogger revolution? Audiences as media producers' Conference proceedings The International Communication Association Conference: New Orleans (2004)

Paulussen S., Heinonen A., Domingo D., Quandt, T. 'Doing it together: Citizen participation in the professional news making process' Conference proceedings, the Future of Newspapers Conference (September 12-13, 2007)

Picone I. 'Conceptualising online news use' eds. Pierson J., Mante-Meijer E., Loos E., Sapio B. Innovating for and by Users. Brussels: Opoce (2008) pp. 145-158

PEW Internet Research Centre. News Consumption and Believability Study Washington: The PEW Research Centre (2008)

Polkinghorne D.E. 'Language and meaning: Data collection in qualitative research' Journal of Counseling Psychology 52 (2) (2005) pp. 137-145

Quandt T.A '"Whole new journalism" - Stuck in the past? A comparative content analysis of online news in Europe and the US' Conference proceedings The Future of Newspapers Conference Cardif (September 12-13, 2007)

Reynolds T.J., Gutman J. 'Laddering theory, method, analysis, and interpretation' Journal of Advertising Research 28 (1) (1988) pp. 11-31

Rogers E.M. Diffusion of Innovations (5 edition) New York: Free Press (2003)

Ryfe D., Mensing D. 'Doing journalism together. Experiments in collaborative newsgathering' Conference proceedings, the Future of Newspapers Conference Cardif (September 12-13, 2007)

Scholz T. 'Market Ideology and the Myths of Web 2.0.' First Monday 13 (3) (2008) http://www.uic.edu/htbin/cgiwrap/bin/ojs/index.php/fm/article/view/2138/1945

Schultz T. 'Mass media and the concept of interactivity: an exploratory study of online forums and reader email' Media, Culture & Society 22 (2000) pp. 205-221

Stefanone M.A., Jang C.-Y. 'Writing for friends and family: The interpersonal nature of blogs' Journal of Computer-Mediated Communication 13 (1) (2007) http://jcmc.indiana.edu/vol13/issue1/stefanone.html

Technorati. State of the Blogosphere 2008. Day 1: Who are the Bloggers (Research Report) San Francisco: Technorati (2008a)

Technorati. State of the Blogosphere 2008. Day 2: The What and Why of Blogging (Research Report) San Francisco: Technorati (2008b)

Thorson E. 'Changing patterns of news consumption and participation' Information, Communication & Society 11 (4) (2008) pp. 473-489

Ugille P., Paulussen S., Raeymakers K. 'Citizens as producers. Audience participation in the professional news room' Conference proceedings Etmaal van de Communicatiewetenschap Amsterdam (Februari 7-8 2008)

Vermaas K., Segers J., Gillebaard H., Kaashoek B., Ongena G. Breedband en de Gebruiker 2007. Eindrapportage (Research report) Utrecht: Dialogic (2008)

World Association of Newspapers. World Digital Media Trends 2008 (Special report) Paris: World Association of Newspapers (2008)

Stijn Bannier

The Musical Network 2.0 & 3.0

Introduction

In this chapter I will examine some changes brought to the musical network by Web 2.0 and which changes we might expect from Web 3.0 and to what extent the user of the internet – being the consumer of music, a music artist or any other actor involved in the musical network – is actively involved in those changes. This chapter presents a theoretical reflection concerned with the relationship between users, internet, technological innovation and the music industry.

First the musical network and the transition from Web 2.0 to Web 3.0 will be further explored. Second, the four musical networks are examined in detail and with relation to the development of Web 2.0 and Web 3.0. To what extent are the different actors influenced by those changes and do the power relations within the musical network shift? The chapter explains the changes brought to the musical network by Web 2.0 and which changes we can expect from Web 3.0.

The musical network

In Time – space (and digital) compression: software formats, musical networks, and the reorganisation of the music industry, Leyshon (2001) discusses various geographical and organisational consequences of the emergence of a new technological assemblage within the music industry. He distinguishes four networks inside the musical network of the music industry: networks of creativity, reproduction, distribution and consumption, as can be seen in figure 1. He derives his notion of the musical network from the theories of Attali and Scott. Attali (1984) introduces the musical network by explaining how the economy of music operates through networks based upon the composition, representation, and repetition of musical forms. Next to this, Leyshon notes that Scott's idea – distribution, consumption and above all production are all bound to physical spaces (1999) – is not true anymore, because of the digital music culture.

The network of creativity in Leyshon's musical network comprehends the creation and recording of music. Besides the artist, other actors are involved in the creation of music, such as the fans and the recording company. The recording company establishes the links to the network of reproduction and distribution and the fans establish the links to the network of consumption. The musical network thus consists of four overlapping networks with interrelationships among the different networks, as can be seen in figure 1.

Leyshon's approach of the musical network can be read in view of the Actor-Network Theory (ANT). ANT departs from networks of relationships and interactions between actors (material and semiotic) and networks (coming together to act as a whole). The actors influence each other (agency) and together these actors are able to make a change or create an idea or technology. Leyshon uses digital technologies to explain new possibilities in the musical network and sees this development not merely as a physical one. An outlook also phrased by Latour (1998, 3) when explaining ANT:

> "The notion of network, in its barest topological outline, allows us already to reshuffle spatial metaphors that have rendered the study of society-nature so difficult: close and far, up and down, local and global, inside and outside. They are replaced by associations and connections (…)."

Leyshon considers this connection between the musical network and new technologies too, since the industry has evolved in lock step with, although is not determined by, several technological advances.

Despite the fact that his model has been subject to the criticism that some networks should be regarded more as linear structures (Wikström, 2010), these networks endure because of technological advances. These advances, addressed in this chapter, are Web 2.0 and Web 3.0 and will be further elaborated in the following section.

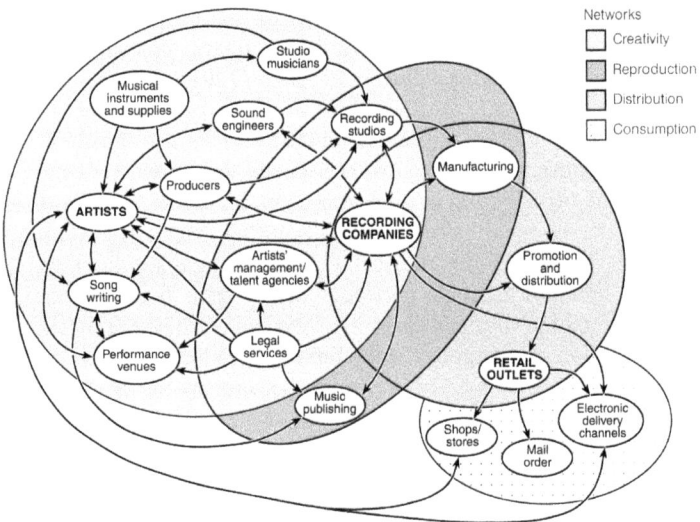

Figure 1: The musical network (Leyshon, 2001, 61)

From Web 2.0 to Web 3.0

The term Web 2.0 is used to describe the evolution (Skiba et al. 2006; Knowles 2007) from a "read-only" World Wide Web towards web sites and web services based on participation, collaboration and sharing between users (O'Reilly 2005; Rollett et al. 2007). These concepts transcend the former dichotomy of creators and consumers of content. Content is now based on the harnessing of data and outputs of users. Web 2.0 applications allow users and websites to consume and remix data from multiple sources. These applications and websites emphasize interaction, community and openness (Millard & Ross 2006). Examples include applications such as weblogs and wikis, technologies such as social tagging and social networking and websites such as YouTube, MySpace and Flickr.

Inventor of the World Wide Web Tim Berners-Lee saw the web not only as a common information source, but also as a place to "work and play and socialize" and where computers can "help us analyse it, make sense of what we are doing, where we individually fit in, and how we can better work together" (Berners-Lee 1998, 1). With coining the term Web 2.0, the future of the World Wide Web is also widely discussed. The World Wide Web seems to evolve further. To what extent can a Web 3.0 arise and what does it signify?

To analyse the web and make sense of what the users are doing, Berners-Lee et al. (2001, 1) see a semantic web as the future of the web:

> "The Semantic Web will bring structure to the meaningful content of Web pages, creating an environment where software agents roaming from page to page can readily carry out sophisticated tasks for users."

The semantic environment will make use of data and metadata, i.e. data on data, the semantics of information and services on the web. These semantic aspects (or semantic web) are part of the technologies that might be incorporated in Web 3.0. The web will become more intelligent and will be able to satisfy and fulfil the requests of users. Adding content and metadata to Web 2.0-applications and organising and processing these data in a Web 3.0 application should make the internet easier to use (Borland 2007).

Although Web 3.0 is seen as the symbiosis of web technologies and knowledge, some theorists are more critical. Among others Lassila & Hendler (2007, 93):

> "Although many aspects of the Semantic Web are yet to be explored, and much research remains to be done, this technology is clearly transitioning into a serious player in the modern Web universe. We might not like the term "Web 3.0," but we enthusiastically embrace the technologies it is bringing to the field."

Evans (2007) foresees several practical problems with Web 3.0 too. Firstly, the semantic web becomes more and more complex and machines cannot understand everything the user puts in. Secondly, the democratised production of content by the users is being ignored by processing data and generating metadata and thus content in a Web 3.0-application. And finally, Evans indicates that a forced pursuit of the semantic web prevents the dynamics of the World Wide Web. These dynamics let the static Web 1.0 evolve to the user-generated Web 2.0. He thinks the internet will evolve to a more hybrid web (he already speaks of Web 4.0) provided by mobile technologies and using physical objects. Something Berners-Lee et al. (2001, 1) also forecasted, since "the Semantic Web will break out of the virtual realm and extend into our physical world". This means a hybrid web, spun from a number of technological threads, all helping to make data more accessible and more useful (Borland 2007) using recommendation and personalisation (Kiss 2008). This chapter defines Web 3.0 as the future of the World Wide Web, in the course of which a hybrid world originates by applying several technological developments. This will happen, assuming that, through recommendation and personalisation, data and content will be made more accessible and useful for users. In what follows, the four musical networks will be explored, explaining the changes, brought to the musical network by Web 2.0 and 3.0.

Creativity

The networks of creativity occur between "a relatively large number of actors, institutions, and technologies" (Leyshon 2001, 61). On the one hand they comprehend the artist's side and its surrounding actors like musicians, producers, venues and instruments. On the other hand they consist of the record company's side and its surrounding actors such as Artist & Repertoire (A&R) managers, producers, studio engineers and recording studios. In between these two sides representatives such as booking agents or managers are also involved. New digital technologies and especially the internet change the musical network and new connections have become available for new actors and new networks. Examples are internet companies that assert new and unsigned acts and music portals that introduce music and specific genres.

These portals are often artist platforms aimed at creating an online representation or social network for the artist. Web 2.0 applications such as MySpace, Facebook and SonicBids make it possible for artists to present themselves in a professional way to audience and record companies. The artist is able to create a profile and upload the home-recorded music as an MP3 file to the internet. This fits in with the "prosumer" principle, since new media easily facilitate amateurs or consumers to produce professional content themselves:

> "Digital technologies have made possible a dispersal and diffusion of music production that has fundamentally changed the nature of popular music market. The apparatus of analogue music production, orchestral studios, 20-foot sound desks and 2-inch rolls of tape can all now be collapsed into a sampling keyboard, a couple of effect units, and a computer. (…) The PC itself is in many ways the ultimate figure of media "prosumer" technology. It is a

technology of distribution, of consumption, as well as a technology of production." (Lister et al. 2003, 33-34)

But amateurs can produce not only professional content. Bruns (2007, 99) coined the term "produsage" to describe a "new hybrid form of simultaneous production and usage", where he refers to users that contribute to Web 2.0 sites by adding comments or giving ratings. Both the networks of creativity, reproduction, distribution and consumption contain prosumers and produsers and their input and this validates the importance of the user in the musical network influenced by Web 2.0 or the musical network 2.0. In accordance with the Web 2.0 concept of "the long tail" – a large number of unique items, each in relatively small quantities (Anderson 2004) – the musical network 2.0 makes it possible to create an online platform for these niches, in contrast with the future absolute musical uniformity, foretold by Adorno & Horkheimer (1944).

Coming back to Web 3.0 – the future of the World Wide Web, in the course of which a hybrid world originates by applying several technological developments – the networks of creativity can witness some interesting innovations. The artist platforms and social networks will be elaborated in the light of the prosumer/produsers concepts. On the one hand the semantic web can be unified in the existing Web 2.0 applications and on the other hand composing music can take place in a hybrid space, combining the physical and virtual spaces.

Artist platforms (for both amateurs and professionals) usually miss a direct or clear link to the music industry, but with the semantic web the artist platforms can address A & R managers and other people of the music industry. Now the Web will think on behalf of the users and the user can easily search for and find suitable artists for a record company or booking office. Because of the semantic metadata, facets as style, genre and life span can be defined and used in the search. With the Web 2.0 "remixability" concept – information of various websites can be recombined to gather new information – Web 3.0 makes it possible to comb several artist platforms for appropriate artists.

As yet, the networks of creativity were discussed by means of shifting relationships between artists, consumers and record companies, but proceeding from the purely creative aspect, the prosumer concept give new possibilities to artists through Web 3.0. Musicians are able to easily and affordably record professional productions and because of that new enterprises are started at the internet. Artist platforms like Sellaband, where artists have to earn $ 50.000 by selling parts to their fans to record and release an album, or online collaborative and jamming applications like Kompoz, Ninjam or Kalabo bring the physical world into the virtual. This merger can be explained on the basis of hybridity.

Hybrid spaces emerge when it is not necessary anymore to step out the physical space to have contact in a digital environment. The border between both worlds blur and the spaces, separated before, are hard to disperse. A hybrid space is a conceptual space where the borders have disappeared. These borders fade away by means of the use of mobile or digital technologies as an instrument. Hybrid spaces however, are no products of technology. They are constructed by mobility and communication and are shaped in social networks that surface concurrently in the digital and physical world (De Souza e Silva 2006). These spaces are not longer bound to a specific location, but they are the result of the alliance with the mutual spaces. Within, it is possible to perceive the physical space and simultaneously feel the connected digital network. Technologies drift away and become invisible, because the connection feels so naturally, people forget to think about them (De Souza e Silva 2003). When interactions take place in media spaces, they take place in hybrid spaces and "in action is framed simultaneously by the physical space, the virtual space and the relationship between the two" (Harrison & Dourish 1996, 72).

Georgina Born gives an outline of the changing forms of musical creativity through the theories of Adorno, DeNora, Hennion and Gell. Sellaband, Kompoz, Ninjam and Kalabo also change the forms of musical creativity in the light of Born's findings (2005, 26). She poses that collaborating on the creation of music will improve the compositions and that collaboration creates ideal conditions. Digital music media like the above mentioned web applications give surplus values, since "digital music media both extend these potentials and afford entirely new modes of collaborative authorship. Through their capacity to "decompose" aural and visual objects into basic binary representations, digital media re-open creative agency".

The possibilities of digital music media and collaboration are being put in the light of ANT by Kendall (2004, 4), when he indicates "as cultural and creative animals, we are locked into hybridity", since "the human and the nonhuman (…), are constantly in dialogue". Kendall declares how technology had produced and changed the music practice. Musicians and music technology are part of a complex web of interests, actions and many more actors according to Kendall.

Web 2.0 and Web 3.0 change the relations between the artists and the fans to that degree that on the one hand both artists and fans are more involved as users with the creation of content in Web 2.0 and 3.0 applications and on the other hand the traditional actors of the music industry, such as record companies, recording studios and their staff and managements, are left aside. Hybrid Web 3.0 applications create a direct connection between fans and artists and as prosumers/produsers, artists are able to produce their own albums. The prosumer/produser seems to be an important actor in the other networks too.

Reproduction

Influenced by the "prosumer" principle, the networks of reproduction changed too. The introduction of the MP3-format in 1992 as audio compression standard implied the possibility to store musical sounds as computer files, to copy and reproduce them on personal computers, and to transmit them over the internet. This development had profound effects on all participants in the musical network, from the artist and recording companies through to the ultimate consumer (2002). Again, this trend is not limited to the networks of reproduction:

> "Since the mid to late 1990s, we have witnessed a period of change where the traditional models of music production, distribution and consumption have been profoundly challenged on an unprecedented scale. (…) Production tools have been democratised to the point that many musicians are now producing music with desktop tools in domestic environments. This has seen an explosion in content from both music professionals and "prosumers", i.e. those whose online activities are located somewhere between the professional musician and the consumer. Ultimately, we have moved from an economy of scarcity, controlled by a finite array of publishers, to a theoretically limitless economy of abundance." (Knowles 2007, 7)

The MP3-format means that there is no physical sound carrier for music and thus, the physical aspect is transferred to music players like the PC, notebook or portable MP3 player. Auslander (2001, 82) speaks of "the disappearance of specific physical objects and the consumption of music as pure digital information" and next to that "musical sound becomes a commodity in itself, unmoored from physical support in a way that was never previously possible".

With regard to the possibilities of Web 3.0 in the networks of reproduction Knowles (2007, 7) mentions an interesting problem, since Web 2.0 concepts made users generate content, but "we now need tools to filter, navigate and establish relationships between elements in this vast field of content". Web 3.0 technologies of all times should be able to bring relieve and solve this problem. After all, the semantic web is able to make data and content more accessible and usable. Essentially this is already possible at the moment an MP3 is produced. This partly happens by means of ID3. ID3 is a table of metadata, included in an MP3 file, where data such as song title, artist, track number, file format and classification are given. Under the influence of the Web 2.0 concept "Users add value" several applications also provide the possibility to add key words or "tags" to music, which create "folksonomies" and "tag clouds". The semantic web leaps onto these possibilities and combines the data and metadata from tags provided by the user. On the one hand this requires an immense form of data mining to gather content. On the other hand complicated programs and algorithms are necessary to create new data and metadata and add these to existing content. Nowadays, research projects are already far advanced with respect to machine listening to and analysing of music and high-level parametric control of musical information. This makes it, for example, possible for a computer to describe which variations Brian May played on the riff in Tie Your Mother Down and how they diverged or how several pianists interpret Bach's Goldberg Variations. It is only a matter of time applications with these capacities will be publicly accessible.

As already argued, Web 2.0 allows both fans and artists to create the online data. The only drawback is that consumers cannot see the wood for the trees with this huge amount of user-generated content. At this point Web 3.0 developments bring relief. Machine-generated semantic metadata combined with better search capabilities allow the user to get better search results. Still, at this point the user has less control of the generation of content, as Evans (2007) already foresaw. Now, the user has not completely control anymore of the content creation, something that also has consequences for the networks of distribution.

Distribution

Because music can be spread digitally and non-physically, the most important new actor within the networks of distribution is the internet and the "Internet distribution channels may help to support traditional networks as much as undermine them" (Leyshon 2001, 70). Those internet distribution channels include both legal distribution, such as online MP3 sales through iTunes Store, and illegal distribution, through for instance P2P networks. Next to that, within these networks a growing amount of prosumer/produser-weblogs can be found. According to the "long tail" (Anderson 2004) every musical genre or style is represented online and websites promote and distribute music in their own way. Furthermore social networking sites such as MySpace, Facebook, Last.Fm and Hyves make use of social tagging and other commenting systems to allow users to show their appreciation for certain songs or artists. Users and artists collaborate to promote and distribute new music and new artists by taking part in social networking sites.

Influenced by the latest developments such as the MP3 format and the prosumer/produser-principles, record companies do not have monopoly power anymore in the networks of creativity, reproduction and distribution (McLeod 2005). Within the networks of distribution Knowles (2007, 7) sees Web 2.0 as an actor with a lot of agency:

> "The cost of distribution has been reduced to free, or near-free levels through digital distribution services, file sharing, peer-to-peer and social media networks. New large-scale web services have emerged which link music producers to consumers via artist similarity, taste profiling and recommendation data as well as linking listeners with shared tastes and interests."

From 1999 (Napster) there was an increase of P2P-networks and social networks. According to Biddle et al. (2002, 9) in The Darknet and the Future of Content Distribution this provided the development of many small networks independent of each other and the assembly of these networks should lead to one new coordinated network:

"In the absence of a global database, small-worlds networks could again become the prevalent form of the darknet. However, these small-worlds will be more powerful than they were in the past. With the widespread availability of cheap CD and DVD readers and writers as well as large hard disks, the bandwidth of the sneaker net has increased dramatically, the cost of object storage has become negligible and object injection tools have become ubiquitous. Furthermore, the internet is available as a distribution mechanism that is adequate for audio for most users, and is becoming increasingly adequate for video and computer programs."

Not only is this a matter of the unification of a number of networks, but also on of the integration of physical products, such as external storage units or MP3 players, into the new network. Once again this points to the hybrid space of Web 3.0. This hybrid prospect with physical products corresponds to Evans' concept of Web 4.0 (2007), even surpassing Web 3.0. This integration of physical products into the musical network leads to an "internet-of-things":

"The Web is on the verge of experiencing a massive evolution. From an internet of nearly one hundred million computers, the Web is soon to become an internet of nearly 100 *trillion* things. Devices such as PCs, PDAs, phones, beepers, sensors, switches, wearable computers, telemetry sensors, and tracking agents are expected to connect to the internet, flooding it with all kinds of information." (Traversat et al. 2003, 282)

This integration of physical products within the musical network and the internet could for instance get the user's listening behaviour not only from the Last.Fm player, but also from an MP3 player or include music videos and radio stations, CD's and vinyl listened to analyse. This combination of Web 2.0, Web 3.0 and Evans' prophecy of a Web 4.0 should lead to an infinite offer of music and should recommend unknown music to the user. Off course, personal taste and emotion are hard to include in this analysis and it's questionable whether an application will ever approach the human choice for a certain kind of music or artist. On the other hand, as already stated, Web 3.0 will make data and content more accessible and usable. This could also offer new feasibilities for social networking sites like MySpace, Facebook or Last.Fm. Facebook already works with recommended friends, as does Last.Fm with artists and events. At this very moment these recommendations are based on cluster analysis of data, but with the addition of metadata these results could be improved. For instance, Last.Fm could combine their cluster analysis of user-generated content and tags with machine created musical information, like genre, tempo, song key and strength, to give even more definite results.

The huge amount of user-generated content of Web 2.0 will be distributed even better because of the Web 3.0 filtering techniques to recommend data. The user, although not completely in control of the content creation, does well by this development, as the data and content will be recommended and personalised and this more accessible and useful.

Consumption

The networks of consumption cover those places in which musical products are purchased. Actors in these networks are organisations, shops, delivery systems and consumers. Since music is created, reproduced, promoted and distributed in the other networks, they have a large influence on the networks of consumption. Combined with the user-driven Web 2.0 applications the users, the main actors in the networks of consumption also influence the other networks more and more. The physical space of the networks of consumption – Leyshon mentions the record shop – is replaced by the virtual space, the internet. Web 2.0 sites make it possible for users to get acquainted with new music, to discuss artists with each other, to buy new albums and to look for concerts. Since Web 2.0 applications anticipate user input, music related Web 2.0 sites instigate a lot of interaction between artists and music fans. More and more artists concur in the possibilities of Web 2.0 and ask their fans to create a music video for their new single or to design artwork for a new album, completely on the strength of the prosumer.

Compared to Leyshon's conception of the musical network, where networks of consumption are only barely linked to networks of distribution and creativity, gives the introduction of Web 2.0 and its concepts a reconsideration of the musical network. The consumer not only influences the networks of consumption as user, but also influences networks of creativity as prosumer, networks of reproduction, at the moment MP3's are created, and networks of distribution, as produser, at the moment music is promoted and distributed through Web 2.0 applications. The democratisation of producing tools and the growing professionalization as a result, centre the prosumer in the musical network and make the networks of consumption affect all other networks. However, it remains to be seen to what extent the user keeps the same role in the emerging Web 3.0 technologies.

In particular the user seems to take advantage of Web 3.0, yet the user is not the only one to add value to the web application. Complex algorithms process data, generate metadata and add content to the Web. Combined with the content obtained via Web 2.0 applications, this will influence the networks of consumption. The connection between large amounts of structured information and user and context related indicators will lead to the enrichment of the information. Enrichment refers to relations between similar information (text, video, audio, ...), facilitating content (public transport, parking facilities, restaurants, ...) and user generated content, but also relations between data, metadata, user profiles and contexts. Web 3.0 applications will combine Web 2.0 concepts, which let users generate content and create and update appropriate profiles, and Web 3.0 concepts to create personalised and enriched content for the user. In real terms this means that the user will create a personal profile and update it with data such as personal interests, musical preferences and visited concerts and events. Through hybrid filtering algorithms, meaning content-based and collaborative filtering are combined, metadata will be created for the content and the user will be provided with personalised, enriched content and the application recommends certain concerts, artist or events. For the artists this means that their music will reach the appropriate fans and users will easily find their favourite artists and music.

Conclusion

In this chapter Leyshon's idea of the musical network is examined in combination with the changes brought to the internet by Web 2.0 and the possibilities Web 3.0 has to offer to the overlapping networks of creativity, reproduction, distribution and consumption in the musical network. Besides that, I examined how the role of the users changes, in which manner they are influenced by the developments of Web 2.0 and 3.0, and to what extent the user could be more involved online, adding more content and metadata on the one hand and getting more and better content on the other.

Within the networks of creativity 2.0 online artist platforms, social networks, prosumers and produsers are offered a chance. They play an important part with respect to creativity in the musical network. Next to that artist platforms offer more possibilities for artists to get in touch with interesting and important actors of the music industry and vice versa. Web 3.0 and the semantic web offer artist platforms and social networks better search results and usability of the websites. The interactive creative process is able to become hybrid, since the internet makes it possible to compose collaboratively online. The most important development in the networks of reproduction is the arrival of the MP3 format and the changes it brought about. Again, the prosumer and produser are able to produce their own MP3's. Given that Web 3.0 is also about creating and processing metadata and adding this to existing content, MP3's will also be supplemented with metadata and tags, not only user-generated, but also automated by algorithms and automated processes. The advent of MP3 influenced the networks of distribution too. Both P2P networks and social networks are the most important actors, given that the user is able to promote and distribute music easily, fast and roughly.

Web 2.0 made it possible for the user to influence the musical network as a whole. The networks of consumption were suddenly connected to all the other networks. Before, record companies and other actors of the music industry influenced every network, now the World Wide Web user influences these networks. The same developments can be seen with the advent of Web 3.0. However, not only user-generated content will emerge at Web 3.0-application, data and metadata are also created by the applications themselves to provide the user with personalised and enriched content. Since Web 3.0 applications build on existing Web 2.0 applications and concepts, the user still has influence on the musical network. Both the consumers and the artists will create content online and use the existing Web 2.0 applications. The future will nevertheless not only show the gathering of as much user content as possible, new Web 3.0 applications will analyse and process these data, replenish it with metadata, enabling the consumer to use the internet even better. Web 2.0 and Web 3.0 concepts are brought together and within the musical network the consumer and artist obtained more agency as users of the World Wide Web. Conversely, the record companies and other actors of the music industry in the musical network saw their power and agency within the networks decreasing. For one thing user profiles and user-generated content are accumulated and for another thing these profiles and content are processed to generate personalised and enriched recommended information, to make the internet more accessible and useful for the user. In conclusion we can say that however the user lost part of the online content generation possibilities, it will be interesting to research the user, being consumer or artist, and to what extent the user will benefit of the upcoming Web 3.0 developments, but also to what extent other actors, who will provide the Web 3.0 applications and programs, will have a more important role at the World Wide Web.

References

Adorno T., Horkheimer M. The Culture Industry: Enlightenment as Mass Deception (1944) http://www.marxists.org/reference/archive/adorno/1944/culture-industry.htm (accessed July 8, 2010)

Anderson C. The Long Tail (2004) http://www.wired.com/wired/archive/12.10/tail.html (accessed July 8, 2010)

Attali J. Noise: The Political Economy of Music Minneapolis: Minnesota University Press (1984)

Auslander P. Looking at records (Revision of a paper presented at the 'Uncommon Senses' conference in Montreal, Canada) Tdr-the Drama Review-a Journal of Performance Studies 45 (1) (2001) pp. 77-83

Berners-Lee T. 'The World Wide Web: A very short personal history' (1998) http://www.w3.org/People/Berners-Lee/ShortHistory (accessed July 8, 2010)

Berners-Lee T., Hendler J., Lassila O. 'The Semantic Web: A new form of Web content that is meaningful to computers will unleash a revolution of new possibilities' Scientific American 284 (5) (2001)

Biddle P., England P., Peinado M., Willman B. 'The darknet and the future of content distribution' proceedings of the 2002 ACM Workshop on Digital Rights Management (2002) http://msl1.mit.edu/ESD10/docs/darknet5.pdf (accessed July 8, 2010)

Borland J. 'A smarter web' Technology Review 110 (2) (2007) pp. 64-71

Born G. 'On musical mediation: Ontology, technology and creativity' Twentieth-century music (2) (2005) pp. 7-36

Bruns A. 'Produsage: Towards a broader framework for user-led content creation' eds. Fischer G., Giaccardi E., Eisenberg M., Candy L. Proceedings: Creativity & Cognition 2007: Seeding Creativity: Tools, Media, and Environments (Washington, DC, 13-15 June 2007) New York: Association for Computing Machinery (2007) pp. 99-106

De Souza e Silva A. 'From simulations to hybrid space how nomadic technologies change the real' Technoetic Arts: A Journal of Speculative Research 1 (3) (2003) pp. 209-221

De Souza e Silva A. 'From cyber to hybrid: Mobile technologies as interfaces of hybrid spaces' Space and Culture 9 (3) (2006) pp. 264-266

Evans M. The Evolution of the Web - From Web 1.0 to Web 4.0 University of Reading: Reading (2007)

Harrison S., Dourish P. 'Re-place-ing space: The roles of place and space in collaborative systems' Proceedings of the 1996 ACM conference on Computer supported cooperative work ACM: Boston, Massachusetts, United States (1996)

Kendall G. 'Towards a sociology of nonhumans: technology and creativity' eds. Bailey C., Cabrera D., Buys L. Social Change in the 21st Century Conference, Centre for Social Change Research: Queensland University of Technology (2004)

Kiss J. 'Web 3.0 is all about rank and recommendation' The Guardian 4/2 (2008)

Knowles J. A Survey of Web 2.0 Trends and some implications for tertiary music communities (2007) http://eprints.qut.edu.au/9747/1/9747.pdf (accessed July 8, 2010)

Lassila O., Hendler J. 'Embracing "web 3.0"' IEEE Internet Computing 11 (3) (2007) pp. 90-93

Latour B. 'On actor network theory: A few clarifications' (1998) http://www.nettime.org/Lists-Archives/nettime-l-9801/msg00019.html (accessed July 8, 2010)

Leyshon A. 'Time-space (and digital) compression: software formats, musical networks, and the reorganisation of the music industry' Environment and Planning A 33(1) (2001) Pion Limited: London pp. 49-77

Lister M., Dovey J., Giddings S., Grant I., Kelly K. New Media: A Critical Introduction London: Routledge (2003)

McLeod K. 'MP3s are killing home taping: The rise of Internet distribution and its challenge to the major label music monopoly' Popular Music and Society 28 (4) (2005) pp. 521-531

Millard D., Ross M. 'Web 2.0: hypertext by any other name?' HYPERTEXT '06 Proceedings of the Seventeenth Conference on Hypertext and Hypermedia New York: ACM Press (2006) pp. 27-30

O'Reilly T. What is Web 2.0. Design Patterns and Business Models for the Next Generation of Software (2005) http://www.oreillynet.com/pub/a/oreilly/tim/news/2005/09/30/what-is-web-20.html (accessed July 8, 2010)

Rollett H., Lux M., Strhmaier M., Dosinger G., Tochtermann K. 'The Web 2.0 way of learning with technologies' International Journal of Learning Technology 3 (1) (2007) pp. 87-107

Skiba B., Tamas A., Robinson K. Web 2.0: 'Hype or reality ... and how will it play out?' (2006) http://www.armapartners.com/files/admin/uploads/ W17_F_1873_34977.pdf (accessed July 8, 2010)

Traversat B. Abdelaziz M., Doolin D., Duigou M., Hugly J.-C., Pouyoul E. 'Project JXTA-C: Enabling a web of things' Proceedings of the 36th Annual Hawaii International Conference on System Sciences (HICSS'03) - Track 9 - Volume 9 IEEE Computer Society (2003) pp. 282-290

Wikström P. The Music Industry: Music in the Cloud Cambridge: Polity Press (2009)

Enid Mante-Meijer, Jo Pierson and Eugène Loos

Conclusion: Substantiating User Empowerment

Introduction

Current transitions in the media and technology landscape have gone hand in hand with a shift from mass media and personal media to media for "mass self-communication" (Castells 2009). This is illustrated by the way that Web 2.0 or Social Media tools (like social network sites and micro-blogging) are becoming commercially engrained in Western everyday life, and the belief that the user is in the driver's seat of socio-technical innovation (Jacobs & Pierson 2009). This shift in ICT, from unidirectional to conversational media has lowered the technological thresholds for everyday users to cooperate for their own benefit, to participate in online environments and social network sites, to co-create business value and possibly to become "prosumers" (Toffler 1980) or "producers" (Bruns 2008). This has created new opportunities and heightened expectations on user empowerment in different societal arenas of everyday life. Actual and potential impact of these applications is found in multiple domains and/or sectors: media, entertainment and ICT; work and enterprises; governments and administrations; politics and society; education and learning; inclusion and segregation; health; mobile and identity (see chapter *Punie*).

However, we observe a discrepancy. On the one hand, the instruments and means for empowering users through Social Media are proliferating, reinforcing the idea of users effectively becoming empowered. On the other hand, we find that empirical evidence about what user empowerment really consists of is to a large extent lacking. With the collection of chapters in this book, we attempt to further stimulate the debate on user empowerment in a Social Media culture and provide empirical answers to a selection of key questions.

Rationale of the book

New media technologies

Tools and technologies for media and communication are undergoing major changes, based on economic transitions and digitisation. This is accompanied by an intensified state of convergence between the formerly strictly divided sectors of audiovisual media, telecommunication and computer industry. The traditional one-way broadcasting media landscape is evolving into a converged media ecosystem, transformed by internet 2 based technologies and applications (Pascu et al. 2007). One of the more highly visible manifestations is the proliferation of information and communication technologies (ICT) like "Social Media", also denoted as "Web 2.0" (O'Reilly 2005) or "participative web" (Vicker & Wunsch-Vincent 2007). The term "social computing" is also used (Pascu 2008). The latter highlights the link with the computer and internet sector, but at the same time indicates that something is changing in the socio-technical field. In a recent European report on the impact of social computing on the European society and economy, Punie et al. 2009 define social computing as: "(...) a set of open, web-based and user-friendly applications that enable users to network, share data, collaborate and co-produce content."

These types of new media technologies are gradually becoming an integrated part of everyday life in major parts of Western society (Haythornthwaite & Wellman 2002), and in some countries have already been fully domesticated. This is particularly apparent in the communication options opening up via internet, where increasingly complex and rich ways of interaction between people are enabled by Social Media applications like (micro) blogging, wiki, podcasting, social tagging, online social gaming, and in particular through social network sites (SNS).

On the one hand, this has lead to the belief that the shift in ICT, from unidirectional to conversational media (Spurgeon 2008), has lowered the technological thresholds for everyday users to cooperate for their own benefit (Saveri et al. 2005), to participate in online environments and social network sites (Boyd & Ellison 2007), to co-create business value (Prahalad & Ramaswamy 2004) and possibly to become "prosumers" (Toffler 1980), "producers" (Bruns 2008) or producing users (Ratto 2000). Another characteristic of Social Media or social computing is that it promises to enable user-centric, collaborative knowledge sharing, community-building activities using the internet (Punie et al. 2009). This discourse has created expectations about new opportunities for users in new media developments and technology design in different societal arenas. On the other hand, critical scholars like Van Dijck & Nieborg (2009), Fuchs (2010) and Schäfer (2009) argue that the changes in the internet landscape and their alleged societal impact are often overrated and part of a rhetorical debate. The discourse on these transitions is then framed by the celebrative manifestos and management books that have helped to boost the internet industry after the bubble burst at the turn of the century.

Mass self-communication

In order to better understand and balance the oppositional perspectives, we frame our discussion within Castells' notion of "mass self-communication". Castells (2009) describes how current transitions in the media and technology landscape go together with a shift from mass media and personal media to media for "mass self-communication". He sees the latter as the novel quality of communication in contemporary society (Castells 2009, 55):

- Mass communication, because Social Media tools can potentially reach a global internet audience.

- "Self-communication", because the message production is self-generated, the potential receiver(s) definition is self-directed and the message or content retrieval is self-selected.

However the different forms of communication (mass media, interpersonal communication and mass self-communication) complement rather than substitute each other. The notion of "mass self-communication" is a good signifier for the techno-dialectic changes taking place in communication and media production, diffusion and consumption, on macro and micro level. Castells situates the current ICT and internet landscape as a conflict between the global multimedia business networks that attempt to commodify the internet and the unprecedented autonomy for communicative subjects to communicate at large, labelled as the creative audiences or users:

> "Yet, this potential autonomy is shaped, controlled, and curtailed by the growing concentration and interlocking of corporate media and network operators around the world." (Castells 2009, 135)

Nevertheless Arsenault & Castells (2008) stress that the greater communicative autonomy of the media consumers could help them to become media citizens, thus restoring the balance of power vis-à-vis their would-be controllers.

In this regard the rise of mass self-communication also intensifies the move towards "networked individualism", where the individual person becomes the portal or hub for different networks around him or her (Haythornthwaite 2002). On the one hand, this gives media consumers freedom and leverage in how, when, what and with whom communication takes place. However, on the other hand, the increased level of individual control inevitably implies more responsibilities, given the possible heavier consequences. There is, for example, a substantial chance that online user practices via Social Media are more persistent in time, have a broader geographical reach and are picked up by unwanted receivers. This means that the vulnerability of people engaging in mass self-communication will change and possibly increase.

Defining user empowerment

The pros and cons of "mass self-communication" are linked to notions of respectively "user empowerment" and "user disempowerment". Empowerment in the general sense is defined as "enabling people to control their own lives and to take advantage of opportunities" (Van der Maesen & Walker 2002, 6) or in other words "a process, a mechanism by which people, organisations, and communities gain mastery over their affairs." (Rappaport 1987, 122). The notion of empowerment has a long tradition, especially in social welfare literature. In this book we have applied the notion within the domain of media and ICT from an interdisciplinary perspective. Different levels of empowerment can be identified, more in particular on an individual level and on a community level. However, we prefer to take an integrated perspective, the so-called social-ecological approach. This is defined as:

> "The interaction between people and their environment, based on mutual respect and critical reflection, by which individuals as well as controlling institutions change in such a way that individuals get a bigger influence on people and institutions that prevent them to acquire an equal position in society" (Delahaij 2004) [Translated from Dutch]

When applying this perspective of empowerment in the realm of mass self-communication and Social Media, we start from the following citation by Robin Mansell (2002, 409):

> "(...) the implications of the new media are contradictory. Once connected, there are no grounds for simply assuming that citizens will be empowered to conduct their social lives in meaningful ways. There is, therefore, a growing need to examine whether the deployment of new media is consistent with ensuring that the majority of citizens acquire the necessary capabilities for interpreting and acting upon a social world that is intensively mediated by the new media."

The notion of "capabilities" refers here to the work of Sen (1999), who takes a normative egalitarian view by stating that people have certain entitlements in the welfare state. We then define user empowerment in relation to Social Media as the capability for interpreting and acting upon the social world that is intensively mediated by mass self-communication.

In order to truly assess whether users are thus empowered or on the contrary disempowered by Social Media tools, we distinguish three levels at which (dis)empowerment takes place: inclusion, literacy and privacy.

- First, there is no automatic link between social computing and user empowerment, as not all users are able, willing or even permitted to get involved and participate by means of or through digital media. This refers to the issues of access, digital inclusion, infrastructure and regulation. We need to ask questions like: How is the Social Media field regulated and organised? Do we (still) need laws on media pluralism, when the people have access to a multitude of media channels? To what extent are (vulnerable) groups in society included/excluded and how do these groups experience their inclusion/exclusion? How can digital media be used to increase levels of inclusion?

- In addition, we need to be aware that not all users are capable of getting as involved with media technologies as they would like to be, due to a lack of digital media literacy. This means we need to ask questions like: To what extent are people competent/capable/literate in the use of Social Media? How can these internet-based media be put to use for enhancing digital literacy?

- Third, even if they have access and are media literate, the question remains as to what extent users are self-reflexive and sufficiently aware of changing privacy and surveillance aspects, i.e. realize how their digital activities are being monitored, processed, analysed and commodified by third parties. Key questions in this regard are: Are people aware that the use of Social Media is never for free but always part of an exchange (of personal data) with (often American) private companies? How do consumers/users perceive the blurring boundaries between the public and the private and how does this relate to privacy protection? How do they perceive the tradeoff between convenience/personalisation and disclosing private information?

So empowering people in the context of mass self-communication means enhancing the capabilities for genuinely understanding Social Media and their impact on private life as regards the levels of inclusion, digital literacy and privacy.

Users in the driver's seat of new media technologies

Jacobs & Pierson (2009) use the car driver metaphor to explain the diverse roles users may have in the shaping of technology. The driver determines the speed, the direction to go, and what to do to avoid accidents. He may make use of his GPS or may rely on his own feeling of direction to reach his goal. He bases his actions on his view of the road and his surroundings, on the actions of passengers and fellow road users and their vehicles and the signals the car is giving him, formal or informal. Passengers may play an active role in showing the way, warning of dangers and keeping the driver awake, but may also be content with just being driven to the goals the driver sets. The technology of the car, however, is a given fact. The user can choose the make, the colour and the size, and at the most influence the accessories he thinks useful when he is buying the car. *Who* drives the car is dependent on the situation: it may be a paid driver, an expert on car driving or just an ordinary citizen, the user of the car. In the end Jacobs & Pierson (2009) reflect that perhaps "rafting" would be an even better metaphor for illustrating the role of users. There is only one driver in a car, while collaboration and coordination may also be needed. This kind of collaboration is institutionalised in a rafting or rowing team, albeit with a coxswain giving direction and tempo of the raft.

These metaphors illustrate the situation experienced by users of ICT when they decide to make use of information and communication technology to manage their everyday life. Users of ICTs may choose the type of ICT they want to use. They may play the role of passenger, allowing themselves to be driven or steered by some expert front(wo)man, or they may sit in the driver's seat themselves and determine the direction they want to go, or even find new, innovative routes to reach their goal. Users differ greatly in skills and opportunities to make use of the technology. Empowerment then means that people gain the skills and knowledge that will allow them to overcome obstacles in life or work and gain control over them in their own lives and in society as a whole. But how much influence do users actually have on the creation and development of ICTs? Which roles are open to them and what does that mean when talking about empowerment of users?

Real user empowerment in production and use?

Thus we observe that instruments and means for mass self-communication by users through Social Media are proliferating, reinforcing the idea of users effectively becoming empowered. However, empirical evidence about what user empowerment really consists of is, to a large extent, still missing. This discrepancy formed the starting point for bringing together a collection of empirical research findings in this book, scrutinising to what extent users are really becoming empowered in relation to new media technologies.

This leads us to the following key questions in relation to user empowerment, as indicated in the chapter by *Punie*: Is the user now becoming an actor amongst many other actors with an influence (as part of a rowing or rafting crew)? If so, how far will this influence reach? (Castells 2009; Fuchs 2009) Or are users actively taking over the control from others (becoming the driver of the car)? There is also the question of what the consequences of these possibilities of user empowerment are for individual and society, as well as what the dangers and challenges are.

Let us look more closely at these questions and let us try to give answers in the light of the different views represented in this volume. Based on *Punie's* division, these views can basically be divided into two perspectives. First, the views which see the involvement of users as active contributors to the technological design and innovation process. This perspective typically has links with the fields of Science and Technology Studies and related constructivist research traditions. Second, there are the contributions that distinguish between the participation and (co)creativity of users in the more general media domain, highlighting that changing roles of users are having an impact on relations of power and control in the (new) media sector. This perspective is often situated in domain of Cultural Studies and the work by e.g. Jenkins (2006) and other scholars studying phenomena like fan culture.

The involvement of users and their role in ICT innovation

It is clear that during the last twenty years the recognition of the importance of user involvement in the development process has changed enormously. ICT is in a high degree a social technology. It is supposed to be used by users in order to regulate their everyday lives, to communicate with others, to play a major role in the way they (have to) do their work, and to structure their leisure and entertainment. ICT provides users with an enormous wealth of choices to make. More and more, users play a leading role in the success or failure of technology. Logically this makes the user an important partner in the development process. Two questions may be asked in this respect:

• What is the active involvement of users in the creation and development of new ICTs? It is clear that the initiative mostly lies with the technologists and policy makers (Norman 2009). The pace of technology itself and the ever growing possibilities offered by technology dictate what will be developed. Economic necessity and policy drive the search for solutions for an ever more differentiated and complicated society and decide which innovations will be pushed. Nevertheless, especially in the communication and media sector, users are more and more able to play an active role in the content contribution.

• Do users *want* to be active controllers in the development of ICT and new media technologies or are they passive consumers, lurkers or even non-users?

Changes in user involvement and empowerment

During the past two decades, the knowledge about adoption and use of new technology and the possibilities to involve users in the development of the technology has grown tremendously. In their chapter *Mante-Meijer and Loos* provide an overview of many of the variables that enable or constrain the individual to make use of new technologies: capabilities of the individual, his macro, meso and micro social environment, his preparedness to take risks, the availability of intermediaries and the quality of technology itself determine the way individuals and communities make sense of the technological innovations and translate them into their everyday practices. The chapter shows the complicatedness of the process and the conditions for success or failure of the push of technological innovation.

But the willingness to adopt is not the only perspective that is important in the world of the new media. Web2.0 and next generations offer ample opportunities to the user for playing an active role himself in the development of his everyday new media. When we talk of empowerment, we visualize a user who actively participates in on-line environments, who co-creates business and may become a producing user.

In their chapter *Frissen and Slot* use the term "bricolage" to describe this process of actively shaping the online environment. When users decide to play an active role in creating new developments in the media domain, their behaviour is comparable with what Levi Strauss calls the "bricoleur". The "bricoleur", according to Lévi Strauss, uses all the concrete materials he encounters in everyday life and all the earlier experiences of himself and others around him, to make sense of the world he is living in and to find solutions for the problems he is confronted with. He thus creatively and intuitively combines and recombines the bits and pieces that are available in the "treasury" of his everyday surroundings. By using what is concretely available, he often – more or less accidentally – creates something new. If we look at the developments in the media domain over the last decade, users have taken up more active and creative roles in the media value chain. The role hitherto played by consumers in the media had been more or less a passive one. Consumers constituted a mass audience. In the twenty first century, however, rapidly growing numbers of ordinary users started to manifest themselves as professional amateurs, tinkering with the digital building blocks available to them in the rich treasury of materials and experiences that the web offers.

User approaches on ICT design and development

Different models for user roles

The above suggests that technological innovation is meeting with a new challenge: changing the existent top-down design by bottom-up methods of research and practices, both in the development stage, and in the phases of testing, experimenting and evaluating applications (see for example the chapter by *Stewart, Coyne, Travlou, Wright and Ekeus*). The goal is to let people work with them, let them develop online collectives and communities and see what happens.

In their chapter on Rethinking the role of Users in ICT design *Kerr, De Paoli and Storni* examine change from the perspective of control or drift, envisioned in two models: the first clearly defines roles for user groups while the second leaves these roles more open. In both cases, technology and license systems work together to prescribe certain user roles and define the degree to which users may become involved in use. These two perspectives, or models, might represent opposing ideal types of users' scripting, where, on one side, we have a more managerial, top down approach to ICT design, while on the other we have a decentralized, peer-to-peer approach. Conceptualizing the relationships between these two models and exploring other models is one of the challenges for ICT researchers. These relationships cannot be taken for granted, at the risk of falling into subtle forms of reductionism, determinism and essentialism. Therefore we need to assess whether we are really witnessing the growth of a more open approach to design, or whether there are forces acting to restrict such approaches. What are the consequences for the social relations of production? Will the more open approach give rise to the empowerment of certain privileged user groups, and not to others? What actors, technologies, policies and licensing systems are needed to ensure that users are truly empowered in meaningful ways?

This gives rise to another question: is such open research possible in practice? Steen (2008), in his dissertation on the fragility of human centred design, remarks that user participation in the design process is by no means easy. Nowadays, designers, technologists, marketers and social scientists are combined into multidisciplinary teams during the design process of a new service. There is often room to involve users as partners during this process and several approaches have been developed. Steen (2008) talks about human centred design, participatory design, and empathic design. The participatory role of users ranges from the employment of lead users as experts, to co-design as part of the team and contextual design in which the user is brought directly into the development process. In empathic design, the user is observed in a kind of "living lab" in which the researchers try to empathise with him and with his experiences and emotions. The problem, signalled by Steen (2008), is that there is no guarantee that the users' contributions are really taken into account during the design process. The technological aspects are often defined a priori; moreover, economic considerations weigh heavily, and the project's client may have different ideas about what he wants to do with the results. Workshops with users have an agenda, defined by the designers and technologists. This means that it is easy to overlook the things that really matter to potential users. In contextual design and empathic design, the world of the user and his experience of this world are central to how the design is conducted. However, according to Steen, these approaches still present the danger that preconceived ideas, and foreground knowledge play a role.

Apart from difficulties resulting from different methodology, different languages and different interpretations (see chapter *Stewart and Claeys*) the role of the user as a partner in research is a rather vague one. Although the user, as part of an interdisciplinary team, has become a partner in the earlier stages of the design, his roles vary from expert advisor during the development stage to guinea pig when testing the almost finished product. *Stewart and Claeys* show that it is not so easy to create real interdisciplinary outputs, as each discipline has its own and widely divergent approach to formulating questions and providing answers.

Also, users themselves differ greatly in their needs, interests, expectations and practices (see chapters *Kerr, De Paoli and Storni*; *Vangenck, Pierson, Van den Broeck and Lievens*). These findings were consistent with the experiences reported by *Marttila, Hyyppä and Kommonen* in their chapter on the development of a P2P software tool for very different communities of users. Keeping the participants motivated when the technology needed was not available in time turned out to be a challenge. In addition, it turned out to be essential to include early as well as periodical activities dedicated to developing a shared co-design framework and language. Nurturing the co-design approach and concretizing the value of each of the co-design partners' efforts to the design process is important, as the lack of common design philosophy may blur the design goals and decrease the partners' motivation.

Steen (2009) shows that even when the intention is to give the user the more leading role, the practice is, that business, marketing and policy considerations win out over the interests of the end-user.

User participation in practice: differentiation in situation, roles and creativity

Apart from the *actual possibility* for the user to take part in the development of technology, an important question is: do users *want* to be active controllers in the development of ICT and new media technologies, or are they passive consumers, lurkers or even non-users? In practice, an enormous differentiation in user roles and creativity can be seen. What separates users with the ability to interact with the media and to take active control from those lacking this ability?

Active users recognize that the internet can serve as a useful medium to remain in control. However, the user's social situation must encourage the use of the medium.

In their chapter *Szekely and Urban* show in their Hungarian study that where there is a large group of non-users, negative stereotypes about users abound: "they just sit in front of the computer and they have only virtual relationships. (…) They only use the internet and do not care for anything else." Although interestingly, non-users in theory accept the information and communication functions of the internet as such, they are averse to the entertainment aspects. These are considered harmful, causing serious addiction. In brief, only limited use of the internet is morally acceptable from the perspective of non-users. Age group and life stage explain the difference between use and non-use, but also education, economic situation and ethnicity are very important explaining variables.

The *felt need or want* to make use of ICT is an important factor in the adoption of the technology and its subsequent use. Non-users' main reason for non-use is that they do not need it, making any activity in this area unnecessary. In their chapter *Ely, Frohlich and Green* point to an important variable that determines the level of activity in the realm of ICT use: changes in life circumstances bring about changes in social, cultural and economic capital. Important changes are, for example, the changes in life phase (single, living with a partner, having children, retiring out of the workforce, but also abrupt events, such as losing a job, becoming widowed, etc.). During such changes, "old" and "new" technologies and practices are linked to users' abilities and knowledge in connecting and reconnecting, and to people's shifting values and priorities. For example, *Ely, Frohlich and Green* studied the impact of relocating from one place to another. When moving, people must find solutions for a plethora of technical and social problems caused by the change. At these times, people (users) are both empowered and disempowered by their ability or inability to enrol friends, family, neighbours, helpdesks, manuals, websites, bank accounts, and the technologies themselves, in order to meet their needs and desires. Hence both technical and social possibilities are actively explored to fill in the gaps by the loss of the old environment and contacts. Digital-Do It Yourself is then an important means to find solutions. Here, however, despite the promise of technological progress, the design of products and services (and in particular the interfaces to them), the material "soup" of artefacts, the assumptions of gender and the limits of users' own creativity, "do-it-yourself" might run up against the limits of its empowerment.

Another example of creative and active use of the possibilities of ICTs in situations of felt need, is given by *Törnqvist* in her chapter. *Törnqvist's* cases of the hunting and bird watching communities show that creative use takes place within larger systems and institutions. The social context plays a significant role in the introduction, development and use of ICT, and partly dictates whether this is going to be successful or not. Here again, the importance of structures, communities and pockets of local orders are stressed as important enablers for individual creative actions. Here, the need was to share information on activities of the hunting, respectively the bird watching associations. The fact that those activities take place in sparsely populated areas, gave rise to the creative use of mobile media as a means to send the information to the members just in time, wherever they were. Creative knowledgeable members became producing users by developing a device tailored to their particular goals. Secondly, micro level users expanded the use of existing equipment by their practices in their specific contexts. The cases show that the implementation and use of ICT takes place in the interaction between individuals in social communities of practice. Without knowledge of the social and cultural structures in which the innovation will be used, a company that is external to the community cannot successfully start an innovative process.

Does the ever increasing creative activity online in the internet society mean that, in the future, "the consumer is dead?" (Shirky 2000). In her chapter *Slot* concludes that this needs to be somewhat nuanced. Even online, users can still be classified as consumers of content. They read newspaper articles on websites using a tablet (e.g. Apple iPad), watch television shows on their computer screens, listen to music and play online games – on the internet, every user is also a consumer. The fact that consumers are enabled to take on other roles online can be seen as a complementary development rather than a complete turnaround. Therefore, it can be argued that because of the internet and networked media, users are enabled to take on other roles *besides* being consumers. Perhaps they can best be labelled as *extended consumers*. Instead of only focussing on the user as a producer (or prosumer), or creator of content, the active-user concept can be broadened to include all kinds of roles. Users can be consumers, producers and controllers at the same time. Looking more closely, the findings suggest that the level of user participation can be nuanced. Low-level and more traditional participatory activities, such as consuming content, communicating and customizing, are among the most popular user roles. The variety within these roles is large and users often engage in several of these activities. On average, far fewer users engage in truly creative and high-level user participation, like making websites and uploading self-made videos, than in easy and low-level activities. Generational differences play an important role in the measure and the ways in which the internet is used. Younger users tend to be online longer each day and engage in more activities than older users. Older age groups, however, are also taking on many active online roles. It can be concluded that they might be online less often and engage less frequently in activities, but that they still engage in a large variety of user roles. It seems that online, the traditional consumer role has extended significantly into multiple user roles, and this has challenged existing user/producer relations.

User empowerment: Are users actively taking over the control?

Roles of empowered users

Web 2.0 and 3.0 have heightened the expectations about user empowerment in different societal arenas of everyday life. As *Punie* writes in his chapter:

> "Actual and potential impact of these applications is found in multiple domains and/or sectors: media, entertainment and ICT; work and enterprises; governments and administrations; politics and society; education and learning; inclusion and segregation."

These creative expectations are currently being realized, especially in the media industry and in particular in the domains of music and news production. There we find concrete informal networks of prosumers and producers that actually influence existing formal networks.

This development of user activity in creating and distributing content is turning, according to *Proulx and Heaton* in their chapter, media industries' traditional models upside down. New ways of user involvement have developed, in which the user holds a more central position in the development of media. Four tactics characterize this veering towards "participative culture" practices (Jenkins 2006). First, users are positioned at the centre of the apparatus, encouraged to produce and distribute their own content online: this tactic is generally referred to in terms of user-generated content (UGC) or user-created content (UCC) (Vickery & Wunsch-Vincent). Second, such participation appears to be facilitated by the limited level of cognitive and technical exertion required to wield the tools of these new platforms – notwithstanding the persisting inequalities in access to and appropriation of these tools – to create a context which favours increased creation and content-sharing among casual internet users (Leadbetter & Miller 2004). Third, these changes are grounded in the development of online collectives and user communities, networked and structured in an apparently non-hierarchical manner (Surowiecki 2005). Fourth, these transformations spawn new economic models (Gensollen 2006) founded in large-scale aggregation of often minimal individual contributions, a market rationalisation of informational goods' production and distribution that is rooted in exploratory approaches to serendipitous discovery – users stumbling across content that they were not seeking out *a priori* (Auray 2008).

We see an example of the changing roles of the users in the musical network that took place under the influence of Web 2.0 and 3.0 (*Bannier* in his chapter). Web 2.0 made it possible for the user to influence the musical network as a whole. The networks of consumption were suddenly connected to all the other networks. Before, record companies and other actors of the music industry influenced every network; now, the World Wide Web user had become an important power in these networks. The same developments can be seen with the advent of Web 3.0. Within the networks of creativity, chances are offered to 2.0 online artist platforms, social networks, prosumers and producers. They play an important part with respect to creativity in the musical network itself. In addition, artist platforms offer more possibilities for artists to get in touch with interesting and important actors of the music industry and vice versa. Web 3.0 and the semantic web offer artist platforms and social networks better search results and usability of the websites. The interactive creative process is becoming more hybrid, since the internet makes it possible to compose collaboratively online. The most important development in the networks of reproduction has been the arrival of the MP3 format and the changes it brought about, now that prosumer and produser are able to produce their own MP3s. Both P2P networks and social networks are now the most important actors in the media industry, given that the user is able to promote and distribute music easily, fast and widely. The result is that the record companies and other traditional actors of the music industry in the musical network saw their power and agency within the networks decrease. For one thing, user profiles and user-generated content are accumulated and, for another thing, these profiles and content are processed to generate personalised and enriched recommended information, to make the internet more accessible and useful for the user.

Limitations on becoming a produser or prosumer

Despite the fact that the new technologies indeed enhance the opportunities to play an active role in classical forms of media production, this type of user participation is hampered by the traditions and ideas of the profession itself. Paulussen et al. (2007) suggest that, despite the differences in context, mainstream media in any of the four countries that they studied, tend to develop very limited opportunities for audience participation. The professional culture of journalists and traditional producers is suggested as forming the main factor preventing the development of participatory projects, while marketing and business strategies somehow push for the exploration of such proposals.

Another question is: who are those active creative prosumers? Are they incidental participants, taking part for their own pleasure, or are they serious lay professionals who want to participate within or outside the existing media? What drives them to take on the active role of producer/prosumer? In his chapter *Picone* shows that production and consumption of news are very distinct activities in the mind of the consumer and that the nature of the news item (content) plays an important role in the willingness to participate, along with a social reflex and self-confidence, and, not insignificantly, writing skills, and the perceived potential public. Self-empowerment through online news participation is not self-evident. According to *Picone*, the consumption - production dimension does not imply linearity. A consumer is not inexorably bound to become a producer. First, the need to publicly articulate an opinion must be felt. Then there is the intrinsic motivation, ranging from just fun to passion. Finally, there is the personal dimension of the authority of the producer, his or her self-confidence and his or her feeling of self-fulfilment by becoming a producer of news. How this choice making turns out, is dependent on the effort it requires to participate in the news. Time also plays a role here, as the more effort produsing demands, the more time it takes. Depending on these conditions, the individual considers whether or not to invest time and effort in contributions. The non-self-publication – self-publication dimension appears to be so strong that simply reducing the effort is not enough reason to participate. Here the "want" dimension, illustrated earlier in this chapter, becomes very important.

As Jenkins (2006) and Van Dijck & Nieborg (2009) have underlined, producers also influence user behaviour. Who stands to benefit most from user activity? Is it the user, or is most user activity simply a marketing ploy used by commercial players to obtain personal data? Are users able to influence the way these parties behave? Internet users are increasingly aware that their personal data is being stored and used to gain a profit (*Slot* in her chapter). In 2010, Facebook users started a Facebook Users' Union, which demanded that Facebook gives its users a say in how the money earned from user data is spent (Kiss 2010). Up until August 2010, this Facebook group had gathered approximately 1,100 users. It will be interesting to see if this group grows and if these users can make a difference. The coming years will show to what extent users are truly empowered online.

Concluding remarks: impact and challenges for future society

Consequences for society: limiting factors for empowerment

In the introduction of this book we formulated the following two questions:
1) Are users now becoming actors amongst many other actors with an influence?
2) Are users actively taking over the control from others in certain areas?
The answer to the first question is: partly yes, partly no. To a growing extent, users are becoming actors amongst other actors with an influence, but this influence is hampered by a host of structural and social variables. The answer to the second question is that, in the Social Media world, there are some signs of users using their power actively in such a way that they become a factor not to be overlooked. But traditional professionalism limits their possibilities.

We have now arrived at another question formulated in the introduction of this book: What are the consequences of these possibilities of user empowerment for individual and society and what are the dangers and challenges?

Punie mentions in his chapter a number of positive impacts Social Media may have on society. Social Media have the potential to improve internal work processes, products and services. They provide new tools for social support and social inclusion and empower civil society organizations that fight social exclusion. They can supply tools that support, facilitate and enhance learning processes and outcomes. They have as such a positive impact on multiple facets of public health and health care. It cannot be denied that, indeed, Social Media have this potential.

However, there are also many limiting factors. The diverse contributions of this book show the obstacles to be overcome in order to realize this potential.

- First, there is the **role of the structure of society**. Policy makers and technologists should be more aware of the role of the social structure and the necessity to make choices, in order to generate more realistic expectations and to create technology that is more adapted to the diverse types of possible users of the society they are a part of. This is in line with the classic notion of constructive technology assessment (Smit & Van Oost 1999).

- Second, there is **the complexity of the processes of adoption, use and appropriation**. In their chapter *Mante-Meijer and Loos* presented an extended model, based on Giddens' structuration theory offering insight into the very complex processes of adoption, appropriation and practical use of technological innovation. The very structures of society, the way they influence the interpretations and sense making about new technology and the way this sense making is translated into practices is the core of the model.

- **Enablers and constraints** play an intermediate role in the relation between societal structure and practices. They help to decide whether the potential user makes the choice to adopt and develop different practices or whether he defers use of the opportunities. Related to choice en risk taking are the perceived cost and value. Other factors are: the capabilities of user and technology itself, the personal needs and wishes of the user himself in his everyday life situation, the influence of significant others in his environment and the cultural, economical, political, institutional structures of which he is a part, that define his norms and values and habits and wishes.

- **Intermediaries of various sorts** are necessary to bridge the gaps between the local setting of users and producers. It is important to understand the role of intermediaries that emerge from communities of users that support and represent them. Examples in this respect are so-called warm experts (Bakardjieva 2005) like family members, neighbours and friends, children to parents, but also community workers, teachers, etc. It is also necessary to understand how these intermediaries can be supported themselves, and their value in the innovation process.

- **"Innovation" has different shapes and meanings for different persons**. The challenge is to obtain technology that is meaningful in the everyday lives of the citizens of Europe. As users differ widely in social cultural background, in life stage and educational background, what is an appropriate solution for one person might not be one for the other. Moreover, it would be unwise to discard the old (analogue) alternatives prematurely by trying to force people into one digital mould.

- **Involving users in the development of technology** is not just asking some experienced users to try out the technology before it reaches the market. Although several techniques have been developed to involve the future user in the development process, and although especially the current developments in Web 2.0 and 3.0 offer ample user friendly opportunities to empower users to give voice to their interests, there is still the danger that the differences in goals of the diverse players in the field will make the outcomes less than optimal. It is important that the ideas, experiences and creativity of those who may represent future users are incorporated into this speculative research. As the investment decisions and innovation pathways are often based on ideas created by researchers in laboratories, the incorporation of ideas and creativity of users make it likely that eventual products and services will be more successful. It is important that these laboratories bring together a diversity of research skills, listen to and find inspiration in people as well as technology or business visions (see chapter *Proulx and Heaton*).

Consequences for society: dangers and challenges

The presented cases offer a general overview of the attitudes and the behaviour of users in situations where they are invited to play an active role in ICT society. They also show a number of factors that influence successful user participation and user co-production. However, they also raise a few questions about the high expectations for the degree of participation in the near future and the beneficial effects for society. What, for example, is to be expected in the future about The Golden Age of Information Society (Slot & Frissen 2007)? These researchers argue that in the Web 2.0 era, it no longer suffices to think of users as "end-users", as they have moved to the heart of the value chain. But to what extent is such an expectation justified? Are we approaching a "golden age" of user empowerment?

It is clear that in the last two decades, the world has gone digital on a large scale. Internet has opened the gates for obtaining information from anywhere. Networks enable us to organize around all kinds of issues we think important, or we want to know. They also enable us to come into contact with others, whom we have never met and probably never will meet. We are able to voice our opinions on a global scale and thus have influence. The internet empowers people in regions where they used to have no opportunities by enabling them to voice their opinions and conduct transactions and create business value by making use of the internet networks.

In the globalizing world, the possibilities and opportunities to make life easier, more pleasant and more effective have grown tremendously. The means that everyday life nowadays differs in many respects from life in the eighties. However, technological advancements do not in themselves create a better and more just society. At the moment, not only has the world become global, the problems of the world have also globalized and are far from finding easy solutions. Are ICTs as beneficial as assumed? What about user empowerment in the future?

In the following pages, we point out some complications, dangers and challenges that the Information Society has to meet and has only begun to solve:

- **The digital divide**

When we talk about the digital divide, we think in the first place of age as the leading factor. Older people have long been held to be, at the very least, reluctant or even "clumsy" users of ICTs. In reality, age does play a role, but, more importantly, experience with computers, frequency of surfing, education and gender go a long way towards explaining the degree of effectiveness and efficiency in use of the technology and search behaviour on the web (Loos & Mante-Meijer 2009). Slot & Frissen (2008) show that differences in the use of internet between young and old people is more a matter of type of use than use or non-use. Also, gender differences disappear with practice.

But the access to ICT differs, as it is related to economics, policy and education. In Europe, for example, we still see large differences, especially between Northern, Southern and Eastern countries in the accessibility of broadband networks and services. Learning and teaching how to make use of e-technology is a challenge, both for the individuals who make use of it, and for the groups and organizations that want to employ ICT for their own production processes and for their communication within the organization and with clients and partners outside the organization.

The technology must not only fit the capabilities of the user, it must also match his/her ability to handle the websites and to make use of interactive tools or networks that are offered. There is also the fact that the introduction of e-tools changes the processes people are used to. There is a large gap between what the user actually is able to do and what is expected from him by technology and by policy (Van Deursen & Van Dijk 2009). Contrary to general belief, they found that this gap is true both for young and old.

The creation of an infrastructure for obtaining adequate digital literacy is more than just teaching people how to use ICTs, or how to navigate the web to obtain information. Training in critical and analytical capabilities should be a part of this programme. It is a necessity to empower citizens, now and in the future.

It is an often-heard statement that the digital divide will disappear when the older generation passes away. We do not expect this to happen. As the development of technology will always run at a quicker pace than society, it is very probable that each time there will be people that lag behind, simply because they participate less in the new developments than others. New technology demands new capabilities and new practices. These have to be learned, implemented and used in order to become part of everyday life.

- **Cultural differences**

The large cultural differences in (traditional) norms, values and habits within and outside Europe (e.g. Scandinavia vs. Italy or Spain) form a challenge for achieving equal opportunities for citizens. Large differences in the adoption and appropriation of ICTs accompany those differences. This problem is becoming more complicated with the immigration of people from regions in the world that differ even more in these respects. What do these cultural differences mean for the ways technology will be used?

- **The lack of easy to navigate and clear websites**

The creation of websites is a free enterprise of the organization or persons who want to be on the web. Loos & Mante-Meijer (2009) show that the ways websites are constructed and the type of information wanted play a role in searching, or in the abilities to look for information on websites. Websites differ strongly in degree of complicatedness and user (un)friendliness. It is important to obtain some sort of standardization in the lay-out of websites, for example, in the placing of search boxes and click possibilities, from the perspective of "design for all". This would make for a better accessibility of the website. Also, people with impaired reading or intellectual capabilities should be able to find the information they are looking for. Here again, it is important to do user interface and user experience testing with real (everyday) users, and not with the technicians themselves

- **Conflicts between internet users and professional corporations**

The rise of mass self-communication has led to "citizen journalism" practices. Here we see two conflicting logics: professional and market logic and a social emancipatory logic (Proulx 2009). Citizen journalism includes the production, processing, and distribution of journalistic information by internet users who are not professional journalists using the tools of the relational Web. From the humble status of reader, the internet user moves to stand with the editor and the commentator: users become editors of news, commentators of current events, or they recycle the information (in other formats). How to safeguard professional standards and to assure the veracity and credibility of the contributions?

- **Safeguarding the trust of the users in digital society**

Digital crime issues threaten user trust in e-society. The same is true for spam and privacy infringements. After 9-11-2001, the discussion about how to safeguard privacy has become entangled with the emphasis on collecting, saving and coupling information on individuals. The risk of unwanted mistakes and misuse grows with the saving and linking of large chunks of data. The recent near sabotage of a Delta flight illustrates the problem. All information on the terrorist was available in the databases, but these had failed to be correctly linked, which shows that databases as such cannot guarantee that the right connections are made. Policy should be very keen on the aspect of preserving privacy. Attention should be focused on data protection and methods of data mining, misinterpretation and also on the fact that what is on the Web will never disappear. This also means that the notion of "vulnerability" with regards to disclosure of private information is changing in an online Social Media context.

- **Energy issues**

An aspect that does not attract sufficient attention, but that might become a great problem, is the enormous costs of energy to maintain all the ICT products and networks, especially when ICT is subjected to strong political aspirations to become accessible for all citizens on their own conditions.

Röpke (2009) focuses on the ongoing process in which ICTs are integrated in everyday life and the impact this has on energy consumption. The use of the computer and the internet has been integrated into work and education (telework, e-learning, schoolwork, home offices, video conferences). Their use has also been integrated into reproductive work, aspects of the intelligent home, security, childcare, do-it-yourself experiences, leisure and into civil society. This rapid technological change has led to growing demand for ever more powerful computers and equipment and a continuing diversification of devices and appliances. Apart from this direct energy consumption, the indirect energy consumption, for example for the production of ICT equipment and increased waste handling due to the rate of renewal for ICT equipment, should not be ignored. These aspects of the ICT push merit closer attention, as do the possibilities of a better management of ICT consumption by extending the life span of computers, better power management, and by looking for energy efficient devices.

This raises a closely related point, namely the vulnerability of society due to the growing dependence on electricity. In the West, for example, one heavy snowstorm leaves numerous households without heating and cooking possibilities. At such times, many computers and computer-related tools also go down, with sometimes serious consequences for society. This is also seen when during power outages due to disasters, criminality or otherwise.

- **The transformation of society in relation to digitization**

ICTs invade citizens' social institutions across the board. It is important to be alert to the consequences for the social fabric of society, relations within families, the education of children, care for the older people, for the less fortunate and for those unable to keep pace with technology, etc. Not everybody can or wants to participate fully or even partly in the digital world. What about the voluntarily excluded, or the drop-outs? Multichannel approaches should always be available. And, in the same vein: what is the impact of virtual reality on the construction of offline realities?

Final remarks

Like all technology, ICT has two faces: it is important to develop long-term views on what to stimulate and what to avoid. What type of society do we wish to have, for example, in 2025? It is therefore important not only to look at the techno-economic future, but also to take into account the fact that people will always be people, with the same basic needs as they have nowadays.

The internet enables people to share knowledge of all kinds, and to partake in all kinds of discussions. As a Dutch newspaper recently concluded, it enables people to look critically at everything happening in the world, as well as at that which governments want to communicate to citizens (NRC, 20.02.2010). This may have a beneficial effect, because it forces politicians to create more transparency, but it can also have a disruptive and chaotic effect, as it leaves room for all kinds of "fairy tales" that are convincing because people want to believe them, but which are in no way, or only partly based on real facts (e.g. religious debates or moral panics on the inoculations against Mexican flu). Taking a much more historical perspective would help. Although history does not repeat itself in the same way, we could learn from what happened with the introduction of the telephone, the TV, the mobile phone or other older media. To find answers to these problems and dangers and to those still unknown and undiscovered, poses a challenge for modern society today and in the future.

References

Arsenault A. H., Castells M. 'The Structure and Dynamics of Global Multi-Media Business Networks' International Journal of Communication (2) (2008) pp. 707-748

Auray N. 'Le Web 2.0: des communautés aux solidarités' Web participatif : mutation de la communication?' Congrès de l'Acfas, Québec (May 6-7, 2008)

Bakardjieva M. Internet Society: The Internet in Everyday Life London: Sage (2005)

Boyd D.M., Ellison N.B. 'Social network sites: Definition, history, and scholarship' Journal of Computer-Mediated Communication 13 (1) (2007)

Bruns A. Blogs, Wikipedia, Second life, and Beyond: From Production to Produsage New York, Oxford: Peter Lang (2008)

Castells M. Communication Power Oxford: Oxford University Press (2009)

Delahaij R. Dossier Empowerment: Empowermentmethoden bij Allochtone Jongeren Utrecht: Forum: Instituut voor multiculturele ontwikkeling (2004)

Dijck, J. van, Nieborg D. 'Wikinomics and its discontents: a critical analysis of Web 2.0 business manifestos' New Media & Society, 11 (5) (2009) pp. 855-874

Fuchs C. 'Social software and Web 2.0: Their sociological foundations and implications' ed. Murugesan S. Handbook of Research on Web 2.0, 3.0, and X.0: Technologies Business, and Social Applications Vol. II Hershey, PA: IGI-Global (2010) pp. 764-789

Gensollen M. 'La culture entre économie et écologie: l'exemple des communautés en ligne' ed. Greffe, X. Création et diversité au miroir des industries culturelles Paris: La Documentation Française (2006) pp. 285-312

Haythornthwaite C.A. 'Strong, weak, and latent ties and the impact of new media' The Information Society (18) (2002) pp. 385-401

Haythornthwaite C.A., Wellman B. 'The Internet in everyday life' eds. Wellman B., Haythornthwaite C.A. The Internet in Everyday Life Oxford: Blackwell (2002) pp. 3-41

Jacobs A., Pierson J. 'Users in the driver's seat of innovativeness in digital media development? Reflections on current conceptualisations The good the Bad and the Challenging 2009' Cost Action 298 Copenhagen (May 13-15, 2009)

Jenkins H. Convergence culture. Where Old and New Media Collide New York and London: New York University Press (2006)

Kiss J. 'Facebook should be paying us' The Guardian Monday 9 August (2010)

Leadbeater C., Miller P. The Pro-Am Revolution. How enthusiasts are Changing the Way our Economy and Society Work London: Demos UK (2004)

Loos E., Mante-Meijer E. 'Getting access to website health information: Does age really matter? Digital media technologies revisited' Conference University of the Arts, Berlin, Germany (November 19-21, 2009)

Maesen L.J.G. van der, Walker A.C. (2002) Social Quality: The Theoretical State of Affairs Amsterdam: European Foundation on Social Quality 24 (2002)

Mansell R. 'From digital divides to digital entitlements in knowledge societies' Current sociology 50 (3) (2002) pp. 407-426

Norman D. Technology first, needs later http://jnd.org/dn.mss/ technology_first _needs_last.html (2009) (assessed September 28, 2010)

O'Reilly T. What is Web 2.0? Design Patterns and Business Models for the Next Generation of Software 2005 http://www.oreillynet.com/pub/a/reilly tim/ news/2005/09/30/what-is-web-20.html (assessed November 28, 2009)

Pascu C. An Empirical Analysis of the Creation, Use and Adoption of Social Computing Applications: IIPTS Exploratory Research on the Socio-economic Impact of Social Computing Seville: Institute for Prospective Technological Studies, 80 (2008)

Pascu C., Osimo D., Ulbrich M., Turlea G., Burgelman J.C. 'The potential disruptive impact of Internet 2 based technologies' First Monday, 12 (3) (2007)

Paulussen S., Heinonen A., Domingo D., Quandt T. (2007) 'Doing it together, citizen participation in the professional news making process' The good, the bad and the unexpected' Cost Action 298, Moscow (May 23-25, 2007)

Proulx S. 'La confiance : ce qui fait lien au temps de l'incertitude informationnelle' eds. Lobet-Maris C., Lucas R., Six B. Variations sur la Confiance: Concepts et Enjeux au Sein des Théories de la Gouvernance Brussels: Peter Lang (2009) pp. 111-124

Prahalad C.K., Ramaswamy V. (2004) 'Co-creation experiences: the next practice in value creation' Journal of Interactive Marketing 18 (3) (2004) pp. 5-14

Punie Y., Lusoli W. Centeno C., Misuraca G., Broster D. (2009) The Impact of Social Computing on the EU Information Society and Economy Seville: IPTS European Commission - Joint Research Centre (2009)

Rappaport J. 'Terms of empowerment/exemplars of prevention' American Journal of Community Psychology 15 (2) (1987) pp. 121-148

Ratto M. 'Producing users, using producers' Paper presented at Participatory Design Conference New York (November 28, 2000)

Röpke I., Gram-Hanssen K., Jensen J.O., 'Households' ICT use in an energy perspective' eds. Gebhardt J., Fortunati L. Experiencing Broadband Society Berlin: Peter Lang (2009)

Saveri A., Rheingold H., Vian K. 'Technologies of cooperation' Palo Alto: Institute for the Future, 31 (2005)

Schäfer M.T. 'Participation inside? User activities between design and appropriation' eds. Boomen M. van den, Lammes S., Lehmann A., Raessens J., Schäfer M.T. Digital Material Tracing New Media in Everyday Life and Technology Amsterdam: Amsterdam University Press (2009) pp. 147-158

Sen A. Development as Freedom Oxford: Oxford University Press (1999)

Slot M., Frissen V. 'Users in the information society: shaping a golden age?' eds. Pierson J. Mante-Meijer E., Loos E., Sapio B. Innovating for and by Users, Luxemburg: OPOCE (2008)

Smit W.A., Oost E. van De Wederzijdse Beïnvloeding van Technologie en Maatschappij: Een Technology Assessment-benadering Bussum: Uitgeverij Coutinho (1999)

Spurgeon C. Advertising and New Media. London: Routledge (2008)

Steen M. The Fragility of Human Centred Design, Dissertation TU Delft, IOS Press Amsterdam (2008)

Surowiecki J. The Wisdom of Crowds. New York: Anchor Books (2005)

Toffler A. The Third Wave New York: Morrow (1980)

Urban A. 'Mobile television: a hype or a real consumer need?' eds. Pierson J., Mante-Meijer E., Loos E, Sapio B. Innovating for and by users Luxemburg: OPOCE (2008)

Vickery G., Wunsch-Vincent S. Participative Web and User-created Content: Web 2.0, Wikis and Social Networking Paris: OECD (2007)

Editors and contributors

Editors

Eugène Loos (e.f.loos@uva.nl) holds a PhD in international business communication from Utrecht University in the Netherlands. He is currently a professor of Old and New Media in an Ageing Society in the Department of Communication Science at the University of Amsterdam and senior lecturer at the Utrecht School of Governance, Utrecht University. He is also a member of the research schools ASCoR (Amsterdam School of Communication Research) and the Netherlands Institute of Government (NIG). As a linguist, he has conducted research and written several books and articles in the field of organisational (intercultural) organization. Currently his research focuses on the role of digital media related to accessible information for older people. His international books include *The Social Dynamics of Information and Communication Technology* (Ashgate 2008, co-edited by Haddon and Mante-Meijer) and *Innovating for and by users* (Office for Official Publications of the European Communities 2008, co-edited by Pierson, Mante-Meijer and Sapio). In 2010, he published his inaugural lecture *De oudere: een digitale immigrant in eigen land? Een terreinverkenning naar toegankelijke informatievoorziening* (Boom/Lemma 2010), which questions the gap between "digital immigrants" and "digital natives" (http://www.uu.nl/faculty/leg/EN/organisation/schools/schoolofgovernanceusg/research/publicmanagement/Pages/ELoos.aspx).

Enid Mante-Meijer (enid@mante.nl) is currently an emeritus professor in the Utrecht School of Governance at Utrecht University in the Netherlands. As an (organisational) sociologist, she taught methods and techniques of social research at Leiden University, and was, up till March 2002, senior researcher at the Dutch Telecom research department, KPN Research. She was also part of the European network COST 298. In 1999-2002 she was project leader of a large European research project, sponsored by Eurescom, on information and communication technology and users. Since 2005, her main field of research has been consumers of ICT, both in an individual and institutional context. In 2008 she published *The Social Dynamics of Information and Communication Technology* (Ashgate), co-edited by Haddon and Loos, and *Innovating for and by users* (Office for Official Publications of the European Communities), co-edited by Pierson, Loos and Sapio.

Jo Pierson (jo.pierson@vub.ac.be) is senior researcher at SMIT (Studies on Media, Information and Telecommunication) (http://smit.vub.ac.be) - part of IBBT (Interdisciplinary institute for BroadBand Technology) - and holds a PhD in social sciences (communication studies) since 2003. He teaches bachelor and master courses on socio-economic issues of the information society, on digital media marketing and on qualitative research methods in the department of Communication Studies (Faculty of Arts and Philosophy) at the Vrije Universiteit of Brussels in Belgium. His core scientific expertise is situated in the field of user empowerment and innovation strategic research on the meaning and use of new media. His research focus is on involving users in the technological development process based on ethnographic study and the Living Lab approach. Other research areas include online privacy and dataveillance, co-creativity, interactive digital television, ICT in small businesses and digital media marketing. In 2008 he published *Innovating for and by users*, co-edited by Mante-Meijer, Loos and Sapio (Office for Official Publications of the European Communities 2008). More information on: http://www.imuses.be

Contributors

Stijn Bannier (stijn.bannier@vub.ac.be) graduated in 2005 with a Bachelor's degree in Dutch, History and ICT / Informatics from the teacher's training department of the Leuven University College in Belgium. He subsequently graduated cum laude as Master of Arts in New Media and Digital Culture from Utrecht University in the Netherlands. In 2008 he joined IBBT-SMIT (Studies on Media, Information and Telecommunication), Vrije Universiteit in Brussels. He is active in several e-culture research projects, varying from digital libraries and music video games to cultural profiling and multi-touch interfaces. His main research interests are digital music culture, video games and the hybrids of new media.

Laurence Claeys (laurence.claeys@alcatel-lucent.be) is a sociologist who received an M.A. in Sociology and an M.A. in Gender Studies in Belgium. She obtained a PhD in Communication Sciences at the University of Ghent, also in Belgium. She works at the Ambient Media Applications team of Alcatel Lucent Bell Labs, Antwerp, where she conducts research on innovation, and corporate and end-user adoption of new technology, especially ICTs, in the field of the internet, tangible media and ambient application. She studies the social and cultural impacts and effects and processes involved in new technology innovation and strongly believes in interdisciplinary work. Laurence Claeys is also an affiliate researcher at IBBT-MICT.

Richard Coyne (richard.coyne@ed.ac.uk) researches and teaches in digital media, the philosophy of information technology, and design theory. He is author of several books on the implications of information technology and design with MIT Press and Routledge. His most recent book is called *The Tuning of Place: Sociable Spaces and Pervasive Digital Media*, with MIT Press. He is also completing a book for the Routledge Thinkers for Architects series entitled Derrida for Architects. He is currently Head of the School of Arts, Culture and Environment, a school within the University of Edinburgh that covers architecture, history of art, and music (http://ace.caad.ed.ac.uk/richard/).

Stefano de Paoli (stefano.depaoli@nuim.ie) is a postdoctoral researcher at the Sociology Department, National University of Ireland Maynooth, where he is working on a research project on the Future of the Internet. He has worked in Science and Technology Studies since 2004, focusing on an investigation of software licenses. Recently, his research interest has embraced massive multiplayer online games and trust in the future internet (http://www.nuim.ie/nirsa/people/postdocs/stefano_de_paoli.shtml).

Henrik Ekeus (henrikekeus@hotmail.com) is a musician, artist and software engineer. With a background in computing, he went on to study Sound Design and Composition at Edinburgh University, where he also worked as a research assistant for a number of years. His work has featured at numerous festivals and events and includes acoustic and electronic compositions, installations, sound walks and film soundtracks. He is currently a PhD candidate at Queen Mary University of London where his research explores the nature of generative processes in the arts and their role as creative driver and intermediary between artistic form and artist.

Philip Ely (pely@ucreative.ac.uk) is associate dean and head of the Business & Community School at the University for the Creative Arts (UCA), UK. He is a PhD candidate at the University of Surrey's Digital World Research Centre/Department of Sociology. He is former director of Digital Media at branding consultancy Design Bridge, Controller of Interactive Design at Granada Media (now ITV), and held senior design positions at Global Music Network, Telstar Entertainment Group, The Brilliant Agency and IBM (Personal Systems Europe). He has a particular research interest in both everyday innovations of users and the creation of new innovative businesses.

Valerie Frissen (valerie.frissen@tno.nl) is a senior strategist at TNO in the Netherlands and professor of ICT & Social Change at the Faculty of Philosophy at Erasmus University Rotterdam. She is interested in the social impact of ICT. One of the themes in her publications and lectures is the role of users in innovation processes. This was the central theme of her inaugural lecture *The Domestication of the Digital World*.

David Frohlich (d.frohlich@surrey.ac.uk) is director of Digital World Research Centre at the University of Surrey and professor of Interaction Design. He joined the Centre in January 2005 to establish a new research agenda on user-centred innovation for the consumer market. Current work includes a mixture of PhD, Industrial and Research Council projects exploring a variety of new media futures relating to photography, literacy and communication (http://www.dwrc.surrey.ac.uk). David worked for 14 years as a senior research scientist at HP Labs, and has held visiting positions at the Universities of York, Manchester and the Royal College of Art.

Nicola Green (n.green@surrey.ac.uk) is senior lecturer in New Media and New Technologies in the Department of Sociology, University of Surrey. Her research interests have crossed disciplinary boundaries in work on technologies, new/media, embodiment, identity, culture and gender. Her research projects have spanned virtual reality technologies, mobile multimedia, surveillance, the internet, and environment. Her recent publications have been included in *Surveillance and Society*, *The Information Society, Journal of Consumer Culture*, and *Information, Communication and Society*. She is co-editor of a collection entitled Wireless World (Springer-Verlag 2002), and is co-author with Haddon of the recent *Mobile Communications* (Berg 2009).

Lorna Heaton (lorna.heaton@umontreal.ca) is associate professor in the Department of Communication at the Université de Montréal in Canada. Her research focuses on collaborative work. She is particularly interested in how new media reconfigure relationships between designers and users in terms of power and expertise, and in questions of innovation in socio-technical infrastructure.

Kati Hyyppä (kati.hyyppa@taik.fi) is a researcher and doctoral student in the Media Lab of the Aalto University School of Art and Design in Finland. Her research focuses on interaction design in the context of collaboratively used, socially enriched digital audiovisual media.

Aphra Kerr (aphra.kerr@nuim.ie) holds a PhD and is a lecturer in the Department of Sociology at the National University of Ireland Maynooth. She has been researching the regulation, production and consumption of digital media on European and national projects for the past ten years and is currently working on a nationally funded project on Future Communications Networks and Services. Her publications include The Business and Culture of Digital Games (Sage, 2006) and journal articles published in Media, Culture and Society, New Media and Society, The International Journal of Cultural Studies, Convergence, Fibreculture and Information, Communication and Society (http://sociology.nuim.ie/AphraKerr.shtml).

Bram Lievens (bram.lievens@vub.ac.be) is a senior researcher at IBBT-SMIT (http://smit.vub.ac.be) in Belgium where he coordinates the user research team. He has a bachelor's degree in social and cultural work as well as a master's degree in communication science. His expertise is focussed on people centered technology development as well as user evaluative projects. Currently he is working on different interdisciplinary projects regarding new and emerging technologies, services and applications within the domain of Future Internet. Bram Lievens also works for the iLab.o - the Living Lab facility of the Institute of Broadband Technology, where he is coordinating different user oriented Living Lab research projects. He has published on these topics in various journals and conferences. He moreover acts as a project reviewer for the Flemish agency for Innovation by Science and Technology on a regular basis.

Kari-Hans Kommonen (khk@uiah.fi) is the director of the Arki research group in the Media Lab of the Aalto University School of Art and Design in Finland. The Arki group studies how everyday life is changing as it becomes more digital, and explores how digital technology and software can be designed to better serve and support people in realizing their own interests.

Eugène Loos See editor

Enid Mante-Meijer See editor

Sanna Marttila (sanna.marttila@uiah.fi) is a researcher and a project leader in the Media Lab of the Aalto University School of Art and Design in Finland. Her doctoral research deals with participatory culture in the context of audiovisual media. As a designer ,her interest is to support and facilitate open and collaborative design activities.

Ike Picone (ike.picone@vub.ac.be) was appointed as a researcher at the SMIT Research Group of the Vrije Universiteit of Brussels in April 2006. His research focuses on qualitative approaches to study news use and participation in a digital and social media environment and is framed within the IWT-SBO project FLEET (FLEmish E-publishing Trends). His study will also result in a Ph. D. With his paper *Conceptualising Online News Use* he won the Junior Researcher Award at the COST 298 Conference The Good, the Bad and the Unexpected in Moscow, May 2007. He has contributed to the books *Innovating for and by users* (Office for Official Publications of the European Communities 2008) and *Jonge Honden: Is er nog toekomst voor de journalistiek?* (2009).

Jo Pierson See editor

Serge Proulx (proulx.serge@uqam.ca) is professor at the École des medias of the Université du Québec à Montréal (Canada). A sociologist by training, he has authored over 100 articles on the uses of media, technologies and communication. His research program concerns the transformation of communicational practices and social ties in the present context of the mutation of capitalism.

Yves Punie (Yves.Punie@ec.europa.eu) is a senior scientist at the Institute for Prospective Technological Studies (IPTS), a European Commission Joint Research Centre (JRC) (http://ipts.jrc.ec.europa.eu) based in Seville. Currently, he is leading the IPTS research and policy activities on ICT for Learning and Skilling and is also involved in projects on ICT for Inclusion and Governance as well as on assessing the socio-economic impact of web 2.0 or social computing. A number of these projects have a strong foresight component. Before joining the IPTS in 2001, he was interim assistant professor at the Free University of Brussels (VUB) and a senior researcher at SMIT (Studies on Media, Information and Telecommunications). He holds a PhD in Social Sciences from the VUB on the use and acceptance of ICT in everyday life, also known as "domestication". In general, his expertise is on the social impact of ICT, its potential and use (http://ipts.jrc. ec.europa. eu/publications/index.cfm; http://is.jrc.ec.europa.eu/ pages/EAP/eLearning. html; http:// is.jrc.ec.europa.eu/pages/ EAP/ SC.html).

Mijke Slot (mijke.slot@tno.nl) is an innovator at TNO in the Netherlands. She conducts research projects in the field of social media, changing user roles and relations between users and producers/organisations in the media sector. Furthermore, she is a lecturer at the International Bachelor Communication and Media at Erasmus University Rotterdam and academic director of a post-academic media seminar. She is currently finishing a PhD thesis about changing user roles in online media services.

Cristiano Storni (cristiano.storni@ul.ie) is a lecturer and researcher in Interaction Design and Science and Technology Studies at the Interaction Design Centre in the Department of Computer Science and Information Systems, University of Limerick, Ireland. He is concerned with design research (theories and methodologies), science and technology studies, and interaction design in various fields. Recently, he focussed on Web 2.0, the Internet of Things and Open source hardware projects. He is currently investigating self-care practices and technology – especially in the context of chronic disease – and envisioning their future.

Levente Szekely (szekelylevente@excenter.eu) is a sociologist and PhD student at Corvinus University of Budapest. He worked for the Information Society Research Institute (ITTK) at Budapest University of Technology and Economics (BME). He is a former editor of the Information Society Quarterly and Infinit (Information Society – Internet – Information Technology) Newsletter. Currently he is the research director of Excenter Research Centre, co-editor-in-chief of New Youth Review (quarterly social science journal) and board member of the *Child and Youth Basic Program* (GyIA). He is the author (or co-author) of nearly 40 scientific publications (journal articles, book chapters, reports) and more than 30 mostly online articles. Research areas: media consumption, new media, youth, education, information society.

James Stewart (j.k.stewart@ed.ac.uk) is a research fellow and lecturer at the Institute for the Study of Science, Technology and Innovation (ISSTI) at Edinburgh University. He trained in electrical engineering and received an MSc and PhD in Science and Technology Studies at the same university. He works in the field of innovation studies, especially ICTs, including the Internet, mobiles and emerging applications of these technologies. His primary research interest is the role of users in innovation, how the eventual users of technology directly, and indirectly shape our technological environment.

Eva K. Törnqvist (eva.tornqvist@liu.se) is a senior lecturer at the Department of Thematic Studies Technology and social change, Linköping University, Sweden. She is also director of studies and the director for Centre for Man, Technology and Society, CMTS. Her research interests are primarily communication and learning in environments and situations where coordination and cooperation are of importance. Examples of research topics are: how knowledge produced in one specific environment is formulated and presented so that it also becomes accessible and usable in other environments where the conditions and assumptions are partly different; how altered technical options affect information and communication conditions and how users incorporate ICT in their everyday practice.

Penny Travlou (sp.travlou@gmail.com) is a research fellow / lecturer at the Edinburgh College of Art. holding a PhD from the Department of Geography, University of Durham. Her research interests lie in the field of cultural/urban geography. Her research is interdisciplinary with a particular focus on theories of space and place and their implementation in research. She has worked in various projects looking at how people use and experience public space using a multi-method approach. She has also been involved in projects that look at the use of ubiquitous technology in the experience of public and virtual space using ethnographic methods (i.e. participant observation and interviews).

Agnes Urban (agnes.urban@uni-corvinus.hu) is an assistant professor at the Corvinus University of Budapest. She earned her Ph.D. degree at the same university in 2006; the title of her thesis was *The Market of New Media Services*. She is the author of several publications, including academic papers and book chapters, especially about the diffusion of new media services. She participated in the COST A20 project (Impact of Internet on Mass Media) and in the COST 298 Action (Participation in Broadband Society). Her primary interest is the field of digital television, broadband internet, mobile television and the change of media consumption habits. She is interested both in business aspects and policy implications.

Wendy Van den Broeck (wvdbroec@vub.ac.be) is a researcher at SMIT (Studies on Media, Information and Telecommunication) – part of IBBT (Interdisciplinary institute for BroadBand Technology) and located at the Vrije Universiteit of Brussels. She recently finalised her PhD on the domestication of interactive digital television. Her main expertise and research interest is in the domestication of new media technologies in the home context, with a focus on TV related services. She actively publishes on these topics.

Marinka Vangenck (marinka.vangenck@gmail.com) graduated magna cum laude with a Master's in Communication Sciences from the Vrije Universiteit of Brussels in 2007, with a thesis on the perceptions of Flemish politicians about the political interviews in the popular Flemish magazine Dag Allemaal. During her studies, she did an internship at the communication department of the Belgian Minister for Interior Affairs, Patrick Dewael. From November 2007 to July 2009, she was part of the SMIT-team. Here she worked on the MADUF-project, doing research into the possibilities and challenges of mobile television and the URBAN-project, which dealt with city navigation through 3D visualisation. Currently, she is working as an assistant to a Flemish liberal Member of the Brussels Parliament. In this capacity, she is responsible for both administrative and communicative tasks, as well as for the preparation of political dossiers.

Mark Wright (mark.wright@ed.ac.uk) is a senior research fellow at the School of Informatics, University of Edinburgh and research fellow in Virtual Environments for the Arts at Edinburgh College of Art. His role is to act as a catalyst for research and development between informatics and the Arts and Humanities in interaction design and the creation of new forms of digital media. Key themes are mobile locative media, social networks, virtual worlds and haptic design media.

Participation in Broadband Society

Edited by Leopoldina Fortunati / Julian Gebhardt / Jane Vincent

This series publishes peer-reviewed monographs and edited volumes by internationally renowed scholars in the field of the 'social use of information and communication technologies (mass media included)', 'communication studies' and 'science and technology studies'. It provides an editorial space specifically dedicated to the collection of work that integrates new research regarding theoretical discourse, methodologies and studies from multiple disciplines such as sociology, anthropology, psychology, geography, linguistics, information science, engeneering and more.

The editors particularly welcome texts elaborating new theories, original methodological approaches and challenges to existing knowledge. Proposals aimed at scholars, professionals and operators working in the diverse field of participation in broadband society are invited from all disciplines.

Vol. 1 Leopoldina Fortunati / Jane Vincent / Julian Gebhardt / Andraz Petrovčič / Olga Vershinskaya (eds.): Interacting with Broadband Society. 2010.

Vol. 2 Julian Gebhardt / Hajo Greif / Lilia Raycheva / Claire Lobet-Maris / Amparo Lasen (eds.): Experiencing Broadband Society. 2010.

Vol. 3 Leslie Haddon (ed.): The Contemporary Internet. National and Cross-National Studies. 2011.

Vol. 4 Hajo Greif / Larissa Hjorth / Amparo Lasén / Claire Lobet-Maris (eds.): Cultures of Participation. Media Practices, Politics and Literacy. 2011.

Vol. 5 Fausto Colombo / Leopoldina Fortunati (eds.): Broadband Society and Generational Changes. 2011.

Vol. 6 Jo Pierson / Enid Mante-Meijer / Eugène Loos (eds.): New Media Technologies and User Empowerment. 2011.

www.peterlang.de

www.ingramcontent.com/pod-product-compliance
Ingram Content Group UK Ltd.
Pitfield, Milton Keynes, MK11 3LW, UK
UKHW021822140426
5217IPUK00004B/50